THE MEN WHO BUILT BRITAIN
A HISTORY OF THE IRISH NAVVY

This history is dedicated to
Tom Beresford, navvy,
born County Waterford, 1913,
died Kent, 1978.

the
men who
built britain

a history of the irish navvy

Ultan Cowley

WOLFHOUND PRESS

Published in 2001 by
Wolfhound Press Ltd
68 Mountjoy Square
Dublin 1, Ireland
Tel: (353-1) 874 0354
Fax: (353-1) 872 0207

British Library Cataloguing in Publication Data
A catalogue record for this book is available from the British Library.

ISBN 0-86327-829-9   Hardback
ISBN 0-86327-890-6   Limited Edition

5 4 3 2 1

Front cover image: Courtesy McNicholas Construction
Back cover image: Sir Robert McAlpine Ltd
Cover design: Graham Thew Design
Typesetting and book design: Wolfhound Press
Printed and bound by MPG Books Ltd., Bodmin, Cornwall

Contents

Acknowledgements   7

Foreword   9

Introduction   11

Chapter 1   The Culture of Migration   19

Chapter 2   Canals, Bridges, Embankments and Cuts   33

Chapter 3   Paddy and the Big Ditch   47

Chapter 4   The Long-Distance Kiddies   71

Chapter 5   Twilight of the Navvy   88

Chapter 6   The Haemorrhage   109

Chapter 7   McAlpine's Men   132

Chapter 8   Public Works   151

Chapter 9   Private Fortunes   184

Chapter 10   Forgotten Men   211

Notes   252

Appendices   257

Bibliography   263

Index   267

Photographic Acknowledgements   272

Acknowledgements

I wish to express my gratitude to all those who have contributed to the making of this book:

Tommy Flanagan; Brendan MacLua; P.J. Leyden; Una Leyden; Michael Forde; Michael Watt; Brendan Butler; Pete Johnson; Paula Johnson; Jimmy Johnson; Sister Elizabeth Cahill; Deirdre Carroll; the staff of Irish Community Care, Cheetham Hill, Manchester; the management and staff of the Irish World Heritage Centre; Don Wilson; John Kennedy; Mervyn Busteed; Tom McGuire; Geraldine Lyons; Caroline Tierney; Fiona Clarke; Brendan Byrne; Mike Harding; Paul Farrell; Mark Flanagan; Kevin Madden; Vinnie Short; Michael Walsh; John Bilek; Colin McNicholas; Sir William McAlpine; Sir Malcolm McAlpine; John Cox, F.I.H.T.; John Docherty; Malcolm O'Brien, M.B.E.; Edna Beasley; Frank Duggan; Dudley Barrett; Carol Morgan; Mike Chrimes; Nobby Clarke; John O'Hara; Noel O'Donnell; Pat Flavahan; Joe McGarry; Alex McDonnell; Anne Doherty; Stephen Nealon; Brendan Kennelly; Kevin Stapleton; Martin Gibbons; Patrick O'Sullivan; Eileen Doyle; Helen Naughton; Michael O'Callaghan; Seamus Bonner; Noel J. Farrell; Billy Morrissey; Bill Brennan; John Neary; David Brooke; Eamon Corcoran; Jim Neary; Jim Gallagher; Frank Munnelly; Peter Hennity; Christy Cahalan; Liam Walshe; Ronnie and Freda Plant; Billy O'Grady; Fr Kieran O'Shea; Fr John Brady; John dePaor; Jim Bailey; Kevin Stapleton; Thomas Handley; Tony Murray; Howard Stevens; Moywest Ltd.; Nick Molnar (Sir Robert McAlpine Ltd); Malcolm R. Paul (Lowery Ltd); D.B. Feehely (P.J. Carey Ltd); K.T. Clancy (The Clancy Group); Ray O'Rourke; M. Purcell (The Murphy Group); Kelly Communications Ltd; Dermot Gleeson (M.J. Gleeson Group plc); Patricia Howard Cowley; Ruanne Cowley; Benjamin Cowley; Tansy Cowley.

The phrase 'The Men who Built Britain' was coined by Martin Doyle, of the *Irish Post*, in an article on my 1995 revue, *A Tribute to the Navvies*.

Publisher's Acknowledgement

Seamus Cashman and Wolfhound Press wish to thank Mr Michael Watt for his generous enthusiasm and financial support for this publication. The publisher also thanks Emer Ryan and David Houlden for their commitment to the book.

'... and woe to he
who called for tea
with McAlpine's Fusiliers.'

Foreword

When Ultan Cowley approached me in the summer of 1995 at a function in my then home town of Glenealy, a village at the edge of the Wicklow Mountains, with a proposal to write the history of the Irish Navvy, it was a subject that in a vicarious way interested me, and the challenge to do this book was taken up. I thought that Ultan would probably disappear and the project would never get off the ground; it did, thanks to his dedication and magnificent perseverance. The reason for underwriting a project like this, apart from being able to afford it, was that I had spent a number of years labouring on construction sites and in the 'oil patch' in a number of different countries, but the most intense period of this 'vocation' was in London in the late 1950s and 1960s, and my general welfare had often been cared for by itinerant Irish navvies.

Ultan, a consummate Irish historian, was inextricably besotted with his project — mud, wheelbarrows, concrete, reinforcing steel, dumpers and shovels. Our series of meetings spanned several years and oftentimes I became concerned that he was being too inclined to the romantic. Which he was and is. But there was no real need to worry, for he also understood the pragmatic side of this kind of lifestyle and work.

I can only speak with experience of the late 1950s and 1960s, but it was mostly a bastard of a job — dirty, often dangerous — and a hard and bleak life interposed with wonderful moments of comradeship, happy drinking bouts and the odd scrap. I deduced that a lot of the Irish navvies had no idea where exactly they were geographically and, more often than not, they did not care as long as there was good overtime, the ability to sub and occasional craic.

During my internationally itinerant days of navvying about the world, I worked with navvies of many nationalities, but particularly Irish. And gradually, by not only working but socially habituating with the Paddies, I began to understand the intensely lonely times that these men experience away from their family and friends, and the paradoxical dark and light side of Ireland which frequently surfaced in these men's dispositions and personalities.

There are many stories, sad, romantic and otherwise, that I could relate about working with the Irish navvy, but one of the most poignant comes from a number of years ago, when I became an underwriting member of Lloyds (heaven forbid). I went as a celebration with my then underwriting manager, the quintessential Englishman,

Michael Watt, driving, with Irish navvy Boscoe Boylan, El Adem, Libya, 1960.

ex-RAF Wing Commander Brian Bell, to a pub off St James Square, London, formerly called The Bell (no relation). We were later going on to a celebratory lunch with three other newly elected members of Lloyds at Wheelers across the road. While we stood at one end of the bar drinking the inevitable gin and tonics, Bell became concerned about a donkey-jacket clad figure at the other end of the bar, who kept looking over at us 'furtively'. Eventually donkey-jacket made his way towards us. 'Is that you, Kiwi? Do you remember me ... Gill?' My mind returned to a job some twelve or so years before at Grey Coat School in Victoria, London. Totally ignoring not only my drinking companions but the preceeding lost twelve years between us, Gill went on to inform me that our mutual buddy, Corky, had died unceremoniously at a London doss house after a night of serious boozing — the fated end for many an Irish navvy. Where I had been for the intervening years was totally irrelevant to Gill, and suddenly the hedonistic Southern California, where I was then living, seemed curiously irrelevant to me as well. Gill was interested solely and proudly in indicating that he would create an opportunity to join back up with him on a job over the road, and particularly to appreciate that he was these days the ganger, and that, therefore, not only could he guarantee me the start, but that he could fix up the mightily important 'sub'.

Gill did not say a hell of a lot more. He didn't really need to. He downed his drink and, taking one final fixed stance, said, 'Now don't forget, Kiwi: 8 a.m. Monday. I'll get you the sub Thursday and we'll have the craic on Friday night.' And he walked out of the pub, never to be seen again.

Brian Bell asked me why I had not explained to Gill that I certainly did not need the job, and that, by the fact of supposedly having money (I had sold my share of an oil-drilling business), I had now become an established member (in my case, temporarily) of a British institution which was, equally supposedly, run by the cream of British business society (later to be proven a load of bullshit). I did not and could not reply to Brian, as there is no answer to a question like that if you have never toiled with the lads. No use explaining the special world that then existed amongst the labouring construction workers. Anyhow, there was a limit to a non-Irish navvy getting to grips with any of the philosophical aspect of Gill's seriously poignant personal directions.

There are hundreds of men like Gill to whom this book should be dedicated, but space and memory prohibit it. However, one of these men with whom I worked in the early 1960s at El Adem, Libya, on a job for JC Gammon Ltd, was Tom Beresford. He encapsulated and personified all sides of the archetypal Irish navvy — tough, hard-working, frequently cantankerous, sometimes both lucid and confused, he was also, equally paradoxically, someone who cared fiercely and firstly for family, then for his mates and then nothing for anyone. Although nostalgia for the navvy world is inappropriate, my fifteen years of being a blue-collar worker were a hell of an experience, and there's an uncertain temptation to say that I am grateful to have been part of it. Although I now have everything and more that a navvy could wish for, on reflection, I believe that oftentimes I miss the company of these men.

This record of Irish navvies deserves to be made. Although the scope of this account is confined to Great Britain — the area of the Irish navvy's greatest social impact — it serves also as a representation of the Irish navvy throughout the world.

Irish navvies oftentimes received bad press — some of it deserved, some not — yet the construction companies always took them on. To those who built Britain, these were valuable men. This is part of their story.

Michael Watt
Resolute, Canadian Arctic
29 August 2001

Introduction

Teacher's question: 'Who made the world?'
Child's response: 'McAlpine, sir — and
my Daddy laid the bricks!'

This parody of the classic catechism question was a popular joke in the west of Ireland — the heartland of emigration — during the 1960s. It refers to the reputation acquired over the previous half-century by the Scottish civil engineering firm, Sir Robert McAlpine & Sons, for employing large numbers of Irishmen on contracts throughout the British Isles.

It was Sir Robert McAlpine, known affectionately as 'Concrete Bob', who said, 'The Scots make the best gangers, the Irish the best labourers, and the English the best clients', and who is also reputed, to have said, on his deathbed, 'If the men wish to honour my death, allow them two minutes' silence; but keep the Big Mixer going, and keep Paddy behind it'.

So many Irishmen were employed with McAlpine that a famous song, 'McAlpine's Fusiliers', was written in their honour:

It was down the Glen came McAlpine's Men,
With their shovels slung behind them.

Prominent amongst other British construction companies which employed large numbers of Irishmen were Taylor Woodrow, Tarmac, Mowlem, Balfour Beatty, Laing, and Wimpey. The latter employed so many Irish labourers in the postwar era that their name became a witty acronym for 'We Import More Paddies Every Year'.

So common were Irishmen in Britain's postwar construction industry that many British people, to whom building workers were known colloquially as 'navvies', seemed to believe that all navvies were Irishmen — some even suggesting that all Irishmen were navvies! The Irish were credited not only with postwar reconstruction, and the civil infrastructure of the new Welfare State, but also with the canals, railways, docks, harbours, roads and utilities of the Industrial Revolution. This book sets out to discover how the Irish earned that reputation, whether they deserved it, and what price they paid for it. It does so against the well-documented contexts of Irish

Rowing to work on the M1 motorway, 1959.

Donegal navvies, circa 1910.

emigration, and British civil engineering, over two and a half centuries. In the written histories of both these subjects the Irish navvy has, to date, been no more than a footnote.

Wherever possible, I have employed the personal reminiscences of Irish labourers, their families and associates, to ensure that they are remembered in their own words and that Paul Ricour's observation — 'To be forgotten, and written out of history, is to die again' — will never apply to this special breed of men.

Definition of a Navvy

The commercial canal system laid out in the British Isles in the eighteenth century was known as the 'Inland Navigation System'. The diggers of these canals, officially entitled Excavators, became known colloquially as 'Navigators'. This was later abbreviated to 'Navvies'. These canals were constructed mainly

between 1745 and 1830, by which time there were almost 4,000 miles of navigable waterways throughout the British Isles.

Railway building began in 1830, assumed a frantic pace for fifteen years, and then proceeded intermittently until the turn of the century. The construction methods pioneered by the canal builders were adapted to railway construction and the navvies effected a smooth transition from the former to the latter. They carried the name 'navvy' along with them.

In 1845, when railway building was most intense, 200,000 navvies were employed; the combined strength of the British Army and Navy at that time was 160,000. By the turn of the century the navvies had built almost 20,000 route miles of railway in Britain alone, but great Victorian contractors such as Peto and Brassey built railways on every continent, using local labour stiffened with a corps of professional navvies from Britain.

Well into the mid-twentieth century unskilled building and civil engineering workers continued to be called navvies (albeit often in a disparaging tone — 'as drunk as a navvy', and so on). From the mid-1960s onwards, however, the rapid development of mechanised excavating, earthmoving, and cable-laying technology made traditional navvying skills largely obsolete.

The term 'navvy' was dropped from British official statistical data in 1960. For some time prior to this construction workers had become reluctant to describe themselves as 'navvies' since by this time navvying had lost much of its former mystique. Two centuries earlier, however, navvies had just been emerging as a new labouring élite, at the cutting edge of the Transport Revolution, and any man elevated from the rank of common labourer to that of navvy had borne the name with pride.

The Transport Revolution

Energy is the essence of activity. Long before the canal era human energy had been allied with animal energy (oxen and horses) and elemental energy (wind and water) in the production and distribution of raw materials and manufactured goods.

Freight was dependent on the packhorse, which could carry two to three hundredweight, or on large wagons drawn by teams of horses carrying one to two tons, depending on the roads. Sailing ships could transport goods via coastal waters but were restricted by poor berthing facilities, costly servicing via 'lighters', and, of course, adverse weather. By loading goods onto barges however, one horse acquired the capability of drawing up to thirty tons via river towpaths, or as much as fifty tons along the still waters of a canal.[1]

This innovation undoubtedly helped trade enormously. Its real significance, however, lies in its relationship to another form of energy critical to British eighteenth-century industrial development — coal.

A good canal should have coal at the heels of it.
(Francis Egerton, Third Duke of Bridgewater)

From the mid-eighteenth century, as the population of Britain's cities grew, so also did the demand for coal. Required initially for domestic use, the milling,

Serious shovel men — navvies working on the Manchester Ship Canal, 1890.

metal-smelting and heavy-engineering industries also became heavy consumers of coal following the development of the steam engine.

Coal wagons drawn by horses along wooden or iron rails were already in use in the mines themselves. It took no great leap of imagination to envisage horse-drawn barges moving coal, via canals, from the rural coalfields to the new domestic and commercial consumers concentrated in the burgeoning cities.

The commercial canal thereby facilitated the concentration, at the point of optimum utility, of the essential energy needed to power the Industrial Revolution. Industrial output in turn could then be distributed throughout Britain via canal and, more significantly, from landlocked industrial areas such as Manchester to seaports for export.

The Newry Canal, in County Down, was the first commercial canal in the British Isles commissioned for the transportation of coal. Begun in 1731 and completed in 1742, its purpose was to transport coal from the Lough Neagh coalfield to Newry port for shipment to Dublin. It was intended to challenge the prevailing 'mainland' monopoly on the Dublin coal trade.[2]

The engineer for the Newry Canal, Thomas Steers, and his assistant, Henry Berry, were later instrumental in the construction of the Sankey Brook Navigation which opened in 1757 ('an artificial cut and not simply a river improvement'). This system linked the Lancashire coalfields with the Mersey Estuary.

It was this project which inspired the Third Duke of Bridgewater to build the Bridgewater Canal connecting his Worsley coalfield with Manchester and Liverpool. The enormous commercial significance of the Bridgewater Canal, opened in 1760, was dramatically demonstrated by the subsequent reduction in the price of coal at Manchester — from seven pence to three-and-a-half pence a hundredweight — a saving to the consumer of 50 per cent.

Later the Grand Trunk (Trent & Mersey) Canal reduced the cost of goods freighted between Manchester and Litchfield by 75 per cent while, by the

Above: Castlefields, Manchester. Spanning the eighteenth-century Rochdale and Bridgewater canals, two nineteenth-century railway viaducts frame the twentieth-century Merchant's Bridge — built in 1995 — which links Catalan Square with Slate Wharf.

Founded by the Romans, Castlefields now encompasses three centuries of British civil engineering history, including the world's oldest railway station.

Navvy with full load — Manchester Ship Canal, 1890.

turn of the century, the cost of transporting pottery between Etruria and Manchester had dropped from a road-freight charge of £2.15s. to a canal-freight charge of 15s. per ton.

When the Bridgewater Canal opened in 1760, cotton manufacturers had increased their imports of raw cotton by a factor of fifteen, and Liverpool's trade had grown by 300 per cent over the previous forty years. The new summit-level canals were especially welcomed by the Pennines manufacturing region, 400 feet above sea level, and hungry for more raw materials and the coal with which to process them.[3] By 1775, 37,000 tons of coal were being shipped into Manchester alone each year.

If we accept the Newry Canal as the earliest commercial link in the eighteenth-century Inland Navigation System — connected commercially and via its engineers with those built later on 'the mainland' — then the Irish 'excavators' employed throughout the eleven years of its construction must be regarded as the first true navvies.

However, here begins the enduring mystery of the place of Irish navvies in the subsequent history of British construction and civil engineering. No evidence remains linking the Newry navvies with later public works in Britain. Yet common sense suggests that such valuable experience, at a premium on canal projects, could not have been allowed to go to waste. However, contractors, themselves often former navvies, took such little account of the labourers in their employ that Anthony Burton, historian of the canal builders, has stated, 'Of all the men concerned in canal building, the workmen retain the greatest degree of anonymity.'[4]

Origins of the Navvies

The skills deployed at all levels in the building of the Inland Navigation System were novel, in the main, and mostly learned by a process of trial and error. At the outset it was engineers such as Thomas Steers and Henry Berry who developed, on the waterways of the North-West, the techniques necessary for the building of cuts, embankments, locks, and impermeable channels. Their work on the Mersey and its tributaries, the rivers Weaver and Irwell, the Sankey Brook Navigation, and the Newry Canal, paved the way for the Bridgewater and other major canals that followed.

It was in large part by appreciating and overcoming the engineering difficulties involved in canal construction that the civil engineering profession came into being in Britain. The majority of the early British civil engineers began life as day labourers, progressing to trade apprenticeships, evolving into mechanical and ultimately civil engineers.[5]

George Stephenson (b. 1781) was the son of a colliery fireman who earned twelve shillings a week. George was set to work as soon as he was able, herding cattle at twopence per day, and later picking shale from coal at his father's place of work. At the age of fourteen, he was appointed assistant colliery fireman and earned one shilling per day.

John Rennie (b. 1761) was the son of a Scottish farmer. After some years as a shepherd, earning free shoes and stockings and five shillings a year, he entered a millwright's workshop as an apprentice at the age of twelve.

James Brindley (b. 1716) was the neglected son of a Derbyshire farm manager. Barely able to write or do arithmetic, he was a farm labourer until, at the age of seventeen, he also became apprenticed to a millwright.

These men developed their engineering skills by dint of inquiring minds, application to the practice and principles of mechanical engineering, and trial and error. Rennie, and especially Brindley, built the first canals in precisely this way.

Road-making, in 1920s Manchester.

In the seventeenth century, when a campaign to drain the waters of the Fens was seriously undertaken, the great Dutch hydro-engineer Vermuyden was recruited. The ditching and embanking skills which he taught the local population eventually produced the famous 'Bankers' of Lincolnshire. These were to become a civil-engineering élite, in constant demand as excavators over the next one hundred and fifty years.

The Bankers, however, comprised only a minority of the men who built the first canals. The rest were tradesmen-turned-contractors, and local agricultural workers seeking more money or a change of work. Amongst the latter were small groups of Irish farm labourers, who came to England and Scotland to earn the rents for their Irish holdings as migratory harvesters, and who, in some instances, stayed on to become navvies. In common with their English counterparts, they learned the art of canal building as they went along. Possessed of few technical skills, like the Bankers, they were nonetheless acknowledged masters of the drain-digging spade known as a 'graft' — a specialised tool which became so synonymous with excavation that it was itself often referred to as a 'navvy'.[6] This early association of Irish migrant labourers with British civil engineering was to have profound and lasting consequences for the history of the Irish in Britain.

1 The Culture of Migration

My rents and taxes were too high,
I could not them redeem,
And that's the cruel reason why
I left old Skibbereen. (Anon)

Almost a century has passed since Arthur Redford, serving with the British Army in Macedonia during the First World War, first noted the phenomenon of seasonal migration amongst peasants in the Balkans. As he observed, 'at first sight (they) might seem as deeply rooted to the soil as the feudal serfs of a mediaeval manor'.

He concluded that this was a widespread practice which embraced 'the regular movement of Vlach shepherds between their winter and summer pastures, the temporary sojourning of Albanian field-labourers in the plains of Thessaly, the annual exodus of Bulgarian harvesters and gardeners to Romania, Hungary, Serbia and Russia'.[1]

Much has since been written on this phenomenon which, as Redford himself acknowledged, was nowhere more significant than in Ireland. The title of a recent Irish publication, *Ireland: The Emigrant Nursery and the World Economy*, underscores the continuing importance and extent of labour migration in Irish society.[2]

In terms of its contribution over three centuries to the economies of Britain, her Empire, and the United States, Ireland has indeed been an emigrant nursery. In the eighteenth and nineteenth centuries the relationship between British employers and Irish labour was essentially symbiotic.[3]

Towards the end of the eighteenth century Irish migrant harvesters began to arrive in Britain in ever-increasing numbers for seasonal farm work, as agricultural 'improvements', responding to industrial and urban growth, generated demand for supplementary labour. 'Before the Famine, as many as one hundred thousand migrants annually plied back and forth across the Irish Sea'.[4]

The Great Famine

At around the same time, Ireland's population had been growing rapidly — from three to four million in the fifty years from 1735 to 1785, doubling from four to eight million between 1785 and 1841, just over another half century.

This dramatic rate of growth has been ascribed by L.M. Cullen not so much to the spread of the potato as a dietary staple as to a 'Europe-wide phenomenon' of fewer famines, declining death rates from epidemic diseases, and the widespread use of early smallpox vaccination.

This growth resulted in

... a disproportionate increase in the population of smallholders in ... the barren lands of the west [where] farming was organised more on a subsistence than on a commercial basis.

If the population of these regions increased, however, their incomes did not. In the absence of commercial cash crops, smallholders and labourers were dependent on wages, but wages were often unavailable, because the majority of holdings were too small to necessitate hired labour and supplementary income from textiles was at best intermittent. 'The background to the Famine ... is as much an industrial as an agrarian one'.[5]

The North-West, West, and extreme South-West of Ireland were largely smallholding regions where economic isolation and poor soil combined to dictate subsistence rather than a commercial or cash crop economy. The people here tended to marry earlier than those with more valuable patrimonies, and readily subdivided their already meagre holdings, or settled wastelands, which were in turn subdivided by their new occupants.

On most of these tiny holdings only the potato, a holistic staple unique in its nutritional sufficiency but notoriously prone to blight, could produce enough food to feed a family. Survival for many therefore depended entirely on access to enough land for this crop — and the means to rent it.

This situation gave rise to a system whereby holdings were sometimes let at auction to the highest bidder, often without any prior attempt at improvement, or any real correlation between the rents demanded and the holding's productive capability. Rents were, in fact, often pegged to English rather than Irish agricultural wage rates.[6]

From about the middle of the eighteenth century however, with population expansion generating increased demand for food, labourers and smallholders could often earn the necessary cash by hiring out as harvesters — either in England or elsewhere in Ireland. Limerick, for example, was sometimes referred to in parts of Kerry and west Clare as,

A place or state of punishment wherein it was necessary to labour before saving up the rent for home or the fare for England.[7]

Even a century later cash was such a scarce commodity west of the Shannon that a witness before the Irish Poor Law Commission in 1847 remarked:

Money is, in truth, not to be found in almost any part of the country and its value is so little known that it is no uncommon thing for a peasant who becomes possessed of a bank note to pledge it at a pawnbrokers' for so many shillings as he may want, and pay the interest on the loan.[8]

Land — The Key to Survival

Bearing all this in mind, the extreme vulnerability of large sections of the population of rural Ireland at this time becomes starkly obvious. In Ireland the census of 1841 specified four distinct economic divisions of the population, defined according to means. In rural areas, size of holding was the main criterion.

Division One specified ownership of substantial property or farms in excess of fifty acres. Division Two embraced tradesmen, and farmers with between five and fifty acres. Division Three covered urban and rural labourers and those with holdings up to five acres. In Division Four an insignificant residue was defined as 'means unspecified'.

Only 30 per cent of Ireland's rural population came within Divisions One and Two; the remaining 70 per cent were either tradesmen, labourers, or smallholders with five acres or less.[9]

Crucial to the economic well-being of the latter was the potential of the regional economy to generate paid employment. Where farming practices were labour-intensive, as in regions of intensive tillage, or where the textile industry provided out-work, as in the linen- and wool-producing areas, supplementary income was available to labourers and lesser smallholders.

In the absence of either of these sources of paid employment, however, survival could become precarious. This was especially true for the landless labourer dependent on 'conacre' (the annual sub-letting of small plots — usually for eleven months) to grow the family's staple crop — potatoes.[10]

While it would be misleading to suggest that the entire rural population of pre-Famine Ireland was disadvantaged, it is clear that the growing labouring and smallholding class was extremely vulnerable to fluctuations in both agriculture and the textile industry.

In the century before the Famine, linen, cotton, and wool were widely processed by domestic spinners and weavers throughout much of Ireland. However, both the woollen and linen industries had been in decline in Munster prior to the end of the eighteenth century. The introduction of power-spinning from the 1820s onwards gradually concentrated employment for farmer-weavers in and around Belfast and the North-East, with domestic spinning ultimately declining even in Ulster.[11]

Inevitably the regions along the western seaboard, where subsistence rather than commercial farming prevailed, suffered most. The traditional occupational mix of farming, fishing, and weaving was curtailed, placing more emphasis on soil fertility.

'Lazy beds' in the Wicklow uplands.

Across the country an economic pattern based on land use emerged. Areas of good land were occupied by a comfortable farming class, able to diversify production, and hence resistant to early marriage and the subdivision of holdings. Bordering these were regions of somewhat poorer land where the size of holding was the main determinant of prosperity.

Beyond these the very poorest land was tenanted by an expanding population of vulnerable cottiers given to recklessly early marriage, subdivision of already meagre holdings, and the colonisation of barren bogs and uplands.

The first of these regions covered roughly east Leinster and Ulster minus counties Donegal and Fermanagh. Here approximately one-third of the population came within Divisions One and Two, with the remainder divided between tradesmen, artisans, and better-off labourers.

The second region comprised parts of counties Sligo, Leitrim, and Roscommon, the western counties of Leinster, and Munster excepting west Cork, west Kerry, and Clare. Here also, upwards of one-third of the population had Division One or Two status, but the many smallholders with five acres or less were more badly affected by the absence or demise of domestic textile spinning and weaving.

The third region, broadly speaking the western seaboard, conformed to a similar pattern. Relatively prosperous inland towns, and farms on good land, approximated to the income levels of the second region; while in a coastal belt, running from Donegal to west Cork, the bulk of the population lived at or below subsistence level.

Irish harvesters in Scotland, 1890.

Of the western coastal counties, Mayo was by far the poorest, with only 15 per cent of the population falling within economic Divisions One and Two of the 1841 Census. Not for nothing was the phrase, 'Mayo God help us' coined to describe the lot of its people.

Approaching the middle of the nineteenth century therefore, wherever poor soil and an absence of paid employment were prevalent, smallholders and landless labourers were forced to depend on the potato for food and on seasonal migration for a significant income.

In this way, for the maintenance of farms and families at home, the pattern of migration and emigration, became an established fact of life in the west of Ireland. It remained so for well over a century. It was from this socioeconomic background in Ireland that the Spailpín, the Tattie Hoker and the Navvy emerged in Ireland.

Spailpíns and Tattie Hokers

The system of subsistence farming practised by the Irish on the western seaboard revolved around seasonal activities such as fishing, peat-cutting, and potato-growing. Each activity allowed for long periods of relative inactivity, sometimes giving uninformed observers a strong impression of inertia and sloth. The potato cycle, in particular, was considered anathema to champions of the Protestant work ethic because it seemed to enable individuals having access to land to survive almost effortlessly.

The reality, however, was that confinement of an expanding population to impoverished holdings — often for inflated conacre rents — precluded almost any other means of subsistence. Such rents, in fact, were often deliberately pegged to English as opposed to Irish agricultural wage rates.

Rents in the areas of high migration were higher then elsewhere — the Griffith valuators indicate that

Mayo tenants were paying rents for bad land, and reclaimable waste, which would have been unlettable anywhere else.[12]

The lack of paid farm work at home affected the level of skills which Irish labourers could deploy in the search for employment abroad. An English railway engineer building in Ireland wrote the following:

The Irish labourer, as the soil produces him, is totally and utterly untaught. A man who has in him the makings of an excellent workman, but who has never handled a pick or shovel, never wheeled a barrow, and never made a nearer approach to work than to turn over a potato-field with a clumsy hoe, is in no position to make a dock or a railway. He has to be taught, and to be set to work ... alongside of a steady workman. For this purpose a nucleus of English workmen is indispensable.[13]

It is interesting to contrast the previous quotation with the following:

Brindley ... found plenty of labourers in the neighbourhood accustomed to hard work ... a superior class.... 'Wise', or 'Cunning' men, bloodstoppers, herb-doctors, and planet-rulers, such as are still to be found in the neighbourhood of Manchester. Their very superstition, says our informant, made them thinkers and calculators. The foremanbricklayer, for example, as his son used afterwards to relate, always 'ruled the planets to find out the lucky days on which to commence any important work and', he added, 'none of our work ever gave way'. The skilled men had their secrets, in which the unskilled were duly initiated — simple matters in themselves, but not without their uses.[14]

The Irish agricultural labourers of the eighteenth century were far less sophisticated than Smiles' 'superior class' of English agricultural workers. Relatively few were employed directly by their landlords, thus receiving neither the security of an arrangement to discharge rents via day-labour, nor the benefit of hands-on experience in farming skills and practices.

Within Ireland a certain level of demand for harvesters existed but it was quite inadequate to meet the financial needs of the labouring and smallholding class. That class increased disproportionately in the final decades of the eighteenth century, and up to the Great Famine, and the majority had no alternative but to migrate to mainland Britain in search of seasonal work. These men were usually adept in the use of the sickle, the standard tool for cutting grain, and also of the spade or hoe.

> *Reaping corn was done with a saw-toothed hook (a sickle). The smaller men were considered best for the latter work, giving rise to the saying, 'Not all big men reap the harvest!' They carried or hitched on a bit of plaited straw in order to identify themselves as looking for work, and were referred to as 'Men of Straw' — men without means.*[15]

An English farm labourer has left us the following description of cutting corn with a sickle in the late nineteenth century:

> *Corn was cut with a 'badging' hook and hay was cut with the scythe. A man could cut half an acre of corn a day and bind it into sheaves, but usually the farmers banded themselves together and worked in groups of from twelve to twenty....*
>
> *Gangs of 'paddies' contracted at so much a field. They used a sickle with a thin curved blade, a yard long, having teeth like a bread knife, which would cut nearly half a sheaf at one stroke.*[16]

With their sickles wrapped in straw, men would leave for England or Scotland, after putting in their seed potatoes, to harvest successive farm crops — hay, corn, oats, and potatoes — up to the end of November or early December. Then they would return to Ireland. Some, usually young single men, might remain abroad

and seek employment as unskilled labourers on public works.

In west Donegal, a boy would progress from hiring out, at eight-to-fourteen years, as a farm labourer in the Lagan (the two-hundred square mile region of rich farmland between Letterkenny and Derry), to heading soon after for 'College Green' — the green fields of Scotland. Amongst the migrant labourers of west Donegal, it was said that he had gone away 'to complete his education' (College Green being the location of the University of Dublin — Trinity College).

Initially workers headed for the Lothians, and gradually moved northwards as grain crops ripened, but only after the railways penetrated to Wigtownshire, Ayrshire, and Fifeshire in the 1840s were they able to access the more lucrative eastern potato-growing areas.

The economies of certain districts in the west of Ireland, such as Achill, Belmullet, Swinford and the Inishowen Peninsula, became so bound up with the harvesting cycle that many of their inhabitants continued to migrate *en masse* well into the twentieth century.

> *... as soon as they had their work finished at home around about St John's Day (21st of June) or perhaps before that, all of them were off to Scotland and they wouldn't come home until November 28th and a lot of the young boys wouldn't come home at all — they would spend the winter wandering.*
>
> *When those men came home then and their wages with them; the place where there would only be one man and he struggling with life trying to keep a wife and family. He would have to pay out the majority of his wages to the shops for the amount they took on credit the spring before. There was no worse or harder time for the creatures than the springtime. Whatever wages the man had earned in Scotland was spent by then; and the crop [of potatoes] had to be sown and the turf cut and twenty things like that to do and the creatures with empty pockets. There is a saying and you would hear it from quite a few people at that time: 'Hardship doesn't come until the spring, or until the grey crow have two eggs'.*[17]

This dependence on income earned in Britain, and the fact that as much as half of every year might be spent abroad, led some official commentators to regard the harvesters as, in effect, English rather than Irish labourers. That, however, did not in any way diminish people's sense of belonging, or their attachment to 'home'. The collective character of seasonal migration reinforced this attachment.

Britain, who relied on them to bring a workforce or 'squad', inevitably leading to recruitment of relatives and friends from within the gaffer's own community in Ireland.

The tradition persisted in parts of the west well into the twentieth century. John Neary, born near Swinford in County Mayo, described the same cycle in the 1920s:

The Derry Boat, c. 1910. Harvesters throughout the North-West of Ireland sailed for Scotland from ports such as Westport, Ballina, Aranmore Island and Derry.

Throughout the latter part of the nineteenth and the first half of the twentieth century, entire townlands on Achill Island put in their potatoes, locked their doors, and headed for Scotland every June. They might be absent from their homesteads for up to five months of the year. Only the very old and the very young remained.

A network of connections bound succeeding generations to the same cycle. Fathers brought sons over with them as soon as they could work; 'gaffers' established relationships with individual farmers in

In my small village of seven or eight houses, the leader of every house in the village went; they all went ... my father was travelling abroad for forty-two years ... the farms around would only be fifteen or eighteen acres, two of it bog, and a thatched cottage; we was one of them, five or six kids, go for water to the well, drawing turf, a couple of donkeys, two cows.... It was the English pound note, or the American dollar that kept you alive, you had nothing else. When your kids got old enough — like me, I was the oldest, it was off to the sugar beet, to send money home.[18]

Above: Scottish and Irish farm labourers, *c.* 1910. The three on the extreme right are brothers from Donegal.

Ten years on, the same financial pressures still governed events in this part of Ireland. John O'Hara told a similar story:

The farmers had any amount of food, but they hadn't the wherewith to buy clothes and shoes for the youngsters at all. But then, you could have as much money, over here, for a week's wage, as you'd get for the bullock after keeping him for two or three years. So as soon as you were big and strong, and fit to come over here, about sixteen or seventeen, there was no other way out.... You had to keep up with men that was twenty-one, twenty-two, twenty-three; they might have mercy on you the first year you'd come over, but after that there was no mercy — you done the same as the others.

The pattern here was: you hit for Blackburn on the 15th of June, because they'd be gettin' in the hay around that time. 'Twas hilly country; for some reason, on the sunny side of the hill, the hay was ready first, they'd have you up at four in the mornin', daylight ... out mowin', openin' up oul' headlands, so as they could get the grass-cutter 'round about. Back in then, you might have to milk five or six or maybe more cows, they'd give you breakfast then ... Out again then, and you'd be savin' hay or whatever....

If you had good weather, and you got the hay in in a fortnight, they'd give you the month's wages, so as they wouldn't be feedin' you; you'd bargain for the month ... they might give you oul' kale, or rhubarb, or boilin' water with a bit of sugar, and oul' black tay. For some reason they thought the black tay was the proper thing to give to Paddies. But you weren't savaged so bad there....[19]

Nobby Clarke was also a Spailpín and Long-Distance Kiddy, but his home place was East Galway. His account of the harvest cycle, also during the 1930s, closely resembles that of John O'Hara:

The Hay Country was all right — we were fairly well treated in the Hay Country. But, as soon as the sun shone, you had to be out, five o'clock in the mornin', 'til you couldn't see at night-time.... Pay (in 1934) was £40 for the month ... for the seven days, bar while you went to church ... 'twas all the time you had off. And, if it was rainin', you got a scrubbin' brush and you had to be scrubbin' the stalls where the cows were.

Get paid then and head for Lincolnshire, when the hay was over. You had maybe to wait a couple of weeks for harvest, but you got 'Dyke Roadin' — cuttin' the grass in the dyke with a sickle, till the harvest started.

Livin' in an oul' hut, make the 'bed' with a fork, canvas to throw over you, and when you started harvestin' the peas, there was what they called 'smut' on it — you'd be like a Sweep in the evenin', when you come in.... The rivers, or dykes, were too deep, and you'd be afraid to go in, so one'd strip off, and catch the other by the two wrists, and duck him up an' down, so he could clean himself, and dry each other with a flour bag.

So we left there when the harvest was over, and we went to the 'taties, to a place called March Chapel, outside Grimsby.... Six of us in a gang ... we slept in an oul' blacksmith's shop, we got the bed of

Scottish and Irish tattie hokers, Scotland, 1910.

straw to lie down, and we made the cookin' with the bellows, where they used to shoe the horses. And it was a great thing to blow up the coals in the mornin' to make the fire.... When we had everythin' done for the 'taties, and the beet, and everythin' pulled, we headed for London, and into oul' headins (tunnels).[20]

So long as demand for harvesters was strong in Britain, and rents in the west of Ireland continued to exceed the productive capacity of holdings, seasonal migration persisted. The first edition of the *Labour News*, in 1871, stated the following:

Crops (in Oxfordshire) are very abundant and hands very short. At Farringdon, Berks., are placards about for 200 men wanted on one farm. No hands to be got, and I was told the price offered is from 14s. to 20s. an acre. This year there is a scarcity of labourers, and as much as 8s. 6d. per acre has been paid for simply tying and shocking corn.

John Neary (left) and family in the 1920s.

Latest advice from Lincolnshire states that, 'in the district of Spalding the harvest has progressed somewhat tardily through the scarcity of reapers.'

Around Boston work is retarded for want of hands, and wages are very high. The Chambers of Agriculture Journal *says, 'the extent to which reapers have been in request this year is almost unprecedented'.*[21]

At this time half the populations of the Poor Law Unions of Dunfanaghy in Donegal and of Claremorris in Mayo were dependent on remittances, as were three-quarters of the population of Swinford. As much as 20 per cent of the population of County Mayo, in fact, relied heavily on emigration.

It would appear that the 1860s and 1870s were the peak periods of migration, providing an income of between £0.8 million and £1 million to the economy of the west and north-west.[22]

Inheritance or Exile

The dominant rationale, the necessity to earn money to maintain the family holding, was reinforced after the Famine by the replacement of separable inheritance with the 'stem system', whereby only one child could inherit. This automatically meant that the remaining children either had to leave the family home or else remain on sufferance as (often unpaid) 'assisting relatives'.

The home nest could eventually maintain but one, and the hard road for the others, was the constant saying in this neighbourhood. And, in the majority of cases, it was the youngest who generally settled down in the homestead.

Even giving sole possession to one son could not guarantee the viability of the holding. One or both parents (and possibly other siblings) might continue to be dependent on the farm for some time, and it could even happen that the inheriting son would seek tempo-rary work abroad to make ends meet. The homestead, of course, often had to accommodate up to three generations and might be subdivided itself.

> *When my father got married, his mother was a widow, and she told him, 'Well now, I'll have half the land, and I'll keep the big room, and ye can share the kitchen'. So we had to live in one room, and we had nothing. We got a pound or fifteen shillings every week from my father in England. He used to go away at the end of May ... he'd cut the turf, and get all crops laid and everything, and be gone until Christmas.*[23]

Inevitably also, many parents came to see these remittances as a form of private pension, giving rise to the cynical perception amongst some emigrants that they had been 'bred for emigration'.

There was indeed much incentive to produce children with this in mind; after all, remittances from seasonal migration to Britain, substantial though they were, merely maintained certain local communities in specific regions. Ireland as a whole, however, benefited enormously from mass emigration to the New World in the aftermath of the Famine. Between 1876 and 1921, 84 per cent of Irish emigrants went to the United States while only 8 per cent went to Britain.

> *Official returns revealed that over £34 million was sent to the United Kingdom by North American emigrants between 1848 and 1887, the bulk of it going to Ireland.*[24]

Journalist John Healy recounted how his grand-mother in County Mayo exhorted each of her daughters, when leaving for the United States before the First World War, to:

> *Keep your mouth and your legs closed, and send home the slates.*[25]

This obligation to 'send home the slates' — that is, accept responsibility for maintaining the family and the home — often rested heavily on young shoulders. The Donegal poet and erstwhile tattie hoker and navvy, Patrick MacGill, expressed his resentment in print at this unfair and unequal burden.

He wondered why his parents seemed unable to exercise any restraint or contraceptive control over their sexual activities if the fate awaiting their chil-dren was emigration and an unending struggle for survival. Not alone was he forced to 'fight for crumbs with the dogs in the gutter', but he was simultaneously expected to remit funds for the maintenance of this siblings who, he felt, were 'taking the very life-blood' out of his veins. Nevertheless he felt elated at the pros-pect of well-paid work in Kinlochleven, which would enable him to meet this onerous obligation.[26]

Most Irish emigrants, however, sent remittances home regularly in order to fulfil their duties and maintain contact with home and family. Between 1939 and 1969, almost three billion pounds in postal orders was sent back to Ireland from Britain alone. Money remitted in the form of cheques or cash was almost certainly as much again, perhaps far more.

Even for these dutiful emigrants there were no guarantees. Wives absconded with, or frittered away, a lifetime's savings; mothers left 'The Place' to a favoured son who'd stayed at home, at the expense of those who left; sometimes all the children emigrated, the parents died, and the holding was sold or abandoned. (In the west of Ireland today, these same abandoned homesteads are much in demand as holiday homes for the new urban élite, anxious for a taste of 'the simple life' from which so many of their own forebears fled.)

John Neary, in colourful language, described the consequences of these commonplace tragedies:

> *Pat Devaneys lost two, we lost two, Shearins lost two, Horkins three, in my village.... You know where they went, but nobody wants to talk about it ... from one family, one died in the Kip-house, another's dead from the drink.... You go back, but the flower of youth is gone; you've got grey hair, and you're goin'*

down the little boreen, to see your mam again; but your mam is gone, and the crows is flyin' in the bloody chimney, and your house is open to every cow in the village, to use it; there's nobody there anymore....[27]

In 1996 *The Irish Post* reported the extraordinary case of an Irish labourer, Eddie O'Donnell, aged seventy, who was found by a local council official living in a cowshed on a Cheshire farm. He had been in

Moved to a Local Authority flat, in a nearby town, he informed reporters that he preferred his old quarters:

It's nice to be comfortable, but I really preferred my old place. I had a log fire burner, to keep myself warm and cook at the same time, a table and a bed. I never wanted any mod cons like television. I was quite happy to just read my book. I never had any problems with the rent. I just used to ask the farmer what I owed him for this, and paid up.

An abandoned homestead in the Wicklow uplands.

residence apparently since 1971, when he and two other Donegal men had arrived for harvest work, and he had stayed on when his companions left. He had no running water to hand and used an outside toilet in the farmyard.

The farmer claimed that Eddie never complained.

He used to doss down here all right. I told him I wanted to demolish the cowshed and that he would have to find somewhere else to stay. He never complained to me. He always seemed to be quite happy. To be honest, I didn't know he'd moved out.

The Irish Post had earlier highlighted the case of Paddy Folan, who lived rough in woodland near Kingsdown in Kent for forty years, until 1994 when the local housing association persuaded him to accept a one-bedroom council flat. Paddy was illiterate and unsure of his date of birth. Villagers who had given him casual employment over the years reckoned him to be at least seventy-five. He was believed to have been born in Coventry, of Connemara Gaeltacht parents, and still retained some knowledge of the Irish language.

These men's resistance to rehabilitation may have had more to do with a reluctance to resume contact with the outside world, and certainly with their families, than with any attachment to primitive living conditions. As John Neary, recalling a period of homelessness spent 'on tramp' in England in his youth, expressed it:

How could I go home in my condition? Pride is a heavy burden.

In a sense they resemble remnants of a species which has gone down an evolutionary cul-de-sac — migrant harvesters had been of declining importance in Britain since the closing decades of the nineteenth century. Even though tattie hokers were still going to Scotland in the 1960s, and unskilled Irish labour was being recruited for the beet 'campaigns' from the 1920s through the 1950s, numbers declined throughout. The former were mostly female, while the latter tended to be either married men with small farms or single youths who usually progressed rapidly into construction work.

The overall transition, driven by economic factors on the one hand and societal change on the other, spanned a period of around fifty years. Beginning in 1879, a combination of economic recession and restructuring of British agriculture precipitated an overall decline in labour-intensive tillage in England.

By this time also, pressure was growing for the children of poorer rural families in Ireland to opt for permanent emigration.

The result was an increase in permanent emigration to the industrialised centres of population in Britain, in an attempt to secure unskilled but remunerative employment such as was available in construction and civil engineering:

Where seasonal migration was particularly relevant ... the permanent emigrants became the main financial source for these communities. Seasonal migration had helped to maintain traditional economic and social structures in the west of Ireland. Permanent migration brought this rural economy into line with the rest of Ireland.[28]

The perception in rural Ireland, particularly from the 1940s onwards — that Britain offered jobs and a better standard of living — was exacerbated by the lack of accessible off-farm employment and the links to friends and relatives already in Britain. In predominantly smallholding areas such as the West and North-West, even the prospect of inheritance was increasingly unable to offset the attractions of emigration.

If the family farm was no longer seen to offer an acceptable lifestyle to the inheriting male, how much less attractive would it appear to a female sibling or a prospective marriage partner? With young women leaving in increasing numbers, how many young men would be prepared to pay the price of life-long celibacy for their patrimony? The answer increasingly seemed to be — very few.[29]

Even where remunerative off-farm jobs could be found for wages on a par with those in Britain, enquirers were informed that any man worth his salt would exhibit sufficient spirit to follow the crowd who had already emigrated.[30]

Nevertheless, the tenacity with which seasonal migration persisted in parts of the west of Ireland, especially amongst married men with smallholdings, is surprising. A television documentary made in 1972 depicted a remote community near Bangor Erris in County Mayo where seasonal migration remained endemic.

> *Once or twice a year you see a lot of taxis pulling up there; all you see is suitcases going on them — you won't see half of those fellas coming back, because there's no place to come back to....*

Whereas in the 1950s harvesting had been the attraction amongst Erris men, this quickly gave way to labouring on the building sites of Britain.

> *I first came over in 1957 and I worked for the farmers, and I worked in London, Coventry, Birmingham, Luton, Cardiff, Southampton.... You came over around the middle of April usually. I go home in the summertime, 'round the middle of July, spend maybe a month or six weeks at home, then come over again at the back end of the year; go back again at Christmas, do a bit of work on the bit of land....*
>
> *Really it's not livin' at all — you got married to be with your wife, but in our area there's nothin' in it — you've just got to leave to make any sort of decent livin' at all.... 'Twas a hard, tough life on both man and woman — you lost a lot, with your wife and then with your family.... I'd love to stay there but I wouldn't be able to keep my wife and family without the work I get in this country.... My children will have to do the same as I'm doing, I suppose....*[31]

'Only women, children, and old men.' Waterford, 1957, three generations bring in the harvest.

2 Canals, Bridges, Embankments and Cuts

Stretches the future before them
Clouded and bleak as their past
These are our serfs — and our brothers
Slighted, forsaken outcast.

It would be wrong to give the impression that Irish migration to Britain in the nineteenth century was confined to seasonal labourers from the western seaboard. Both rural and urban Irish from all counties moved freely between Ireland and England, especially following the Act of Union (1800), and pursued such occupations as they were trained to or could access on arrival.

Recent research into local concentrations of immigrant Irish in Victorian Britain shows a wide diversity of occupations, ranging from beggars and street-traders to shopkeepers and civil servants, and the presence of substantial numbers of migrant textile workers indicates significant emigration from Munster, Leinster, and east Ulster.[1]

Nevertheless, in specific locations taken at random, the evidence indicating a preponderance of unskilled labourers from Connaught, throughout most of the century, is almost overwhelming. Carl Chinn's study of returns from the 1851 Census for Birmingham showed that

Folk from Connaught were dominant in the streets of highest Irish concentration from which there is information about counties of birth.[2]

Chinn also found that one of the largest groups of Irish workers in the city at that time were harvesters, described by a member of the Birmingham Town Mission as:

... poor shoeless and shillingless bogtrotters from Connaught.[3]

Even the labourers, according to the Census enumerators, represented twenty-seven different types, falling into three broad categories. Similarly, a recent comparative study of concentrations of Irish in the North-West and North-East of England, coincidentally also at the time of the 1851 Census, found that,

> ... *the majority of Irish-born males were engaged in manual labour.*

Further, this study found that a comparison of Irish residents recorded at specific addresses during the Censuses of 1841, 1851, and 1861 suggests a highly mobile labour force, again with a significant cohort of seasonal agricultural labourers.[4]

In the closing decades of the nineteenth century, however, mechanisation and the downturn in British agriculture accelerated the decline of the market for harvesters from Ireland. This had far-reaching consequences for the subsistence farmers of the West. Survival now hinged increasingly on undivided holdings coupled with the emigration of the non-inheriting children and/or remittances from those working abroad.

Many agricultural labourers remained on English or Scottish farms as permanent hands but many more sought employment as casual labourers in mills and factories, mines, construction projects and 'Public Works'. The latter term was used until after the Second World War to denote major state-sponsored civil engineering projects such as transport networks, dams and reservoirs, docks and harbours, and public utilities.[5]

The Irish had always to some degree been employed in these areas even during periods of strong demand in the agricultural sector. The harvesters and tattie hokers were so widely distributed throughout Britain that they inevitably acquired a keen awareness of the variety and extent of demand for unskilled labour. This knowledge was shared amongst themselves and passed on to others.[6]

The harvesting cycle was drawing men from Donegal, Sligo, Roscommon, Leitrim, Mayo, Connemara, Kerry and elsewhere to the Lothians, Peebleshire, Selkirkshire, Roxburgh, Wigtownshire, Lancashire,

Yorkshire, Derbyshire, Lincolnshire, Cambridgeshire, Berwick and Warwickshire.[7]

The South and West of England attracted fewer Irish harvesters after the Famine although the annual exodus of hop-pickers to Kent in fact contained very many Irish who had settled in London's East End over several generations (the 'Lambeth Walk' is derived from an Irish jig). Likewise, in Scotland, native-born Irish tattie hokers faced increasing competition in the later nineteenth century from the Irish populations of the larger Scottish towns and cities.[8]

This highly mobile but transient workforce annually traversed a large part of Britain and contributed both labour, and word of work, to the more settled Irish communities that were already *in situ* in the urban and industrial centres of population. In 1851 Liverpool's Irish-born population was 22.3 per cent, Dundee's 18.9 per cent, Glasgow's 18.2 per cent, Manchester and Salford's 13.1 per cent, Paisley's 12.7 per cent, Bradford's 8.9 per cent, and London's 4.6 per cent.[9]

The total Irish-born population of Britain in that year was 727,326 — up by 308,070 from the figure in 1841. Ten years later the figure was 806,000, or 3.5 per cent of the whole. By 1901 it had fallen, by 1.7 per cent, to 632,000. This drop reflects the rising numbers emigrating from Ireland (albeit often via Liverpool) to the United States, Canada, and Australia.

> *Between 1876 and 1921, eighty-four per cent of Irish emigrants went to the USA, seven per cent to Australia and Canada, and only eight per cent to the United Kingdom.*[10]

The harvesters, of course, are not included in the above figures but neither, by the same token, are many of the equally transient and elusive Irish casual labourers who were (or contrived to be) unavailable to the census enumerators on the day/night when each census was taken. In recognition of this difficulty, nineteenth-century enumerators were sometimes allowed to make an educated guess as to the numbers engaged in public works on sites difficult to access or encompass. Amongst these were a great many Irish.

> *The coming of the Irish to Pollokshaws, now a suburb of Glasgow, was a result of that undertaking* [the Glasgow–Johnstone Canal,1807–1811]. *So ... the Irish in Paisley were considerably increased in number by the arrival of many of their countrymen when work ceased on the canal.... After the completion of the canals ... many of the Irish migratory labourers found further employment on road-making, which was proceeding apace ... and on the construction of docks.*[11]

Between 1813 and 1849 the quays around the river Clyde were lengthened from 941 feet to 10,238 feet and, according to Handley, '700 of the 1,000 or so stevedores employed at Glasgow harbour in the '30s were Irish — building the harbours of the Clyde'.[12]

Ardrossan, Stranraer, Ayr, Leith, Dundee, Aberdeen and Arbroath all constructed docks in the years following the completion of the Caledonian Canal (1818–1822). Between 1799 and 1901 Liverpool's great central dock system was an ongoing source of constant employment for the Irish.

> *A good portion of them were Irish, but there are others who are Lancashire men ... [the Irish] are the most reckless violent sort of people that can be imagined.*

Given that this judgement emanates from a hard-bitten policeman, one might suspect that, in his encounters with the Irish, he was 'meeting his own thought' as modern writers on self-development might put it. The same witness stated that

> *The principal technical and managerial skills possessed by a Ganger were two in number: his left fist and his right.*[13]

On the prolonged construction of the various great docks serving the port of London, the Irish, in addition to labouring, also figured prominently as stevedores.

The London dock strike of 1889 was, in fact, led by London-Irish activists.

> *Ben Tillet, whose mother was Irish, was the dockers' leader. He later stated that almost half the dockers involved in the 1889 strike were Irishmen or the sons of Irishmen.*[14]

Nevertheless 43.4 per cent of the Irish population of Britain in 1871 were living outside the sixty-three largest towns and cities. The Irish were merely finding their niche in that great surge of muscle-powered building, construction and commerce that characterised the phenomenal growth of Britain's economy in the nineteenth century.

> *Twenty years after the great Famine ... England was the greatest industrial nation in the known world. Half the world's coal was raised from her pits; half the world's textiles came from the Lancashire mills; one third of the known world's output of manufactured goods travelled on British ships.*[15]

Handley's researches led him to assert that the Irish were to the fore in every aspect of public works

Spoil wagon servicing mechanical excavator 'steam navvy', Manchester Ship Canal, 1889.

throughout nineteenth-century Britain. He tends, however, to equate the term 'navvy' with 'Irishman' and consequently gives the impression that the growth in demand for navvies may be taken to mean a concomitant increase in the employment of Irish labour.[16] Given the paucity of nineteenth-century sources recording the actual names and birthplaces of individuals employed in construction, however, it is difficult to produce tangible evidence for this assumption. Nevertheless Handley cites sufficient evidence for the employment of the Irish in this capacity, and this, when coupled with the density of, and demand for, Irish labour in Britain at this time, makes it difficult to deny the logic underlying his arguments.[17]

What was the nature of these 'public works' which, in the nineteenth century, generated so much employment for the Irish, and fatefully familiarised them with the rudiments of civil engineering?

Roads

Several of these turnpikes ... have been set up of late years, and great progress has been made in mending the most difficult ways, and that with such success as well deserves a place in this account.

Daniel Defoe, *A Tour throughout the Whole Island of Great Britain*, 1723

The work of the great Scottish engineer, Thomas Telford, was so extensive and varied that it usually generated demand for such Irish labour as was available locally. As engineer to the Ellesmere Canal (1793), the Shrewsbury canal (1795) and the Caledonian Canal (1803–1820) he employed many Irish labourers whose peregrinations via Liverpool and Glasgow had brought them into proximity with these projects. Dargan, the foremost Irish nineteenth-century railway contractor, was employed by Telford in England in his youth.

Telford's work as a road-builder in Scotland is credited with advancing the Highlands 'by at least a

century'. Here he built nine hundred miles of roads and over eleven hundred bridges and, in the rest of Scotland, a further thirty bridges and three hundred miles of roads. On these, as on the docks and harbours he built in Aberdeen, Leith, Banff, Wick, Ardrossan, Glasgow, Kirkwall, Dundee and elsewhere, a great many Irish found employment.[18]

Telford, of course, also built roads in England. It is singularly appropriate, given the long association between twentieth-century Irish emigrants and the port of Holyhead, that Telford's Holyhead Road should have used Irish labour. A bridge still stands, taking a spur of the A5 across the Llangollen Canal, which is known locally as 'The Irish Bridge'.

Telford's specifications for the Holyhead Road give us some idea of the labour-intensive nature of road-building prior to the twentieth century:

Upon a level bed prepared for the road materials the bottom course or layer of stone is to be set by hand in the form of a close, firm pavement. The stones are to be set on the broadest edges, lengthwise across the road, and the breadth of the upper beds is not to exceed four inches in any case. All the irregularities of the upper part of the said pavement are to be broken off by a hammer, and all the interstices to be filled with stone chips, firmly wedged together with a light hammer. The middle eighteen feet of pavement is to be coated with hard stone as nearly cubical as possible, broken up to go through a two and a half inch ring, to a depth of 6 inches, 4 of these 6 inches to be first put on and worked by traffic, after which the remaining 2 inches can be put on ... the whole of the material to be covered with one and a half inches of good gravel.

These activities could proceed only following the excavation and levelling of the road surface, work which in Telford's time was carried out solely by the use of pick, shovel, wheelbarrow, horse and cart. A ready market for Irish labour on road-making and repair works all over Britain has existed from Telford's

time to the present. The ballad, 'England's Motorways',
is a contemporary folk memory of Irish involvement in
the building of the motorways. Tarmac-laying is
almost an Irish monopoly in Britain today and many
emigrant Irishmen have recently returned home to
deploy these skills in expanding the trunk road
network in Ireland.

Canals

*A transport system remarkable for sound workman-
ship and the quiet dignity of its architecture.*

Duckham, Baron F.,
'The Founding of Goole....'

Roads entailed much ancillary work such as the
construction of bridges, cuttings, culverts and embankments, but prior to the twentieth century they

rarely equalled in extent and complexity the work
necessitated by the building of canals. The 3,360 miles
of canals (excluding the Manchester Ship Canal) built
in the British Isles in the eighteenth and nineteenth
centuries represent a Herculean achievement given the
technology of the time.

*The men who did the hardest work in railway
making, were those who had been engaged in a
similar kind of work, requiring cuttings and
embankments, — namely, in the formation of
canals.... Indeed, the work to which they had been
accustomed was such as required, in some respects,
even more care and attention than railway work; for
the best of brick-work and masonry, and well-made
earthworks, were necessary to make a canal secure ...
the common labourer at canal making had received
a training which more than fitted him for his share
of the work on railways.*[19]

A hand-built road, c. 1928.

Interior of puddle trench.

The construction of a canal involved many operations other than digging — itself no mean task. Quarrying, brick making, joinery and ironwork employed artisans for stonework, building locks, bridges, gates, drawbridges, arches and tunnels, and laying rails and pipes.

These canals were usually sixteen feet bottom width, five feet deep, with dual towpaths ten feet wide and eighteen inches above water level. The navvies not only excavated the channel using picks, shovels, and wheelbarrows, they also lined the bottom and sides with impermeable clay.

Installing this clay lining was known as 'puddling'. The material used was loam mixed with coarse sand or fine gravel (for this purpose, unlike in the making of pottery, a certain degree of porosity was desirable to avoid shrinkage and cracking if the clay dried). Once the canal had been excavated to the specified dimensions, a further two or three feet were excavated from the bottom for the 'puddle ditch', and usually another foot from each side, as a base for the impermeable walls or 'puddle gutters'.

The clay was made plastic with the addition of water worked through it by navvies using spades to compact and homogenise it. Nine inches of puddle clay were spread over the floor of the canal in manageable

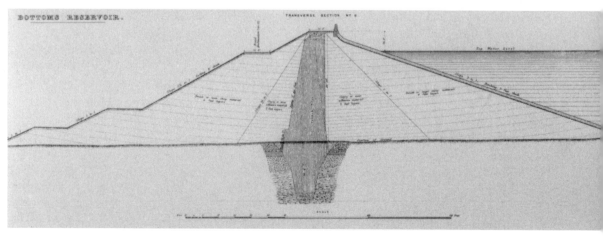

Above: Puddleclay wall, Bottoms reservoir, Derbyshire, 1869. Sunk 36 feet into solid rock, this 'plug' of impermeable clay was built up in 6-inch layers to a height of 80 feet inside the timbered puddle trench which spanned the entire length of the dam's base.

lengths, and chopped inch by inch, until it bonded with the bottom of the trench. A line of navvies advanced side by side, chopping as they went, and laboriously tamping down the clay with their boots to eliminate bubbles. For this arduous work they wore clogs, or strong boots, with sacking wrapped around their ankles and lower legs. (During construction of the cut-off trench for the Silent Valley Reservoir in County Down, in the 1920s, clay puddlers were issued with a pint of linseed oil daily to waterproof their leather boots).

When the first course of clay had dried sufficiently to withstand a man's weight, the next was added, and so on, until the required depth had been filled. Once the base was in, the 'puddle gutters' were started, from a depth of one foot down in the sides of the 'puddle ditch'. The gutters obviously could not be walked in to drive out air but common sense suggests they were beaten with spades or bats.

Despite the widespread use of concrete from the 1890s onwards, puddling continued to be employed as a sealing technique for dams and reservoirs, well into the twentieth century. As late as 1964, on the Chew Valley Reservoir in the South-West of England, the heeling-in of puddle clay had to be resorted to when power ramming failed to deliver the required standard of workmanship. In a 1,553-foot-long cut-off trench five feet wide, forty-eight feet below ground level, labourers heeled in no less than 14,000 cubic yards of puddle clay. At Killylane Dam, County Antrim (1956–1960), the contractors again employed this technique, and for similar reasons. These may well be the last recorded examples of the application, on a major civil engineering project, of a traditional navvy skill in constant use for over two hundred years.

The nerve and endurance needed to work in the claustrophobic conditions of these narrow trenches, to depths of perhaps one hundred plus feet (as in the case of Woodhead Reservoir, Derbyshire, 1848–1877), laboriously laying down puddle clay in six-inch layers, may now be only guessed at. None of the labourers concerned has left a personal record or written commentary of their efforts.

Heeling-in puddle-clay, Chew Valley Reservoir, 1960.

Another arduous, but much more dangerous, technique employed in canal construction was the barrow run. Here, if the canal was too deep for spoil to be thrown off the shovel onto the bank, a strong plank (or two bound side by side) was laid from the floor to the rim of the trench. A horse-gin, or 'jenny' was set up above. A line was then extended from the horse (or team of labourers), via gin or pulley, to a wheelbarrow in the trench. When the barrow was filled horse or men drew the barrow up the plank with the navvy guiding it behind.

A man could go up and down nearly twice in a minute if others filled the barrows and, in this way, a hundred barrow loads could be lifted in an hour. Overloaded barrows, weak lines, nervous horses, drunken navvies or slippery planks were all hazards that could, and often did, lead to accidents.

An English innovation was the technique of filling up the hollows from the heights — in other words,

Above: The Kilsby Tunnel. Tunnels were bored from both ends and also from the bottom of air shafts sunk at intervals from the surface. Men and spoil were winched up in containers. If a container snagged on the sides the men inside might fall to their deaths. The longest shaft at Woodhead was 579 feet deep.

Below: Navvies on barrow run.

taking the spoil from cuttings and using it to fill up the intervening valleys to the level required for the line. This technique was later adopted by Continental railway engineers.

This was necessitated by two facts that differentiated railways from canals. The lock system allowed barges to rise in steps over elevated terrain. Early locomotives, however, lacked sufficient horse-power to draw heavy trainloads up steep gradients; therefore the lines had to be laid as near to level as possible. Another option for canal builders in hilly country was to travel around the contours. The promoters of railways, however, were spending far greater capital sums than had been entailed in canal building and could afford neither costly land acquisition nor protracted construction periods. The most direct route attainable was therefore the chief aim of their engineers.[20]

Spoil from excavations was moved by wheelbarrow out to a distance of fifty or a hundred yards, before being tipped; beyond which the distances involved became too great for barrowing to be economical. After this point flat-bottomed rails were laid for spoil wagons drawn by horses. The horses drew these wagons at speed to the end of the embankment where, the horse being decoupled and led aside, the wagon shot forward until it collided with buffers.

At that stage a 'bankend man' with a shovel tripped the hinged door on the end of the wagon, just before it tipped up, and its load was propelled over the leading edge of the embankment. In theory the empty wagon fell back on the rails and was returned to the cutting for a refill. Excessive speed, a sticky load of 'muck', or incompetence could, however, result in muck, wagon, and perhaps even horse and driver going over the side all together.

Excavated material was classified as either 'rock' or 'soft'. One accepted definition of 'rock' was 'Any material other than earth or clay, that requires to be quarried or blasted'. 'Rock' was priced at three times the rate of 'soft'. Rock excavation was achieved by placing gunpowder charges in drilled holes.

Drilling was done using a pointed hexagonal steel drill known as a 'jumper'. One man, in a crouching position, held the 'jumper' above the point to be drilled while two strikers alternatively struck the top of the drill with fourteen-pound sledge hammers swung in a 360-degree arc over the shoulder. After each blow the jumper was turned a fraction. In this way a hole could be drilled to a depth of three to five feet. If, as often happened, a poorly tempered drill-bit broke off in the hole, the work was halted so that the bit could be extracted. For this a special device was used: a slim steel rod with two flexible flat blades welded to it was pushed into the hole until the blades extended down each side of the broken tip. A second rod had a ring attached at right angles to it; this ring was slipped down over the first rod until it encircled the blades and tightened their grip on the broken bit. Then both rods and bit were easily removed. This device was known as a 'bitch'.

A shaky hand on the drill, or a misjudged arc on the sledge stroke, could have disastrous consequences for the man on the jumper. The charge and fuse were usually rammed home using a copper or iron ramrod. Copper was safe but soft and wore out quickly. Quite often, however, the iron rod made sparks which prematurely ignited the gunpowder, 'firing' the rod back at the workman, and perhaps killing him instantly. Too short fuses were equally lethal, while the rock might not split or fall as expected, causing injury to those nearby. Haste and carelessness resulted in many accidents around these processes.

Another dangerous practice was undercutting banks, to encourage the soil to fall in, instead of laboriously digging it out in the normal way. A man was stationed on top of the overhang to warn of an impending collapse while his workmates were still undercutting the bank; inevitably warnings often came too late, or not at all, and men were killed by collapsing soil and rock.

Overall, a casualty rate of one or two deaths per mile of railway was considered unremarkable, and in this way the tone was set for the cavalier macho mentality, characteristic of both labourer and

Above: Hand-drilling using sledge hammers and 'jumper'.
Below: Construction of embankment, Manchester Ship Canal, 1888.

contractor, which to a degree still pervades the construction industry to this day.

It is a well-known fact that until the First World War it was statistically more dangerous to be a navvy than to be a soldier, even during periods of sustained fighting.[21]

Navvies' wages, for these hazardous undertakings, ranged from one shilling and sixpence per day in 1803 to two shillings and six pence per day in 1814. As late as 1845 harvesters, in contrast, were earning only an average of one shilling and ten pence per day. By that time, railway navvies earned on average three shillings and nine pence per nine-hour day.

Forty years later, on the Manchester Ship Canal, wages were still at the same level. In summer, however, a twelve-hour day was not unusual on public works, and this brought wages up to way beyond what an agricultural labourer could hope to earn.

Handley gives detailed figures for food prices from mid-century to the First World War. These show tea and sugar halving in price from five shillings per pound for tea and seven shillings per pound for sugar in 1850, to two and six and later to three shillings and five pence in 1875. In the 1870s potatoes cost from sixpence to sevenpence a stone, and bread sixpence per 4lb loaf. Butter increased modestly over the same period, from one-and-twopence to one-and-sixpence per pound. Handley states that prices fell by 20 per cent in the 1890s and remained stable thereafter until the First World War. Rents for a single apartment in Glasgow in 1875 were around three shillings per week.

A contemporary Scottish newspaper investigation estimated the average working-class family income at twenty-five shillings per week. Handley, however, quotes the Edinburgh Dean of Guilds to the effect that earnings of even sixteen shillings eluded the average common labourer.

The labourers have four pence per hour just now (1885). They had five pence some years ago, but now they work nine hours a day and six on Saturday; that is fifty-one hours a week, and that at four pence an hour amounts to about 18/-; but from that you have to deduct broken (i.e. wet) time.[22]

Railways

They were the nomads of the New World and their muscular strength laid its foundations.
Trevelyan, G.M., *English Social History*

As already noted, in addition to the annual agricultural influx of harvesters and tattie hokers, throughout the nineteenth century there were Irish workers in factories, chemical works, warehouses, mills, and mines:

The boundless coal-fields beneath us, and the boundless mines of labour, so to speak, existing for us in Ireland, form together one of the great secrets of the almost unparalleled prosperity of this part of Scotland.[23]

Many, as we have seen, were engaged in construction of every sort. With few exceptions, however, none of the many nineteenth-century building activities that employed Irish labour has caught the imagination of the public to the same degree as railway building.

*In eighteen hundred and forty-five
Poor Paddy was more dead than alive,
Poor Paddy was more dead than alive,
From workin' on the Railway.*

Samuel Smiles, writing about the building of the Liverpool–Manchester Railway (1830), wrote:

They were drawn by the attraction of good wages from all parts of the kingdom; and they were ready for any sort of hard work. Many of the labourers employed on the Liverpool lines were Irish; others were from the Northumberland and Durham railways, where they had been accustomed to similar work; and some of the best came from the fen districts of Lincoln and Cambridge, where they had been trained to execute works of excavation and embankment.[24]

Although many lines were built largely with local agricultural labour these tended to be lesser routes through easy well-populated country. On major lines, either in urban centres or remote thinly-populated regions, professional navvies were the norm. By

definition, these men went wherever demand led them, and travelled light.

Navvies were in demand in the urban centres because, despite a surfeit of unskilled labour, the male inhabitants were even less suited to construction work than the agricultural labourers of the countryside.

In 1901, Earl Grey stated that,

Of 11,000 men who had volunteered from the Manchester district for service in South Africa, 8,000 were rejected as unfit to carry a rifle and endure the fatigues and privations of a campaign; of the 3,000 who were accepted, only 1,200 were pronounced by

Navvies filling 'sets' of wagons, Manchester Ship Canal, 1890.

the Military Authorities to be up to the standard of what a soldier ought to be.[25]

To be a navvy a man had to be strong, beyond even the norm for the agricultural or casual labourer.

There has been a large influx of agricultural labourers, also plenty of Irishmen, and those who have not had previous experience have less chance of securing a job than those hardy fellows who have moved about the country on public works for a lifetime.... We have, in fact, met numbers of men of splendid physique, Samsons in their way, who may literally be said to have been born navvies.[26]

Some idea of the labour involved in railway construction is conveyed by the following information. Trains of muck-shifting wagons on a railway were known as 'sets'. Usually fourteen such 'sets' were filled in a day. A wagon held two and a quarter cubic yards of spoil. Each wagon was filled by two men.

Railway engineers of the time employed Irish as well as British labour both in Britain and Ireland, and F.R. Conder canvassed their opinions on both. His conclusion make interesting reading:

The English navvy ... is a man with whom there is some satisfaction in working ... to whom you can attribute any failure to elevate him into a position of permanent comfort and respectability, not to any inherent infirmity of nature, but to want of early training, and to the potent influence of strong drink.

Ironically, these words, if written about the archetypal twentieth-century Irish navvy, would have been accepted without comment by many British observers who subscribed to the belief that an English operative was far superior to his Irish counterpart in terms of skill, dependability and sobriety. Yet Conder goes on to remark that:

It is otherwise with the Irish labourer.... In England or America he becomes a hard-working and reliable operative. His natural ability, far above that of the average Englishman, when directed in the right channel, enables him to take a high rank in the republic of labour.[27]

According to Stephen Ballard, an agent for the great railway contractor Thomas Brassey,

'Steam Navvy', Manchester Ship Canal.

The labour which a navvy performs exceeds in severity almost any other description of work ... each man has to lift nearly twenty tons of earth on a shovel over his head into a wagon. The height of lifting is about six feet. This is taking it at fourteen sets a day; but the navvies sometimes contrive to get through sixteen sets, and ... some men ... will accomplish this astonishing quantity of work by about three or four o'clock in the afternoon, a result I believe not nearly equalled by any other set of workmen in the world.[28]

Another famous Victorian railway contractor, Samuel Morton Peto, in his Address to the Crown at the opening of Parliament in 1851, said of the Irish navvies:

I know from personal experience that if you treat him well, and show you care for him, he is the most faithful and hardworking creature in existence; but if you find him working for fourpence a day, and that paid in potatoes and meal, can we wonder that the results are as we find them? [A reference to current unrest amongst Irish navvies on certain lines] But give him legitimate occupation, and remuneration for his services, show him you appreciate those services, and you may be sure you put an end to all agitation. He will be your faithful servant.[29]

This testimonial to the Irish navvies mirrors a similar one praising the Irish harvesters of the time :

... wandering Irish labourers, who slept on the straw in barns and sheds, had wheat bread for their sole substantial nourishment, and took home £10 or £12 at the end of the half-year.... They are most efficient labourers, and a more industrious, cheerful, easily-managed and well-conducted class of men is nowhere to be found.[30]

Navvies, of course, could not have performed the feats of strength expected of them on a diet of wheaten bread; the navvy consumed on average two pounds of beef, two loaves of bread, and five quarts of ale per day — when he could get them. This was another incentive for Irish labourers, used to a monotonous diet of potatoes and buttermilk at home, to elevate themselves to the status of navvy.[31]

Trevelyan wasn't exaggerating when he described the navvies as nomads. They had few ties, if any, and they tramped the length and breadth of Britain following contractors or seeking out 'the big money'.

Spoil wagon with 'bank-end' man, Manchester Ship Canal, 1887.

During the railway-making period, the navvies wandered about from one public work to another — apparently belonging to no country and having no home.... Working together, eating, drinking, and sleeping together, and daily exposed to the same influences, these railway labourers soon presented a distinct and well-defined character, strongly marking them from the population of the districts in which they laboured. Reckless alike of their lives as of their earnings, the navvies worked hard and lived hard.

The unskilled casual labourer of the nineteenth century in Britain led an uncertain existence based on intermittent employment at a variety of jobs throughout the year. Industry, commerce, and construction were all very labour-intensive; the common denominator was brute force. When demand slackened in one sphere of activity, the labourer switched to another, sometimes relocating in the process.

Railway building was, by definition, a uniquely mobile process and such men as found it congenial and profitable had to become itinerant to remain employed at it. The Irish had a particular predilection for wandering. This lifestyle fostered values that the settled community, rooted in the timeless and unvarying routines and rituals of rural England, found disturbing. The resulting tensions are reflected in the writings of many contemporary observers:

> *They lived but for the present; they cared not for the past; they were indifferent to the future. Their pay-nights were often a Saturnalia of riot and disorder, dreaded by the inhabitants of the villages along the line of works. The irruption of such men into the quiet hamlet of Kilsby must, indeed, have produced a very startling effect on the recluse inhabitants of the place. In short, the navvies were little better than heathens....*

> *For their lodgings, a hut of turf would content them; and, in their hours of leisure, the meanest public house would serve for their parlour. Unburdened, as they usually were, by domestic ties, unsoftened by family affection, and without much moral or religious training, the navvies came to be distinguished by a sort of savage manners, which contrasted strangely with those of the surrounding population.*

> *Yet, ignorant and violent though they might be, they were usually good-hearted fellows in the main — frank and open-handed with their comrades, and ready to share their last penny with those in distress.*[32]

In 1847, when the so-called 'railway mania' was at its peak, there were approximately 257,000 navvies employed building railway lines. By 1850, following the collapse of this speculative boom, the numbers employed had shrunk to a mere 36,000.[33]

Nevertheless railway building continued, albeit at a slower pace, for another eighty years. Between 1825 and 1840, the total route mileage built was 1,484; by 1850 it was 6,084, and by 1860, 9,069. By 1870 it was 13,563, creeping up at a slower pace to reach the peak of over 20,000 route miles by the 1930s. Over half of the total railway network in Britain had been laid out by the early 1860s.

The numbers of navvies waxed and waned throughout the nineteenth century but the tribe continued to attract new members and those who enlisted became part of a race apart — an outlawed breed, 'savages in the midst of civilisation'.

That other outlawed breed — the Irish — frequently threw in their lot with them. ('Even the wild Irish navvy has a soul to save', claimed the Salvation Army.) In the course of a lifetime's service these Irish men evolved into a unique labour élite, known throughout Britain's construction industry as 'The Long-Distance Men'.

3 Paddy and the Big Ditch

Thomas Carlyle's remarks, penned in 1846, on the 'better behaviour' of Irish railway navvies vis-à-vis their English counterparts indicate a transitional phase, amongst the Irish labourers, from harvesting to navvying:

> *The Yorkshire and Lancashire men, I fear, are reckoned the worst; and, not without glad surprise, I find the Irish are the best in point of behaviour. The postman tells me that several of the poor Irish do regularly apply to him for money drafts, and send their earnings home. The English, who eat twice as much beef, consume the residue in whisky, and do not trouble the postman.*[1]

The ingrained harvesters' habits of abstemiousness, thrift, and diligence were obviously still very much in evidence amongst these Irish navvies but they no longer worked in family groups. Their habits and outlook were changing as they became part of that great army of unskilled casual labour powering Britain's burgeoning economy.

The population of Great Britain — England, Wales, and Scotland — almost quadrupled between 1801 and 1911. Within one generation of the Battle of Waterloo, half of England's population had shifted from a rural to an urban environment, and this trend accelerated thereafter. The resulting expansion of housing, factories, offices and commercial premises, plus their ancillary services and utilities, created much employment for labourers and tradesmen.

> *Ireland is our market for labour, the supplies of which are regulated on the same principles which regulate the supplies of articles of consumption and commerce;*

In the present state of the labour market English labour would be almost un-purchasable if it were not for the competition of Irish labour. The English labourers have unfortunately been taught their rights till they have almost forgotten their duties ... and in that case we are frequently able to put on the screw of Irish competition;

English labourers will not allow others to work, and therefore we have very great assistance from the Irish;

We employ the Irish not because we prefer them but because the English have not been sufficient to supply the largely and rapidly increased demand for labour in this town.[2]

Casual work by definition demanded flexibility from unskilled labourers, and those whose movements were not constrained by family ties had the advantage of unrestricted mobility. Since the construction industry in particular was predicated on finite projects, in varying geographical locations, the latter were best placed to work in it.

The greatest of the 'public works' in the first half of the nineteenth century were, of course, the railways. The Irish, as migrants, benefited from their eminent suitability to the nomadic lifestyle of the railway builders. However, the prejudice they often encountered in Britain as religious, political, and cultural 'aliens' was exacerbated by the hostility of the settled community towards the often brutalised and lawless navvy.

The women shun us like lepers are shunned. The brainless girl who works with a hoe in a turnip field will have nothing to do with a tramp navvy. The children hide behind their mothers' petticoats when they see us coming.

'The Big Ditch'. The Manchester Ship Canal —
the greatest engineering feat of the Victorian Age.

Author Dick Sullivan had a navvy father and a mother born on site of navvy stock. Notwithstanding his Irish-sounding name, in his book, *Navvyman*, he writes:

> The Irish were cast out even by the outcast navvy: they were the minority within the minority, the outsiders inside the outsiders. Although they made up only 10 per cent of the whole, the Irish were the common factor in about a third of navvy riots.[3]

David Brooke, perhaps the greatest living authority on the railway navvies, while he acknowledges the notorious riots between the Irish and the Scots and English navvies, cautions against inferring too much from these.

In a study of lines coincidental with the censuses of 1851, 1861, and 1871 he points out that on many lines Irish navvies, present in small numbers over long stretches of the works, did not seek common housing as a means of protection. In fact, they often shared their accommodation indiscriminately with English navvies.

Dr Brooke qualifies this, however, with the observation that the lines to which he refers did not coincide with the years of heavy railway building prior to 1841 'when the number of Irish at work in England was probably at its greatest'. At such times, he suggests, the latent xenophobia of the English may have been inflamed by the sight of the culturally exotic Irish assembled en masse and, allegedly, working for lower rates of pay.[4]

Statistics quoted by Jackson (*The Irish in Britain*, 1964), however, suggest that the numbers of Irish born in Britain rose from 419,256 in 1841 to 727,326 in 1851 and peaked, at 806,000, in 1861. The period 1835–1847 saw the greatest spurt of railway building and this had passed before the major Irish influx following the Famine.

It is unlikely, in any event, that many of those Irish who emigrated to avoid starvation in Ireland would have had the necessary strength and stamina for railway building.

'Samsons in their Way'

Some of the work is given out on 'Piece', and men of trained muscles make good wages. An ordinary figure is 6d. per day, and sometimes it adds up to as much as 7s. The 'Piece' men work in gangs of about five or six, and their chief business is soil-stripping. A square of perhaps a hundred feet is marked out for one of these gangs, and the cutting and wheeling are undertaken at so much a yard.

The members of the gang share on equal terms, the leader getting no more than his companions. In making up a gang care, of course, is taken that each man can do his share of the work, and in this way groups of fine brawny fellows get together, and sometimes keep together for twelve months at a stretch.

The average navvy stands over six feet tall, and weighs fourteen or fifteen stone, and this magnificent engine of labour can be had for, at the outside, seven shillings a day. The common man, who works under a 'ganger', and not for his own hand, receives four and a halfpence an hour, which adds up to three shillings and nine pence if the day's work is unbroken. The trained and seasoned Excavator, however, working in a 'butty gang', may earn as much as 8d. an hour.[5]

An Irish engineer, Samuel Roberts, working on the Cong Canal in 1848, had this to say about the quality of labour employed on it:

> *I have never witnessed more want of power of exertion among the labouring classes in this part of the country when work began ... the greater portion of them are so perfectly destitute and so wretchedly fed, that it would be impossible to enable them to realise a rate of wages calculated to support them in a proper manner without paying prices which the economical execution of the work would not permit.*[6]

However, the Irish labouring in Britain on public works, and who were not Famine refugees, were a different matter.

David Brooke quotes Sullivan and his own earlier study as evidence for his statement that

> ... the majority of the worst (episodes of navvy violence) occurred in the north of England and Scotland, and involved conflict with Irish workers. Moreover, they belong to the 1840s, the most intense years of Irish immigration.[7]

However, as Brooke himself admits, the navvies began to acquire a reputation as troublemakers from as early as the canal era of the eighteenth century and they were regarded with fear or contempt by the middle and upper classes from the very inception of the railway age.

> The term navvy is simply an abridgement of the word navigator, which savours too much of the sound of the word alligator to be pleasant, and in fact some people have a rough idea that the navvy is a sort of human alligator, who feeds on helpless women and timid men, and frightens children into fits.[8]

This view emanates from a clergyman who had spent some years as a missionary on railway projects and who might, on both counts, have been expected to be more charitable.

Equally bizarre, given his occupation, were the views expressed by Lt Peter Lecount, an assistant engineer to Robert Stephenson on the London & Birmingham Railway (1838):

> Possessed of all the recklessness of the Smuggler, without any of his redeeming qualities, their ferocious behaviour can only be equalled by the brutality of their language. It may be truly said, their hand is against every man and, before they have been long located, every man's hand is against them; and woe befall any woman, with the slightest share of modesty, whose ears they can assail — Crimes of the most atrocious character are common, and robbery without an attempt at concealment has been an everyday occurrence, wherever they have been congregated in large numbers.[9]

Fifty years later, however, during the construction of the Manchester Ship Canal, a local newspaper commented favourably on the calibre and behaviour of the navvy workforce:

> We hear good accounts of the navvies' conduct. The old prejudice has not quite worn out against them but respectable people who have had navvies as lodgers are, we hear, astonished to find them so tractable, so intelligent, and so well-behaved. Of course, all are not alike but it is clear that it is time to judge them as men and not, as did the reporter who, when describing a loss of life by thunderstorm, wrote, 'Three men and a navvy were killed.'[10]

The Irish on the Ship Canal seemed to be even better behaved; the old Lancashire man referred to above who had been employed on this project said of them,

> We had hundreds of Irishmen on the canal, hard workers and all; you'd never hear them swear — once in a blue moon, not like our buggers.[11]

Far from being troublemakers, the Irish were, if anything, more often sinned against than sinning:

> Many difficulties arose with the men, especially in consequence of the feuds that existed between the English and the Irish navvies; and eventually the latter were driven off the field, and were afraid to return unless they were especially protected at night by the police. The engineer promised that they should be taken care of — and he arranged it with the authorities that three policemen should be placed at his disposal.

These he directed to appear at certain points of the works, and in certain attitudes and positions, at certain times; and, taking an Irishman under cover of the night to these points at the right moments, he showed one after another of what seemed to be a little army of constables. The three policemen grew into a multitude; the Irishmen were satisfied of the abundant sufficiency of the protection afforded, and they returned to their work.[12]

An Outlawed Breed

'Race riots' notwithstanding, by and large the navvies of the nineteenth century seem to have placed greater emphasis on the differences between themselves and the settled community than on their individual nationalities, and, by and large, made common cause in the face of hostility and exploitation.

In the semi-autobiographical writings of the Donegal navvy poet and writer Patrick MacGill, for instance, his fictional alter ego Dermod Flynn is the only navvy who is identified by his country of origin. MacGill is almost unique, amongst navvies, for his written articulation of the strong sense of alienation of this outlawed breed:

Stretches the future before them, clouded and bleak as their past,
These are our serfs — and our brothers,
Slighted, forsaken, outcast.[13]

So harshly were the early railway navvies treated in fact that, in 1845, conditions on the construction of the Manchester and Sheffield Railway's Summit Tunnel at Woodhead, in Lancashire, finally provoked a public outcry.

It appears from the evidence ... that the construction of railways, as at present conducted, is accompanied with very great risk to the men engaged; that the losses in killed and wounded are nearly proportional to the losses of an army in a campaign; that the men are crowded together to an undue and injurious extent; that their moral condition is most deplorable, especially as regards sexual immorality and drunkenness; that there is much vagabondage among the class; and that there is great reason to fear that, when these works are discontinued, the dispersion of such a class among the general community will be attended with similar mischief as the disbanding of a small army.

At the summit level tunnel the killed may be stated at 3, and the wounded at 14, per cent. The deaths (according to the official returns) in the three battles of Talavera, Salamanca, and Waterloo, were only 2.11 per cent of the privates; and in the last forty-one months of the Peninsular War, the privates killed in battle were 4.2 per cent, and by disease 11.9 per cent.

... It was stated that a large proportion of the accidents at the summit level had happened from the drunkenness either of the sufferers or of their fellow-workmen. The precaution of preventing any man working while drunk would at once be adopted if it were the contractor's evident interest to be very careful.... The contractors or sub-contractors have often an interest in the sale of drink; and sometimes they even pay wages in 'drink tickets' instead of money.

What happens is that, first as many of the workmen procure lodgings among the residents as can possibly be taken in, and far more than can be properly or even safely accommodated; the rest erect for themselves temporary abodes of the rudest description, often little better than mud hovels. Sometimes, indeed, the accommodation is so scanty that the men are divided into night and day gangs, in order that one set of beds may serve for two sets of men. As a natural, nay almost inevitable consequence of such overcrowding, the common decencies of life are grossly disregarded, and the condition of the women may be imagined.[14]

Above: 'Frying Steak on the Shovel' — Installation, Castlefields, Manchester. If no pots were to hand, Navvies (and farm labourers) often cooked on their shovels, which were kept spotless.

There are three railway tunnels at Woodhead. The first was driven between 1839 and 1845, the second between 1847 and 1852, and the third between 1949 and 1954. The first tunnel is three miles and thirteen yards long. All but one thousand yards of it is lined with masonry because of the unstable nature of the rock (millstone grit, shales, red sandstone, slate and clay). The depth of the longest of the five air shafts is 579 feet below the surface of the moors above.

The navvies at Woodhead 'bivouacked in huts run up with loose stones and mud and thatched with ling from the moors, and slept on truckle-beds in groups of twenty' — this at an altitude of 1,500 feet. In high summer that site, even now, is too chilly to visit without a jacket, and in winter a man could die of hypothermia if caught out without shelter overnight. An average of 1,100 men worked on the project, usually up to their ankles in mud or water, and dry clothing was a rarity in any season.

Wages were good, because conditions were atrocious and few men were attracted to the works, but payouts happened only every nine weeks. Men were obliged to feed themselves and their families using food tickets redeemable at the contractor's 'tommy shop'. These establishments were operated by traders on behalf of the contractor and usually sold inferior goods at exorbitant prices. In fact, in the face of the uncertainties and vicissitudes of railway building they often represented the most certain source of profit for the contractors and their agents.

Paid in Beer

At Woodhead, while food tickets were available to the navvies only at specific times, beer tickets were available on demand. Inevitably, off-duty navvies not only drank excessively, but also often went to work intoxicated while their families went hungry.

'Truck' (see quotation below), first introduced in the Scottish coal-mines in the eighteenth century, was a feature of public works in the canal era but was outlawed by the *Truck Act* of 1831. Unfortunately this Act made no reference to railway workers, simply because these did not yet exist, and so the railway contractors were exempt from its remit. By the time the *Truck Amendment Act* was introduced in 1887 railway building had become much more systematised and the large and reputable contractors then operating had all but eliminated it. However, this was too late for the thousands of navvies who had suffered its abuses over the previous half century.

The provident contractor raised a little city of turf huts, and accommodated his workmen on the spot. Their daily wants were met by the ticket system, or what was better known as the 'tommy-shop'. Near the labourers' shanties was provided an emporium, furnished with all their habits led them to procure. Ale in abundance, spirits, bread, meat, fat bacon, tobacco, shovels, jackets, gay crimson and purple waistcoats, boots, hats and night-caps, were all to be obtained of the convenient 'tommy-shop' keeper, who, though apparently an independent tradesman, was

*in fact a mere nominee and dependent of the
contractor. Political economists would have been
delighted at the ease with which the wants of the
labourers were supplied without the need of money.
Credit was always at their command. Even the
newly-arrived and penniless 'navvy', provided that
his boots were sound, could obtain a shovel on credit
— that necessary implement of toil being all, except
stout thews and sinews, that he was called upon to
furnish....*

*The pay was, generally, monthly. On a large sheet,
the detail and the total of every man's time, calculated
in quarter days, was entered by the contractor's
timekeeper. The rate of wages, varying from 2s.6d. to
4s.9d. per day, was added. The total earnings of the
month thus arrived at were entered in the next
column. In the following came the amount drawn on
tickets, or shop credit. The final column contained the
cash balance due to the workman. It was extraordinary to see with how small an amount of actual
specie the monthly pay was discharged....*

*The profit of these tommy-shops was very large
— often the main part of the gain of the contractor....
If 8 to 12 per cent was the profit which a contractor,
who was his own foreman, could secure on the
nominal cost of his work, the profit made by the
shop out of the nominal cost price might amount to
from 30 to 40 per cent. In fact, in some instances, the
poor men were shamefully ground down.*[15]

Demand for Irish Labour

We must assume that the Irish navvies suffered the
same vicissitudes as their English or Scots counterparts, but in what numbers we may only guess.
Jackson, in *The Irish in Britain* (1963), claims that, 'The
Irish provided a large pool of available and willing
labour and ... appeared particularly well-suited to this
work', and cites the evidence of a witness before the
Select Committee on Emigration from the United
Kingdom (1827).

*It is a fact that if an extensive drain, or canal, or
road, or any other thing were to make, that could be
done by piecework.... I should not feel in the least
surprised to find, that of a hundred men employed
at it, ninety were Irish.*

Jackson points out the difficulties inherent in
assessing the actual numbers of Irish involved. He
cites the wide seasonal variations in railway building,
as compared with those affecting harvesters, and,
consequently, the longer intervals between return trips
to Ireland (which were officially recorded).

He also refers to the high incidence of recruitment
of Irish labour from mainland centres of population,
rather than directly from Ireland, and the poor record-
keeping of sub-contractors vis-à-vis the labour force.
Nevertheless he gives the impression that the lifestyle and conditions of the navvy, which he goes on
to describe, affected Irish labourers in significant
numbers.

Concerning the issue of Irish labour depressing
English wages, Redford alleges a dearth of Irish in
railway building during the period between 1831 and

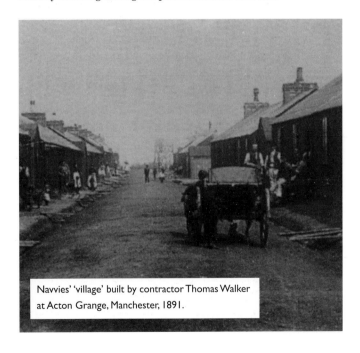

Navvies' 'village' built by contractor Thomas Walker
at Acton Grange, Manchester, 1891.

1841, and states that 'for the years of depressed trade after 1836 it was possible to get English labour as cheaply as Irish'.[16]

Even if this were so, why should the contractors not have used the desperation of the Irish as a lever to depress wages still further, rather than being content merely to rely on the scarcity of jobs to keep wages low? Such restraint would have been most uncharacteristic of employers in that era of raw capitalism.

Redford, however, also states that contractors were discouraged from employing the Irish by 'violent opposition from the English labourers', which 'led to serious disturbances'. However, the only serious incidents of this sort occurred in 1845–46, when there was a construction boom employing over 250,000 navvies. Both arguments cannot be applied to the same time frame.[17]

Strike-Breakers

The exotic character of the Irish poor, distinguished by accent and dialect, dress and appearance, customs and religion, made them conspicuous targets for English or Scottish discontent and xenophobia. Their destitution led them to accept both inferior housing and lower pay and left them vulnerable to charges of undermining the material and moral standards of their native counterparts.

Redford goes to great lengths to justify with citations the contemporary perception of certain sections of British society that the Irish had only 'potatoes and paws', where the Scots had 'oatmeal and brose and horn spoons', and the English 'meat and bread and knives and forks'. Therefore, there were fears that the 'wheat-fed population of Great Britain' could be 'supplanted by the potato-fed popula-tion of Ireland'.

He cites the many instances of strike-breaking and undercutting involving Irish labour in the industrial centres, around milling particularly, with special emphasis on the Famine influx. Describing the influence of the Irish immigrants' 'lower standard of living' as 'evil' he asserts that,

> *With this lower standard of living went a lower efficiency as workmen, and a worse moral tone. The Irish were less provident, and more given to drunkenness; they were slovenly, careless, and stupid. On this account they were not usually put in charge of power-driven machinery, and were necessarily given the lower-paid work. They formed a submerged class, always tending to drag down their neighbours to a lower level of living.*

He does, however, make some small concession by distinguishing between the 'industrious and sober' agricultural and rural Irish labourers and 'those working in the great industrial centres'. Here Redford seems to strain somewhat after a certain bias, which contrasts strongly with his conclusion that,

> *It was, indeed, generally assumed that Irish labour was indispensable to the prosperity of both the manufactures and the agriculture of Great Britain; and the Irish undoubtedly proved useful to the employers in keeping down the level of wages.*[18]

That conclusion speaks for itself; whether utilisation of Irish labour did depress wage levels or not, the consistent demand for Irish labour in Britain in the past two centuries speaks volumes for the quality and constancy of their work. Rather than Irish labour 'lowering standards', it could be argued that their application and hard work set standards which the British conspicuously and consistently failed to match.

Certainly there is a belief still prevalent amongst older and recently retired Irish construction workers, some of them formerly in senior positions, that English labourers performed poorly when compared with their Irish equivalents.

In the words of one Irishman who, after thirty-nine years in the industry, retired with the rank of Senior Administration Manager,

I must say that, having worked with many nationalities over the years, my own countrymen always were Top of the Pile. They had no equal when it came to hard graft, sheer guts, and pride, yes pride, in a job well done and the fact that they were Irishmen, the greatest grafters in the world.[19]

David Brooke, in correspondence, has stated that his researches revealed no concrete evidence for undercutting by Irish railway labourers in the nineteenth century,

I have never been able to reach any conclusion on the accuracy of the allegation that they worked for lower rates.[20]

'Paddy on the Railway'

That is not to say, of course, that such was never the case or that the rumour of it would not have been sufficient to have led to conflict on site. Such conflicts, however, were never so inevitable or endemic as to prevent the employment, albeit sometimes segregated, of the Irish. What Brooke's research does show, however, is the distribution and extent of Irish railway labour between 1841 and 1871 (1891 in Scotland) as of each census.[21]

Table V in *The Railway Navvy: 'That Despicable Race of Men'* (1983), lists the Places of Birth of navvies working on lines on England in 1841, 1851, 1861, and 1871, in Wales for the years 1851, 1861, and 1871, and in Scotland for the years 1841, 1851, 1861, 1871, and 1891.

Over the entire period, on lines where the Irish were recorded in any numbers, the lowest figure given for Irish-born (for the South-Eastern Tunbridge Wells-Hastings Line, in 1841) is 1 per cent. The highest figure, on the Edinburgh & Bathgate, Glasgow Extension (1871), is 76.9 per cent.

The highest percentage of Irish recorded on an English line was 54.5 per cent (Border Union Line, 1861). The two next highest percentages in England

were 50.2 per cent (Border Counties, 1861), and 33 per cent (Newcastle & Carlisle, Alston Branch, 1851).

The highest figures for Wales were 46 per cent (Merthyr, Tredegar & Abergavenny Line, 1861), 36.7 per cent (Taff Vale, Dowlais Branch, 1851), and 21.3 per cent (Vale of Neath, 1851). The lowest figure recorded was 5.1 per cent (Oswestry & Newtown Line plus part of the Shrewsbury & Welshpool Railway, 1861).

In Scotland the three highest figures recorded for the Irish are 76.9 per cent (see above), 68.7 per cent (Edinburgh & Bathgate, Coatbridge Extension, 1861), and 65.8 per cent (Monkland, Bo'ness Extension, 1851). The lowest recorded figure for Irish railway labourers in Scotland was 2.4 per cent (Inverness & Rosshire Line, 1861). As late as 1891, when Robert McAlpine was building the Mallaig Extension to the West Highland Line, 32.6 per cent of the workforce were Irish.

In England between 1841 and 1871, out of a total of around forty-eight lines, the Irish were present in numbers exceeding 20 per cent on only six. This would suggest that they accounted for only around 12.5 per cent of England's railway labourers during the period when the majority of her railways were built. From the above figures it will be noticed that, where the Irish are present in the greatest numbers, it is on North-of-England lines close to the Irish immigrant centres of Liverpool, Manchester, and the Scottish borders.

J.A. Patmore, in a study of Irish navvies on a North-of-England railway project coincidental with the 1851 Census, makes the following observation:

The biggest single group was that born in Ireland, some 26 per cent of the total.

Statistics such as this may have contributed to the popular perception of the Irish as quintessential railway navvies. Closer analysis of the Returns however gave Patmore cause to qualify these findings:

Such evidence as is available, however, suggests that these labourers were in no sense members of a regular gang, or even previously experienced in railway construction. The children of many of the

Irish labourers were all born in Ireland, with the exception of the youngest, though many families seem to have been resident in Knaresborough since the beginning of the contract five years previously. A typical entry in the returns is that of an Irish railway labourer of thirty nine, with a daughter of nine born in Ireland and a daughter of four, and a son of two months, born in Knaresborough.[22]

In Wales between 1851 and 1871, where a total of eleven lines were under construction, the Irish exceeded 20 per cent on only four. This accounted for approximately 30 per cent of the labour force and of course the Irish were concentrated in South Wales. There they commenced work in the mines and iron-works and later migrated to railway building in search of better pay or work out of doors.

In Scotland, however, where returns were available up to 1891, twenty-one lines were built and the Irish were present in numbers exceeding 20 per cent on no less than fifteen of them. They approximated therefore to over 75 per cent of the workforce and 'dominated the railway scene in those parts of Scotland which were their customary areas of settlement'.[23]

This forms the basis for Brooke's assertion that,

... in the East and West Lowlands, the hub of Scotland's industry, the supremacy of the Irish as railway navvies stood unchallenged by either men from the resident population or migrant Scots.[24]

Brooke goes on to assert, on the basis of his analysis of the census returns covering the entire United Kingdom, that 'only the ubiquitous Irish can be described as a truly international force in railway construction'. In correspondence, he has drawn my attention to his findings that

There were some Irish workers on Mackenzie and Brassey's contracts for the building of the Paris & Rouen Railway in 1841–43. Further, some were present on Mackenzie's work for the Marne-Rhine Canal at Einville.[25]

These findings seriously undermine the time-honoured claim by the Irish in England that 'we built the railways'. Oddly enough this claim is not as a rule disputed by the English. They thereby deny their ancestors the enormous credit due to them. Railway historians, as opposed to popular writers on the subject, are generally in agreement that the great majority of nineteenth-century railway navvies in England were from the northern counties, and Lancashire, with the Irish, Scots, and Welsh (in order of importance) forming much smaller minorities. Where the Irish were undisputed masters of railway building was in Scotland and the United States.

The Irish navvies, individually, ranged far and wide across the British Isles in search of work. Thomas Ryan was returned in the 1971 Census as a resident of the navvy village of 'Jericho', at Batty Green on the Midland Railway's Settle–Carlisle Line, near Ribblehead Viaduct in the Yorkshire Dales. According to the Returning Officer's records Thomas had a son James, aged ten, born in Ireland; a son Francis, aged eight, born in Gloucestershire; a daughter Mariah, aged five, born in Gloucestershire; a son Michael, aged four, born in Scotland; and a daughter Anne, aged one, born in Huddersfield, Yorkshire.[26]

Dick Sullivan's book, *Navvyman*, embraces the mainstream scholarship of Coleman, Brooke, and Handley but the writing reflects his navvy father's prejudice against the Irish. He writes, for example that '... most of the miners [on the Settle — Carlisle Railway] were from Devon or Cornwall, with some Irish, *the only place on numbers One and Two contracts where they were tolerated*' (my emphasis).[27]

If, as Sullivan claims, Thomas Ryan was part of a very small Irish minority on the Settle–Carlisle Line, then he appears to have had no great anxiety about his English and Scots co-workers. He and his family remained there at least long enough for his youngest child, born nearby, to reach her first birthday on site and he had previously worked both in the West Country, where Irishmen were thin on the ground, and in Scotland where there was much anti-Irish sentiment. This calls into question the accuracy of Sullivan's claims regarding the proportion of Irish involved in railway building elsewhere.

Irish navvies were recorded on the Manchester & Birmingham Railway, the Edinburgh & Glasgow Railway, the Staffordshire & Worcestershire Railway, the Bolton & Preston Railway, and the Midland Railway as well as many others. It is impossible to give numbers other than where confirmed by census figures.

Brooke points out that the Irish contingents were usually unskilled or semi-skilled, citing the Border Union and West Highland lines where 'over ninety percent of the Irish worked as labourers, excavators and navvies', as opposed to 69 per cent and 48 per cent, respectively, of English and Welsh.[28]

This is reflected in Wilhelm Westhoven's account of the division of labour on the building of the Forth Bridge (1883–1890) which, when opened, was the largest bridge ever built and employed 4,600 men during construction. 'Scots, English and Irish were about equally represented, and though the latter furnished very few skilled hands, they were mostly very hard workers and very conscientious and reliable men'. Westhoven was a section engineer and photographer on the project and wrote a history of its construction.[29]

Aside from a few such first-hand accounts by literate participants it is unfortunate that, as J.H. Trebel observed in an article on Irish navvies in *Transport History*, apart from census returns the only significant source of information on railway navvies was the contemporary provincial press. When it came to the Irish, the British press rarely mentioned them, other than as lawbreakers and troublemakers. Consequently such sources are a poor indicator of the numbers involved in railway construction.[30]

The Forth Bridge, Scotland; when it opened in 1890, it was the largest ever built and the first with an all-steel superstructure.

Press coverage, however, served Handley very well in assessing the range and extent of Irish involvement in building, construction, and public works in Scotland although his research extended much further to include a multitude of official sources. He concluded that 'navvying in Scotland in the nineteenth century depended for its labourers more on Irishmen than on native workers'.[31]

Southern Scotland in the late nineteenth century shared with the North of England the doubtful distinction of being a rapidly industrialising region with a dearth of unskilled labour. The rural Irish had been migrating seasonally to both regions since the eighteenth century and responded in ever-increasing numbers to this demand for brawn and muscle.

David Fitzpatrick has pointed out that, 'Between 1840 and 1910, the urban sector of the rapidly-growing English population rose from 48 to 79 per cent; natural increase and rural–urban migration alone could scarcely have generated this transformation', his point being that Irish immigration was essential to the rapid expansion of cities and industrial undertakings.[32]

The Irish found employment not only in industry and construction but also in the British Armed Forces. James Graham, an Irishman, was chosen as the bravest non-commissioned officer at the Battle of Waterloo. It has been estimated that about 40 per cent of the non-commissioned ranks in the British Army in 1830 were Irish. By 1868 there were 55,000 Irishmen in the British Army; in 1896 there were still about 25,000 Irish in service.

In addition to servicemen and the ubiquitous 'harvesters', many of whom subsequently became navvies, Ireland also produced men who started life as railway labourers at home and continued to work on railway building works in Ireland all their lives.

One such man was Patrick James (PJ) Doyle, born near Enniscorthy in County Wexford around 1830. He became a railway engine-driver in later life but worked on construction rather than train driving. His granddaughter, Eileen, recalled stories of his career told to her by his widow in later life.

Imagine if you can a rural Ireland in the middle & late 19th century when the railways were being built. All transport was horse-drawn — the heavier loads being hauled around the countryside by steam traction-engines. She would say that she had a child born in all four corners of Ireland. They used to move from section to section with all their possessions & the four children packed into a cart they owned. They would then rent a cottage near the next site which would sometimes be quite primitive.

Sometimes there would not be a proper cooking-stove and Grandma had to use a cauldron-type pot, with chains, slung over an open fire. I don't think she often had the comfort of living in a town but I do know they were living in Dublin at the beginning of the century. The railway eventually reached Keady, Co. Armagh, where her husband died — I think about 1909. There her wanderings ceased & it became the family home for the next nine years or so until she came to England to live with her second son (my father) who had married & settled down here.... How my grandfather Doyle came to adopt this nomadic life is a mystery to me. It might have been for economic reasons or maybe he just had 'itchy feet'. I incline to the latter theory as it is a trait he passed on to most of his descendants.[33]

Eileen Doyle's father, Joe, and her uncle, Jim, both became mechanical engineers in construction and, in fact, worked with Patrick MacGill, the Donegal-born 'Navvy Poet', at Kinlochleven Dam in 1908. What the work of a 'Mechanical Engineer' involved was, in fact, the operation and maintenance of all mechanised plant — steam cranes, steam navvies, locomotives, etc. — involved in civil engineering and construction. These men were crucial to the smooth running of large-scale operations and consequently, unlike labourers and navvies, were retained from contract to contract and paid a special rate.

The Welsh labourers [on a McAlpine contract] *once went on strike because they said they did not see why*

Irishmen and Scots were paid higher wages. This was settled by Sir Malcolm McAlpine calling a mass meeting of all the workers and addressing the strikers, with aforesaid Irish & Scots standing behind him on the platform — my father and his two brothers with them.

He told the strikers bluntly that when they could operate the machinery, repair it, dismantle it, oversee its transport to the next site and erect it again, they would get more money. Until then they could take it or leave it, as he was prepared to bring in outside labour to do their jobs. They went back to work quietly and there was no more trouble.

When Sir Robert McAlpine built the Waterford–Rosslare Line, between 1900 and 1906, the firm employed many local Irish labourers. According to Sir Robert's descendant Sir Malcolm H.D. McAlpine,

[We] *built on contacts made then to attract a lot of Irish labour between the wars, hence the 'McAlpine's Fusiliers'. A number of them rose to foreman and manager status and this rightly encouraged further recruitment at labourer and craftsman level.*[34]

Joe Doyle was with the previous Sir Malcolm for some years. Prior to 1933 he was a works manager for McAlpine's on the construction of Heraklion Harbour and power station in Crete. It was a sore point with Joe that Sir Malcolm never saw fit to send anyone out from head office to inspect the works. At one point, according to Eileen, Sir Malcolm '... got as far as Athens on holiday, but had not thought it worthwhile to travel out to the island, which would have made a good impression on the local harbour authorities'.[35]

Conclusion

It seems to be impossible at this remove to quantify the Irish input into British nineteenth-century railway building. Undoubtedly scholars prepared to identify lines built coincidentally with census years (the returns for 1901 will soon become available to the public), and search the returns for districts where building was taking place, could roughly quantify the Irish presence on such lines at those times. Even exhaustive research such as this, however, cannot be conclusive, for the reasons already given.

At least we do have the personal testimony of one of the greatest railway contractors of the age, Sir Morton Peto, as to the special qualities of those Irish whom he had employed throughout his career.

Peto was second only in importance to Brassey in extent of contracts and numbers employed — in 1850 he employed 14,000 men, more than the entire New Model Army which fought under Cromwell at Naseby. Brassey himself built 6,415 miles of railway, 1,940 miles of it in Britain, and on his death his British estate was assessed at £3,200,000. Brassey had other interests besides construction but the bulk of his fortune was amassed through the building of railways.

It was in recognition of the tremendous achievements of railway builders such as Brassey and Peto that the great engineer, Robert Stephenson, remarked, 'The contractors left even the engineers little more than the poetry of engineering'.

The part played by the navvies in all of this is best appreciated by reference to Lt Peter Lecount's contemporary description of the labour involved in the building of the Great Pyramid of Giza as compared with the construction of the London and Birmingham Railway:

The labour expended on the Great Pyramid was equivalent to lifting 15,733,000,000 cubic feet of stone one foot high. This labour was performed, according to Diodorus Siculus, by 300,000 men; according to Herodotus, by 100,000 men; and it required for its execution twenty years.

To build the railway 25,000,000,000 cubic feet of material (reduced to the same weight as that used in the pyramid) was lifted one foot high, or 9,267,000,000 cubic feet more than for the pyramid. Yet this had been done by 20,000 men in less than five years.

Lecount also expressed this achievement in another way:

If the circumference of the earth were taken in round figures to be 130,000,000 feet, then the 400,000,000 cubic feet of earth moved in building the railway would, if spread in a band one foot high and one foot broad, go round the equator more than three times.[36]

When we recall the observation made by the journalist with the *Illustrated London News* in 1851 that, 'The navvy proper deals only with the pick, the shovel, the crowbar and the wheelbarrow', we can imagine the amount of sheer physical effort required to build this railway alone. It then becomes easier to understand why the Irishman, that consummate artist of the pick and shovel, was celebrated in song as 'Paddy on the Railway', though in what precise numbers we may never know.

Living Hard

In the first half of the nineteenth century (and even much later) navvies on remote works had to accept very rudimentary contractors' housing or, more usually, improvise their own.

The gangs of navvies had, in this lonely wilderness [Dove Holes Tunnel on the Buxton–Manchester section], to extemporise habitations for themselves, by the erection of conical mud huts, or cave-houses of two or three rooms each, cut in the solid rock, or by cottages built of stone.[37]

According to Benjamin Blyth, a former railway engineer and President of the Institution of Civil Engineers, the standard contractors' specifications for navvy accommodation, having laid down the dimensions of the huts, stated:

Each bed to contain not more than two men, and to be at least six feet long and four feet wide.[38]

The contractors' huts were normally built of wood and turf, twenty to thirty feet in length, and twelve feet in width. They might be divided by a gable and have a fire at each end. The beds were in tiers, two rows of three down each side, with a four-foot passageway down the middle of the hut. A hot plate for cooking was usually supplied. Patrick MacGill vividly described the situation as late as 1900, at Kinlochleven:

Usually three men lay in each bunk, and sometimes it happened that four unwashed dirty humans were huddled together under the one evil-smelling, flea-covered blanket.[39]

That MacGill was not exaggerating for effect is borne out by the evidence of Alfred List, given before the House of Commons Select Committee on Railway Labourers in 1846. The huts on the Hawick branch of the Edinburgh to Berwick line:

... are erected in bad situations, mostly on the brae [hill] face; part of the brae forms the back walls, and the roof not impervious to rain; they make a sort of gutter for the water to run from them; within they have a disagreeable smell, the air being insalubrious and fetid.[40]

In Scotland, where the Catholic Irish were often precluded by their religion from obtaining lodgings with the local inhabitants along the line, self-built huts were commonplace where Irish labourers were present in any numbers. The *Glasgow Herald* newspaper reported one such community along the banks of the Union Canal between Edinburgh and Falkirk:

... certain edifices have been erected which strike the traveller with no little astonishment. These are huts erected by Irish labourers.... One of them, with the exception, perhaps, of a few sticks, is composed entirely of rotten straw; its dimensions would not suffice for a pig-sty, and its form is that of a bee-hive, only it is more conical ... a Hottentot kraal in comparison with it is a palace. In the midst

Above: Enumerator's return for district adjacent to Ship Canal works, 1891 census. Note occupational distinction made between 'excavators' and 'general labourers'.

of so much misery the children appear healthful and frolicsome, and the women contented and happy.

Twenty years later, according to the *Kilmarnock Journal*, little had changed for the Irish labourers building the railway from Dalry to Kilmarnock:

On going along, it is curious to observe indications of the hardy habits of the Irish engaged upon the laborious work of excavation ... they have built themselves about a dozen turf huts of about ten feet by eight and thatched them with the same material ... peeping out of their low doors and strolling in the neighbourhood, healthy, well-clad women and rosy-cheeked children were seen in abundance.[41]

Of course, unless religious barriers or the proscriptions of local landlords intervened, the local inhabitants usually welcomed the additional income to be derived from lodging itinerant navvies. If anything, they tended to cram too many into already overcrowded hovels, and they made handsome profits from their newfound lodgers.

The huts for accommodation of the navvies are not yet constructed and the cottages of Eastham and the neighbourhood are crowded with lodgers — so much so that in some cases the Nuisance Inspector has had to turn men out of houses that were overcrowded.[42]

These problems resulted in navvies building their own extemporised dwellings. They attracted much media comment — not, as might be expected, because they were unfit for human habitation, but because they afforded amusement to the editor and his readers.

For example, an illustration from a London newspaper covering the building of the Manchester Ship Canal shows a stone-built circular hut, with no door, with a sod or grass roof and a crude stove-pipe chimney, about four and a half feet high and six feet wide. A navvy is emerging in a crouching position with a woman's face peering out behind him. The caption reads:

A hut on the canal — as yet we have not been able to learn whether this is a discovery in the line of 'hut dwellings'; but it is certainly a curiosity in its way. How it came here, or where it came from, we cannot learn. It may be from Ireland; it may be from Africa. Perhaps Mr Stanley [Foreign Secretary] *or Mr Balfour* [Prime Minister and former Chief Secretary for Ireland] *can settle the question.*

The same edition featured an even more anti-Irish illustration showing a *Punch*-style Irishman, dressed in knee-breeches and a Leprechaun hat, pointing to a roughly lettered wooden sign on a mud hut, which reads: 'NO IRISH ALLOWED IN THIS BIN' (A 'bin' was a small on-site shelter for boys).

'BEGORRAH THIN, AND PHWAT DO THEY MANE BY THAT?' the Irishman exclaims. The editor comments:

We can excuse Pat's surprise and indignation, seeing that the edifice bears so striking a resemblance to his own native hut, from which he was so recently evicted. Go in, Pat; take peaceable possession and defy the 'Pours of Parlimin.'[43]

Common sense suggests that, in rural areas, railway labourers would readily have found accommodation with agricultural labourers (often being 'off the land' themselves and merely seeking a change of work), artisans, and small shop- and innkeepers. There was little class distinction between these, in fact, and they had far more in common with the itinerant navvy than with the 'respectable' middle classes who looked down on all of them. Married men, especially, sought out permanent housing for their wives and children wherever possible in preference to the temporary shelters available on site.

This was the pattern in the vicinity of the works along the line of the Manchester Ship Canal.

The village of Cadishead ... had suffered greatly due to the depression in the fustian-cutting trade ... the canal found employment for much of the surplus labour. A large proportion of men employed on the Irlam and Cadishead length of the canal took up abode in the village.

Similar benefits accrued to the other villages alongside the works. Accordingly, lodging-house keepers, publicans, shopkeepers and tradesmen all reaped the benefit and the villages thrived on their newfound prosperity.

These largely Methodist communities, dotted along the route, soon lost their trepidation in their delight at catering to the navvies' needs for food and accommodation.[44]

The *Pall Mall Budget* of 12 April 1888 commented:

The labourers are not at all the sort of people the Eastham folk dreaded they would be. Fine, big, stalwart fellows many of them are, capable of any amount of hard work, but by no means the rough and brutal navvies whose incursion was so much feared.

In the urban areas married Irish householders who had settled down locally accommodated many Irish labourers. The Salford painter Harold Reilly recounts how, in 1954, he met an old Irishman living in Eccles in the vicinity of the Ship Canal. Named Tom Kirk, he had navvied on the project and was ninety-three years old when Reilly made his acquaintance. He claimed that his grandfather, also a navvy, had worked on the Manchester to Liverpool Railway in 1828 and had conceived Tom's father on one of his rare visits home. Tom still lived in the old family home and recalled many Irish navvies lodging there in his earlier years.

Construction of the Manchester Ship Canal lasted from 1887 to 1893 and overlapped the 1891 Census. A scrutiny of the returns for districts contiguous to the works revealed many examples of this practice.[45]

At 5 Timothy Street, Eccles, in the Parish of St Andrew, John Kilgarriff, an Irish bricklayer's labourer, and his wife Anne, both aged forty, had six single Irish Ship Canal labourers lodging with them. Numbers 1, 11 and 13, Timothy Street were all lodging-houses, containing a total of nineteen Irish Ship Canal labourers.

Number 225 Ellesmere Street, Eastham, at the seaward end of the canal, was a Model Lodging House. On census night it held no less than twenty-one Irish 'general labourers'. Four days later the *Eccles & Patricroft Journal* was reporting that there was 'no early prospect of the creation of a village of huts, but there is no stint of accommodation in Eccles, Patricroft, and Barton. The Model Lodging House at Patricroft is full'.

One week later the same paper was still reporting on the situation of the labour force.

In Hollins Green only a few of the navvies can be lodged. They therefore proceed in some cases as far as Cadishead and Irlam on the Lancashire side of the river, and on the Cheshire side some go to Lymm, which is further still, to lodge, the distance thereto being four miles at least.

The same newspaper gave a detailed account of the rules governing the fifty lodgers at the Model Lodging House in Patricroft whose proprietor was a W.S. Cordingly:

The Regulations, which are posted in the kitchen, common to all, say the house is closed at 11 o'clock — 10 o'clock on Sundays; that no drinking is allowed in the house, that persons smoking in the bedroom will be expelled, that washing clothes on a Sunday, and

gambling at any time, is strictly prohibited. Females are not yet accommodated. A number of Ship Canal men have lodged here. Some, on finding a prospect of permanency, have left and sent for their wives. The lodger provides, and as a rule cooks, for himself, the proprietor having fixed up a large stove.

Sometimes Irish widows set up as boarding-house keepers and specialised in catering for Irish labourers. These would become widely known and their addresses would be passed on by word of mouth. It did not, of course, follow that they could be counted on to treat their countrymen fairly or well but, in that event, their reputations also went before them.

At 171 Irlam Moss, Margaret Smith, a sixty-one-year-old Irish widow from Dunmore, County Galway, ran a boarding-house. On the night of the census she had eight Ship Canal and twelve general labourers in residence — all Irish.

In marked contrast Winifred Connor was the 'Head of Household' at 83 Liverpool Road, Irlam, on the night of 16 April 1891, when the Census Enumerator called. A widow born in Mayo, she had three daughters, aged twenty, eighteen and sixteen, employed as fustian cutters, one son of fourteen employed as a farm labourer, another son aged, twelve, employed as a ship canal labourer, and two sons aged eight and six returned as 'scholars'. She had no lodgers, no husband, and no man's wage coming in.

Number 85 Liverpool Road, Irlam, was rented by Dennis McDermott from Galway, aged twenty-four, and his wife Catherine, aged twenty-nine (born in Irlam of Irish parentage). They had no less than ten Irish ship canal labourers, aged between nineteen and thirty-five, lodging with them. At an average rate of thirteen shillings per lodger per week they were well off indeed. The average weekly wage was twenty to twenty-five shillings per week. Professional navvies, working in 'butty gangs' for 'piece', could earn up to thirty shillings per week.

In both towns and contractors' 'villages' there was a marked tendency for English and Irish exclusively to

Canal Ploddies

1 large potato, peeled
1 medium onion
1 egg, beaten
2oz chopped bacon
1oz self-raising flour
seasoning
Oil to fry

Grate potato and onion coarsely. Add
bacon. Mix in egg and flour, season
well. Drop 3 or 4 spoonsful into pan
and fry, turning until well browned on
both sides. Eat hot.

Boxty.

8oz raw potato, grated
8oz mashed potato
2 eggs, beaten
2 tablespoons of flour
1 onion, grated
¼ cup milk
Seasoning
Oil for frying

Mix all together well, until blended.
Heat oil in frying pan. Drop in 3 or 4
tablespoons of mixture. Cook 3-4 minutes
on each side of pancake until crispy and
golden brown. Serve while hot.

Banana Fruit-cake

2 over-ripe bananas
50g (2oz) margarine
150g (5oz) caster sugar
2 eggs, lightly beaten
225g (8oz) self-raising flour
A pinch of salt

Mash bananas. Cream fat and sugar, adding
bananas. Mix in the eggs, sieve flour and
salt and fold into banana mixture. Grease
and flour a large loaf tin. Fill with
mixture and bake 175°F, 190°C, Gas 5 for
1 hour, lowering heat a little after 30
minutes. Serve sliced and buttered.

Above: Menu for centenary dinner given by Salford artist, Harold Reilly, in honour of Irish navvies on Manchester Ship Canal works. Copthorne Hotel, Manchester, 1994.

monopolise certain streets or settlements. Thus, numbers 125 to 129 Atherton Lane, Cadishead, were all occupied by English families. Of their sixty-four lodgers, not one was Irish. On Ellesmere Street, on the other hand, numbers 120 to 150 were all occupied by Irish families, and between them they housed eighty Irish labourers.

The field huts built by Thomas Walker along the canal were similarly divided. At Ince and Moore/Acton Grange, with eighty-five huts and 1,132 men between them, there were only seven Irish labourers in residence. On the fifty-four-acre field at Ellesmere Port,

however, Walker's huts housed one thousand men and were almost monopolised by the Irish. Thomas Gilmore aged thirty, his wife Sarah, aged twenty-five, for example, occupied hut Number 23, together with fifteen Irish lodgers aged between eighteen and thirty-two. 'Bankfields Farm', also under company housing, had no less than one hundred and twelve Irish labourers in residence.

If it is true, as claimed by the *Eccles & Patricroft Journal*, that 'The huts are each put in the care of a navvy well-known to the firm', and that, as the same paper also asserted, 'The first arrivals and nucleus of the workforce were practically all full-time employees of T.A. Walker, having worked under him on the construction of the Severn Tunnel', then this suggests that Walker did indeed employ many Irish navvies on a continuous basis. Ship Canal Company folklore would lead one to believe so.

Similarly, given the almost total absence of Irish in Walker's huts at Ince and Moore/Acton Grange, one might speculate that a company policy of racial segregation was in place. Walker had a lifetime's experience as a railway contractor behind him at this point (he died in 1889, aged sixty-two) and may well have learned to keep the Irish and English navvies apart in the interests of peace and (economic) progress.

The houses are built of wood, protected on the outside in some cases with heavy waterproof cloth, in others with thin sheets of metal....

In an ordinary case a house of two storeys will take in twelve lodgers. For such a house, the rent is 8s. per week, including 4 cwt. of coal, and the lodgers pay for board and lodging 13s per week, which is not so much as it looks when one remembers the kind of diet they expect.

In other cases lodgers who are not full boarders pay 2s.6d. a week as a kind of sleeping rent, 6d. a week for tea, 6d. for potatoes, and 1s. for pudding, leaving them free to provide their own beef.

In such a household the wife must work as hard as any man on the works. Remote as she is from shops, she need waste no time in making purchases. At all hours of the day butchers' and bakers' vans can be seen picking their way across the network of rails for the convenience of these wives of the pick and shovel.[46]

They look rather larger than one might have expected, with rooms on each side of the front door, and projecting portions behind.... The front door opens directly into the kitchen or common living room, which is furnished with a good fireplace and ovened grate. Opening out of this, to the left, are two little bedrooms for the use of the family, and to the right is a big room for the lodgers. At the back are two other doors, the one opening into a scullery, the other into a pantry with plenty of shelving.... The roofs are coated with a thick waterproof material.[47]

The concentration of people in these huts, however, sometimes defied the imagination. One hut in this settlement was rented by Benjamin Baker, aged thirty-eight, from Plymouth, his wife Ellen, aged twenty-nine, two sons, five daughters, and thirty-four Irish lodgers.

That such enterprise could be rewarding is evidenced by the satisfaction inherent in this song of navvy life on the Ship Canal penned by a man called Morris. He was the head ganger on the Eastham Section, known to his men as 'The Bricklayer Poet', having published a volume of poems about 'The Ways of The Line'.

One of 'Walker's Fragments', Manchester Ship Canal.

I'm a navvy, I work on the Ship Canal
I'm a tipper, and live in a hut with my Sal;
If you ever come to Eastham, call at Sea-Rough
wood
There's a hearty cheer, without the beer,
And 'tommy' that's always good.

We have lodgers, a splendid lot of young men
In the evening around the tables are ten
Some of the lads are strangers, never been out before
But some can tell of a long long spell
Tramping the country o'er.

Tales of daring the older ones would tell
And tales of want when with nowhere to swell
They'd nestle in a hayrick, or shelter in a barn
And tales like these us navvies please
When not o'erdone, to yarn.

Our wives are rough, but yet no one can say
They're hard-hearted; none are sent away
If they only look like navvies, they're welcome to a
share
And told to lay, by the fire 'til day
If there's no bed to spare.

Our work is hard and dangers are always near
And lucky we are if safely through life we steer
But still the life of a navvy, with its many changes of
scene
With a dear old wife, is just the life
That suits old Nobby Green.

The returns also show some unexpected occupations for Irish residents in the region. In Thelwall at 156 Mildespool Causeway, a lodger named Daniel O'Sullivan, single, aged forty-one, was recorded as 'Supervisor, Inland Revenue'. At 22 Frederick Street, Latchford, lived John Rodgers Mahoney, married, aged fifty-eight, a 'Teacher of the Irish Language'. Owen O'Neill, married, aged thirty-four, living near Knutsford Road in a 'Gypsy Caravan' with four children, was returned as 'Horse Dealer'. Given the huge numbers of horses employed in the construction and ancillary work of the canal (200 were employed by Walker alone) he was probably a most prosperous individual.

Mr Joseph Farnham, aged twenty-seven, was returned as 'Missionary', and with his twenty-eight-year-old wife, daughter, and son lodged only one tenant, returned as 'Schoolmaster' (a most respectable Irish enclave which failed to interest the Press). At Hansey Hall Lodge, near Grappenshall, lived Robert Buchanan, 'Police Constable'. There was even an Irish-born prison governor — Mr F. Price, of Knutsford Prison. One man known perhaps to Mr Price was James Tucker, a resident of the field huts at Ellesmere Port, who gave his place of birth as 'No Man's Land'.

Overall, the consensus from about the 1870s onwards seems to be that there was a gradual improvement in general conditions for the railway navvies as contractors became more professional and systematic and the navvies themselves responded to improved conditions. Men such as Peto, Brassey, and Walker held enlightened views as to how best to secure productive work, and provided not only well-built and managed huts but also schools, missions, and, ultimately, field-hospitals.

'Walker's Fragments'

Regarding the latter, the claim is often made that the first navvy field-hospital was built by Robert McAlpine for the labourers on the Mallaig Extension of the West Highland Line (1897–1901) which employed many Irish navvies. Ten years previously, however, Thomas Walker had already provided field-hospitals during construction of the Severn Tunnel, in the early 1880s, and along the line of the Manchester Ship Canal some years later. In fact, the surgeon appointed by Walker to oversee the Ship Canal hospitals, Robert Jones, became so adept at constructing artificial limbs for disabled navvies (known as 'Walker's Fragments' because the contractor always tried to keep them on) that he is recognised as the father of orthopaedic surgery.

Until the carnage of the First World War it was widely recognised as being statistically more dangerous to be a navvy than to be a soldier. As Bagwell observes,

The idea was widely recognised that the public benefits which accrued from canal, railway and port improvements were partly paid for in the human suffering of the navvies.

The Irish on the Manchester Ship Canal, as far as the author could ascertain, numbered upwards of five thousand, or just under one-third of the labour force of sixteen thousand men. This project was unusual in that its enormity made the traditional labour-intensive construction methods prohibitively expensive and therefore impractical.

'The Big Ditch'

Described by L.T.C. Rolt as, 'The greatest engineering feat of the Victorian Age', the Ship Canal was designed to deliver Manchester and its hinterland from the stranglehold of the Port of Liverpool and the Liverpool and Manchester Railway. It was said that goods could be sent more cheaply from London to Bombay than from Manchester to Liverpool.

Oldham spinners could buy cotton in Germany or France, pay the costs of importing via Hull, add railway charges from across the Pennines, and still make a saving on the price they would have paid for the same cotton in Liverpool. On the export side, over half the cost of sending a ton of cotton goods to India was absorbed in railway and dock charges at Liverpool.[48]

The Ship Canal is thirty-six miles long, twenty-eight feet deep, and between one hundred and twenty and one hundred and eighty feet bottom width. The course of the canal intersected two rivers, a canal, many roads and five railway lines. The route was divided into eight sections, each under its own resident agent and engineer, section eight subsequently being subdivided because of its difficulty. The staff and contractors on each section worked independently of each other; this resulted in healthy competition and made any 'combination' of the navvies for strike purposes all but impossible. Subcontracts were given out for bridges, viaducts, and such like.

The Canal was unique in Britain by virtue of the enormous quantity of powered plant employed in its construction. The reasoning behind this was spelt out by the projects consulting engineer, E. Leader Williams, in a paper delivered at the Institution of Mechanical Engineers in Liverpool in 1891:

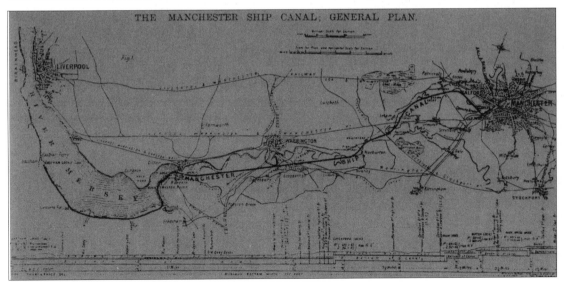

The mechanical appliances being used in the construction of the Manchester Ship Canal are on the largest scale in order to minimise the employment of labour. The number of men and boys employed on the canal has never exceeded 17,000 and about 200 horses have been used. As the excavation amounts to forty-six and a half million cubic yards, of which over ten million are sandstone rock — any available number of men and horses would be insufficient to do the work in any reasonable time.

In the first year of construction these appliances numbered forty locomotives, seven steam excavators, eighteen 'Steam Navvies', twenty-seven steam cranes, fourteen portable engines, 1,780 wagons, four pumping engines, nine steam saw benches, three steam tugs, fourteen 'flats' and barges, 2,500 barrows, 5,000 tons of rail and 70,000 sleepers covering ten route-miles. By 1891 there were 173 locomotives, ninety-seven steam excavators, and 6,300 trucks and wagons. It was said that the amount of plant employed was equivalent to the labour of 120,000 men. Perhaps it was in reaction to this that an Irish navvy on site is reputed to have christened this colossal project, 'The Big Ditch'.

Symptomatic of the level of indifference to the welfare of Victorian working men is the variation in estimates for casualties over the six years of construction. The Company's insurers, the Lancashire and Yorkshire Accident Insurance Company Ltd quoted 154 deaths, 186 permanent disabilities, and 104 partial injuries. The Navvies and General Labourers' Union, on the other hand, claimed 1,100 deaths, 1,700 permanent disabilities, and 250 partial injuries.

A 'Works Insurance Scheme' was in operation, financed from a weekly stoppage of 5d. per man, which paid for the company's three field-hospitals. A navvy injured going to, or coming from, the works, however, got no sick benefits. Injured navvies occupying beds in the company's hospitals were docked half their sick pay. Older and debilitated workers were often excluded from the scheme. A navvy killed on the works was buried by the company for three pounds, but no compensation was paid.

Juries at inquests were composed of tailors, grocers, and other general tradesmen with no technical understanding of construction work. Workmates called as witnesses had to confront the 'walking boss' of the relevant section, and the dead man's ganger, both

Even the traditional barrow runs operated on a grand scale on the Manchester Ship Canal.

seated on the coroner's right hand. Naturally they were loath to criticise company procedures lest they be dismissed. According to the Navvies' Union,

> In nine cases out of ten, we have no hesitation in saying — and we speak from personal, local, and practical observation — that the verdict should be that of manslaughter against the contractors or company.

Needless to relate, the verdict was, in fact, usually one of 'accidental death'.

A story is still told by old men retired from the Manchester Ship Canal Company, concerning the collapse of an embankment during construction, in which eight men were buried alive. Three were rescued but five died. The agent issued the command, 'Count the shovels'. Back came the response, 'Three shovels, sir'. 'Damn and blast,' said the agent, 'I'm five shovels short!' He made no mention of the deceased navvies.

T.A. Walker, at his own expense, provided fifteen mission halls operated by the Navvy Mission Society along the works, which could accommodate from seventy to eight hundred people. There were thirteen missionaries, five of them old navvies, led by an old tunnel miner from the Severn Tunnel contract. The missionaries ran both day and Sunday schools for the children of the navvies, in addition to night schools where navvies were taught to read and write.

Not all of Thomas Walker's navvies appreciated the contractor's concern for their physical and spiritual welfare. In the *Navvy's and Labourer's Guide* of March 1891, the newspaper of the Navvies and General Labourers' Union, George Haley, an Irish navvy who had worked for Walker, wrote the following:

> I have worked from 40 to 50 hours without any rest. On the Severn Tunnel works, Mr. Walker illegally stopped 8d. per week from every man and boy to compensate for the erection of the hospital. With regard to the wooden villages, the late Mr Walker charged every tenant the sum of 10s. per week. Each hut holds fourteen lodgers, the waste wood being afterwards used for shoring purposes. It was true that Mr. Walker read out of the bible to those who attended the mission halls on Sundays, but most of the navvies needed rest after working night and day in that dark, wet hole, with bad, foul air, tainted with naptha lamps, and blasting of dynamite. The navvies were paid but four and halfpence per hour. At one time many poor fellows died there from smallpox. The corpses of these were thrown into old brick carts and taken to the grave like so many dogs. Is this friendship for the navvy? I always speak of things as I find them, and I like to give honour where honour is due. I believe the Gospel of the lord Jesus is destined to uplift the navvy from his present degraded position but I believe the gospel should be imparted in a practical manner, reaching the soul through the body.

Mrs Elizabeth Garnett, evangelist and author of the book, *Our Navvies*, realised the potential for a religious newspaper aimed at navvies. She wrote:

> It is a great pity, and also a sad truth, that the religious papers are not made sufficiently attractive. If there could be such a publication as a newspaper up in all the latest news of the day, with striking illustrations, takingly written, yet with a high moral tone, not a magazine but a news paper, it might possibly in time beat the sporting newspapers, and the Police News, out of the field.

Mrs Garnett was the only female member, during the forty years of its existence, of the Navvy Mission Society's governing committee. Founded in Yorkshire in 1877, at the instigation of the Rev. Lewis Moule, the Society's leadership came from the senior ranks of the Church of England plus certain leading contractors and politicians. The 'missionaries' themselves were recruited by local committees from the ranks of former navvies. Obviously there were no Irish Catholic missionaries enlisted.

The *Quarterly Letter to Navvies*, published by the society, was the outcome of Mrs Garnett's inspiration; she herself edited it until her death in 1917. Space was given to 'Works in Progress', lists of accidents, deaths and marriages, and personal messages. The *Newsletter* became very popular with navvies in Britain and abroad. The project list alone would have guaranteed it a following since this saved men a great deal of speculative 'tramping' in search of work or the rumour of work.

Mrs Garnett not only penned the regular exhortative 'Letter', designed to uplift spiritually the navvies whom she habitually addressed as 'Mates', but she also featured news items of personal interest to navvies and their landladies:

> *Mrs Brown, Hazel Grove, Stockport, a poor old widow, 71, has in nine weeks been sloped by eleven lodgers. One lived with her three weeks, never paid a cent, got her even to buy him tobacco, and went off in her son's boots. Will these mean, bad-hearted thieves pay up or I will publish their names in the* Quarterly.[49]

One of many personal notices concerning navvies sought by deserted wives was the following:

> *June 1882 — Gypsy Tom's wife and child, who he left at East Grinstead, recovering from smallpox, have tramped north. They are at South Cave, on the Hull and Barnsley line, and will be glad to hear where he is. Surely he does not intend to desert them?*[50]

The First World War saw the virtual end of railway building in Britain, and the Navvy Mission Society amalgamated with the Christian Social Union to become the Industrial Christian Fellowship. That body still exists, but the navvies have long since disappeared. Before that happened, however, their peculiar code of ethics — 'The Ways of the Line' — had been adopted by many Irishmen, caught up in the nomadic lifestyle of the life-long labourer on Public Works, over the long twilight of the navvy between about 1890 and 1960.

The Manchester Ship Canal at Manchester, 2001. The Pomona Docks inlets, now waste ground, can be seen on the right of the picture.

4 The Long-Distance Kiddies

McAlpine went by Motor Car
And Wimpey went by Train,
But Paddy tramped the Great North Road
And got there just the same. (Traditional)

Writing in 1970 L.T.C. Rolt described the Manchester Ship Canal (1887–1893) as, 'the greatest civil engineering achievement of the Victorian Age ... unprecedented in its scale and magnitude'. One year later Rolt called the building of the London Extension of the Great Central Railway (1894–1899) 'the final chapter' in the history of the railway navvies. He wrote then that 'no similar work of comparable magnitude was undertaken in Britain until the building of the motorways sixty years later'.[1]

The Great Central ran from Nottingham to London Marylebone, and was a textbook example of Victorian railway engineering at its best, although executed half a century later than the classic works of Brunel and Stephenson in the 1830s and 1840s. Both projects were, however, distinguished by the employment of powered plant such as steam excavators, steam cranes, and portable steam engines for driving mortar mills and powering water pumps on an unprecedented scale.

The steam navvy was estimated to be capable of doing the work of between thirty and eighty men and, of course, was not subject to illness, injury, or discontent. Clearly it would pay any contractor to replace men with machines, provided he had sufficiently large contracts to justify the typical 1890s price of £1,250 per steam navvy. The navvy, it was said, 'deals only with the pick, the shovel, the crowbar and the wheelbarrow'. If these tools became redundant, the navvy's days would be numbered, but such was far from being the case.

Public Works

Not until the building of the motorways, as Rolt remarked, was any civil engineering project on such a scale again attempted in Britain. However, other, lesser, public works proliferated throughout the British Isles, and these collectively employed navvies in far greater numbers than on the high-profile civil-engineering works.

> The next work I shall mention is the Victoria Docks, London, for the making of which Messrs. Brassey, Peto, and Betts contracted. These ... were opened to the public in 1857. They are entered from the Thames, immediately below Blackwall, by a lock, having a depth of water on the cill of twenty-six feet at Trinity high water. They have a water area of over a hundred acres, divided by eighty-foot gates into a tidal basin of about twenty acres. They have vaults for wines, and warehouses for general merchandise, to the extent of about twenty-five acres of floor.
>
> The City warehouses for wines and general goods are in Fenchurch Street, and were constructed with a floor area of about five acres. They are in direct railway communication with the Docks. All the warehouses, quays, dock gates, etc., are supplied with and worked by Sir William Armstrong's hydraulic machinery, and are connected with all the principal railways of the kingdom.
>
> The same firm constructed the Thames Graving Docks, with an entrance from the wet dock of the Victoria Dock, having a water area of about fifteen acres, and hydraulic machinery and lifts for docking and under-docking vessels of all capacities.[2]

It is said by natives of London's Docklands that the boundary walls surrounding Millwall Dock were built to a height of nine feet because 'that was the minimum height above which a docker couldn't throw a sheep'.

Construction of docks and warehousing proceeded apace all over Britain throughout the nineteenth century; developments in the great cities such as London, Liverpool and Manchester, were matched by equally ambitious schemes in lesser cities such as Hull, Newcastle, Newhaven, Glasgow, Greenock, Peterhead, Aberdeen, Dundee, Leith, Grangemouth, Methil, Burntisland and Rosyth. Every dock and warehouse in turn necessitated laying a network of rail links to the main lines for goods distribution.

Referring to the impending construction of Greenock's Victoria Harbour by the firm of Stephenson, McKenzie and Brassey, a merchant testifying before the Poor Law Inquiry of 1844 stated that:

Drag-line excavators and caterpillar earthmovers illustrate how big a breakthrough the JCB and large-wheeled dumper actually were for civil engineering.

We have in contemplation to enlarge the harbour, which will take three years at least. It is not likely that that work will go on without a great immigration of Irish.

'All in all', writes Handley, 'if a navvy had been prepared to travel — and the tribe of necessity were rovers — he could have spent the whole of his working life on reconstruction work in the nineteenth century at the harbours of Scotland'. This held for the whole of Britain.

It was in the provision of public utilities and services that the navvy found the most consistent demand for his unique skills. Excavating and entrenching sewers, water pipes, drains and ditches could not be attempted by the large and clumsy powered excavators and this remained the case until the second half of the twentieth century.

Then there was the Northern Mid-Level Sewer, which Mr Brassey contracted with the Metropolitan Board of Works to make (in 1856). This, though only twelve miles in length, was a work of great magnitude and difficulty, and occupied nearly three years in construction. The line of sewer runs from Kensal Green, passing under the Bayswater Road, Oxford Street, and Clerkenwell, to the River Lea ... this undertaking ... is, by some persons, considered one of the most difficult works that have ever been done in this country. It was necessary to tunnel under houses and streets, and also to cross the Metropolitan Railway with a very large tube.

For the first time ... cranes worked by steam were generally employed in sewers for hoisting the earth from excavations direct into carts in which it was to be removed. The method hitherto adopted had been that of lifting the earth from stage to stage by manual labour. The adoption of the new system enabled the contractors to dispense with a great deal of this manual labour, which is always found to be more costly in London than elsewhere, and it also accelerated the execution of the works.[3]

Stages were usually erected every four feet down. It is therefore likely that the use of steam cranes in such situations was actually welcomed by the navvies. Again, only large-scale projects such as London's Northern Mid-Level Sewer could justify the purchase of these costly machines, the average contract being on a much smaller scale.

The key element in all of these activities was water. As cities grew, provision of adequate supplies of water for industrial and public consumption became imperative, and the first step was the building of reservoirs.

Of all the services that the navvy undertook for the welfare of the community none was as beneficial as the supply of drinking water.[4]

The builders of the eighteenth-century canals had constructed reservoirs retained by earth dams with a core of puddle clay. This technique remained the norm, even as larger and larger dams were built, until the hundred-foot Dale Dyke Dam, constructed for the city of Sheffield, subsided suddenly on being filled for the first time in 1864. Two hundred and fifty lives were lost and afterwards earth dam construction was gradually abandoned in favour of massive masonry constructions.

In 1881 the first large masonry dam in Britain was begun, at Vyrnwy in North Wales, for the supply of water to Liverpool. Completed in 1892, using blocks up to twelve tons in weight, it was then the largest artificial lake in Europe and held 12,000,000 gallons of water. Manchester (Thirlmere, 1894) and Birmingham (Elan Valley, 1904) soon followed Liverpool's example.

Long before this, however, Irish navvies had been building reservoirs in Scotland. Various schemes were instigated by the Scottish local authorities, from as early as 1825, and gathered momentum as urban populations increased exponentially throughout the remainder of the nineteenth century.

Irish navvies, according to Handley, were employed in substantial numbers by the Edinburgh Water

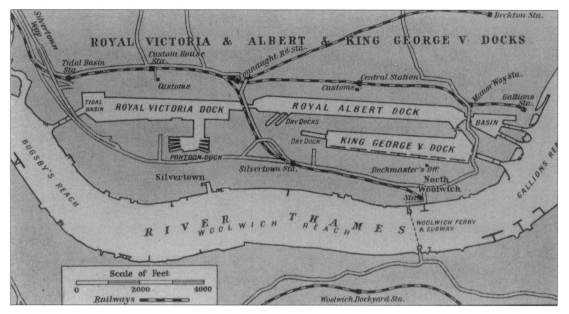

Company in the vicinity of that city from 1819 to 1850 impounding springs and building compensation reservoirs.

In the six years spanning the mid-century, apart from other activity, seven reservoirs were built — big constructions with wide and tall embankments, broad puddle-walls and deep puddle-trenches impounding hundreds of millions of gallons of water.

Following the replacement of the Edinburgh Water Company by a local-authority agency a new spate of reservoir construction began, between 1876 and 1880, for which experienced navvies were in great demand.

In 1895 the city began construction of the Talla Reservoir and ancillary works. The Reservoir had a surface area of 300 acres. Despite the pioneering use of concrete in the Highlands by Robert McAlpine at that time, the cut-off trench (designed to prevent leakage from underneath a dam), here eighty feet in depth, was still filled in the traditional manner using 100,000 tons of puddle clay. This project occupied hundreds of navvies over a ten-year period.

Glasgow, whose population increased five-fold in the nineteenth century, not only had a larger population than Edinburgh but also required enormous quantities of water for industrial use. At mid-century the city was consuming 14,000,000 gallons daily. In 1856 the town council began the enormous Loch Katrine Scheme which took three years to complete.

Three thousand navvies were employed on the eighty tunnels and related works required by the scheme. A service reservoir at Craigmaddie, begun in 1886, took ten years to complete.

On several of these Scottish hydro schemes the initial contractors went bust as a result of the enormous geological and topographical difficulties encountered and the primitive technology then available to overcome them. Not until air compressors arrived in the closing years of the century was hard-rock tunnelling anything less than a grinding struggle little altered from the pioneering efforts of the eighteenth century.

Patrick MacGill, writing about the construction of Kinlochleven Reservoir and Dam around 1910, recorded the navvy's unique perspective on these great public works. He alleged that he and the thousands of other navvies on the works neither knew nor cared for what purpose these massive waterworks were being constructed. They performed herculean labours merely because that was what they were paid for, 'turned the highlands into a cinder heap' and were no wiser at the end that at the beginning.[5]

Less onerous, but equally protracted, was the waterworks programme of Manchester Corporation, whereby no less than eight reservoirs were constructed in the Longdendale Valley amongst the Derbyshire Peaks. The first of these was begun in 1848 but not completed until 1877 — the same year in which the eighth and last was also completed. Together they have a holding capacity of 4,200 million gallons. The first and greatest is Woodhead Reservoir, a name made notorious amongst the navvies of the day by the horrendous conditions endured during construction of the Sheffield, Ashton-under-Lyne and Manchester Railway's Woodhead Tunnel.

Local census returns for the decades 1851 and 1861 record a number of Irish families with male members listed as 'labourer, water works', whose fathers were present during construction of the first Woodhead Tunnel (1839–1845). Modern telephone directory listings suggest that descendants of some of these families may still reside in local villages such as Broadbottom and Tintwhistle.

As Handley rightly points out, these schemes generated knock-on employment for navvies in the urban centres which these water schemes were intended to serve. Water from the mains fed by the reservoirs had to be piped into the towns and cities and thence to the consumer. More running water meant newer and bigger sewers. These in turn meant large-scale resurfacing and reinstatement.

King George V Dock, London, is 800 feet long and 45 feet deep. Each of the steel gates weighs 309 tons.

Simultaneously, gas mains were being laid down and drawn off into dwellings, factories, and commercial premises for purposes of illumination. As with water supply, the early gas works were provided either by private utility companies or by larger industrial concerns with a requirement for such facilities. Between 1805 and 1826 several big gas companies were established in London. The specialist engineers, who pioneered the provision in the capital of public gas supplies (some had formerly operated works in places like Manchester and Stoneyhurst College), in turn contracted to provide gas works for industries and local authorities elsewhere and thus disseminated the new technology throughout the regions.

Hard-rock tunnelling, in Scotland during the 1930s.

The navvies' cemetery, Kinlochleven, Scotland. Like that at Woodhead, Derbyshire, a bleak and lonely spot.

The cradle of the industrial revolution, the North-West of England, was in the forefront of the provision of gas lighting outside London. Lancashire, Cheshire, and southern Cumbria saw the growth of the silk, cotton, coal and chemical industries in such towns as Manchester, Liverpool, Oldham, Rochdale, Burnley, Ashton-under-Lyne, Bolton, Blackburn, Macclesfield, Preston, Stockport, Wigan and Warrington.

Inevitably this concentration of industrial activity precipitated a population explosion; Lancashire alone trebled its population, to reach almost 2 million between 1801 and 1851. The North-West had the benefit of not only abundant water, coal, and iron, but also a steady supply of Irish labour.

Some urban centres also grew up around green-field sites, as a result of individual enterprise (Fleetwood, St Helen's, Widnes), or railway activity (Barrow, Crewe, Poynton). In all these 'company towns' gas and other utilities were provided initially for company use but were subsequently sold to the wider community as much for private profit as for the public good.

After the 1835 reform of municipal corporations improvement commissioners acquired more powers and the 1848 Public Health Act (reformed in 1858) ushered in the Local Boards of Health. These developments quickly gave rise to programmes aimed at improving public health facilities, sewerage, paving and lighting. The 1875 Public Health Act accelerated these programmes and utility companies were either bought over or newly established by local government agencies.

Building Up and Tearing England Down

In London from mid-century, and elsewhere later on, underground railways were also built and these were later supplemented with tramways to facilitate the new commuter traffic. Most early subway lines were constructed by the 'cut and cover' method rather than by tunnelling, and this disruptive activity called for the deployment of large numbers of skilled men. Provision of a safe environment for production tunnelling in soft ground had to wait until the invention by James Henry Greathead of the 'Shield' in 1884.

> The first shock of a great earthquake had, just at the period, rent the whole neighbourhood to its centre. Houses were knocked down; streets broken through and stopped; deep pits and trenches dug in the ground; enormous heaps of earth and clay thrown up; buildings that were undermined and shaking, propped by great beams of wood. Here, a chaos of carts, overthrown and jumbled together, lay topsy-turvy at the bottom of a steep, unnatural hill; there, confused treasures of iron soaked and rusted in something that had accidentally become a pond. Everywhere were bridges that led nowhere; thoroughfares that were wholly impassable; Babel towers of chimneys, wanting half their height; temporary wooden houses and enclosures, in the most unlikely of situations; carcasses of ragged tenements, and fragments of unfinished walls and arches, and piles of scaffolding and wildernesses of bricks, and giant forms of cranes and tripods straddling above nothing. There were a hundred thousand shapes and substances of incompleteness, wildly mingled out of their places, upside down, burrowing in the earth, aspiring in the air, mouldering in the water, and unintelligible as any dream. Hot springs and fiery eruptions, the usual attendants upon earthquakes, lent their contributions of confusion to the scene. Boiling water hissed and heaved within dilapidated walls whence, also, the glare of flames came issuing forth; and mounds of ashes blocked up rights of way, and wholly changed the law and custom of the neighbourhood. In short, the yet unfinished and unopened railroad was in progress, and, from the very core of all this dire disorder, tailed smoothly away upon its mighty course of civilisation and improvement.[6]

All this tearing up of roads and pathways necessitated resurfacing with setts, blocks, cobbles, asphalt, flags or concrete. This was work which could only be done by hand, and the constraints of commercial activity, combined with proximity to the public, necessitated precision work of which only experienced navvies were capable.

'The Power of a Hurricane'

During the closing decades of the nineteenth century it was in these multifarious but mundane aspects of public works, rather than in the more glamorous but somewhat exclusive activities of railway building, that the Irish navvies really found their niche. The extent of the demand for Irish navvies in the labour-intensive areas of Britain's economy was documented as early as 1835:

> The introduction of so large a number of Irish into Great Britain has been ... influenced by the qualities which the Irish bring into competition with the English and Scotch workman. The most valuable of these, and those to which the employment of the Irish has been mainly owing, are willingness, alacrity, and perseverance in the severest, the most irksome and disagreeable kinds of coarse labour; such, for example, as attending on masons, bricklayers and plasterers, excavating earth for harbours, docks, canals and roads, carrying heavy goods, loading and unloading vessels, etc. In these departments of work it has been found by contractors and others more advantageous to employ the Irish than native labourers.[7]

The journalist Henry Mayhew, writing about the Irish poor in London twenty-five years later, said of the Irish labourer: 'In his strength he often resembled the power of a hurricane'.

Handley, commenting on the seeming inconsistency of Irish labourers from an overwhelmingly agricultural background flocking to Britain and congregating in the urban centres, points out that 'the soil for the Irish spelt only poverty, frustration, and eviction'. Because, as we saw in Chapter Five, they were mostly tenants-at-will subsisting on five acres or less, they had little or no opportunity for farming in the fullest sense of the term. Handley puts it succinctly:

They were only labourers. All they knew was how to dig. Indeed, they were experts at delving and trenching, and this skill they acquired on their miserable little conacre patches or in working for the landlord

London Underground extension, 1938.

and his comfortable tenant. When therefore the industrial revolution in Scotland and England beckoned and offered recompense in cash instead of in kind they approached with alacrity.[8]

The almost total absence of cash in their lives prior to emigration ensured that they would make a beeline for paid work abroad. It may also have had some influence on their choice of occupation; whereas casual labour in and around the urban centres of population was likely to be paid for in cash by the day, work on the railways was usually paid fortnightly or even monthly. This meant not only long intervals without ready cash, but also dependence for subsistence on the 'tommy shop' credit account, which, in turn, might mean little or no actual wages on pay-day. Such a prospect would not have appealed to the cash-starved Irish isolated on remote lines far from the urban centres where they might be assisted by communities of their fellow-countrymen.

Without either artisans' skills or education they had no alternative but to accept low-paid and menial work. English commentators, some of them employers, remarked on the curious failure of the Irish poor to transcend their unskilled status even after a lifetime working in England. These comments usually date from the nineteenth century but in the construction industry especially, they would be equally valid in the twentieth. Not surprisingly, of course, they take no account of the legacy of colonialism.

We are still at the beginning of excavating the sediment deposited on Irish minds over the centuries of physical inferiority, much of which still remains, however much we celebrate our new-found 'confidence', now three generations after the treaty, suggesting that the roots of intellectual and psychological dependency had indeed sunk in deeply.[9]

The Irish journalist and political activist John Denvir observed in his book, *The Life Story of an Old Rebel*, that throughout a lifetime in England he had 'never known a bricklayer's labourer who wasn't Irish'. But, he added, it was 'a sure sign that our people are rising on the social scale' when, at the turn of the nineteenth century, the Lancashire Irish no longer monopolised this niche.

The educated Irish such as professionals also emigrated in significant numbers but, whereas the poor Irish were a highly visible alien collective entity, the former simply 'melted away' into the host society and were painlessly assimilated as 'respectable', if somewhat colourful, citizens of the United Kingdom.

Given that the poorer Irish adopted the classic (and sensible) strategy of travelling to areas where their countrymen were established, it was natural and inevitable that they likewise found employment in occupations where their kind already had a foothold. In consequence, they themselves to a degree established 'closed shops' in certain occupations such as stevedoring in London, sugar refining in Greenock, and general labouring on building sites and public works (although they had to wait until the twentieth century to dominate the latter).

'Ready to Labour and to Serve'

However, even success at this level didn't usually facilitate access to apprenticeships for their better-educated children. On the contrary it was generally easier for the second generation to become clerks or industrial operatives than tradesmen. By the end of the nineteenth century it had become clear that the Irish in British construction were never going to gain access to trades until they either controlled management or faced no competition from the British (as was the case during the Second World War).

A curious aspect of the Great Famine was that, despite the loss of some three million people, demand for labour in Ireland did not increase and those remaining still had no alternative to emigration. Continuous prolonged emigration in turn mitigated the necessity for economic transformation and so

Above: London and Birmingham railway works at Camden Town, London, 1837.

preserved an outmoded and unproductive economic system. That outmoded system in turn discouraged domestic investment and industrial development, which might have stimulated demand for labour, and so the cycle was perpetuated.[10]

Between 1850 and 1875 an average 770,000 emigrants left Ireland. The majority of these went to Britain but, as the fare to the New World was about six pounds from Liverpool, many could have left Britain for America soon after their arrival. There is no way of determining how many may have done so. It was a simple matter for a single man or woman to walk to an Irish port, beg the steerage fare to Britain, and earn enough from unskilled labouring to buy a ticket to America in a matter of months.

Between 1876 and 1910 emigration dropped to around 185,000 annually. Recession in the United States, combined with agricultural decline in Britain and an increase in Irish wage-rates, were together inhibiting the urge to emigrate. For those who did emigrate in this period, however, Britain was not their preferred destination. Between 1876 and 1921, 84 per cent of those leaving Ireland went to the United States. With the introduction of the quota system in the United States after 1924, however, numbers making for the US declined rapidly. By 1951 the roles of Britain and the United States had been reversed. Thereafter, 80 per cent of Irish emigrants went to Britain.

The Irish unskilled labourer in Britain towards the close of the nineteenth century was often absorbed into a pattern of casual labour which the prevailing economic system encouraged. Much economic activity was either seasonal or sporadic in character; dock work being a prime example. Gas works — busy in winter, slow in summer — were another.

Agriculture absorbed workers when other occupations were quiet, and vice versa. Construction work was, by definition, intermittent. For the Irish engaged in railway building, however, as indeed for the rural English and Scots similarly occupied, the harvest season often presented an irresistible temptation to abandon navvying for healthier work such as saving hay.

In manufacturing, in agriculture, in the service industries, and in construction, strong men were always in demand. Employment, however, was rarely permanent, and, where it may have been — as in mills, iron works or chemical plants — men formerly accustomed to labouring in the open air often found conditions in such confined work-places intolerable over a prolonged period. Consequently casual work became a way of life for many. As Ruth Anne Harris puts it, 'A person might be a navvy, a tramp, a peddler or a harvester, all in the same year, or at different stages of their work life'.[11]

Donegal navvies building a road in Glencoe, Scotland, 1900.

Tramp Navvies

It rings strangely in our modern ears to hear the term 'tramp' used in relation to a working man; in the nineteenth century, however, that association would not have been unusual. Eric Hobsbawm, in his article, 'The Tramping Artisan', making the observation that 'The story of nineteenth-century labour is one of movement and migration,' deals with the English custom of journeymen-tradesmen going 'on tramp' either as a means of unemployment relief or simply to gain experience and 'see the world'.

This system was prevalent amongst the British trades unions or societies of the eighteenth and nineteenth centuries. A tradesman unable for any reason to continue working in his current situation would receive a document from his local society identifying him as a member in good standing and he would then leave town to seek employment elsewhere.

This document could be presented to an official of the same society, in a 'lodge house' or 'club house' or 'house of call', in another town. The traveller would then receive basic hospitality, in the form of a meal and a bed, plus a tramp allowance sufficient to maintain him through another day's tramp if he failed to secure work locally. In the event that he had to move on, it was the custom for his fellow-artisans who were working to 'pass the hat' for him as well. Travel by any means other than Shanks's Mare was generally frowned upon until late in the century — hence the phrase, 'on tramp'.

Since most working-men's clubs used a room in a local pub for meetings, it was inevitable that these 'tramping artisans' usually made a bee-line for particular public houses frequented by their fellow-tradesmen — hence the plethora of 'Mason's Arms', 'Bricklayer's Arms' and the like, throughout Britain.

The navvies also, in their turn, quickly identified a network of pubs around the country which were patronised by men involved with the construction industry. Here they could be appraised of the availability or otherwise of work and accommodation, and could learn the whereabouts of navvies of their acquaintance.

Where work was unavailable, or a man was only 'passing through', cash was passed to him, without comment, as a matter of course by those in work. It was understood by all parties that the money was not a loan but that the favour would be returned if ever their roles were reversed.

This unwritten code ensured that no man was ever truly destitute, and that navvies could count on each other, if on no one else. This was especially true of the Irish and remains so, to an extent, even today. It goes a long way towards explaining why navvying and construction work became so closely associated with pubs and drink.

The tramping artisan usually followed a well-established circuit which, if he failed to find enough work to settle elsewhere, would eventually bring him back to his original starting-place. So rigid was this system in the nineteenth century that Hobsbawm was able to establish that 'among the compositors this grand tour was about 2,800 miles long in the 1850s, among the brushmakers over 1,200 miles in the 1820s'.

Many trades practised this system and it was looked upon as a very effective method of undermining any attempt by employers at blacklisting or lockouts.

In 1860 it was in use among compositors, lithographers, tailors, coachmakers, bookbinders, smiths, engineers, steam-engine makers, stonemasons, carpenters, ironfounders, coopers, shoemakers, boilermakers, plumbers bricklayers and various other crafts.[12]

It particularly suited the footloose, and young men eager for adventure. Oddly there was, according to Hobsbawm, no provision made for the dependants of married men. Later in the nineteenth century it came to be seen somewhat as the refuge of the work-shy, and the sub-standard craftsman, and therefore as something to be discouraged amongst 'respectable' Victorian tradesmen.

Navvies, although skilled at their rather specialised work, did not possess tradesman status and were ranked at the lower end of the skills hierarchy. They lacked the support of a trades union (except briefly and locally) but substituted pride in their independence, and mobility, for the power of collective bargaining. The freedom to 'jack' (walk off the job) was and, to an extent, still is the prized and jealously guarded prerogative of the construction worker.

While tramping might have been almost unavoidable for an unskilled casual labourer in early life, it was romanticised, and often emulated, by many for whom it was little more than an indulgence. Even the prosaic German industrialist Engels spent a period wandering in rural France before knuckling down to the task of helping Karl Marx to overthrow Capitalism.

These *Wanderjahre*, or years of wandering, were a recognised part of a young man's rite of passage. They have links with a much older vagrant tradition in Europe — that of the pilgrim and the wandering monk or scholar. Up until the beginning of the Second World War it was still possible for an impecunious young man, travelling through Germany, to call on the mayor of a town and obtain an official voucher for supper and a bed at the local inn. The custom of nailing a small tin badge featuring the emblem of the town or city to the traveller's staff, betokening receipt of such assistance, has its origins in European pilgrim rituals of the Middle Ages.

Patrick MacGill compares the archetypal buck-navvy to tramps and vagrants but is careful to distinguish him from the latter as being not alone a workman but a veritable pioneer of civilisation, for which he gets no credit. His true reward, MacGill seems to suggest, is the freedom of the Road and the exhilaration of tramping from site to site with no need of greater shelter than the lee of a hedge in Summer. [13]

Such conditions were little worse than those the Irish harvester habitually encountered on the farms of England and Scotland in the nineteenth and early twentieth centuries, 'Canvas to throw over us, and make the bed with a fork'. In the Bothies of Scotland

and the 'Paddy Houses' of England they slept in sheds normally reserved for farm animals, on upturned seed potato boxes overlaid by straw-filled sacks, and covered themselves with flour bags. Inevitably, they slept in their clothes.

Rats were endemic and, if they didn't consume the harvesters' food, they chewed their buttons, their clothing, and sometimes their extremities. Most of these sheds admitted rainwater and lacked any form of heating. The conditions, in fact, were little better than those encountered when 'on tramp'. In fact, considering the added disadvantage of being an adjunct to back-breaking labour, often in wet clothing, for as much as sixteen hours a day, seven days a week, except for the Sabbath off in Scotland, or, in England, two hours off for Mass on Sundays, conditions seemed grim indeed.

Little wonder, then, that MacGill could romanticise life on the Open Road in poems such as 'Have You (On the Road to Kinlochleven, 1908)'.

> Have you slouched along the meadows, have you
> smelt the new-mown hay?[14]

MacGill, however, had 'seen the two days', and wrote other verse which distinguished sharply between the middle-class Romantics on walking tours and the tramp navvies living by their wits. In 'Padding It' from Moleskin Joe's diary he writes of 'An empty stomach, an empty sack and a long road'.[15]

The navvies, in common with other unskilled casual labourers 'on tramp' in nineteenth century Britain, acquired the traditional skills of the professional vagrant. They learned how to 'drum up' tea at the roadside in a 'billy-can' (the Tate & Lyle Golden Syrup tin was acknowledged by experts to make the finest 'billy') on a fire of kindling. They knew how to hang their food in a bag from an overhanging branch beyond the reach of rats while they slept (in more recent times they would sometimes hang an old alarm clock up in the same way). They became expert at stealing fowl from farms, and on how and when to beg from housewives — after the midday meal, when there might be 'leftovers', or when children, home from school, were being shooed out of the house with cuts of fresh-baked bread and lard to keep them quiet.

Their dress was quite distinctive: big donkey-jackets with two large outside pockets and a concealed 'poacher's pocket'; moleskin or heavy corduroy trousers; double-canvas shirts, velvet or cord waistcoats, braces plus a wide big-buckled leather belt (to strengthen the back while lifting); headgear and a large neck-scarf of coloured cotton tied with the special 'pincher's knot'. This scarf served to keep a man's throat warm in winter, when vigorous effort necessitated an open shirt, and protected the back of his neck from dangerous sunburn in summer.

They picked up a little of the gypsies' lore, and used the more basic of their signs to signal to each other which way a companion had gone at a crossroads, whether policemen were on the watch for vagrants, and when a house was good for begging or was best avoided by the homeless and the hungry.

MacGill picked up some of this lore also, and refers to marking the gateposts of households which responded well to begging, as a signal to his companions who were following behind. He also exhorts them to watch out for laying hens in adjacent hedgerows.[16]

'Savages in the Midst of Civilisation'

Naturally these parasitic habits alienated the settled community, and resulted in the tramp navvies being ostracised. They quickly acquired a reputation for lawlessness and anarchic behaviour that conferred on them the status of bogeymen amongst the rural poor. Dick Sullivan's father described an encounter with a farm labourer while on tramp in Gloucestershire. The rustic inquired whether Sullivan was a navvy; getting an affirmative answer, the man said, 'I'll give you sixpence if you'll show me your tail'. MacGill remarked similarly on the rural public's perception of the navvy. He acknowledged that no woman, young or old, would entertain a navvy, regarding navvies almost as lepers, while children were encouraged to see the navvy as the embodiment of the bogeyman.[17]

Likewise, in *Betty and Billy — A Child's Tale of the Ship Canal* (1889), by E.E. Haughton, navvies are described as, 'A strange army of giants and savage creatures'.

Irish labourers adopting this nomadic lifestyle soon learned 'the Ways of the Line' from their English counterparts, as Pat MacGill's alias, 'Dermod Flynn' learned from Moleskin Joe who, as has been noted elsewhere, is nowhere identified by nationality. We may infer, however, from a scene in *Children of the Dead End* that Moleskin was definitely not Irish:

> *'You hell-forsaken Irish blanket-grabber, you!' Joe was roaring; 'You've got all the clothes in the bed wrapped round your dirty hide'.*

Since the Irish and the Scots rarely got on, the inference must be that Moleskin Joe, or whoever MacGill's navvy mentor actually was, was in fact English.[18]

However, in spite of such alienation and isolation, the Irish labourer continued to maintain ties to home and family, if for no other reason than to honour his obligation to remit money for their survival.

Below: Signs used by tramps and gypsies. Scratched on gateposts, or the side of a dusty road, they acted as a form of 'bush telegraph' for society's nomadic outsiders.

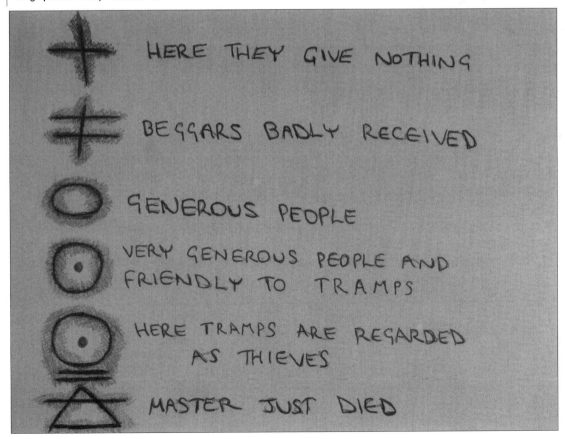

Remittance Men

This expectation of remittance money characterised almost every relationship between the Irish emigrant and his or her family back in Ireland. The 'Emigrant Letter', with its dollar bills, pound notes or money orders, was an indispensable adjunct to daily life in many parts of Ireland up to the 1970s.

It is difficult to overestimate the importance of these letters in such small communities.

Official returns revealed that over £34,000,000 was sent to the United Kingdom by North American emigrants between 1848 and 1887, the bulk of it going to Ireland.[19]

'Long-distance man', London, 1963.

Figures recently released by the Central Statistics Office show that, between 1939 and 1969, £2.2 billion was sent privately to Ireland in the form of telegrams ('the wire') and money orders from Britain alone. In today's money this is worth £5.5 billion. There is no record of the sums remitted in cash or cheques but it must come close to a similar amount. All this cash was being injected into what was a near-subsistence economy.

Not only was the money vital in many instances but the character of the son or daughter, the degree to which they were seen by outsiders to honour their obligations, was judged by the fidelity of their dispatches.

It was still commonplace, in small West of Ireland towns in the 1970s, for butchers to open up at eleven or twelve o'clock on a Friday and Saturday night. The men could then buy the weekend's meat with the cheque just cashed, or large note broken, in the pub-cum-grocery next door.

In one case recounted to me by an emigrant from Mayo the local postman, week after week throughout the year, had to disappoint an elderly widow waiting for a letter from her only son who had gone to England but didn't write home. In this he was not unique; young men are notoriously bad at writing letters, even in this age of universal literacy, and were much worse when education was rudimentary for most. The one time of year, however, when those who had not been in touch with home made an effort to communicate was Christmas. Sure enough, every Christmas without fail, the postman would deliver a letter to the widow, containing twenty pounds, from her son in England. She was always overjoyed by this sign that she was not forgotten and made a point of going into town to show all her friends and neighbours the long-awaited letter. This continued faithfully, for many years, until the widow died. Only then did the postman reveal to my informant, a trusted friend, that the Christmas letters the widow had received were written by himself each year and posted from England by arrangement with a friend.

Where the sender of remittances was male he was often employed at navvying or construction. The money was usually good, relative to what was paid to harvesters, even in the nineteenth century, and it was reasonable to expect that an able-bodied single man would be able to send money home regularly. Many of them did.

Those sending the money often made considerable sacrifices to do so; they endured terrible working and living conditions, deprived themselves of luxuries, and went without holidays or trips back home so that others could have what they believed they needed.

The downside of construction, however, was, as we have seen, the intermittent nature of the work and the nomadic lifestyle it engendered. Added to this were the effects of an all-male, macho culture that fostered attitudes of élitism alternating with bouts of alienation, self-loathing and shame. All of these negative aspects were compounded in many cases by addiction to drink. In MacGill's words, 'I felt that I was a man classed among swine, and that is a very bitter truth to learn at eighteen'.

Banishment

The result was that, in too many instances, a man might find himself failing or forgetting either to write or to remit money, over progressively longer intervals. Finally, he would reach the point where to re-establish contact would have been to face such severe censure that he lacked the courage or emotional maturity to do so. (It should be borne in mind that many of these men left home as little more than boys).

Such a man became an exile in the truest sense: a victim of self-imposed placelessness and banishment. He would thereafter avoid not only his relations, but anyone connected to his place of origin. He usually assumed an alias, and refused to be identified with his place of birth, or even in some instances with Ireland itself.

Perhaps an explanation for so many Irishmen adopting the lifestyle of the traditional tramp navvy was the evolution of a lifestyle built around casual comradeship, ready money, drink and day-to-day existence in a foreign country, which led, inevitably, after many years of wandering from job to job and place to place, to a lonely and anonymous old age in the bed-sits and homeless hostels of Britain's urban ghettos.

Domhnall MacAuligh described the typical fate of those whose lives had brought them to this pass:

> *They're much to be pitied, these old men, moving around from room to room and from camp to camp, without a sinner to mourn them when they die a lonely death in some dirty, broken-down old lodging-house.*[20]

Again the basic humanity of MacAuligh's insights enabled him to express perfectly the typical fate of those whose lives had brought them to this pass:

> *They're much to be pitied, these old men, moving around from room to room and from camp to camp, without a sinner to mourn them when they die a lonely death in some dirty, broken-down old lodging-house. They, worked, and they drank, and they fought while they were in it; and now, as their time draws near, they have nothing to do but stretch their bones in some corner, turn their faces to the wall, and wait for death.*[21]

MacAuligh first encountered these remnants of the Long-Distance Men in the early 1950s. Numbers of them are reputed to have died of hypothermia under the railway arches in east London, during the harsh winter of 1963, when temperatures remained close to freezing from February until early April. By this time, the sun had truly set on the old-time tramp navvy and 'The Ways of the Line'. Those men may have been the last of their kind.

5 Twilight of the Navvy

*You may call yourselves ... all kinds of fine names,
but the real old navvy was far before you as a man.*
Elizabeth Garnett
Navvy Mission Society

In Britain the half-century prior to the First World War was a time of fluctuating demand for unskilled labour, with more troughs than peaks, and this pattern characterised the agricultural as well as the urban industrial aspects of the economy. Throughout this period economic recession, together with changing farming practices, led to a sharp decline in the demand for seasonal Irish agricultural labour in Britain. In Ireland itself, although there was an overall decline in demand for farm labour, wages for those in agricultural employment increased.

These factors combined to reduce the attractiveness of migration to Britain at this time. In certain parts of the West and North-West of Ireland, however, dependence on foreign earnings remained undiminished and people in these areas suffered severe hardship whenever seasonal employment in Britain was unavailable.

'Mayo God Help Us!'

In these regions, population levels during the Famine had not dropped as significantly as in other regions precisely because many of the inhabitants were simply too poor to emigrate. This, in turn, meant ongoing reliance on seasonal migration to finance the renting of marginal lands for the ubiquitous potato crop:

Seasonal migration was a direct consequence of the economic policies undertaken by the landlords, as the latter continued to extract from holdings rents well in excess of what they were capable of producing. Farm rentals were inflated to an artificial level, for it was the level of English rather than Irish labourers' wages which were maintaining rentals at the artificial rate.[1]

By the end of the century ... most farm workers were unpaid assisting relatives or temporary hands who received wages only at peak season. Even among the residue many were paid partly in kind.... By 1911 the 'ordinary' Irish farm labourer might expect to earn about 10s. 9d. weekly, much less than his English counterpart and absurdly less than his relatives employed in foreign cities.[2]

As long as demand in Britain for Irish harvesters was strong, therefore, the pattern of seasonal migration from the West and North-West persisted well into the latter part of the nineteenth century.

Seasonal migration was crucial in the survival of many communities throughout the region.... Up to three-quarters of Swinford's population depended heavily on these remittances, whilst figures lie close to one half in the other two (Poor Law) Unions — Claremorris & Dunfanaghy.... In Mayo up to 50,000, or twenty per cent of the population, relied heavily on migration.

 It would appear that the 1860s and 1870s were the peak periods of migration, providing an income of between £0.8 million and £1 million to the economy of the west and north-west.[3]

A combination of depression and restructuring in British agriculture precipitated a serious cash crisis for the Irish smallholding and labouring class. Depressed British agriculture, in the period 1879–1881, led to extreme hardship in these communities; and re-structuring, across the entire last quarter of the century, led to an overall decline in labour-intensive tillage (except in Scotland).

The result was an increase in permanent emigration to the urban industrial regions and a growing demand on the part of Irish labourers for work in construction and civil engineering.

Where seasonal migration was particularly relevant ... the permanent emigrants became the main financial source for these communities. Seasonal migration had helped to maintain traditional economic and social structures in the west of Ireland. Permanent migration brought this rural economy into line with the rest of Ireland.[4]

The *Labour News*, founded in 1871 to advise labourers of the whereabouts of work and thereby deliver them from the hardship of tramping the country in search of it, was also reporting a great demand for construction workers:

There is a cry out everywhere for manual labour, and in the very heart of London railway works drag on slowly instead of advancing quickly, because men who can work are not to be obtained in sufficient plenty.

The paper followed this with the following:

New Railway Works. — Of the 199 private bills passed during the last session of Parliament eighty-two were railway bills. The works under the latter will clearly, in many cases, give employment to large numbers of men. With an already announced dearth of 'navvies' it is difficult to foresee how the demand will be met without careful organisation of all available resources.

The following advertisement, appearing on the same page, bore this out:

200 ground-workers are wanted immediately, con-stant work, full wages, between Hackney and Edmonton, on the Great Eastern Line. Lucas Brothers, Contractors. Apply on the works.

This was a time of great mobility and variation in supply and demand for labour right across the United Kingdom and the Crown Colonies. The *Labour News* of 22 August 1874 ran many advertisements illustrating this situation:

Advantageous Migration Offer. — A few respectable FAMILIES, Widows with boys over 13 preferred, can

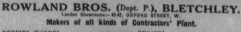

Above: Even in the 1920s Victorian technology was still the norm when it came to plant on site and the labourer's shovel remained — as Patrick MacGill called it — 'a mighty power in the land'.

be shown excellent openings in Lancashire and elsewhere, if they will apply at the Labour Agency, 1, Long Acre, London; or persons interested in the removal of labour which may be in excess in any part of the Kingdom may address themselves, with particulars of families willing to migrate, to the same office, 1, Long Acre'

Under the heading, 'MIGRATION FROM THE METROPOLIS', the paper's office was also at that time promoting the following pamphlet:

'FROM LONDON TO A MIDLAND COTTON MILL', being a report upon fifteen families removed from London to the Manufacturing Districts. Price One Penny; post free, 1½d., from Labour News Office, 1, Long Acre, London.

Simultaneously the paper ran almost half a broadsheet page of advertisements for emigrants to the colonies and the New World. Amongst these were many offers of free passage and/or free landholdings in the new territories. In many cases families were preferred over single men or women but there was much demand also for single agricultural labourers and domestic servants.

Labour News was only one of many newspapers and journals of the period, circulating in both Britain and Ireland, running similar advertisements for prospective emigrants. Through tickets from anywhere in Ireland to destinations in North America or the Antipodes could be purchased from shops in most provincial towns.

There was a general drive to populate the new territories and this is underlined by the fact that the Government of South Australia, in one advertisement, was offering Assisted Passages to 'Artisans, Agricultural Labourers, Miners and Gardeners', whereas 'Single Female Domestic Servants' could avail of Free Passages.

In the years prior to the First World War, as Flora Thompson points out in *Lark Rise to Candleford*, female domestic servants often:

> *belonged to a class which would not be found in service today; for at that time there was little hospital nursing, teaching, typing, or shop work to engage the daughters of small farmers, innkeepers and farm bailiffs. Most of them had either to go out to service or remain at home.*[5]

A third alternative, of course, was emigration, especially to bride-hungry parts of the colonies. While orphanages, poor houses, and even prisons were scoured for suitable females, not all were either destitute or deprived working-class women. Many were from better-off backgrounds similar to those listed by Flora Thompson.

Statistically, at least, there was ample opportunity for Irish emigrants in Britain to find partners of their own race: 'Everywhere the Irish emigrant was more likely than his British counterpart to be an unmarried adult'. It has often been observed that the Irish who emigrated in the nineteenth and twentieth centuries were unusual amongst migratory races in the degree of gender balance which prevailed amongst them: 'The balance of sexes seldom strayed far from parity'.[6]

The Famine, of course, precipitated whole families out of Ireland but it also provided an unusual degree of motivation for such collective action. The pattern before and after the period associated with it conformed more closely to that described above.

In fact, the post-Famine 'stem' system of inheritance and the impartability of land-holding, together with the lack of off-farm employment and general absence of economic opportunity, combined to make emigration an attractive option for young people anxious for marriage prospects. David Fitzpatrick has elegantly outlined this equation:

> *For those remaining in Ireland, non-marriage signified not the triumph of self-interest, but defeat: the 'celibate' had failed either to escape Irish restrictions or to qualify for an Irish match.*[7]

The long-term consequences of this situation for those remaining in rural Ireland are starkly spelt out by Roy Foster:

> *In 1929, the Irish age of marriage was the highest in the world — 34.9 for men, 29.1 for women — while one-quarter of the female population were unmarried by their forty-fifth birthday.*[8]

The last quarter of the nineteenth century witnessed a substantial decline in demand for Irish harvesters:

> *A final conclusion that might be suggested from the rather confused figures is that although the peak period of Irish migration for harvest work was around 1850 for Great Britain as a whole the massive influx into Scotland, and the fairly quick decline of much smaller numbers in the south of England, have masked the fact that the peak period for England when considered separately, was probably in the late 1870's, concentrated in the north and midlands.*[9]

Nevertheless, as we saw in an earlier chapter, men were still migrating from County Mayo to work as harvesters in England a century later. The numbers, however, were minuscule when compared with those of the previous century although, in the 1950s, there was brisk demand in England for sugar-beet workers and a great many men and boys from rural parts of Mayo worked on the beet 'campaigns' of the period.

Only 8 per cent of the Irish who emigrated between 1876 and 1921 went to Britain. Seven per cent went to the Dominions (Australia and Canada). The remainder went to the United States and elsewhere. Existing connections between the Irish of the western seaboard and those in the United States were immeasurably strengthened at this time. An informal migration network evolved which still, today, constitutes a broad and dynamic channel for potential emigrants to the New World.[10]

Of those who migrated to Britain, however, many of the males not enlisted in the British armed forces (still an impressive 25,000 in 1896) were absorbed into construction, in the form of either public works or house building. Inevitably this took them far afield and, if they were married, often resulted in children being born in several different locations.

An entry in the Census of 1871 reads as follows:

Thomas Ryan, Miner/Excavator, Railway, Ingleton Fells, born Ireland;
Children — James (10 years), born Ireland; Francis (8 years), born Gloucestershire; Mariah (5 years), born Scotland; Ann (1 year), born Huddersfield, Yorks.[11]

Ingleton Fells was the location of the 'navvy village' of 'Jericho', at Batty Green, near the site of the Ribblehead Viaduct on the Yorkshire Dales. This viaduct was part of the Settle–Carlisle Line being built for the Midland Railway between 1869 and 1875. Over 2,000 Scots, English, and Irish navvies lived at Jericho and worked on the building of the line.

Dick Sullivan was adamant that 'a common cause of riot' amongst the navvies, apart from drink, was 'an unhesitating hatred of their own Irish minority'. He wrote of the Irish on the Settle & Carlisle Line: 'Most of the miners were from Devon or Cornwall, with some Irish, the only place on numbers One and Two Contracts where they were tolerated'.[12] But again, in the works of Patrick MacGill, we find no references to anti-Irish hostility amongst the navvies with whom he worked in Scotland around the turn of the century.

Other notable rail-related projects on which Irish navvies were present in greater or lesser numbers include the following:

Project	Date Opened
Metropolitan Railway (London; world's first Underground Railway)	10/1/1863
Severn Tunnel (Bristol Channel; @ 4 miles, 628 yds. Longest railway tunnel in Britain when opened, after 14 years' construction)	1/5/1876
Southampton Docks (taken over by London & South-Western Railway)	1/11/1892
Liverpool Overhead Railway (world's first electric overhead railway)	6/3/1893
West Highland Railway	7/8/1894
Glasgow Underground Railway	14/12/1896
Great Central Railway	15/3/1899
Leytonstone–Newbury Park Central Line Extension (Final part of pre-war London Area tunnel construction programme)	14/10/1947

Many things were different in the world of civil engineering in the closing decades of the nineteenth century. Contractors had become more professional, resulting in improved conditions for the navvies; fewer major railway lines were being built, resulting in a greater diffusion of skilled men throughout other public works; and the age-profile of the professional navvy was changing. Terry Coleman's assertion that 'most died at forty' may be less accurate than his statement that 'The few who survived until they were sixty looked seventy'.[13]

Above: Grave of an unknown navvy, Kinlochleven, Scotland. The marker directly behind is inscribed 'Bernard Murphy'.

Tramp Navvies

It might be more accurate to surmise that by the turn of the century navvying, in common with agriculture, was no longer attracting young men; and many of those who were still 'in the game' were veterans of forty years and upwards.

In the last thirty years of the century men in their sixties and seventies were by no means uncommon on the railway contracts of Britain. Even the Irish, who are generally supposed to have been the most youthful of the nationalities, followed this pattern.[14]

Undoubtedly there was still a steady stream of young Irish men supplying the British unskilled labour market. Between 1852 and 1910 around 1,250,000 Irish emigrated to Britain, more or less equally divided between males and females, most of them under twenty-five years, inexperienced and 'full of eagerness to learn how to labour and to serve'.

The growth of the cities, however, combined with the ever-expanding Irish communities therein, was drawing more and more immigrants into urban occupations, albeit of an unskilled nature. Railway navvying was seemingly diminishing in importance to the Irish, even as the English were becoming less dominant within the professional navvy workforce.

It is nevertheless true that, of the Irish resident in England in 1871, no less than 43.4 per cent were resident outside the sixty-three largest towns and cities. Many of these were in small communities such as those already noted in the Pennine villages of Glossop, Broadbottom, and Tintwhistle, which had grown up around the railway, reservoir, and milling works that drew the Irish to these remote rural locations from the 1840s onwards.

The contemporary Irish populations of Lockerbie and Dunblane, to name just two Scottish towns which have coincidentally emerged from obscurity in recent years, derive from itinerant labourers who settled in these communities after building canals and railways nearby in the nineteenth century.

Many harvesters also chose to remain as permanent farm labourers and, like their navvy counterparts, found wives amongst the indigenous population. It would no doubt be a revelation to discover precisely how many 'English' people today, living far from the traditional Irish destinations of Liverpool, Glasgow, Manchester or Birmingham, have unknown Irish ancestors.

Although, between 1890 and 1950, Irish immigration into Britain was much lower than at any time immediately before or after, the majority still came from a rural agricultural background (as late as 1926 over 61 per cent of Ireland's population still lived outside towns and cities). Consequently males often gravitated towards employment in construction or civil engineering where the physical strength, stamina, and endurance in all weathers characteristic of agricultural workers were still valuable assets in this labour-intensive industry.

The civil engineering industry, as has been observed, experienced not only a decline in capital projects of national importance such as railways, but also a consequent diversification into a multitude of utility-related public works. In tandem with this development went an enormous increase in building industry output. The workforce increased from 497,000 in 1851 to 1,219,000 by 1901. Males engaged in building, as a proportion of all occupied males, reached a peak of 1:9.5 in 1901.

The 1891 Census Report contains no less than four foolscap pages listing large and small contracts for impending construction works, including railways, docks and canals, sewerage schemes, waterworks, and large public buildings, spread right across Britain. There was therefore a great deal of intermingling between ordinary unskilled labourers and the old-style navvies of the Railway Age.

Much of this interaction occurred off-site: in workingmen's accommodation as well as 'on tramp'. With fewer British youths drawn to navvying, young Irish labourers were taught 'the ropes' by the older 'Tramp Navvies' as described by Pat MacGill in *Children of the Dead End*. There was an ascending scale of accommodation, rising from hedgerows, via 'The Spike' (the local authority vagrants' temporary shelter), through simple 'digs' and boarding houses, to the Model Lodging Houses of the 1880s onwards and culminating in the Rowton Houses.

Handley gives an exhaustive account of the range and development of labourers' accommodation in Scotland (mostly frequented by Irishmen and Highlanders) which is representative of the situation across the whole of Britain in the nineteenth century:

In 1843 Glasgow had 524 lodging houses in the centre of the town. Those were the registered ones. It was calculated that from 5,000 to 10,000 persons were nightly accommodated in those houses at 2d. or 3d. a head.... The better type of lodgings offered varieties of accommodation according to the price paid. For a shilling a night — almost a day's wages for many a

Glasgow subway, 1894.

lodger — there was a choice of tent-bed and curtains or a feather-bed, sheets, blankets and a piece of carpet in front of the bed. Sixpence procured a tent-bed and curtains or a chaff-bed, blankets and sheets.

For the offer of threepence the lodger had to be content with a tent-bed or chaff-bed, blankets and a coarse half-sheet, and if he could afford only twopence he had to make do with a shakedown on the floor, consisting of a bed of straw and blankets.... police officers reported that they had seen twenty-six beds and about twenty shakedowns in one house and six beds in one room. Three persons frequently shared the one bed and four the shakedown, the number depending altogether on the demand.

Handley quotes from the memoirs of one individual paid to sleep in the kitchen of such a lodging-house to protect the chest of foodstuffs:

During the night rats came by hundreds; as I lay on the chest forty or fifty rats would step from the bed-head on to my breast and from there to the floor. They became uncommonly impudent.[15]

The 'Models'

The first improvement on this basic accommodation came with the formation by a local philanthropist in Glasgow, in 1847, of the Model Lodging House Association. Emulated by various local authorities elsewhere, the new type of lodging-house offered much improved accommodation, ranging from private cubicles, separated by wooden partitions and roofed with wire mesh for ventilation and security, let for sixpence, through dormitory beds for fivepence to bunk beds for threepence-halfpenny.

Soon such lodging-houses were being provided by municipalities throughout the United Kingdom, and the word 'model' became synonymous with lodging-house in the jargon of labouring men everywhere. According to Handley, Scotland, before the First World War, had a total of 423 common lodging-houses. Those in Glasgow alone provided over 13,000 beds. At Rosyth, where the new naval dockyard was being constructed in the early 1900s, a 'model' was specially built to house 600 navvies.

Each 'model' was equipped with a hot plate, consisting of 'a metal top on a large coal furnace built of brick', frying pans and saucepans, and hot water for washing and free footbaths. A full bath cost an extra penny.

The reputation of the improved lodging-houses of Glasgow spread far and wide. Josiah Flynt, a young American proto-sociologist who made an international study of tramps while masquerading as a hobo, wrote the following in 1893:

Glasgow is the best kip town that we found. Its lodging-houses are known all over Great Britain, and as soon as I was well within the city I asked for a 'Burns home'. There are several of these in Glasgow, all belonging to Mr Robert Burns, who was once a workingman, but is now a wealthy proprietor. He built his homes mainly to make money, but also to furnish poor workingmen a cheap and fairly respectable sleeping-place.[16]

The lodging-houses were designed to serve the needs of single men. Married men had to settle for 'apartments' in tenements, or one-room houses — the census of 1861 revealed that 227,000 families, or more than one-third of the population of Scotland, lived in houses of one room.

Other alternatives included 'farmed-out' (sub-let) houses, and 'ticketed' houses whose controlled accommodation levels were subject to unannounced inspection, usually in the middle of the night, by representatives of the local authority. According to Handley, there were more than 20,000 such houses listed by Glasgow Corporation at the close of the nineteenth century. Variations on this option are described in great detail by Handley and, in fact, his three books on the Irish in Scotland are an enlightening and invaluable source of information on the daily life of the Irish emigrant.

After the First World War there was a further improvement in standards of accommodation in the 'models'. MacGill's fictional navvy hero, 'Moleskin Joe', visits one such in Leeds around 1920. He finds a new breed of lodger, dressed not in the moleskins and velvet waistcoats of the old-time navvy, but in Army-surplus khaki. Instead of the time-honoured pipe these men smoke cigarettes. The accommodation is vastly improved and is monitored nightly by sanitary inspectors — some of whom are women![17]

The 'models' never completely displaced the poorer grades of lodging-house. John Neary describes an incident which occurred in a doss-house, in Selby, Yorkshire (Number 7, Wren Lane, run by an Irishman man from Ballina) where he spent a night as a teenager in 1924:

> *The first night in a kip house, I joined the men around the fire. Then a big man came into the room carrying a frying pan which he put on the coal fire. He pulled out a small parcel of meat from his jacket pocket and threw the contents onto the frying pan. As he waited for it to sizzle, he declared in a loud voice: 'Who was the best fighting man before I came in?'*
>
> *A small man next to me whispered that this was 'Big Joyce, the fighting man'. Nobody replied. If we were the long-distance kiddies, then this was the chief kiddie.*
>
> *Fearing there could be trouble that night, I decided to sleep out in the fields.*
>
> *Returning next morning to collect my belongings, I met Big Joyce again. Much to my surprise he greeted me civilly and, having established that I was down on my luck, he took me into a back room where he pointed to various scraps of paper. Written on each piece of paper was a message. I clearly remember that the first one I read stated: 'The Mule is on his way to Donny'. Big Joyce translated for me. It meant that 'The Mule' Durkan, from Swinford County Mayo, was on his way to Doncaster.*[18]

The 'Spike'

A decade later the 'Spike' occupied the bottom rung in temporary lodgings; run by the local authorities, these were the Casual Wards of what were formerly known as Poor Houses, and were mostly patronised by tramps. George Orwell gives a terrifying description of one of these institutions in *Down and Out in Paris and London*:

> *It was a grim, smoky yellow cube of brick, standing in a corner of the workhouse grounds. With its rows of tiny, barred windows, and a high wall and iron gates separating it from the road, it looked much like a prison.... I ... exclaimed, 'But I say, damn it, where are the beds?'*
>
> *'Beds?' said the other man, surprised. 'There aren't no beds! What yer expect? This is one of them spikes where you sleeps on the floor. Christ! Ain't you got used to that yet?'*

Orwell goes on to list the various sleeping options for a homeless person in London in 1931:

1. The Embankment. *One of only three places where one might legitimately sleep out in London at that time. 'You'd be bloody lucky if you got three hours' sleep';*

2. 'The Twopenny Hangover'. *Here lodgers sat along a bench and each might lean over a rope stretched in front of him. 'A man, humorously called the valet, cuts the rope at five in the morning'.*

3. 'The Coffin'. *This facility consisted of a wooden box covered by a tarpaulin. 'It is cold, and the worst thing about it are the bugs, which, being enclosed in a box, you cannot escape'.*[19]

These were all charitable or statutory facilities for those who couldn't afford the sevenpence minimum charge for the lowest type of commercial lodgings. Amongst the latter another hierarchy prevailed, which was measured by charges ranging from sevenpence to one-shilling-and-a-penny per night.

Orwell rightly puts the Rowton Houses at the top of his commercial list. Here, for a shilling, one could have a cubicle to oneself plus the use of excellent bathrooms. Half a crown (two shillings and sixpence) purchased a 'special' which, according to Orwell, was the equivalent of hotel-standard accommodation in 1932.

Arlington House

Lord Rowton, a Victorian philanthropist and one-time private secretary to Benjamin Disraeli, built a series of large hostels for workingmen to provide them with clean and decent accommodation at affordable prices. Arlington House, opened in Camden Town in 1905, was the last to be built. The nine hundred and eighty-five cubicles, each measuring seven feet by five feet, were a great improvement on the common lodging-houses. Despite an onerous disciplinary regime which forbade cooking, card-playing (the navvies' favourite pastime) and drinking, they were still so popular in the 1930s that Orwell described the Rowton Houses as 'always full to overflowing'.

Second best on Orwell's list, in point of cleanliness, were the Salvation Army hostels. Orwell wrote that they 'stink of prison and charity. The Salvation Army hostels would appeal only to people who put cleanliness before anything else'. Here, unless one could afford a private cubicle, dormitory accommodation often meant sleeping in a room containing up to forty beds.

Last, but in terms of sociability and dignity not least, Orwell puts the common lodging-house. They were dirty, noisy, unwholesome and squalid places, but life for the inmates usually centred around a warm homely kitchen where they could 'lounge at all hours of the day or night' and cook whatever they could, buy, beg, steal or borrow.

Orwell paints quite a rosy picture of a typical lodging-house kitchen, which corresponds to descrip-

tions given to the author by several of the older Irish navvies who themselves patronised them in the past:

There was a general sharing of food, and it was taken for granted to feed men who were out of work.[20]

These basic living facilities were ideal for single men, or those working away from home, and remained popular with Irish labourers until very recently. Arlington House, for example, still houses a small minority of men in regular employment although 98 per cent of the current Irish residents (themselves 41.36 per cent of the occupants) are currently unemployed and, in most instances, unemployable in construction because of age and infirmity.

Sixty years ago it was quite a different story in Arlington House. Then also, most of the inhabitants were Irish, but they were mainly young and fit, and in the vanguard of construction work.

Above: Arlington House, Camden Town, London. A classic Victorian working men's hostel which is still in use today.

Above: Wembley Stadium, 1924. The 'White Cliffs of Dover' backdrop in the arena and the surrounding buildings were erected for the British Empire Exhibition.

Patrick Kavanagh stayed there, briefly, during the 1930s and wrote:

Many Irish boys made Rowton House, Camden Town, first stop from Mayo. The soft voices of Mayo and Galway sounding in that gaunt impersonal place fell like warm rain on the arid patches of my imagination.

These boys were true peasants. They walked with an awkward gait and were shy. To me they looked up as to a learned man and asked me questions I couldn't answer.[21]

During and immediately after the Second World War there was a proliferation of such hostel-type accommodation, much of it of mixed quality, but little if any now remains.

'Strong in the Back and Weak in the Head'

Despite the pious hope expressed by Denvir in 1896, that his own maxim, about all bricklayers' labourers being Irish, might become obsolete as they acquired access to skills and education, the Irish in building and construction continued to dominate the ranks of the unskilled and semi-skilled labourers. The following passage, the autobiographical sketch of an English plasterer building 200 houses for Ashton Corporation in 1938, shows the dogged and depressing longevity of this imbalance and the racial prejudices which underlay it:

Here we are. 'Hello, Mick!' Mick's our labourer. Carries a hod as big as a coffin, and chews half an ounce of twist a day. Carries the Madonna in the Whit Sunday procession too. Good sort. Part with the shirt off his back; never knows his own strength. Irishmen make the best plasterers' labourers. They take to carrying things like a duck takes to water. They must have lived clean and healthy in their own mud cabins near the bog. I would not like to be a labourer in our game; they've to be strong in the back and weak in the head. Mick's fetched his shovel and a bucket of water, and is softening the top stuff. It's grand to watch him use that rake which he's now got in his hand. Watch him shove it through the top stuff. He's got some arms on him. See that extra pound that he gets by using his knees for leverage. He's filling his hod now. How would you like to carry it? One, two, four, six big shovelfuls, and one on the top for swank. Watch his run, it's a sort of jog-trot. He's a sort of human horse.

Clomp, clomp, clomp, his big feet are coming up the stairs. He'll be mixing, softening, and carrying all day. He'll hardly get time to stretch his back.[22]

But, behind the scenes, signs and portents of a turnaround were already visible at the century's end.

Robert McAlpine, who began his career as a bricklayer and builder — 'he could lay 2,000 bricks per day, minimum' — encountered the ubiquitous Irish navvy while building the Mallaig Extension to the West Highland Railway, 'the greatest concentration of concrete construction in the world' (1886–1901).

The good impression made on McAlpine by the Irish in Scotland was cemented (no pun intended) by his subsequent experience while building the Waterford–Rosslare Line (opened 1906). As a result, the firm began the practice of actively recruiting navvies in Ireland and, in the words of Sir Malcolm McAlpine, 'built on contacts made then to attract a lot of Irish labour between the wars, hence the "McAlpine's Fusiliers"'.[23]

Aided by these cadres of Irish navvies, McAlpine built such famous British landmarks as the Wembley Empire Exhibition (1924); Wembley Stadium (1922–3), the Dorchester Hotel (1929) and the Birkenhead half of the Mersey Tunnel (1934).

McAlpine has always been greatly interested in the feeding of his men, and on many of his jobs special cooking arrangements are made. Once, when inspecting in the south of Ireland, he became furious because he saw the men eating nothing but bread and jam. He turned upon his foreman, and after swearing at the absurdity of asking men to work when they had eaten nothing substantial, he gave instructions that kitchens should be built and beef and mutton should be served. When McAlpine had finished, the foreman remarked, 'But, Sir, haven't you rather forgotten the fact that today is Friday?' [At that time Catholics were forbidden to eat meat on Fridays].[24]

Around the turn of the century an Irish bricklayer from County Galway, M. J. Gleeson, established himself in the vicinity of Sheffield and in 1903 founded his own construction company there. The firm opened an office in Surrey in the 1930s (thereby positioning itself to avail of the paradoxical domestic and light industrial

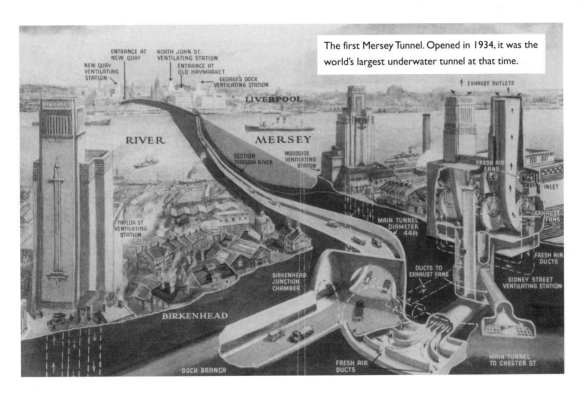

The first Mersey Tunnel. Opened in 1934, it was the world's largest underwater tunnel at that time.

building boom happening in the South-East at a time when the industrial north was in the throes of recession).

The Surrey base became the company's head office in 1960 when M.J. Gleeson & Co. became the first Irish-owned construction company in Britain to obtain a Stock Exchange listing. In the fiscal year 1999–2000 M.J. Gleeson Group plc achieved a turnover in excess of £298 million.

M.J. Gleeson was almost unique, in terms of his success, amongst Irish immigrants working in British construction at that time. Companies like McAlpine, with their propensity for promoting Irish workers to positions of responsibility — 'a number of them rose to foreman and manager status and ... rightly encouraged further recruitment (of Irishmen) at labourer and craftsman level' — were themselves as yet only minor players.

The small men persisted despite the growth of major contractors. There was work on minor lines that no respectable firm would touch; there were sub-contractors like Wimpey, Mowlem and the McAlpines who would later emerge as 20th century giants.[25]

Public Works

The older firms who dominated the industry at this time showed little inclination to elevate the Irish above their accustomed unskilled or semi-skilled status. Irish tradesmen, other than masons, were rare and, perhaps because of 'closed shop' practices amongst British tradesmen, were given few opportunities to 'rise through the tools' and become 'company men'. British clients also were reluctant to give contracts to unknown Irish tradesmen/builders.

The result was a preponderance, amongst the unskilled Irish, of navvies and labourers in the industry prior to the Second World War. More and more of these were employed in construction and on public works contracts such as reservoirs and dams.

By the final decades of the nineteenth century, the navvy was compelled to find an increasing proportion of his employment in the fields of dock and reservoir construction.[26]

As long ago as 1849 the association between cholera and water supply had been demonstrated by Dr John Snow, but slow sand filtering was only introduced in Britain in 1928.

... it is estimated that there are about 2,000 reservoirs containing more than 22,500 cubic metres of water above adjacent ground level. The great majority of these dams are earth embankments.[27]

Typical of such projects was the waterworks in the Derwent Valley in Derbyshire which, early in the new century, attracted many Irish navvies from nearby Leeds, Liverpool, and Manchester, in addition to the local agricultural labour force. The navvy village of Birchinlee provided not only hutments but also a 'dosshouse' in which newly arrived labourers were quarantined (deloused) before being admitted to the permanent quarters of the village proper.

Conditions here were excellent for the time, but so habituated to tramping had the older 'pincher' navvies become that, according to one local resident, some of them preferred to sleep in the large concrete culvert pipes around the edge of the site. Many of these men were Irish and Scots.[28]

The Fylde Water Authority, also in Derbyshire, undertook similar work in the vicinity of Clitheroe. This work, which began in the 1920s continued until 1932 and again employed many navvies who were housed in a specially constructed 'village' close to the works. It was a far cry from the turf huts thatched with heather in which the navvies had been housed at the nearby Woodhead Tunnel works eighty years previously.

The following advertisements in *Labour News*, from the 1920s, give a flavour of the industry this time:

Gorple Reservoir Works, Hebden Bridge, Yorks.:
Good Navvies & Timbermen required. Fully licensed
canteen now open.
Lehane, Mackenzies & Shand Ltd.

(5 May 1928)

WHY DON'T YOU TRY KEY'S CORDS?
Read what a Fellow Workman Says

Alton,
Hants.
29/12/26

Sir,

Please find enclosed PO to the value of 25/- for one
pair of cord Forkstrong trousers. Swansdown
linings — fly fronts. Square pockets. You have had
my measurements for years. My last pair, just
finished, I had October 17th 1923. My work is very
rough, and I think they have done me good service.
Your attention prompt will oblige.

Yours faithfully,

Get Your Cords From Key's !
Patterns Free
Geo. Key Ltd.
Workmen's Tailors,
Rugeley,
Stafford

Good Rock-Getting Ganger Wanted: Must be able to
handle men and explosives. Apply Agent, Betws-y-
Coed Widening Contract, North Wales.

(26 February 1927)

Excavation To Let on Piece Work:
Harbour Deepening at Findochty, near Aberdeen.
20,000 cubic yards shingle and sand. Jubilee Wagons
and Petrol Locos. Provided. Accommodation on site
for Men. Further particulars given on site, or apply to:
W. and G. Sykes, Contractors, Middlesborough

(16 April 1927)

Good Navvies Wanted:
Apply Sewerage Works, Ashford, Kent

(30 July 1927)

Will John Markey, better known as Cleveland Jack,
come home, or otherwise communicate with his wife.
25, Sixth Road, Tyler Point, Brightside, Sheffield

(21 January 1928)

Gorple Reservoir works. Hebden Bridge, Yorkshire.
Fully Licensed Canteen Now Open. Good Navvies
and Timbermen required. R. Lehane, Mackenzie
And Shand, Ltd.

DERWENT VALLEY WATER BOARD.

DOSS HOUSE AT HOLLINCLOUGH.

RULES FOR LODGERS.

(1.) The House is intended for the temporary accommodation of persons seeking employment on the Works of the Board.

(2.) No Applicant will be admitted unless he consents to have his clothes disinfected and to take a bath.

(3.) The price charged is 6d. each per night, which must be paid on entering. In exchange the Applicant will receive a numbered ticket, entitling him to a night's lodging, with use of clean night-shirt, bed, bed clothes and use of common fire.

(4.) Lodgers are permitted to remain in the House one night only, unless on the following day they are successful in obtaining employment on the Works.

(5.) Men who obtain employment are required to remain in the Doss House a week before they will be permitted to take lodgings in the Birchinlee Village, and must each obtain a "Workman's Doss House Ticket" from the time-keeper and must shew it to the care-taker at the Doss House when applying for lodgings on the second and following nights.

(6.) Provisions can be obtained from the care-taker at the following prices:—

Mug of tea, with milk and sugar		-	1d.
Potatoes (per meal) -	1d.	Bacon (per lb.) -	8d.
Bread (per lb.) -	1d.	Porridge with ½ pt. of milk	1d.
Soup - -	1d.		

(7.) Lodgers are permitted to provide their own food and to use the common fire to cook it.

(8.) No one is permitted to bring intoxicating drink of any kind whatever into the House, and anyone infringing this rule will be at once turned out, and, if in employment on the Works, will be paid off and will have no further chance of being engaged.

(9.) Lodgers must strictly observe the rules, and must be quiet and orderly in their conduct. The care-taker is authorised to turn out anyone transgressing the Rules.

(10.) Lodgers are requested to help in the maintenance of order, and in the observance of the Rules.

(11.) The above Rules may at any time be added to or varied by the Board.

By order of the Derwent Valley Board.

EDWARD SANDEMAN,
ENGINEER.

Above: A 'halfway house' on a Derbyshire waterworks project in the 1920s.

PLACES WANTED: Young Man, seeking change, desires situation with contractor as TIMEKEEPER, anything, anywhere. Box 313, Labour News Office, 10, Farringdon Avenue, London, EC.

(30 July 1927)

It is probable, given that he hoped to became a Timekeeper (demanding little in the way of skills or strength, but a modicum of education) that the young man in question came from a middle-class background and therefore was unlikely to end up like 'Cleveland Jack'. Was he running out on a sweetheart? Had he been 'fiddling the books' in some clerkship in the City? Was he avoiding parental insistence that he enter the Army or the Church? Who knows? — many navvies were men who had opted out of 'respectability' for personal reasons. There were amongst them former teachers, ministers, lawyers, soldiers, sailors, criminals and the sons of gentlemen but, as in the Old West, 'The ways of the Line' guaranteed them anonymity, and the comradeship of their fellow-navvies.

Labour News, incidentally, was known in the industry as 'The Jacker's Journal' (to 'jack' being to walk off the job). Another popular nickname was 'Paddy's Bible'. *Construction News* and *The Irish Democrat* were equally important to the postwar Irish working in construction.

Between 1919 and 1939 over four million houses were built in Britain. In 1937 the inter-war record was reached, with a peak figure of 347,000 completions. This era also saw the inception of the 'Garden City' concept, as typified by Welwyn Garden City and Hampstead Garden Suburb, designed to contain the growth of satellite commuter communities.

The slump caused by the Great Depression affected the industry in a patchy sort of way. House building fell off in the industrial north, but carried on apace in the more prosperous South-East. Public works, such as water schemes, were also not affected but large private contracts were severely curtailed. It was a difficult time for professional navvies.

At the height of the Great Depression, in 1932, 27.3% of the construction industry was out of work. RIBA president Raymond Unwin pleaded for everyone earning more than £250 per annum to donate at least 1s. 7d. a week to the Architects' Unemployment Fund.[20]

The old-style navvy suffered much hardship during the Depression but general labourers prepared to seek employment on housing projects could be lucky. At one point during the inter-war period McAlpine's built 3,000 houses in three years for Manchester Corporation — a staggering twelve completions per day — with a workforce of 9,000 men.

Wimpey — 'We Import More Paddies Every Year' — employed the Irish in substantial numbers on ground-works from as early as 1920, when they were commissioned by Hendon Rural Council to lay roads, sewers, and drains for a large housing estate on a greenfield site in Hendon. That project, Wimpey's first major contract, was valued at £50,000.

Another major pre-war Wimpey housing project, Greenford Park Estate in London (1932) provided affordable housing at £550 per unit (deposit £25) to young couples anxious to marry and move out of the parental home. The stereotypical urban working-class

Methil Dock, Scotland, c. 1911. Note the juxtaposition of concrete pier, steam tugs and sailing ships — a time of transition.

girl's response to a marriage proposal around this time was, 'Yes — I'll marry you, as long as I can have my own front door', and the government of the day intended to meet this need.

Wimpey's first significant civil engineering contract was the Team Valley Trading Estate, Gateshead, built in 1936 at a cost of £800,000. This was the site on which Wimpey wagons were first painted the trademark yellow. The company went on to build such distinctive 1960s projects in London as Draper's Gardens, Euston Centre, London Bridge House and Centre Point.

Other inter-war employers of Irish labour included Peter Lind & Co. Ltd., founded in 1915 (Projects included grain silos for Minch Norton in Cork, 1934, and conventional power stations at Bargoed Colliery, South Wales, 1919; Croydon, 1930; Fulham, 1934; Gravesend, 1938; Swansea, 1942); and A.E. Farr Ltd., founded in 1906, although this company made more use of Irish labour on their many postwar projects.

An important employer of the Irish was Mitchell Construction. This company absorbed the tunnelling specialists Kinnear Moodie and Charles Brand & Co., both of which employed many Irish tunnellers, and went on to develop enormous expertise in the construction of dams and power stations. One modest early Mitchell project of uniquely Irish interest was

Waterford Bridge, 'the first reinforced concrete bridge in the British Isles' (1912). Again, their heyday for employing Irish labour was the postwar period, when Irish tunnellers and navvies worked on Mitchell Construction projects as large as any ever built in Britain.

The great Irish post-Famine exodus was directed predominantly to America, but in this the Irish were not unique in Europe. Between 1850 and 1914 fifty-four million Europeans left for the Americas and/or Australia and New Zealand. Of these, perhaps two million were Irish.

Irish emigration gradually tailed off from the late 1880s, with Britain replacing North America as the favoured destination after the 1920s. As we have seen, however, migration from the North-West persisted, because of the ongoing necessity for foreign earnings, while at the same time opportunities for seasonal work were diminishing in Britain.

One country where seasonal work remained undiminished until the outbreak of the Second World War was Scotland. Tattie hokers continued to travel from Donegal and Mayo in significant numbers and, as always, young single men were tempted to remain in Scotland when the harvest season closed and seek employment in construction.

'We Import More Paddies Every Year'

'Tunnel Tigers'

This ready availability of Irish labour in Scotland meant that Ireland was heavily represented on Scottish public works. When, in 1908, the British Aluminium Company's Kinlochleven hydroelectric scheme was initiated, many Irish navvies, including Patrick MacGill, were employed on it. A much larger scheme, also designed to supply energy for aluminium smelting, was begun nearby in 1921 and work continued on it for ten years.

This was the Lochaber Power Scheme, also for the British Aluminium Company. A catchment area of 303 square miles behind Ben Nevis — elevated land with heavy rainfall — was tapped into to feed water to the turbines at Fort William. These turbines generated electric power at a continuous output of 120,000 horsepower.

Loch Treig is the main storage reservoir for the Scheme. It is fifteen miles from the power house at Fort William, and the task of conveying the huge volume of water for this distance involved one of the biggest engineering feats of its kind in the world at that time.

It was decided to drive a tunnel right through the mountain mass from Loch Treig to Fort William. At fifteen miles it was one of the longest tunnels in the world, then surpassed only by two others, supplying water to New York and Los Angeles respectively, and longer by miles than the more famous Alpine railway tunnels. In addition, seven adits, 9 by 8 feet in section, fed water from the northern face of Ben Nevis into the tunnel.

There were many supplementary operations needed to facilitate the project. A three-foot gauge railway, twenty-three miles long was built from Fort William, to transport men and materials to the seven

Mersey tunnel, 1934 — looking towards Birkenhead.

adits, and four 18 by 12-foot vertical shafts. This railway started at sea level and rose to a height of 1,200 feet.

Camps were built to house three thousand men, and other narrow-gauge railways were built to connect the various camps with the works, to link Loch Treig with Loch Laggan, and to link up with the West Highland Railway and the local quarries.

Twelve miles above Fort William, where the River Spean passes over the Monessie Falls, a short tunnel and a pipeline were built to connect with a temporary powerhouse. This generated 4,800 horsepower, at 11,000 volts, supplying electricity for the compressed-air plant installed at each of the adits and shafts. At each entrance a two-stage air compressor delivered air to the working faces via 6-inch pipes.

At the headings, groups of rock drills bored holes eight or ten feet into the face. When twenty or thirty of these holes had been drilled 180 lb of gelignite was inserted. The explosion normally brought down about 150 tons of rock, which had to be cleared by hand, before further drilling could take place. Some of the rock was so abrasive that drills required sharpening after only six inches' penetration.

Three thousand men were employed on the excavation of the tunnel. Approximately two-thirds were from Donegal. The maximum rate of advance was more than 900 feet in four weeks, with a record advance of 91 feet a week in one heading. At peak periods, compressed air was being used at the rate of 17,250 cubic feet a minute.

Battery-driven locomotives hauled trains of spoil to the surface and later brought concrete back in to line the tunnel. The invert was concreted; streams crossing the line of the tunnel (eleven in all) were dammed and their waters diverted via shafts into the tunnel. Then a surge shaft 240 feet deep with a 30-foot diameter was constructed; and the water finally taken by three 70-inch pipes 3,200 feet from the tunnel mouth to the power house at the seaward end of Loch Linnhe.

Another army of men was engaged on the conservation work on the other side of the Ben Nevis

Laggan Dam under construction, Scotland, 1925. Note the operatives scaling the face of the dam.

range. The main features of this scheme were the building of two great dams below Lochs Laggan and Treig and the driving of a tunnel, nearly three miles long, between the two reservoirs.

Laggan Dam is a mass concrete structure, slightly curved in plan, with a length of 700 feet at the level of the spillway. The preparations for this dam included laying a three-foot gauge railway about four miles long across the gorge of the River Spean.

When the work on the foundations had been completed, the concrete monolith was built up, each section being added to in turn to allow time for the poured concrete to cool and to avoid the formation of cracks. The concrete was laid in lifts of about 3 foot 6 inches, that is, in layers about 3.5 feet thick. Every lift was covered with heavy coconut matting which, to prevent cracking, was kept wet until it was removed for the next lift.

The main storage reservoir of the Lochaber Power Scheme is formed by Loch Treig. Water from the Laggan Reservoir is conveyed to Loch Treig by a tunnel which opens at the eastern end of the Laggan Dam. The Laggan-Treig Tunnel has a length of 14,600 feet, or nearly three miles, and is similar to the Ben Nevis Tunnel except that for the most part it was driven through solid granite.

Loch Treig Reservoir has a capacity of 7,800 million cubic feet. The raising of the loch necessitated the diversion of the track for a distance of 1.5 miles and the driving of a tunnel through a rocky shoulder on the side of the mountain. Similar diversion work had to be undertaken before the building of the Laggan Dam — the road to Kingussie had to be rebuilt at a higher level for about a mile of its length.

The sheer scale of this project, undertaken in very inhospitable terrain and under difficult conditions for the period, is most impressive. The men who worked on it, over ten years, must have endured considerable hardship in that climate, given the rudimentary facilities then standard for the industry.

An Irish wit highlighted the poor catering which characterised the early hydroelectric schemes:

Aqueduct, Galloway Power Scheme, 1935.

Above: 'Keep the big mixer going ...'

It was spam and jam
That built the dam
For Wimpey in Loch Shinn.

The fact that working conditions in civil engineering were much more primitive than those in the building industry is often overlooked by men who speak loosely of working 'on the buildings' as navvying; nothing could be further from the truth.

The tunnelling dimension of the project was very significant for the Irish. The earlier project at Kinlochleven, on which Irish navvies had worked a quarter of a century previously, did not entail tunnel work. Lochaber was the first Scottish civil engineering project on which Irish navvies gained experience of hard-rock tunnelling.

Unfortunately the men who were employed here were no longer active when the great series of postwar hydroelectric schemes was initiated in Scotland in the late 1940s. However, the association between Donegal men and hard-rock tunnelling was already clearly established. Donegal men were still travelling in significant numbers to Scotland to work in construction, and it was natural that they should become involved in the later schemes.

Poles, former coal miners displaced after the war, also worked on these projects, and everyone, including the contractors and engineers, learned together. In this respect the civil engineering situation was almost analogous to that which had prevailed when the first canals were built two centuries previously.

Many Mayo men also worked as tunnellers although their associations with the industry in

England, especially around London, led them more often into soft tunnelling work in clay, shale, and sand. The tunnelling experience gained by the Irish in this period firmly established them as the industry's leading miners — the famous 'Tunnel Tigers'.

Other Big Projects

Another major pre-war Scottish hydroelectric project on which Irishmen were employed was the Galloway Scheme, begun in 1929, which comprised five separate power stations, several reservoirs, and a large number of dams, tunnels, aqueducts, pipe lines and other engineering works. The scheme employed over 2,000 men, and was completed in 1936 at a total cost of £3 million.[30]

In England a series of coal-fired power stations was commissioned in the 1930s. Several of these, including Stretford, Radford, Barton and Preston, were built by Gerrards, who also built Risley Munitions Factory between 1935 and 1938. Gerrards, a major employer of Irish labour, was later taken over by Fairclough, now part of the Amec Group.

In 1939 the government banned all new public works, and unemployment in the industry swelled from 200,000, in September 1939, to 359,000 in early 1940. At the same time, numbers employed declined from around one million to 380,000. This situation precipitated about a crisis, which was exacerbated by the introduction of immigration controls from Ireland into Britain. If the Irish remained, especially without employment, they faced the possibility of conscription. If they returned to Ireland, neutral and independent but in dire economic straits and suffering from chronic unemployment, how could they re-enter Britain? How was Ireland to turn this fresh hour of 'England's difficulty' into 'Ireland's opportunity'? They couldn't know it then but, for the Irish in British construction, their finest hour was, in fact, at hand.

Tilbury Docks, London, 1929.

6 The Haemorrhage

The year was 1939, the sky was full of lead
Hitler was headed for Poland, and Paddy
For Holyhead. (Anon)

The decades preceding the Second World War witnessed a bottoming-out of the traditional relationship between Irish unskilled labour and British employers. Migration from Ireland to Britain almost ceased as world recession reduced foreign job prospects and domestic employment increased.

In Britain itself, with almost four million unemployed, as many as 200,000 emigrated to the Colonies each year. Up to fifty voluntary organisations, many of them religious, assisted potential emigrants financially. Government agencies actively encouraged emigration as a means of reducing the dole queues.

In this atmosphere, those Irish who did migrate to Britain were looked upon with suspicion and resentment both by right-wing politicians and by the indigenous working class. Calls were made in Parliament for the introduction of controls between Britain and the Irish Free State, in the form of visas and work permits, but ensuing proposals were considered unworkable and, ultimately, undesirable.

Allegations that Irish immigrants were claiming unemployment benefits could not be substantiated. An Interdepartmental Committee representing the Home Office, the Board of Trade, the Ministry of Health, the Ministry of Labour, the Scottish Office and the Dominions Office found that, in marked contrast to much indigenous labour, the Irish, in particular, were favoured by employers seeking men for heavy unskilled work such as navvying.[1]

Demand for Irish harvesters had been declining for almost fifty years although a trickle still persisted and the sugar beet 'campaigns', started in the late 1920s, did pick up a little of the resulting slack:

CONTRACT FOR LINCOLNSHIRE SUGAR-BEET FACTORY — A new company has been formed, called The Lincolnshire Beet Sugar Co., Ltd, with offices at 77, Gracechurch Street, London E.C. The company has placed a contract with Sir Robert McAlpine and Sons, for the erection of a large sugar-beet factory at Bardney, Lincolnshire. The factory has been designed, and will be constructed, under the supervision of the Dyer Company of America, and is to be completed in time for the 1927 crop.

(*Labour News,* 5 March 1927)

PROGRESS ON SELBY SUGAR FACTORY — Work has commenced on the preparation of the site for the new beet sugar factory at Selby, Yorks. The factory, sidings, etc., estimated to cost £350,000, will occupy a position on the east side of the river opposite the Selby shipyard. Sir Robert McAlpine and Sons are carrying out the work for the Dyer Company of America, whose offices are in Pall Mall, London.

(*Labour News,* 5 March 1927)

The Lowest Ebb

The social and economic climate in which these and several other beet factories were established in Britain, is aptly illustrated by John Neary's reminiscences of his introduction to the life of the Long-Distance Kiddy at that time. When we last met John, he had survived an encounter with 'Big Joyce, the Fightin' Man' in a 'kip' house in Selby in 1929. Not yet seventeen, he tramped the roads of Yorkshire throughout that Autumn and Winter, getting a few days or weeks pulling beet for local farmers and, in between:

Where possible, tramping the roads with five or six other men. We walked single file through the narrow roads to avoid being hit by what traffic there was. Our line of gaunt, dishevelled men must have made a pathetic picture.... I had now been a whole month on the road without work. I decided to go back to Selby in the hope of finding work in the beet-processing factory. I was fortunate to get a job —

Galloway Power Scheme, 1936 — not much 'work wear' in evidence.

shovelling coal at threepence a ton. Not good, but it
was warm work and more regular than I'd ever had.[2]

He was lucky: at the beet factory in Selby he was
befriended by an American engineer, seconded from
the Dyer Company, who took him in hand, gave him a
good job, and set him up in digs, with decent clothes
and a bank account. John Neary, sometime Long-
Distance Kiddy, never looked back.

Most Irish unskilled males migrating to Britain,
however, continued to find employment principally in
construction. House building provided many of the
jobs, whereas civil-engineering projects became
scarcer, despite the fact that the building of the London
Underground network, begun as far back as 1863,
developed apace throughout the first three decades of
the twentieth century and continued to employ
thousands of navvies.

> *No time ... proved as bleak as was the depression of*
> *the early 1930s when seasoned navvies in London*
> *competed for the job of excavating the pedestrian*
> *underpass from Paddington main line station to the*
> *underground system in 1932.*[3]

Protectionism within the industry, and reaction to
the IRA bombing campaign of 1938–39, took their toll
on Irish labour. In addition, the *Prevention of Violence
Act* of 1939 introduced compulsory registration of Irish
citizens for the first time, and also facilitated legal
repatriation. Prospects for the Irish emigrant labourer
within Britain's construction industry had never
looked so bleak.

Then came the war...

> *World War II was a licence to print money as long as*
> *you had that most valuable of raw material: people.*
> *We had people and we exported them faster than*
> *cattle and like cattle and while fathers, sons and*
> *daughters cried all the way to the train and the bus*
> *and the ship, the flow back of emigrant cheques and*
> *money orders evaporated the maternal and wifely*
> *tears so that on the threshold of the Post Office or the*

Acton Railway, 1935.

> *Hibernian Bank below in Main Street you could*
> *smile a little more with every passing week. The old*
> *order was changing.*[4]

What John Healy meant by 'the old order' was the
unequal but symbiotic relationship in rural Ireland
between town and country. The small farmer and
cottier survived from year to year, courtesy of credit
from the local shopkeeper, but nonetheless helped keep
these same shops in business with their intermittent
earnings and remittances.

Each year the shopkeeper advanced seed to the
farmer, or the fare to Britain to the migrant harvester.
During the financial hardship of the Economic War, in
the 1930s, the farmer or cottier spread his custom
across a range of shops in order to avail fully of the
limited ration of credit which each shop could extend.
In this way he obtained sufficient credit to maintain
his family in essentials pending a good crop or the
fruits of a season's agricultural labour abroad.

> *The farmers had any amount of food but they hadn't*
> *the wherewith to buy clothes and shoes for the*
> *youngsters at all.*

This arrangement enabled both smallholders and shopkeepers to survive the worst years of the Depression without permanent emigration. Socially, however, it fostered attitudes of unwarranted snobbery and contempt, on one side, and resentment and inferiority on the other. Arcane but insulting terms such as 'Buff Sham' and 'Rager Cove' were coined in the small towns of the west to denigrate the country boys and girls. These were mocked for coming to school (when not needed for chores at home) in home-made clogs, or bare feet in summertime, wearing altered second-hand clothes bought from stallholders at the marts or handed down from older siblings.

As John Healy pointed out, prior to the war 'townies' weren't usually involved in the seasonal migration cycle; if they left home, it was to work in the cities or emigrate to America. The former implied a better education than the bare minimum which domestic circumstances permitted to the country children, thus demonstrating greater family wealth, while the latter was a prestigious move requiring contacts and resources beyond the attainment of the average smallholder or cottier. The honourable exception to this rule was the 'passage' in the form of a ticket, or cash for same, remitted by a relative who had previously emigrated and become a link in this form of chain migration.

'Dole Beef'

The Economic War was the absolute nadir of deprivation and financial hardship for the cottier and smallholder class in the west of Ireland. As John O'Hara recalled,

> After 1934 things got severe. You could get plenty food — in this way.... Come the springtime of the year you could get a few old swans' eggs, and wheelauns' [black-headed gulls'] eggs.
>
> They'd lay — about a thousand of them would lay in the same patch, up on the bog, and you could go up and pick baskets of them, but they'd last only about a week or two.... Then again, there was other bits and pieces that would come around, like the day that they would tail the lambs — that would be another bit of a feast. Oh, you daren't buy any meat — you couldn't, but then there was 'Dole Beef'.
>
> They used to stop them tuppence out of the shillin', or something, and give them a couple of pounds of meat. Well there was fellas cashin' in on that; I see it on the television nowadays — this 'Mad Cow Disease', well, we had it where a cow would take 'The Staggers', and that went for 'Dole Beef'....
>
> There was the odd bullock killed 'round the place, but they went to the Doctor, or the Lawyer, or whoever; the 'Skins' that was on the dole didn't get anythin' of that at all. But then the 'Skins' that was on the dole never did get a taste of beef very much, so of course anything was a great feast to them![5]

There was, therefore, a certain contempt for the country youth, whose agricultural bondage led him from compulsory involvement in the activities of the family farm to eventual enrolment in the ragged army of hired labourers headed for the harvests of Britain with a father or older brother to show the way.

The Spailpín's humble familial peregrinations carried none of the glamour of the 'American Wake'. Above all, the 'townie' who found a niche at home, however dull or servile, could feel superior to the emigrant whose decision to emigrate, even temporarily, was regarded as an admission of failure, an inability to 'make the grade' in his own country.

The War

The war changed everything. In Britain conscription for the armed forces, coupled with mobilisation of the entire economy for 'Total War', meant a sudden widespread shortage of labour 'to carry out the strategic programme and maintain the essential life of the nation'. Because of its close proximity and traditional role as a labour pool Ireland, North and South, was the most promising source of extra manpower in Britain's hour of need. As John Healy observes in *Death of an Irish Town*:

> *In the mad floodtide of those years there was no distinction between the 'townie' and 'rager sham' from 'up the country'. McAlpine's Fusiliers took them all as they came, put shovels in their hands, and let them get on with it.*

Initially recruitment was in the hands of private agents representing individual employers and, inevitably, the construction industry took full advantage of its traditional links with Ireland to ensure that its needs were met. Irishmen employed by British firms were dispatched to Ireland to enlist men from their own communities, and they sent workers across in large numbers.

Because married men were less inclined to make the necessary commitment to this type of work the emphasis was on young single men, and these were available in town as well as country. A youth with few prospects, accustomed to handling perhaps no more than a pound a week, and living in the shadow of priests and parents, was not going to refuse the prospect of earning up to eight times that amount in an atmosphere of comradeship, adventure, and relative licence abroad.

A study done in County Clare, in the 1930s, reported that some farmers did not allow their sons to handle money earned from farm transactions, and even collected wages earned by their sons on public works.[6]

The outbreak of war brought a ban on all public works but also resulted in the initiation of a series of building programmes for the war effort which, in turn, led to a sharp drop in unemployment in the industry (from 354,028 in January 1940 to 78,334 by October of that year). Until the fall of France, brisk demand for Irish labour on civil-engineering projects, and for harvesters of grain, potatoes, and sugar beet, continued to attract migrants across the Irish Sea.

In June 1940, however, fear of invasion prompted the authorities to introduce controls on travel between Britain and Ireland, and travel permits were issued only for 'business of national importance'. At the same time, anyone returning to Ireland was required to remain there. Irish men already working in Britain, however, ran the risk of being called up for military service, and consequently a great many 'headed for Holyhead', and Ireland.

Very soon the invasion scare passed; even in 1940 tattie hokers were being granted six-month visas to travel to Scotland, and a more relaxed interpretation of the regulations was adopted generally. While British

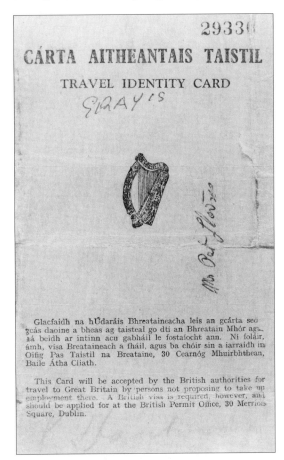

Above: Irish government travel ID, property of Mr Paddy Flavahan.

officials had initially intended to issue visas only to those seeking permanent employment in 'scarcity occupations' such as mechanical engineering, it soon became obvious that even unskilled manual labourers were in seriously short supply, and would remain so unless they could be found elsewhere.

Both governments experienced difficulties with the existing arrangements. The Irish government risked being accused of rendering economic assistance to a belligerent nation while, at the same time, its citizens in Britain were theoretically subject to military call-up. The British, for their part, had no effective control over the selection and recruitment of Irish labour, which was still in the hands of private agents acting independently for individual employers in Britain, without due regard for the national war effort.

In July 1941, therefore, officials of the British Ministry of Labour and the Agricultural Departments met in Dublin with representatives of the Irish government, with a view to negotiating a more efficient and unambiguous system of labour recruitment from Ireland.

The Irish insisted that any such agreement was conditional on Irish men working in Britain being allowed to retain the right to leave the country rather than face call-up and, if in Britain specifically for war work, being exempted completely from compulsory military service. Irish women were also specifically exempted from industrial conscription under the *Registration for Employment Order*.

In return, the British government was empowered to appoint its own labour agent in Dublin who would exercise control over, but not personally engage in, recruitment throughout the country. Actual recruitment would continue to be carried out by individual agents on behalf of private British employers. These agents, however, would be assigned to specific parts of the country by the British government's labour representative in Dublin. They would also be required henceforth to notify their requirements to the nearest Irish labour exchange, from where names of suitable applicants would, in due course, be forwarded to the agents for interview.

To answer charges of 'foreign agents' stripping the country districts of labour needed for agriculture and turf cutting, the Irish government amended the agreement the following October so that British agents, henceforth called 'employers' representatives', could interview only applicants considered by their local employment exchange as eligible for emigration. Such eligibility would also be conditional on suitable employment in Ireland not being immediately available. Only seasonal agricultural workers were exempt from this provision. A further condition of eligibility was a minimum age of twenty-two years.

The scheme was difficult to operate efficiently because of the number of bureaucratic procedures involved. The 'employers' representatives' had to be introduced to the Department of Industry and Commerce by the UK liaison officer, to wait for assignment to a specific area, and then to set up an office there or in Dublin. After meeting with the local employment exchange manager, the employers' representative would hire one or two local men capable of identifying suitable applicants and issuing them with slips introducing them to the labour exchange concerned. Bearers of these slips were asked to complete forms which were then forwarded to the UK liaison officer in Dublin. This individual forwarded such forms as he deemed suitable to the agents who, when they had sufficient to justify setting up interviews, arranged these through the relevant employment exchange. Those selected were medically examined and their names, endorsed by the exchange manager, were forwarded to the United Kingdom permit office.

That office then requisitioned birth certificates, travel documents and the signed consent of wives where appropriate. Only after this process was complete were the actual work permits applied for and obtained. Armed with these, the agent could finally proceed to forward the recruits to their prospective employers. This entailed reserving and labelling railway carriages, appointing gangers to assemble the travellers and take charge of their permits, tickets, and cards, booking hostel accommodation in Dublin where necessary, checking the recruits at their port of embarkation, issuing them with coloured identification badges, and notifying employers of their impending arrival in Britain. Full particulars of each recruit were, of course, forwarded to the UK liaison officer in Dublin.

Despite the assignment of Ministry of Labour welfare officers to Holyhead Port and the important (and disconcertingly busy) railway junction at Crewe, chaos was commonplace. Irishmen would get on the wrong trains and off at the wrong stations in the blackout; parties would fail to arrive or would consist of greater or lesser numbers than was expected.

The establishment of transit hostels in the Midlands, Lancashire, and London helped alleviate some of the stress involved. In addition, a policy of allocating groups of workers to employers able to facilitate them in camps or hostels complete with Irish chaplains enabled the Irish to retain a sense of community and cultural cohesion.

In the early stages, however, the system was both cumbersome and inefficient in that it took too long to bring labour to where it was needed and resulted in a lot of wastage when volunteers dropped out along the way.

Initial demand was for labour in land drainage, civil engineering, and heavy engineering. Construction work was eagerly sought after, and the bigger firms had a good recruitment network already in place. Agents were, however, sometimes unscrupulous in offering unrealistic rates, or otherwise misleading workers in order to meet labour targets for which some were paid on a *per capita* basis. In February 1942, therefore, the Federation of Civil Engineering Contractors introduced a system whereby labour was recruited to a common pool from which the needs of individual firms were met.

For the individual construction worker the new employment prospects were something of a mixed blessing. Some men recall having to grease agents' palms to secure employment or use influence to persuade labour exchange managers to enrol their names for consideration. Many of the rural Irish felt demeaned by, and resented, the unaccustomed regimentation of coloured badges and nameless numbers, designed to facilitate identification by group and destination.

During the summer of 1939, on the Militia Camp Programme, employers were offering the prospect of subsistence allowances, high hourly rates, and plenty of overtime work. Guarantees of 80- to 100-hour weeks were given by some of them. As much as 42 hours' overtime was put in by the 950 men employed at Taunton. The lowest amount of hours' overtime recorded on the scheme was offered to the 1,500 men employed at a camp near Ripon in Yorkshire, but even here each got an average of 12 hours' overtime per 66-hour week.

Frank Taylor of Taylor Woodrow, the Liverpool bricklayer who, like Robert McAlpine, had built up a major construction company while still in his twenties, urgently needed men for a large Ministry of Works job in 1942 and looked to Ireland to obtain them. Taylor sent an Irish agent named Dwyer to County Mayo and, within two months, Dwyer had recruited a thousand men plus a priest and brought them into Liverpool. Taylor recalled:

> *The rate for the job was thought to be 3s. 7d. per hour, and this was what other construction companies were offering. Taylor Woodrow however recruited on the basis of 3s. 5d. per hour to make sure. When the other companies' men got to England and found that the official rate was 3s. 6d. they were angry and discontented. Taylor Woodrow were able to raise the men's rate to 3s. 6d. when they arrived — this made all the difference to their morale and they worked happily. They had good camps and good food, and somehow they got a team spirit that enabled them to work ten hours a day and overtime too.*[7]

De-Lousing

One procedure that the Irish resented was the de-lousing 'medical' instituted in Dublin in 1942, with the consent of the Irish government. This was designed to ensure that Irish emigrants were not carriers of infection, and to reassure not only employers but, perhaps more importantly, owners of accommodation in Britain. Considerable resistance to Irish tenants, encountered especially in the iron-ore mining and quarrying districts, had alarmed officials who ascribed it to the belief that the Irish were lacking in personal hygiene.

In fact, traditional anti-Irish racism, exacerbated by the recent IRA bombing campaign of the 1930s, was at least equally to blame.

We were met at the station in Dublin and taken to the Globe Hotel, where, after a meal, we were rounded up and taken to a swimming bath for a medical! The medical consisted of a close inspection of the hairy parts of the body and the seams of the shirts! I was told that anyone who failed to pass this examination were taken away to be de-loused and scrubbed! The irony of this humiliation was that when most of these workers got to England they had to live, for the most part, in bug and mice infested lodging houses that didn't have a bathroom! I doubt if one in thirty working class homes in Britain at that time had a bathroom and often, the only toilet facilities was a fly-blown lavatory in the back yard!

After the 'Medical', anger was expressed among the twenty or so migrants, not only against the perfidious English but to a greater degree against the Irish Government who allowed such debasement to be practised against its own citizens![8]

The Globe Hotel was located in Talbot Street, Dublin, and three years after Joe Duffy's de-lousing experience there, Peadar Quinn, from Dingle, County Kerry, underwent a medical which hadn't changed appreciably.

It was my first time on a train, Tralee to Dublin, head out the window most of the way, marvelling at the vastness of Ireland. Globe Hotel, Talbot Street, was the destination. Medical, Eye testing etc.[9]

Several correspondents recruited for construction work in England in the decade between 1942 and 1952 reported staying overnight at the Globe Hotel in Dublin.

On February 17 1948 I left my native Kill, Co. Waterford. I travelled on to the Globe Hotel in Dublin and met up with about twenty other chaps from all over Ireland. We had a medical by a doctor who was well into his second bottle of whiskey, and stayed the night.[10]

Women were, of course, also subjected to the same procedures, usually in a different hotel called the 'Fitzwilliam'. They often found the medical examination acutely embarrassing:

Then it came out over the loudspeaker that we were all going to have a medical, so in this huge hall they put up screens the whole way round, and you went behind one screen and got stark naked. And they were only screens and you could see everything behind them. You went in and they made you raise up your arms, they looked under both arms and they looked in your hair and they looked in your private parts, and if anybody had vermin they were sent to the baths.

When we got to Dublin, we were met there and taken to this hotel. I'll never forget that experience, it was terrible. The way they looked at you, we had to strip, take all our clothes off and they looked at every bit of us, at our hair and everything, before they gave us a cup of tea even ... I tell you, if I'd known what would happen, I wouldn't have ventured coming over here, I'd have stayed at home.[11]

Charlie Duffy, a house painter from Ballaghadereen, County Mayo, described his arrival as a volunteer with the Ministry of Labour in 1943:

You went where the Ministry sent you; they might tell you, 'Work in Wimbledon this week', and send you to the top of Scotland next week, if it suited them. I worked ten days for a firm in London when I first came — just enough to settle in. Pack your bag, ten more men with you, we were sent off to the country somewhere, right in the middle of some woods. We didn't know what was goin' on.... There was no paintin' for the likes of me because there was a few old Englishmen doin' it. They were constructin' places like small gasometers: thick walls, lead-lined, roofed with concrete, domed roofs. We never knew what it was....

Suddenly the Yanks walked in and took it over, and ordered us out.... It was a Poison Gas Plant — they were gettin' ready to use it if Hitler used it [gas]. *Everything came in at night, on a little spur line, right to where we were, but always at night. Cigarettes, food, everything....*[12]

Between 1940 and 1944 a total of 160,000 Irish workers, of both sexes, took up employment in Britain. Women numbered between 30 and 40 per cent of the total. Many men originally authorised for agricultural work transferred subsequently to construction and civil engineering, and a significant proportion were employed in mechanical engineering.

The Ministry of Supply, responsible for the production of war materials, rivalled the Ministry of Labour in its efforts to recruit in Ireland and, unlike the Ministry of Works which was responsible for the construction industry, took both men and women. The Government agents it sent to Ireland had semi-fictitious status as the representatives of private industry.

The Labour Officer of Drop Forgings Sub-Control and a member of the Labour Supply Division, for example, recruited for tank-track link foundries, drop forgings, and eventually for the iron and steel industry generally, under the guise of agents for an entity known as 'British Foundries'. Agents of an equally vague corporate entity known as 'British Products'

Above: Access to London Underground wartime air-raid shelter.

recruited for ball bearing, tank production, non-ferrous metals and timber. They were all, in fact, British civil servants employed by the Labour Supply Division. The Ministry of Works, however, got the lion's share of male recruits between 1942 and 1944. The total value of construction work done between 1940 and 1945 was £2,250 million, and the number of operatives employed on the British government's wartime building programme peaked at 570,000 in October 1941.

'Shadow Factory'

Wartime construction programmes were often massive undertakings. Typical of the non-military construction projects on which Irish wartime recruits worked was the underground factory built in a disused quarry at Corsham in Wiltshire for the Bristol Aeroplane Company. This was an Alfred McAlpine project. Valued at seven million pounds, it was the firm's biggest contract to date.

A ninety-acre site had to be excavated without removing a twenty-seven-metre-thick layer of hard limestone. Below this limestone was a stratum of Bathstone nine metres thick which resembled a gorgonzola cheese with its labyrinth of mine shafts. It was intended to remove this stratum and build an underground factory, equipped with workspace for building aircraft engines, dormitories, canteens, reading and dancing rooms, a cinema, a theatre, a hospital and two crèches — in effect, a small town.

McAlpine appointed an office manager in Dublin to recruit for all the firm's UK work, and many of the 10,000 men employed at Corsham were taken on here but recruited mainly from County Mayo by local men employed by the company. Eight hutted camps were built to accommodate the workforce; these were equipped with canteens, a cinema and several bars.

The first phase of the project was completed within the stipulated three-month deadline by dint of working the 'twelve by seven' shift system — twelve hours a day, seven days a week. The factory personnel moved into their underground accommodation and recreation facilities, while the construction workers continued to live in the camps above ground for a further two years.

Another former site agent described an ordnance (munitions) factory, 'ROF 16', on which he worked in the early 1940s for Nuttall's. He said it was six miles square, and employed 3,000 men, ninety dumpers, and thirty-five excavators.

In 1942 eight vast underground air-raid shelters, known as 'Deep Shelters', were constructed in London below existing Tube Stations — four north and four south of the Thames, each capable of accommodating 8,000 people.

Besides factories, housing, airfields and military camps the Ministry of Works also organised the construction of the following facilities: storage depots for ordnance; standard stores for general purposes; storage depots for special articles and materials; cold storage buildings; grain silos; inland sorting depots.[13]

Almost 450 airfields were built in Britain during the Second World War. According to Ronald Cox, most of the concrete paving for these was laid by hand. In an address to the Institute of Highway Engineers in 1982 Mr Cox declared:

> *During this period one hundred and seventy-five million square yards of concrete and tarmacadam paving was laid in runways, taxi tracks and standings. Converted into dual three lane highways, it would be equal to over 4,000 miles.*[14]

There was one notable wartime project from which the Irish were excluded for security reasons. This was the construction of the two Mulberry Harbours, built by the Ministry of Defence for the D-Day landings. Each of these artificial prefabricated harbours was larger than Dover Harbour and was composed of breakwaters, floating piers, and floating roads from piers to land. They were essential to the feasibility of landing in Normandy rather than in the more accessible but heavily defended Calais region.

With D-Day imminent, travel between Britain and Ireland was once again prohibited, and the following September new centralised recruiting procedures came into effect. Enrolment and distribution of Irish workers was henceforth the sole prerogative of the Ministry of Labour. The staff in Dublin recruited volunteers and allocated them according to priorities worked out in advance between Ministry of Labour regional offices and interested government departments, with due regard to the recruits' employment preferences and experience. The Ministry of Labour also paid all recruitment and travel expenses and guaranteed safe arrival and accommodation.

Bomb Damage

Although recruitment for civil engineering tailed off in 1944, the German V1 and V2 rocket bombardment of London in 1945 gave fresh impetus to construction (if the drive to repair the extensive bomb damage may be called 'construction'). The importance of the Irish in this campaign is indicated by the fact that, of the 900 building-repair men billeted in the Kensington Palace Hotel in 1945–6, 600 were Irish.

Of course, as Sir Malcolm McAlpine has pointed out, the Irish navvies who were employed by British construction companies prior to the outbreak of war were also invaluable at this time. They not only formed a nucleus of experienced supervisory staff on site, but also functioned most efficiently as recruiting agents during and after the conflict itself.

Value of Irish Labour

The indispensability of Irish labour to Britain's war effort has been acknowledged officially. Referring specifically to the Ministry of Supply's munitions labour force, the Official History account records that,

Irish labour was valuable ... out of all proportion to its numbers. This was partly because Eire was a source of heavy male labour when British supplies had almost run dry; and secondly because Irish labour ... was mobile and was not subject to the preference rulings under which British labour was allocated. Recruitment in Ireland gave the Ministry of Supply a margin of labour to use at its own discretion for urgent and difficult demands ... the Ministry of Aircraft Production during 1942–44 [also] *found its Irish labour a very useful supplement to meet urgent and difficult demands.*[15]

An enlightening perspective on the value to Britain of Irish wartime labour appeared in *The Times* in June 1946. Captain Henry Harrison, commenting on the Lord Chancellor's public acknowledgement of a 'debt of honour' owed to Irish military volunteers, demanded equal recognition for the Irish civilian war workers for their contribution, not to the war effort, but to the Exchequer.

> *He appears totally to ignore the fact that, since 1940–41, Irish volunteer labour has been admitted to this country on a system of short-term police permits. Thus, for the last five years, these voluntary war workers have been compulsorily paying for insurance from which they would receive no benefit. And the Exchequer has been receiving the workers' and employers' contributions without incurring liability to pay anything — a pure gain of over £2 millions per 100,000 insured Eire volunteer workers.*[16]

Of course, the really substantial gain was to the Irish economy; according to the *Irish Democrat*, in response to a Dáil question in May 1945, the Finance Minister gave the following figures for postal remittances (postal orders and telegraphed money orders):

Year	UK	Foreign Countries (mainly US)	Total
1939	£1,000,267	£588,382	£1,588,877
1940	£1,150,497	£439,380	£1,589,877
1941	£2,200,873	£329,127	£2,530,000
1942	£4,689,324	£301,200	£4,990,524
1943	£6,737,778	£358,423	£7,096,201
1944	£6,924,761	£420,032	£7,344,793
Total	£22,722,510	£2,116,544	£25,100,278

The figure for the United Kingdom does not, of course, take account of sums remitted by cash or cheque, brought home on holiday, or subsequently repatriated in peacetime. Nor does it include the official figures for 1945, the last year of the war. This total, in today's values, amounts to approximately £588,558,116.17.

Not all of this money was earned in the construction industry. Female earnings aside, as the war progressed and labour shortages extended beyond the agricultural and civil-engineering industries, British employers in other sectors and their responsible government ministries reluctantly employed the Irish where these might not previously have even been considered. Nevertheless the preferential distribution system established by the Ministry of Labour in 1942 allocated 50 per cent of all male recruits to the construction industry and, although there were subsequent adjustments downwards in 1944–45, a substantial proportion of Irish males continued to work in construction. This included many who succeeded in transferring from agricultural work after they had been in the country for some time. Wage rates were not hugely disparate but the nature of construction work allowed for substantial overtime earnings, which swelled pay packets.

Certainly John Healy was in no doubt that those Irish employed 'on the buildings' had the greatest financial and social impact on their local communities:

> *In those rural days of 1941, the parting tears and the shame of the going evaporated with the first wired money order and when the wired money orders of £20 and £30 came every two weeks from a pair of young sons you could hold your head higher.*[18]

Healy described the effect of money on both the young emigrants and their social 'betters' despite the latter's oft-repeated put-downs which centred around their being 'unable to amount to anything, from the people they came from':

> *Their money and their earning power were as great, if not greater, than the social hierarchy of the town. They made more than the schoolteachers who could not afford to buy a round of drinks for the house. They had twice the salary in the week of the sergeant above in the barracks. They had maybe more money below in the bank than the bank manager himself had in personal savings for the last ten years.*[19]

The clergy were not so happy with the situation. With some satisfaction, the *Irish Democrat*, organ of the socialist Connolly Association in Britain, quoted speeches by more than one Irish Catholic bishop deploring the tide of emigration to 'heathen England'.

'Employment — even at a quarter of the wages — which could enable a man to live at home with his wife and children, would be much better than that which involved the breaking up of the home', said the Most Reverend Dr Browne, Bishop of Galway, at the annual meeting of the Galway branch of the NSPCC.

Three months later the same paper quoted a more pragmatic commentary on the subject by another senior Irish cleric:

'Emigration on a large scale was a slow bleeding to death of the nation', said the Most Reverend Dr Dignam, Bishop of Clonfert, in his Lenten Pastoral.

'Economic reasons alone compelled young men and women to leave and seek a livelihood abroad, which they might not have at home. And they left unwillingly, in tears. No one could reasonably expect them to remain from a sentimental love of Ireland. If they were given what they got in other countries — constant work, a high standard of wages, good social services, and the amenities of modern life — they would remain'.[20]

There was, however, little likelihood of any such transformation of their prospects at home in the near future, and more and more young people voted with their feet for the blandishments of British life.

The Beet 'Campaigns'

From July of 1946 modifications to the regulations, culminating in the rescinding in December 1947 of the *Passenger Traffic Order* of 1842, allowed intending emigrants to Britain much greater leeway. British employers, particularly in the construction industry,

recommenced direct recruitment in Ireland, but the Ministry of Labour continued to service the labour needs of specific sectors of the economy via its Irish agents. In 1947, for example, this entailed hiring 1,400 men for the sugar beet 'campaign'. Similar numbers were recruited annually for the British sugar refineries. This continued well into the 1950s and many young rural males got their 'start' in England through this successor to the traditional grain harvesting market for Irish seasonal agricultural labour. Peadar Quinn, from Dingle, County Kerry, was one such 'campaigner':

I first left Dingle in September of 1948 at the tender age of twenty years. My first trip was at the 'Beet' Scheme. We were recruited through the local Labour Exchange, summer of '48, to work in Sugar Factories for the British Sugar Corporation. I was to go to Ipswich in Suffolk.

An Identity Card had to be got (a form of passport) with photo, and stamped at the local Garda Station.

At last the big day arrived — my first big break from home; I think the excitement of going, and the chance of making a few pound which we never had the opportunity of here, helped out in the break from home.

The boat — the 'CAMBRIA' — I think, was also a first experience. Factory work was a challenge. Such machinery was only in the imagination before this.

The first bit of lonesomeness struck a week later. It was awful, but it had to be got over.... The campaign lasted three months. I went back the next year for another, then in 1950 went to London to construction work. I travelled around England — Yorkshire, Derbyshire, Durham, Lancashire, etc. — mostly at building, also platelaying.[21]

Peadar's account of progressing from farming-related employment into the construction industry is interesting in that it reflects a pattern which was becoming established amongst a minority of harvesters since the 1920s, but which rapidly gained momentum during and after the war. Also of interest is his destination as a navvy, namely London.

Above: Paddy Flavahan's British ID.

Destination South-East

Demographers of the Diaspora in Britain have commented on the marked shift from Scotland and the North-West of England towards London and the South-East, as the favoured destination of new Irish immigrants since the war.

In fact, the preponderance of Irish in the North-West, which had characterised the first two decades of the century, was diminishing by 1931. By the time the 1951 census figures became available, the ascendancy of London had become decisive; it was the destination of 34 per cent of males and 42 per cent of females. Scotland, once a major catchment area, had witnessed a steady decline over the half century from an Irish minority numbering 4.6 per cent to one numbering merely 1.7 per cent.

Oddly, however, whereas the Irish accounted for only 5.5 per cent of the construction industry labour force in England and Wales in 1951, in Scotland they totalled 25 per cent. Of course, it is important to qualify such figures with the caveat that they do not include those of Irish descent, consisting solely of the Irish-born.[22]

The shift of Irish labour from the North-West to the South-East, however, ought not to have been so surprising. Clearly the pre-war industry had found the bulk of its building contracts in that region, and the move by M.J. Gleeson Ltd from Sheffield to Surrey, in the 1930s, was a rational response to trends in the marketplace. Other major players in the industry made similar moves before the war. John Laing's headquarters had, in fact, been moved from Carlisle to London in the mid-1920s. By the mid-1930s this firm already used no less than fifteen large excavators, employed 3,000 men, and was building 1,000 houses per year.

Hydro Dams

One factor which helps to explain the disproportionately high percentage of Irish in the Scottish construction industry is the major programme of hydro-electrification begun in Scotland soon after the war and continuing right into the late 1970s. This was predicated on the existence of ideal conditions for the construction of reservoirs, dams, and power stations in the Scottish Highlands. Many schemes were initiated by the North of Scotland Hydro Electricity Board which, despite a political policy of local recruitment, relied largely on Irish labour for the hard work entailed in dam building and hard-rock tunnelling.

The influx of Irish labour had diminished only very slowly since the turn of the century because Scottish farmers continued to rely on Irish spailpíns and tattie hokers to harvest their crops. Many went on to work in construction and civil engineering on a seasonal basis, returning to Ireland for part of each year, and so were not returned in official surveys as Scottish residents.

A nucleus of Irish labourers had acquired experience of hard-rock tunnelling on the pre-war Lochaber and Galloway Schemes. Many of these tunnellers came from Donegal — from Aranmore Island, the Inishowen Peninsula, and elsewhere. They belonged to families whose menfolk had traditionally migrated to Scotland as unskilled seasonal labourers, on farms and public work, each generation maintaining its hold on Irish soil by accepting the necessity for seasonal migration and hard physical labour in the service of another country.

When the postwar hydro schemes were mooted it was natural for these same families to throw up volunteers who, if they lacked direct experience of tunnelling, had at least worked with those who had — often their own fathers or uncles. Donegal families associated with hard-rock tunnelling include such names as Campbell, Bonner, O'Donnell, McCole, Docherty and Sweeney.

I was born in Burtonport in Donegal in 1942. My father was a migratory worker; he started on the tattie hoking and progressed into construction, and then mining — tunnelling, in Perthshire in the forties and fifties. I left school at fourteen and worked for local builders; I had been offered a place by the headmaster of the secondary school in Burtonport but my father thought it best for me to be workin'; he was away from June to December and I was the eldest of five. There was no shortage of money.... A man could save £20 a week, which was a lot of money, but now I know they were workin' six and seven twelve-hour shifts; it was just all work and no play. They would go over in June, go up to Perthshire or wherever the tunnelling job was, and they wouldn't see a town from then until Christmas.

I was nineteen when I went back with my cousin George in 1962, the 31st of July. The tunnel holidays coincided with the Glasgow holidays, so all the Donegal folk would be home. At that time you could get from Burtonport to Glasgow for a fiver, between boat and hackney fare. A guy called Docherty would take four or five....

When I arrived I got a job on a dam; I was too young to go underground, and had no experience anyway. There were two twelve-hour shifts — from eight to eight, with two ten-minute and one half-hour break. The work was basically — the dam was a hundred feet high, half a mile long, and they would pour concrete in fifty-foot sections, and raise it maybe one lift a day, in staggered lifts. You'd start with cleaning off the solid rock to make it ready for concreting, then you'd blow off the concrete bays with water and compressed air, getting that ready, working from section to section.... Other guys would come along and pour in the concrete into the encased shuttering. The easiest job I had was being a 'banksman' for the Digger-man or Crane-man, wave or signal with your hands.... The worst job was 'scabbling' — perforating the smooth concrete walls, making it rough for more concrete to adhere to; you had a small pneumatic machine with a pointed edger. Another job was vibrating the concrete mixer; if you were up fifty feet, all you had holding this massive amount of concrete was a few bolts into the solid concrete — if that gave away, you were gone. It did happen ... the guys put in a bolt with a few bars welded onto the end of it, a nut put into the wet concrete, just screw in a long bolt, and that was holding the shutters in place, and behind the shutters was tons and tons of concrete. Leave it for two or three days, then move up another 'lift'.

One day, to save a half-mile walk, myself and another guy came down off a hundred-foot lift on the hook of the crane, me standing on the other guy's foot.... Those crane drivers were always livin' on their nerves; chain-smokin', and sickly-like; climbing up a hundred and fifty feet on these ladders; lifting concrete out of lorries in bins which had to guided into these small compartments where they were pouring the concrete. Sometimes these things came down on the guys; good eyesight and a steady nerve were vital ... they were always Scotsmen — Irishmen never got onto those jobs. They were on good money — maybe £20 a week top line....[23]

Scottish hydro dam under construction, illustrating 'lifts'.

Even before the First World War the Kinlochleven and Ben Nevis hydropower generating systems had conclusively demonstrated the unique potential of the Scottish Highlands for electricity generation. Oddly, however, attempts to extend the concept throughout the Highlands met with parliamentary indifference for a further quarter of a century. Whereas the Galloway Power Scheme was passed through Parliament without difficulty in 1929, the West Highland Bill had been defeated a year previously, a similar Bill for an adjoining scheme having met the same fate in 1927. The Caledonian Power Scheme, which covered the same area as these, was, in its turn, rejected by Parliament in 1936, 1937, and 1938.

When yet another scheme, this time drawn up by the Grampian Electricity Supply Company and approved by a Parliamentary Commission, was rejected by Parliament in 1941, the then Secretary of State for Scotland, Mr Thomas Johnston, established the Cooper Committee 'to consider the practicability and desirability of future development of water power in the North for the generation of electricity'.

The Cooper Committee's main recommendations appeared as the *Hydro-Electric Development (Scotland) Act* of 1943. That Act in turn facilitated the establishment of the North of Scotland Electricity Board, which was empowered to:

Initiate and undertake all future large-scale hydro-electric development in the Highlands and Islands; distribute electricity to consumers outside the area of other authorised electricity suppliers; provide electricity in bulk to these suppliers and larger power users; sell electricity, after the above priorities had been met, to the National Grid; and collaborate in measures for the economic development and social improvement of the North of Scotland district.[24]

The Board's area of operations covered over 20,000 square miles. It was confirmed in its autonomy by the *Electricity Act* of 1947, which nationalised the electricity industry, increasing the Board's powers and extending its territory to cover the whole country north of a line from the River Clyde to the River Tay.

By January 1948 twenty-nine large and small waterpower schemes were in preparation, and work had begun on projects at Lochs Sloy, Tummel-Garry, Cowal, Affric, Glen Shira, Morar, Lochalsh, Gairloch, and Storr. Contracts had been placed worth £13,396,545. Eighty-six of these contracts had been awarded to Scottish contractors. Contractors included Mitchell Construction (incorporating the famous tunnelling firm of Kinnear Moodie), A.M. Carmichael, Tyssen, Duncan Logan, Reed & Mallik, and Nuttall's.

Most of the non-technical labour was either Irish or Polish — many Polish 'Displaced Persons' were ex-coal-miners and had valuable hard-rock tunnelling experience.

Apparently relations between Irish and Poles weren't always either close or cordial. As late as the 1970s there was still a saying current amongst the Poles

in Britain: 'The Pole keeps his money and throws away his pay packet; the Irishman throws away his money but keeps his pay packet' (to show off to his mates the big bottom-line figure).

Over the next twenty years other Scottish hydro schemes associated with Irish labour included Shin, Dalcroy, Invermoriston, Strathfarrar, Foyers, and Loch Awe. Mitchell's was one of the most prominent construction companies in this field. Its projects in Scotland included the Strathfarrar Scheme, Locheil, the Awa Barrage, Glen Moriston, the Nant Scheme, Culligran, Deanie, Crannachroc and the Breadalbane Scheme (for which St Fillan's Underground Power Station was built, which included nineteen miles of tunnel, in the construction of which a world tunnelling record of 557 feet in one week was set by a Donegal team). Mitchell's also built Scotland's first nuclear power station, at Chapelcross.

Dam building continued in Scotland into the 1980s. Projects included Backwater Dam (Balfour Beatty,

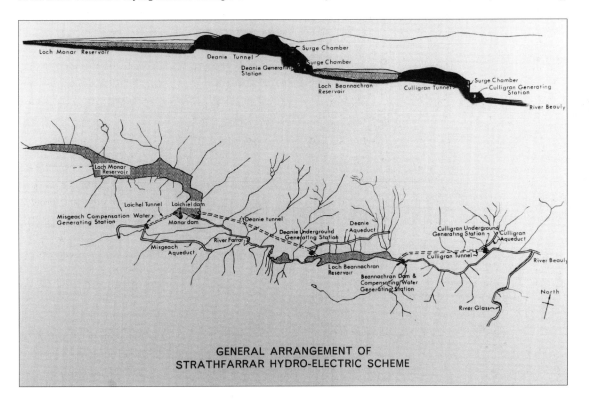

GENERAL ARRANGEMENT OF
STRATHFARRAR HYDRO-ELECTRIC SCHEME

1964–69); Bradan Dam (M.J. Gleeson, 1970–73); Castlehill (M.J. Gleeson, 1975–78); Clunas (Tarmac, 1969–71); Craignafeich (R.H. Cuthbertson & Partners, 1970–72), and Cruachan (J. Williamson & Partners, 1962–65).

The development of North Sea oil in turn generated a massive civil-engineering programme of terminals, refineries, and pipelines along the east coast, which employed thousands of Irish operatives and maintained right up to the 1990s the great traditions of the Irish navvy on Scottish soil.

Progress was rapid over this forty-year period and conditions on site improved beyond all recognition. Initially firms were on a learning curve; they had little or no direct experience of hard-rock tunnelling and dam building on such a scale and in such a remote and inhospitable environment. All concerned — the local authority, the engineers, even the operatives — had to learn as they went along. The situation resembled that which had prevailed in England when the inland navigation system had been laid out two centuries previously (see Chapter One).

Hard-Rock Tunnellers

The authorities had a well-filled war chest, but little understanding of cost control relative to such novel projects. The consulting and site engineers in turn had little practical experience of the work; and, in the euphoric pioneering spirit of the times, everyone concerned felt free to use money and materials as if there were no tomorrow.

If you wanted to put the muck a good bit back the tunnel, you put in the centre holes flat; if you want to leave it at the face, you put them in at an incline, and the muck just sits there; you could hardly get up the top, it would just sit there at the face.

But different shift bosses had different practices; if you drill the holes in the muck you keep the tunnel level — there wouldn't be any bites in the roof; if you didn't there'd be gouges out of it.... As far as I could see the North of Scotland Hydro Board didn't give two hoots whether there were gouges or not because

Scottish hydro-dam world tunnelling record, October 1955. Donegal man Gerry Rogers kept the drill bits sharpened for the record attempt.

Above: Access tunnel leading to Ceannocroc Underground Power Station, Scotland — 'If that's the access route, how big must the power station be?' Tour buses now travel this route daily.

the roof didn't matter; except there were more broken rocks comin' out of it — the guys had to take out more muck....

Like cuttin' butter, you can cut a tunnel to the exact size, within two inches of the specifications, so why take out an extra foot if you can do without it? But this was goin' on all the time — they were takin' out far too much....

There was a practice up in the North of Scotland, where they would drill the top holes as the guy was muckin', for the next round, because you didn't want to be goin' up a stagin'. So you would drill the top four holes off the muck, and then, when you wanted to do the big drillin', they were already done ...

But sometime guys didn't bother — they just drilled from the ground the next time but then you were bringin' down far more muck than you really wanted because when you bore from down here, the bloody thing is goin' to go up in the air, because you can't keep the machine flat if you had it down too low.

But drillin' from the top of the muck was a dangerous job because you might have an old *detonator from the previous blast that was still in the rock and you may or may not see it, because explosives can freeze like solid rock if it doesn't go off.... They didn't care how much explosives was used....*

A typical crew for a twelve-hour shift included:

Tunnel Boss	1
Shift Boss	1
Machine Men	8/9
Eimco Driver	1
Loco Drivers	3
Handyman	1
Drill Doctor	1
Powder Monkey	1

The production sequence was as follows: Drill, charge, withdraw from the face, fire, wait for the 'reek' to clear, muck out. Often, however, men were back at the face before the 'reek' of the explosives had cleared, because:

Cutting with pneumatic axe. Note lack of ear mufflers or other noise protection.

Some ignorant shift boss might say, 'We'll go back in now, lads' — and the smoke wouldn't have cleared, you'd be chokin' and splutterin'; any guy with a good chest usually had to give up after a while.... The 'reek' in most tunnels was terrible; Men were back at the face before the roof was properly scaled.

Some diesel locos, built in the 1930s, were still in use twenty years later. Electric locos were a gift — no fumes and no noise.

Progress in the larger drives of over twenty feet in twelve hours was normal. Progress was largely the result of how well the rounds were 'pulling' (breaking out rock at the face)....

They'll pull as well as they're drilled; if you drill holes off line, they're not going to break. If you drill a hole eight foot, you want it to pull eight foot; but if one hole's goin' that way, another hole's goin' that way, it'll break short, maybe five foot/six foot.

It all depends on how the holes round the centre were; if they were dead on, it'll break nicely into it; it may not matter about the outside holes because when the opening's made, it'll come in anyway. That's how the boys read it that time; the rounds pulled as well as they were drilled; if they weren't drilled well, they wouldn't pull anyway. They were blamin' the rock, but if the rock gets harder, you just put in a few more rounds, if it's softer you can do with less.... The norm was three eight-foot cycles per twelve hours; if you done it in eight hours, nine hours, the rest was relaxation time. But you couldn't go out to the surface and sit there for three hours, like — that wouldn't go down too well. The worst scenario was if there was a Polish shift and an Irish shift — if they didn't get on — they'd start racin' one another, and that was bad for themselves in the long run. They could mess it up. If they used their common sense, it went along nicely, don't get too greedy. Do a certain amount every shift, everybody was happy....

Accommodation was in camps; usually sixteen to a unit (often, in the early postwar period, ex-Army timber huts). A Shift Boss or Tunnel Boss usually got a prime, end spot — sometimes partitioned off. The typical Service-issue pot-bellied stove was gradually replaced, in the 1960s, by electric or oil-fired heating. Food was normally prepared by a catering company — 'poor quality & the minimum necessary'. A well-stocked 'company shop' was provided, but no 'wet canteen' such as would have been normal on major sites in the 1970s. Oil skins and wellington boots were all the clothing provided.

You got subsistence, paid by the Hydro Board; you got coupons every week; say, blue for lunch, pink for breakfast, green for dinner ... you handed this in and got whatever ... soup out of the big pot, porridge out of the big pot, on your plate, as much as you wanted ... I remember, even at that age, awful stomach problems, especially after being on the night shift. The food wasn't good — stodgy, and made on a massive scale, dished up.... The dining-room/canteen would hold maybe a hundred men. There were seventy or eighty on each shift....

We were on the dam; the other guys were away on the tunnel sections — they were the elite. We were only Mickey-Mouse.... About sixty per cent were Irish; a lot men from Peterhead, Banff, all up along the east coast; they called themselves 'The Seagulls'

— very hard to understand; quite a few from the Western Isles as well ... didn't seem to have many locals....

One would get to church every Sunday; the company would put on a bus to take you to church. We'd be in the local pubs as well.... There was quite a bit of gambling — poker and the 'Crown & Anchor Board'. Young lads would be warned by relatives to stay away from that.... It was illegal — shady characters would take the easiest jobs possible on the site, save their energies for the weekend, gambling.... Some guys would lose their week's wages. 'The Gambler Docherty' was a famous card-sharp who was said to have been driven out eventually.... Paid in cash in an envelope.... Keep it on you at all times, even underground.... Most Irish people operated through the post office — they never went to Scottish banks as far as I could see. I always sent it by registered post. The post office came to the site for the purpose ... every Friday evening on some sites, such as Dalmally.

There was a TV room, and the papers every morning, in the sixties.... The pubs were dangerous places to go on the weekends; quiet places with names such as 'The Tight Line', overrun by wild Irishmen and east coast Scots, all boasting about their tunnelling feats....

I never remember walkin' around the place; you were just confined to the bloody camp; it was just a wilderness of moorland and bog, I never seen any guys go for walks over the hills or anything, the terrain was too rough.... So it was down to the little village, or take the Saturday bus to Oban, twenty miles away ... beautiful little town, didn't appreciate the Irish guys drunk on a Saturday night!

Any guy workin' in the smoky conditions of the tunnel for twelve hours a day for more than a year, wouldn't look in physically great shape. You'd get very drawn and white.... You'd see them coming a mile away; if a guy came home from Scotland to Ireland, you'd know without askin' him, that he was workin' on the tunnels, underground in diesel smoke conditions. Machines that could lift fifteen to twenty ton of muck; big scoops ... pouring out diesel. That didn't operate on that Mitchell scheme, but it operated on the Nuttall scheme further down.... A combination of dust and diesel fumes isn't for the weak-hearted; a lot of guys weren't able to tolerate it.... I've heard of Donegal guys in the fifties having to come home, with chest problems. High noise levels — five or six or more machines operating in a small area. You'd communicate by sign language.... I remember a night on the Awe Barrage in 1964, listening to the Sonny Liston–Mike Tyson fight on a little transistor, six miles underground....[25]

By the 1960s, Britain's economy was booming, and the push to provide conventional and nuclear energy throughout the United Kingdom was in full swing. Enormous projects — oil terminals, refineries, and power stations, were built throughout England and Wales, as well as Scotland. The men who pioneered the Scottish projects could now command big money, provided they were prepared to follow the work and endure the often-spartan conditions. The legend of the 'Tunnel Tigers' began to grow.

Gradually a new breed of 'Long-Distance Men' emerged, to succeed the old-time tramp navvies, as the eccentric élite of the construction industry. But behind them, by the late 1950s and early 1960s, marched a huge army of Irish building labourers, 'McAlpine's Fusiliers' — the shock-troops of the drive to rebuild Britain.

This page: Mitchell
Construction Company
camp, Scotland, 1960s.

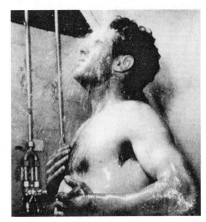

7 McAlpine's Men

*Come all you true brave Irishmen
And listen to my song
Don't ever work for Wimpey,
McAlpine or John Laing
For they'll put you behind the mixer,
You'll be doggin' in the sand
And you'll rue the day, you sailed away
From Mary Horan's Land.*

The slow haemorrhage of emigration which had characterised the two decades preceding the Second World War reflected the continuing failure of the Free State either to establish domestic industries, capable of creating dynamic urban centres, or to transform the archaic economy of the poorer agricultural regions.

Country people could feel inhibited about seeking employment in the towns, even where work was available. Julia Griffin, the daughter of an estate herdsman with nine children, was born near Athlone in 1935.

> *I went to school until I was thirteen when my sister got married. Then there was no one to help my mother, and we still had five boys at home ... so I never went back to school. There was a factory in the town, but my mother wouldn't hear of us looking for a job, although we had nothing, and we were terribly poor, still you just didn't work in a factory if you were country people like we were.*[1]

On a macroeconomic level, given that the alternative to inheritance must of necessity be emigration, the population could not hope to attain the critical mass essential to viable large-scale manufacturing. Without such a prospect there was little hope of generating jobs and therefore of creating significant demand for goods, services, and professional activities. At the same time a shrinking population meant a diminishing tax base and reducing State investment in infrastructure. So dire was the demographic picture that a serious contemporary examination of the crisis was given the doom-laden title, *The Vanishing Irish*.[2]

'No Irish Need Apply'

For those choosing to emigrate to Britain in the 1920s and 1930s the prospects, if they lacked skills or secondary education, were bleak indeed. They could in the main expect to go into catering or service, if female, and labouring, factory work, or the armed forces, if male. Few industries were open to the idea of employing Irish labour, and many trades operated a 'closed-shop' policy, which also excluded the Irish. Earnings in any of these occupations were meagre and promotion slow, and anti-Irish sentiment was rife.

In the 1920s it was fermented by the War of Independence; in the 1930s, after a modest lapse, it was rekindled by the IRA bombing campaign; in the 1940s it was again inflamed by Irish neutrality during the Second World War. The massive wartime labour recruitment campaign in Ireland had the eventual outcome of extensive Irish permeation of British industry, on an unprecedented scale, and the self-evident necessity for Irish labour to assist with reconstruction also had an ameliorating effect on anti-Irish sentiment. This was tempered, however, by hostile reaction to the sheer extent of Irish immigration in the two decades following the end of the war. The arrival of the New Commonwealth influx of non-whites, in the 1950s and 1960s, diverted xenophobic attention away from the Irish for a time.

The so-called 'Troubles' in Northern Ireland, beginning in the late 1960s, once again provoked anti-Irish racism in Britain but by then legislation had outlawed its more overt and gratuitously insulting manifestations such as, 'No Irish need apply' employment, and 'No blacks, no dogs, no Irish', relating to rented accommodation.

The two decades after Independence, however, were perhaps the most unrelentingly harsh period for emigrants to Britain. Men with families to support had difficult choices to make and no avenue held out much hope of comfort and security, let alone prosperity, unless they could use Britain as a stepping-stone to the United States. Few of those with dependants could hope to do so.

Instead, if they worked in construction they often lived lives of unrelenting labour and hardship, by today's standards. By their own lights, however, and in comparison with life in the remoter parts of the west of Ireland, they managed to achieve a frugal comfort for which their children at least appear grateful. The following unsolicited letter from Scotland recounts a typical Irish labourer's life of the period:

My father, Patrick Kelly, was born in Ardara, in Donegal, in 1922 and was a navvy all his life.

I can remember he had to go to the North of Ireland for work to feed his family as there was no work where we lived. He was arrested by the Garda three times as he did not have a work permit. The first and second time he was taken from the house we were all young and very scared. The boys who played football with him paid his fines, but the third time he was sent to prison. The only crime he committed was to try to feed his children.

Sewerage tunnel, Manchester Main Drainage Scheme, 1920s.

When he came out of prison we came to Greenock in Scotland and he worked in many building sites in all weathers. He also travelled all round Glasgow. He was a very good worker and timekeeper. I was always so proud of him.

When they started building the Telephone Exchange in Greenock more than fifty years ago my dad worked there from start to finish.

He used to take my son, his grandson, to work with him when he was 16 and learned him all he knew. Now my son Daniel has got his own small construction business in Glasgow.

My dad worked till he was over sixty years old, and never complained; he enjoyed every minute of it. He died when he was sixty-eight years old.[3]

Coming, as most of them did, from large families or the care of institutions, Irish emigrants often suffered from loneliness and homesickness. Many, in the beginning, regarded life in England as merely the lesser of two evils.

It was 1937 and I was seventeen when I came to London and I soon got a job. I was lonesome and so on, but I was too proud to let them know at home that I had made a mistake, so I had to bury my pride and stay![4]

West Cork hill farm.

Discrimination

The ingrained class discrimination which had thrived under colonial rule persisted in Ireland until relatively recent times, and this was reflected in the lack of educational opportunities for children of working-class parents, prior to the *Education Act* of 1967, which provided free secondary education for all.

I was born in County Kerry, my father was a farmer. You left school at fourteen in them days, so I worked around the farm and that. Well that was it, there was nothing else to be done, there were no jobs. That's why all the Irish came over here, wasn't it, because the farms wouldn't keep them all, the farm was only for one and they all couldn't get the farm, could they?

Well I got fed up with home and I wanted to travel. I didn't see much of a future at home and everybody was coming to England, they were all going to the labour exchange, all signing on to come over here for jobs (1946). So I decided to do it; and I came and I was sorry after!

I went to the labour exchange at home and signed on. That was for a job in England, and you had to take the job they gave you.... Your fare was paid; the only thing you had to get was a permit. Well, you'd get your photograph taken and went to the police station. You had to stay in your job for so long, you couldn't leave when you came over here and you had to report to the local police station with your travel permit.[5]

The only avenue through which a child of parents unable to pay school fees might gain access to secondary education was a scholarship. These were fiercely contested, and anyone capable of winning one was clearly an exceptional scholar, fully deserving of the opportunity thus provided.

Pat Burke, born in County Cork in 1918, was one of six children whose father did outdoor maintenance work for the county council. A bright lad, he won a scholarship to a fee-paying college in Fermoy, run by the Christian Brothers.

The Christian Brothers, evidently, talked my father and mother out of it. They pointed out that it would be a big financial burden to my family if I went, because although I'd won a place, there's books and uniform to be paid for, and everything else, and that a boy could go out and earn his keep, be put to a trade. And they evidently talked my father and mother into thinking that it wasn't very wise to send me to college.[6]

Domhnall MacAuligh's equable temperament saw him safely through a stint in the Irish Army, many years on British building sites, and minor cult status as a successful author and contributor to print media as diverse as *The Irish Times, Building* magazine, and *Ireland's Own,* while still working as a navvy. Nonetheless, even he is mildly reproving of Ireland's endemic class system, as he describes heading back to England by boat after a short break at home in the early 1950s:

Coming into Dun Laoire I saw men in white clothes playing cricket and, somehow, I felt annoyed. A young man and his girl were walking by themselves down below us in the golden evening sunlight. It's well for you, my friend, that every day you arise can be spent round about this place.... The quay is lined with little sailing boats, and wooden rowing boats. The wealthy own them, those who can stay behind here.[7]

In many cases children were separated from their parents, when families were broken up, in order to distribute the burden of rearing amongst the extended family or the agencies of the State. Such children were often sent in their mid- to late teens to places of employment in Britain, as student nurses, domestics, catering staff or labourers. Their plight is becoming better understood and appreciated in contemporary Irish society as the media and individual survivors make their stories known.

Many children placed in the care of the State, or of religious institutions supported and sanctioned by the State, subsequently emigrated or were placed in employment abroad because no effort was made to rehabilitate them at home. Even some who were placed with families or employers in Ireland were indirect victims of the endemic emigration that was de-populating the countryside and of the Establishment's essential indifference towards it.

In the order of values, it seems more important to preserve and improve the quality of Irish life, and thereby the purity of that message (Christianity) which our people have communicated to the world, than it is to reduce the number of Irish emigrants.... High emigration, granted a population excess, releases social tensions which would otherwise explode and makes possible a stability of manners and customs which would otherwise be the subject of radical change.[8]

Professor James Meenan maintains that the noted Irish capacity for hard work abroad is a consequence of the stark and simple fact that, in the immediate post-war period, it was much easier to earn a proper reward for hard work in Britain, the United States, or Australia than in Ireland. In the absence of the option to emigrate, however, their natural desire for higher living standards would have caused the Irish to maximise their natural and human resources and achieve greater economic efficiency.

He points out that the decision to emigrate is essentially, for the majority of emigrants, a free choice based on an independent assessment of the economic realities in Ireland and, presumably, leads to improved circumstances abroad.

As such, the option to emigrate is in a sense a national asset and, in a democratic state, should not be arbitrarily curtailed. He also observes, however, that 'emigration has prevented the emergence of an immense surplus of labour and an inevitable driving down of all salaries and wages'. He concludes:

It has allowed those who remain at home to enjoy a standard of living which is not justified by the volume of their production. In the short run at least, emigration has done a great deal to make life in Ireland more leisurely and less disturbed by class warfare. If it ended suddenly, that life would become much more competitive and much less remunerative.[9]

As late as 1964 the number of pupils in full-time education by type of school was as follows:

First level (6–14 years)	496,068
Second level (14–18 years)	129,365
Third level (17+ years)	16,819[10]

Given that 82 per cent of emigrants in 1961 had left school before the age of fifteen (in other words on, or prior to, completion of their Primary cycle) it is clear that only a tiny minority of those included in the figures for second and third levels quoted above went on to emigrate.

Professional and white collar workers, who were twenty per cent of the working population in 1961, were shown to have obtained sixty-five per cent of the university places awarded on the result of the Leaving Certificate examination that year, whereas the manual workers, accounting for twenty-five per cent of the working population, gained only two per cent of university places.[11]

Little wonder then that the unforeseen liquidity of so many of these 'children of the dispossessed' caused such social tensions in the small towns of rural Ireland once the wartime emigrants began to return on visits home:

It could be abrasive and often was: the social ramparts of a small town never crumble under such an assault without its woundings. For this was ignorant money challenging and blitzing impoverished, educated gentility. One retreated in the face of the 'ignorant bosthoon of a spailpeen' who

told you 'put your money where your mouth is' in too many arguments and who, very fast, had produced his own slide rule for success: the money he had below in the bank.[12]

Of course there was always an innate tension in the relationship between those who emigrated and those did not. Ruth Anne Harris contends that permanent emigration, irrespective of the degree of success that may have followed from it, was regarded as failure by those at home. The purpose of emigration was considered to be the acquisition of the means to return permanently.[13]

This generalisation is, however, difficult to accept outside the narrow social and temporal confines of the migrant harvester traditions of the nineteenth century. As this system of subsidising Irish family holdings declined, from the 1890s onwards, increased dependence on permanent emigration implied different standards for the evaluation of emigrants' goals and their achievement.

'When are You Going Back?'

Those with whom I have discussed the question, who had first-hand knowledge of the issues, occasionally expressed some resentment of the indifference and opportunism displayed towards them on visits to Ireland:

Q:. How long are you staying / When are you going back?

A: 'Well, I thought I might look around for something while I'm home....'

Response: 'Sure, there's nothing here — you're better off Over ... would you have the loan of a few pounds before you go ?'

A few emigrants expressed guilt because they'd 'run out' on those at home but countered it with the assertion that, 'Everyone was going at that time; you'd feel strange staying behind,' meaning that anyone with any 'go' in him would have done the same. Most offer the explanation that the family holding could not sustain the numbers of children reared on them and off-farm employment in Ireland was unavailable.

Many who remained, and prospered, have repressed guilty feelings around the plight of emigrants by describing them as 'shiftless', 'unreliable', 'lacking staying-power' or 'unable to settle down for the long haul'.

We are only now finding out the true extent of this deep-seated tension and its ultimate consequences for Irish society. One small western townland, situated close to John Healy's home place, holds in its annals the kernel of this story.

Between the towns of Charlestown, in County Mayo, and Tubbercurry, in County Sligo, lies the small parish of Curry. Between 1841 and 1851 the population of this townland was reduced from 202 to a mere forty-three. The Great Famine, and its criminal mismanagement by the British government, was responsible for this sudden decline. Between 1901 and 1981, however, the population of this same townland, which had recovered to number 339, dropped to the level of 106 souls. This time the slow haemorrhage could be blamed on no one but the Irish themselves (this was the same place from which John O'Hara was to leave for 'The Hay Country' in 1943).

The Hay Saved and Tubber Bet

In 1932 Matt Gallagher, a noted footballer and the second eldest son of a small farmer from the village of Cashel, in the townland of Curry, borrowed the fare to England from his older brother Eddie who had emigrated to America three years earlier. He went harvesting hay in Yorkshire, and potato picking in Lincolnshire, and returned home in December. He was one of the stalwarts of the Curry football team and so, in 1933, after the county championship, 'with the hay saved and Tubber bet', he returned to England. Five of his six brothers joined him over the following ten

years. Taking full advantage of the wartime demand for construction workers, Matt and his brothers established a small bomb-damage repair and construction business that quickly grew into a major house-building concern in house-hungry postwar Britain.

Returning to Ireland in the 1960s, they established a business empire. This embraced Gallagher Group Ltd., Merchant Banking Ltd., Home Builders Ltd., City Inns Ltd., Abbey Homesteads Ltd., Paramount Homes Ltd. and Home Rentals Ltd. One brother, James, became a Fianna Fáil TD for South Sligo in 1961.

Veterans, Bala, 1957.

Someone strongly resembling Matt Gallagher gave the historian J.A. Jackson an insight into the experiences which coloured his perceptions of class distinction in Britain, and amongst the Irish themselves, and between them and the British. On the gulf between middle-class and working-class Irish he said:

There was simply no meaningful contact. We stuck to our circuit and they stuck to theirs. Occasionally, we might meet an Irish architect or doctor at some

Irish medical golfers, National University of Ireland Club, London, 1950s.

Church function, but they always struck me as being embarrassed when we met ....

Mind you, we were all very sensitive and unsure then.... from two things: coming from rural Ireland, and the education we had there. In the country, you see, we hardly ever met English people, and our Christian Brother education was very anti-British ... all this brooding thing of history.... Now ... I'd prefer to do business with an Englishman any day of the week; they're more honest than the Irish and they keep their discretion as well as their delivery dates. And they don't have the malice the Irish have towards each other, resenting the fellow that gets on in the world....[14]

Those emigrating to Britain in the immediate post-war period to work in construction were essentially little different from those who had preceded them. The sons of landless labourers or small farmers, with little or no formal education or vocational skills, they left with little by way of preparation or instruction, and few resources other than the informal network of community and county contacts that they already had abroad.

As noted by John Healy, however, the 'harvester' class of rural migrant for whom emigration was almost hereditary was now being joined by youths from the small towns of the regions traditionally associated with emigration.

Well over half of total Irish emigration between 1911 and 1957 was provided by six southern and western counties: Cork, Mayo, Kerry, Donegal, Galway and Tipperary.[15]

The most significant difference between pre-war and postwar migration was the enormous increase in numbers. Because of the war there was no British census in 1941 but numbers that early in the war weren't very different from the late 1930s. Between 1931 and 1951, however, the number of Irish-born in Britain increased from 381,000 to 627,000. In the single decade 1951–1961 over 400,000 emigrated from the Republic of Ireland to Britain. Nearly half of these were males between the ages of eighteen and twenty-five.

If the profile of the early postwar emigrant was little changed, however, the prospects awaiting him or her in Britain had altered dramatically. The visible signs of anti-Irish sentiment were still there but they no longer held any official or commercial significance.

The extensive wartime recruitment of Irish labour across a wide spectrum of occupations other than the traditional ones of agriculture, domestic service, nursing, the armed forces, construction and unskilled labouring opened many doors to postwar Irish emigrants which hitherto had been closed against them.

In construction, the relatively small group of pre-war Irish operatives employed by established firms such as Wimpey, Laing, Gleeson, Taylor Woodrow, Mowlem and McAlpine had proved an invaluable asset during the period of intensive wartime building and civil engineering. They not only assisted with the recruitment of their fellow-countrymen in Ireland but they also provided a supervisory corps of gangers and foremen with whom the new Irish labour force felt more at ease. The Doyle brothers, Joe and Jim, were classic examples of this type of Irish pre-war 'company man'.

There were, however, important differences between the two generations. The older men came almost exclusively from small-farming backgrounds and had found their way into construction via seasonal harvesting. They were all veterans of the 'tramp navvy' tradition, and had become imbued at an early age with the values of the Victorian railway navvy, the 'Ways of the Line'.[16]

The desire on the part of the professional navvies for 'freedom to go wherever they want to' was, of course, fostered by the nomadic nature of the civil-engineering industry and was ingrained in any man who became habituated to the lifestyle.

Although this restless spirit continued to take hold of many Irish who worked in construction, long after the tramp navvies had disappeared, the postwar Irish construction worker, unlike his pre-war equivalent, now had prospects. He could command good money and, in an industry where the Irish were becoming dominant in groundworks, he could establish himself in business in his own right provided he had the necessary ruthlessness, energy, and ambition. Before the Second World War, unless he was a tradesman, an Irish construction worker had virtually no possibility of achieving either of these things. Navvying for most Irishmen was a dead-end job whose arcane compensations few could discern or appreciate.

It was natural for such men, inured to hardship and able to survive on a level unimaginable to anyone who has never lived rough, to hold the 'townies' and 'greesheens' of the postwar exodus in mild contempt.

Demolition, London, 1952.

Many had been attracted to construction work from harvesting, not because the money was better (prior to the Second World War it actually wasn't), but because it offered such basic amenities as a bed (albeit perhaps shared) and access to washing facilities, which weren't available in the bothies and 'Paddy Houses' of the agricultural sector. Both occupations, of course, were out of doors and allowed men the important freedom to wander at will.

'Dull, Drab ... Backward and Lonely'

There had always been the stick of unemployment and the carrot of adventure to lure a young man away from the Irish countryside and onto the boat; now there was the attraction of good wages and the companionship of his peers who had already left. The authors of the *Report on Emigration* (1954) clearly grasped the effects which the widespread emigration of the 1940s was having on the population:

The average unskilled worker from this country has in recent times been able to secure in Great Britain a greater material return for his labour ... to the young mind, rural areas appear dull, drab, monotonous, backward and lonely....

Tradition and example have also been very powerful influences.... For very many emigrants there was a traditional path 'from the known to the known'.... This path they followed, almost as a matter of course, and without even looking for suitable employment in this country....

Road works, Manchester, 1938.

Apart from tradition and example, there is a widespread awareness of the existence of opportunities abroad, and a realisation of differences between conditions at home and in other countries.... The publicity given to the success of Irish emigrants, often in highly coloured and romantic terms, tends to cause dissatisfaction with what may seem to be the more prosaic conditions at home, especially in remote rural areas.[17]

John Healy described the effect that 'McAlpine's Fusiliers' had on his community when they came home for holidays:

Our town was the first town in Mayo; through it came all the traffic bound for Ballina, which itself filtered the traffic out to Belmullet and Erris and North Mayo. Now in the month of December bus after bus — often in convoys — would pull into Charlestown....

They drank their way home, those two hundred miles across the face of Ireland....

They came in new suits and flashy ties.... Only their accents and their honest Irish faces had not changed.[18]

The Men with 'the Gimp'

A former Irish nurse from South Tyrone recalls seeing as a girl the same convoys of buses coming through Dungannon bound for Derry and Donegal, in the winter of 1952:

I saw bunches of great big men come down the street, with their shirts open to the waist, wearing neck-scarves tied with the 'Pincher's knot', heavy corduroy trousers with braces and wide leather belts fastened by big brass buckles, and hob-nailed boots. They walked with a gimp and they were roaring for drink. My older brother was one of them — he boasted that they were the Milestone Inspectors, the Long Distance Kiddies....[19]

Many of these of course were the hard-bitten tunnellers from the early Scottish hydro schemes of the 1940s and 1950s, former harvesters and tramp navvies, veterans of the hungry 1930s and a different breed from the raw recruits about whom John Healy wrote.

However, by the late 1940s the latter were a veritable multitude. Construction was still very labour-intensive, either because projects were so enormous, as in the case of such public works as power stations, oil terminals, and hydro schemes, or because construction methods were technologically undeveloped, as in house building and commercial development.

Technical development in the construction and civil-engineering industries during the 1940s and 1950s was very uneven. While powered plant had been introduced piecemeal during the 1930s, in road making, its dissemination was hindered by the need to create employment and the consequent retention by local authorities of traditionally labour-intensive methods of road maintenance and construction right up to the outbreak of war.

Although the first D8 dozer, with a rated capacity of 115 HP, was introduced from the United States in 1934, and crawler tractors with rope-operated scrapers were in service towards the close of the decade, labour was so cheap that trenching could be undertaken by hand as cheaply as by machine and most road maintenance still relied on large gangs equipped with a minimum of plant.

When war broke out, road maintenance was put on a 'make and mend' basis for the duration and the only new roads commissioned were for military use. Such resources of plant and expertise as were not devoted to military service were directed towards building airfields.

After the entry of the United States into the war American road-building methods and equipment become widely disseminated throughout the United Kingdom. The first mechanical tarmac/asphalt spreader was introduced for airfield construction in 1941.

Cromwell Road, Extension, London, 1938.

Such equipment was used mainly on wartime airfields and later on the construction of the strategic bomber bases between 1950 and 1955. Any other available large earth-moving plant was confined to open-cast coal mining and was broadly similar to the traditional 'steam navvy' of the railway age. During the first decade after the war, in fact, it was not unusual to see American Sherman tanks, fitted with scrapers, adapted to earth-moving tasks, and their wheeled transporters used for moving extra-large units of plant and machinery.

Not until the mid-1950s, when the British government elected to launch a national motorways programme, did the civil-engineering industry begin to undertake the serious acquisition of modern excavation and earth-moving machines.

In construction proper, and the groundworks (including demolition) preceding it, progress towards mechanisation seemed steadier and more consistent. Cranes, 'steam navvy' excavators, and even pile-driving steam hammers had been available since the nineteenth century and the development of tracked excavators, scrapers and loaders had evolved from steam to diesel-powered models between the 1880s and the 1930s. At that time the first dump trucks, built by Euclid, were introduced along with the American Le Tourneau motorscraper. It was not until 1953, however, that the first backhoe loaders, JCB Mark 1 and Case, were developed.

Hydraulic excavators, replacing the venerable rope-operated models, arrived following the merging in the 1950s of the great British firm of Ruston with Bucyrus of the United States. The acronym 'RB', preceding various digits, has become synonymous with excavation ever since. Over the following decade Hymac, Poclain, Demag, JCB and Atlas introduced a variety of hydraulic excavators. Not until the 1970s, however, did the articulated dump truck, developed by Volvo and Moxy, arrive to complement fully the hydraulic excavator as the supreme large-scale earthmoving tools.

Rural road works, 1938.

The 'RB1'

To the average Irish unskilled labourer working in construction during the period between 1940 and 1960, little in terms of mechanical development was evident. For him the most familiar piece of equipment was still the 'RB1' — the humble shovel. Following the end of the Second World War he was rarely expected, unlike his pre-war counterpart, to supply his own tools, but pick, shovel, and wheelbarrow were such intimate adjuncts of his labours that even in the 1960s a man could still get into trouble for taking another man's wheelbarrow.

In 1948 Sean O'Ciarain, an erstwhile tattie hoker in Scotland, got 'the start' with John Lawrence, Builders, on the Springboig Housing Scheme at Carntyne. He was put to work under a ganger named MacEnroe, digging drains for sewer pipes, having been issued with a shovel and a pickaxe.

All the digging on that site was done by men with picks and shovels. There was not a mechanical digger in the place.... All of MacEnroe's men were Irishmen and they were good men at digging trenches.... And

cutting out the spade work.

Everything needed in the building industry, from heavy diesel tractors to the smallest of contractors' tools, can be supplied on sale or hire by Wards whose skilled operators and up-to-date hire fleets all play their part in cutting out the spade work in building today.

THOS. W. WARD. LTD.

HOLD THE MOST MODERN AND COMPREHENSIVE FLEETS OF CONTRACTORS' PLANT AND EQUIPMENT

Albion Works - Sheffield

GRAYS · GLASGOW · BRITON FERRY

London Office: Brettenham House, Lancaster Place, Strand, W.C.2

they were very particular about keeping their shovels clean.... The older the man the more tidy a worker he seemed to be, and the more careful regarding his tools and the materials he worked with.[20]

Sean's work was typical of what was expected; it was an integral part of all building work, along with digging out and concreting foundations, all of which was done by hand.

Trenches on a housing project were seldom deeper than six feet or shallower than three. They averaged 18 inches in width, which left little room for manoeuvre, and apart from keeping the sides straight and remaining on course, the most difficult part was 'bottoming' — finishing off the bottom so that the pipes would lie at the correct gradient for connection to the main sewer.

It was vital to 'throw the muck well back' — in wet weather or bad ground, a heap of 'muck' left too near the edge of a trench might cause the side to collapse.

Two common exhortations from gangermen were: 'Dig deep, lads', and 'Throw it well back'. These McNicholas cable workers have learnt well.

Wet clay is very heavy and a man can be suffocated in a trench even a few feet deep if he is bent over or loses his footing when the walls collapse. No one knows how many men have lost their lives in this manner but everyone in the industry has a story about it.

'Throw it Well Back'

Digging out the foundations was more laborious, but allowed for teamwork, whereas a man trenching with others before and behind was constantly under pressure to keep up. Of course any Irishman coming from a small, boggy, west of Ireland farm would have lots of experience at digging drains. As such he would have been in constant demand in British construction. Nobby Clarke, an old Long-Distance Man, told me that, before the War, a navvy was expected to bring his own shovel, fork, foot-iron and 'graft' (drainmaker's spade). Not only were trenches dug for housing, and all types of serviced buildings, but they were also the conduits for pipes and cables — water and gas pipes, telephone, electricity, and television cables — and countless Irishmen were employed laying them.

Before building could commence, however, post-war Britain had to demolish all the old and bomb-damaged stock that the war had rendered uninhabitable. Many of the Irish recruited by the Ministry of Labour in the last months of the war had been directed towards demolition and repair work in British cities because there were so few Englishmen available with the necessary skills.

'Demolition Men'

One man who 'seized the time' was Kerryman Bill Fuller. Emigrating to London in the 1930s, he established the Buffalo Ballroom (now the Electric Ballroom and still in his possession) in Camden High Street. When the Blitz began he assembled a corps of Irish men, 2,000 strong, to deal with the bomb damage. So prominent did he become in demolition that it was said of him in London, 'What Hitler didn't knock down, Bill Fuller did'. McNicholas also began in bomb-damage repair.

Hostels

At a conference of Irish building workers held in the Holborn Hall, London, in February 1946, men from no fewer than twenty-six different hostels were represented. They issued 'A strong demand for the continuation of the payment of lodging allowances for Eire workers who were not allowed to bring their families to Britain' during the war.

They also raised the issue of the payment of unemployment benefit and workmen's compensation if, and when, they returned to Ireland. With the arrival of peace and the imminent release of ex-servicemen, civil defence, and war industry employees to civilian occupations (in 1945 still some nine million people) the Irish who had been recruited during the war on temporary work permits might be sent home to face indefinite unemployment. These were strong fears to be taken into consideration.

The Doncaster Bypass, 1959.

Six months later, following attempts by the Hostels Corporation to increase rents from 25/- to 30/- for men and from 20/- to 25/- for women, a dispute led to the Residents' Association calling a national rent strike.

When the Corporation retaliated by refusing the residents permission to use the canteens, the latter withdrew their ration books and began to cook their own meals outside the hostels. The extent of this type of accommodation is indicated by the spread of participating hostels; these included London, Birmingham, Coventry, Oldbury, Redditch, Brockworth, Slough, Pontefract, Falkirk, Swindon, Malvern and West Bromwich, amongst others.

So pervasive was the Irish presence that it was feasible for the Hostels Corporation to attempt a 'divide-and-rule' strategy by claiming to the press that 'Irish trouble-makers' were the source of most of the agitation. It was a plausible argument given the density of the Irish in British hostels. The *Irish Democrat* estimated that there were nearly 30,000 Irish building operatives living in London's industrial hostels in August 1946. The enormous London hostel at Onslow

Square, off the Fulham Road, housed over 2,000 Irish labourers in August 1947, about 75 per cent of the total.[21]

The Irish demolition workers resident in the Onslow Square Hostel were earning £4. 15s. 6d for a forty-four hour week in 1947. The hostel dwellers paid 30s. per week for bed, breakfast, and an evening meal. Rationing was still in force (and remained so until 1954) and each individual was allowed paltry weekly quantities of food such as three pounds of potatoes, one ounce of bacon, two pints of milk. It was poor fare for a navvy.

It was possible for migrant agricultural workers in the mid- to late-1940s to swap a ration card for a month's supply of what were known as 'Emergency Coupons', which were about the same size as the old English pound note. These were negotiable in any shop whereas to use a ration book it was necessary to register with a specific shop or other supplier. John O'Hara remembers:

We found out this dodge — like young lads do; we always got paid in big, blue pound notes ... we couldn't spend all we were gettin', ye see, because

beer was rationed, fags were rationed, and all the rest of it.... So — we were working late one evenin'.... We used to go into the grocer or the butcher, or wherever, and the game was — the first thing they'd ask you — they wouldn't ask, 'Have you money?' they'd ask, 'Have you coupons, Paddy?' and we'd say, 'Well, I think I have', and you'd pull out this wad of notes, and go searchin' through them.... And he'd say, in a sharp tone of voice, 'Stand over there in that corner, Paddy — I can't be moidered with you, I've got customers to serve' ... and as soon as he had the shop clear, 'What do you want, Paddy?'.... We often used to get about three pound of beef, that time, for a £1 — we were livin' like kings!

But we tried it one time in that Maggie Thatcher's shop, in Grantham, and it wouldn't work — no way! You wouldn't be entertained at all. The oul' father was some sort of a preacher — there was a big church, as you go down the London Ramp towards Peterborough, and he was some sort of a — a preacher, or somethin' — he was the gangerman there, anyway. That wouldn't come off there — it wasn't her, it was her oul' father.[22]

Considering that the Second World War had cost Britain some £7,000 million — one quarter of her national wealth, and that £1,500 millions of this represented bomb destruction and damage to property, it is not surprising that there were good opportunities in the fields of demolition and reconstruction.

Reconstruction

Demand for housing had, by 1948, reached an unprecedented level. There were 700,000 fewer houses than in 1939 — 475,000 houses had been destroyed by bombing —and in the three years following the end of the war there were 11 per cent more marriages, and 33 per cent more births, than in the three years preceding the conflict. The attainment of full employment also fuelled people's expectations in regard to new and better-quality housing. Initially priority was given to bomb-damage repair, local-authority housing, and educational facilities.

Consequently the major established building firms of the day were able to move from a situation of asking themselves, 'Have we enough work?' to one where the question became instead, 'How can we cope with the work?' Companies such as Wimpey, Laing, Sir Robert McAlpine & Sons, Richard Costain, Taylor Woodrow and Wates expanded their workforce and hired thousands of Irishmen in the process.

Paradoxically, however, productivity fell steadily between 1937 and 1951 and, in fact, pre-war levels weren't equalled until the late 1960s. Given the proliferation of work and the shortage of labour, men were allowed to remain on site during wet weather or delayed deliveries rather than being laid off. Poor-quality labour was being hired, and, without undue fear of the consequences of dismissal, output was not what it could have been.[23]

A McAlpine demolition site near St Paul's, London, 1952.

Wages had increased by almost half in the course of the war, and earnings, under the impetus of the war effort, were boosted even further. The cost of living rose by 29 per cent so the balance was in the workers' favour. From 1945 onwards, 'rained off' operatives were given half pay and the thirty-two-hour guaranteed week was introduced. Holidays with pay and extended notice of dismissal were other measures introduced for the first time. In 1948 the working week was reduced from forty-eight to forty-four hours. The labour rate, which was 1s. 4d in 1940, had risen to 2s. 5d ten years later.

Housebuilding

During the General Election of 1945 Labour's Aneurin Bevan had rashly promised to build 'five million homes in quick time' but, with the severe shortages of resources confronting the new administration in which he was Minister for Housing, this was a tall order. Nevertheless, in 1946, 55,400 new houses were built; in 1947, 139,690; and in 1948, 227,616.

The financial crisis of 1947, following on the worst winter in living memory, curtailed building for some years. However, Bevan also introduced other measures which, in addition to indirectly alleviating the housing shortage, also assisted the construction industry.

The Housing Acts of 1946 and 1949 removed the limitation on local authorities building 'only for the working class', while the Labour policy of encouraging the erection of temporary prefabricated dwellings resulted in 157,000 such 'prefabs' becoming available between 1945 and 1950. Some of these dwellings were EFM (Emergency Factory Made) bungalows which, despite the scepticism of the orthodox builder, in many cases still stand. Other 'permanent non-traditional' house types included Airey, Cornish Unit and Wates (pre-cast concrete); Laing 'Easiform' and Wimpey 'No-Fines' (in-situ concrete); and BISF and Unity (steel

Early post-war housing estates, south-eastern England (also opposite page).

frame). Together these accounted for some 16 per cent of all new homes in the decade from 1945 to 1955.

The *New Towns Act* of 1946 established a series of development corporations charged with building totally new towns at various locations throughout Britain. This innovation, a variation on the 'Garden Suburb' concept of the 1920s, took some years to bear fruit but was ultimately very successful.

'A Certain Vision'

Anyone with even the rudiments of a building trade could find a niche in the chaos of demolition and reconstruction of the early postwar period. Bernard McNicholas, chairman of McNicholas Engineering, recalled how his father and uncle, from Bohola in County Mayo, got started:

They were knockin' about in South London doin' labouring work when my uncle started doin' bomb damage repair work in 1945. They must have had a certain vision other people that came across didn't have ... apart from just doin' the daily routine of the job they looked around them and weighed up the situation. If someone was earning more than they were, how was he doing it? He probably developed from a labourer into a foreman, got an idea of what was happening on the site, and subsequently became a sub-contractor. When they made some money, they ploughed it back into the business in the form of a wagon or a van or whatever was required, and built up the business that way.[24]

This is sound reasoning but it also oversimplifies the processes, both practical and psychological, involved in transforming the average young Irish countryman from a labourer into a contractor. For the

100,000-plus males who had come over since 1940, and the thousands more who were arriving every month, the circumstances were too confusing and the conditions too basic to allow much opportunity for taking stock.

Tom Durkin, who was a veteran of the struggles of the 1930s, described the situation in the construction industry in London immediately after the war:

> After the war there were jobs goin' a beggin'; men worked three weeks on, one off, from 7 am to 6.30 p.m., seven days a week.... You could get a bed in a cubicle for a shilling a night — forms for 6d, but you might fall off in the middle of the night. The partitions between the beds were made of corrugated iron....

These were mostly men from large families who now found themselves cut off from their traditional support system. In England they were noticeably different from others around them by virtue of dress, deportment, accent and religion (despite it being said, with reference to racist English attitudes towards the Irish, 'No one knows you're black until you open your mouth'). Consequently the only social group they could depend on was centred round work. If, therefore, they had no home life, they inevitably congregated wherever that group could be found — namely, in the pub.

> When you come over here you have no home, you pay for your week's lodgin's, get a bed, your meals maybe, but at night you're not wanted there, you don't fit in, your culture is different, you go out at night and spend your money in the pub because there's nowhere else much to go to, because there's camaraderie there, and there's people, it's a social kind of a life....[25]

For Irish working men in Britain the pub had always been a unique institution. In every urban centre there were 'Irish' pubs — albeit called perhaps 'The George', 'The Crown' or 'The King's Head'. Here they could network — meet old friends, get news from home, locate contacts, find lodgings or be given 'the start'.

They had simply adapted one of the great institutions of the old railway navvies to their special needs as an ethnic minority.

Contractors' agents, and subcontractors, used the 'Irish' pubs as their recruiting grounds. Men were picked up at the pubs and dropped off at the pubs and, inevitably, spent their day's wages there instead of going 'home'.

> I started drinking — I drank for forty years — everything I earned — good money. It was into the van in the morning, out of the van in the evening, no such thing as, 'Will we go to the Cafe?'; out of the van, into the pub ... you might have a few drinks, or you might do the session.[26]

In the late 1940s the Irish 'subbie' was not yet an industry phenomenon, but many of those who were only finding their way, as humble navvies, were indeed, as Bernard McNicholas put it, 'weighing up the situation'.

The three most distinct Irish elements in the industry were, however, already in place — the steady, solid 'company men', mainly employees of reputable building firms on housing contracts, from which they went home to good digs each evening after work; the new breed of 'long-distance men', who went exclusively for the big money on remote civil-engineering projects such as dams and power stations, where accommodation was mainly in camps and there was nothing to do but work and save; and the 'lumpers' who worked for labour-only sub-contractors, were paid cash day and drank it each night, and had no National Insurance stamps and little or no involvement with the Revenue Commissioners.

In the construction and civil-engineering industries, the Irish were now a force to be reckoned with. Henceforth, in the early stages of any project — demolition, main drainage, foundations, groundworks — the Irish would be predominant. The only question seemed to be: Who would be the ones to find the gold in the streets?

8 Public Works

I stripped to the skin with The Darky Flynn,
Way down in the Isle of Grain.
With Horse-Face Toole, well you knew the rule,
No money if you stopped for the rain.
McAlpine's god was a well-filled hod,
Your shoulders cut to bits and seared,
And woe to he who called for tea
With McAlpine's Fusiliers.

Jackson's assertion that 'Only 5.5% of the total labour force in the building industry in England and Wales in 1951 was in fact Irish-born' (25 per cent in Scotland), while statistically accurate, may be misleading.

Apart from the fact that it omits those of Irish descent (always an important constituent of the Irish presence), it suggests that they were an insignificant element in the industry overall, but that was far from being the case. To appreciate their importance one needs to understand the structure of the industry at that time and the different functions men performed within it.

These statistics embrace a multitude of small one- and two-man operations, such as repair and maintenance firms and modest builders, as well as the medium to large construction companies, and those engaged in civil engineering.

The largest 0.1% of firms carried out the same proportion of work, almost a quarter, as that carried out by the smallest 90% of firms.[1]

About one-fifth of the roster of a typical large construction company in Britain in the 1950s was represented by administrative, professional, technical and clerical staff. Many such firms embraced plant and transport, joinery, planning, work-study, design, bonus surveying and site-safety services.

Apart from the board of management, the firms required estimators, buyers, planning engineers, contract managers, surveyors and clerical staff — all off-site. On site (and there could be hundreds of sites involved at any one time) were project managers, site managers, site agents, section foremen and general foremen. Of these essential personnel, only the very last named were at all likely to be Irish (there were exceptions but, prior to the 1970s, not enough to matter statistically).

This still leaves the trades to be accounted for. A small number of Irish tradesmen had found employment in Britain before the war, and their numbers increased during the wartime recruitment drive. In Ireland, however, parental hardship, poor technical education facilities, and Irish 'closed shop' trades union practices meant that until the 1970s, most Irish building workers began their careers in Britain as unskilled labourers.

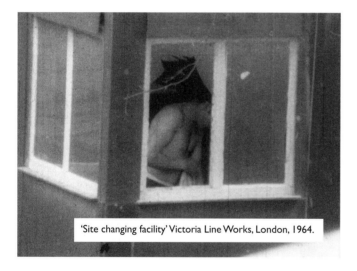

'Site changing facility' Victoria Line Works, London, 1964.

Plant operators, in the early postwar period, were also invariably British, although this became one of the favoured Irish avenues of advancement for men who wanted steady employment and better prospects.

Nomadic Irish

The quid pro quo in the larger firms for access to these jobs was unswerving loyalty, willingness to travel, and length of service. Loyalty to the firm was a quality more commonly found amongst the English, with their traditions of service, but it was outweighed, in the estimation of most civil-engineering companies, by the premium placed on willingness to travel, and this trait was more characteristic of the migratory Irish.

An English company agent, probably with Dick Hampton, filmed during construction of the M1 motorway by Philip Donnellan for his 1965 documentary, *The Irishmen*, had this to say concerning the nomadic qualities of Irish labour:

He's a nomad in the sense that the industry likes to think of him that way. The trend today of every industry is to accept that it has an obligation to try to give employment nearer home — his actual home....

Our industry tries this, as far as it can — 'regionalisation', as we call it ... but, in fact of course, because of a man's particular skill in one job or another, you are obliged to say to him, 'Finish this job, and then go to another job'; and this means changing home.

Well of course, this nomadic character in an Irishman, as we have just described it, this is an asset ... I think he's nomadic in that sense.

But of course his home is, essentially, Ireland — he always remembers this....[2]

This is a conveniently circular argument — the agent extols the nomadic character of the Irish labour force, while at the same time making it clear that willingness to travel is a prerequisite for the job. It has been suggested that this particular speech indicates anti-Irish racism, or is, at best, patronising, but that is to overlook the whole history of the navvy and the fundamental nature of the civil engineering industry.

Coincidentally, thirty years later, another Englishman, also an agent with Dick Hampton in the early 1960s, reiterated this position:

Back in 1964 I could guarantee to deliver two hundred Irishmen to anywhere in the country to start on Monday morning; not anymore. The 'Travelling Man' has virtually disappeared....

When we built the M4 we had no local labour — they wouldn't work on it, and we wouldn't have them anyway; they were useless. You wanted the 'Paddy'; he was experienced with the pick and shovel, used to getting his hands dirty, used to working hard. These local guys would want to go home at 5 o'clock, for a cup of tea or whatever, whereas Paddy would work through. He'd understand the sort of game you were in....[3]

The résumé recited by an anonymous worker in Donnellan's documentary typifies both the career of the archetypal postwar Long-Distance Man and the sadly foreshortened youth of many Irish emigrant labourers:

I come from the West of Ireland and I came across to Scotland when I was fourteen-and-a-half years of age. I worked on the hydro-electric schemes there until I turned twenty, when I came to England.

The first place I landed there was Peterborough, where I worked on a power station. I went on then to Falconbury Airfield, which was a seven-and-a-half-million-pound contract — we were there for four-and-a-half years.

I then went on to the Preston By-pass, and then on to the M1; finished on the M1 and then went to Rossmore; completed that and went to the M6; completed that and went back to an airfield in Scotland again. We completed that and I was working on the M1 since then.

There was an *esprit de corps* amongst the Irish labour force, on the big civil engineering schemes of the 1950s and 1960s, which some men regarded as a form of 'company loyalty' but which others interpreted as mere pragmatism — following 'the big money'.

We're a nation of travellers — when we joined a company, the company looked after us, and we travelled with the company. Whereas the Brits became domiciled and, when the work left the area, they stayed on, we went with the work — we 'followed the money' and travelled in mass.[4]

It was possible for an Irish man to prosper with the big British companies but civil-engineering sites were so hazardous in the immediate postwar period that a man was lucky to live long enough to enjoy the fruits of his success.

In 1954, after a stint with Wimpey in Newcastle, forty-two-year-old Mayoman Peter O'Neill was offered a three-year contract in Australia. The firm was building the first major uranium mine in the Northern Territory, together with a company township ironically called 'Bachelor', and the scale of the project was such that his contract was renewed for a further three years. He was also promoted to Foreman-Driver.

Site caravan, M4, 1963.

Peter was delighted since this opened up the possibility of settling permanently in Australia. He sent for his family in Ireland. They joined him in June of 1957 and settled in Bachelor. His son joined Peter on site and his daughter, Rosaleen, found employment in the Company Store. Another daughter attended the local school. The family seemed to have landed on their feet.

Unfortunately, on 19 November of that year, Peter was electrocuted while investigating the cause of a fatal accident on site four days previously. He was, according to Rosaleen, the only Irishman killed on this project. Afterwards his family were obliged to return to Ireland.[5]

John Cox, known throughout the industry as 'Mr. Motorway' for his lifetime's experience of road building and pioneering work with Tarmac on the early motorways, claims that,

> *Motorways changed the whole structure for construction workers. They could travel seventy miles each way to work, and did.... It wasn't unusual for me to drive 300 miles on a Friday night, from say Edinburgh to Wolverhampton. But often motorways started as by-passes, and men could live locally in digs; we didn't need to have camps. Camps were only for very isolated places — dams etc.*
>
> *On the Preston By-Pass, in 1956–58, all my senior chaps in the field were Irish — Works Managers and General Foremen, and they were very good. Many of the men I started with used to go home once a year — at Christmas. It was a very sad life for them — living in digs, as most of them did. They had come over before the war, and were very experienced. The next move, of course, was when we introduced on-site caravan parks, because the men were bringing their wives along with them.... They wanted a better quality of life....*[6]

McAlpine's

Tarmac, like Wimpey, was known to employ the Irish in large numbers, but the biggest British employer by far of Irish labour was McAlpine. Given that McAlpine was a Scot, a race traditionally hostile to the Irish, this may seem strange. Malcolm O'Brien offered this explanation:

> *At one time, in the 1920s, the company were going to the wall, and Sir Robert McAlpine called a meeting of the workforce. He told them he wouldn't be able to pay wages for two or three months but, if the men stuck by him, he'd turn the company around and reward their loyalty. Obviously the local men, many of whom probably had families to support, had to leave and find a wage elsewhere; but the Irish, who really had no choice in the matter but didn't say so, said they'd stick with the company.*

It is said that, as a direct consequence of this incident, there is an unwritten law in McAlpine's that if two men apply for a job, and one is Irish, the Irishman gets hired. In fact, according to industry sources, McAlpine's has always shown great loyalty to its Irish workforce. This has resulted in strong Irish representation at supervisory level. According to Malcolm O'Brien:

> *If you visit a McAlpine project, the Construction Manager, or General Foreman, and all the gangers, are always Irish.*

Undoubtedly the McAlpine family, beginning with the founder Robert McAlpine, has always held Irish labour in high regard and their hiring record ever since the early part of the century certainly reflects this. That is not to say that McAlpine paid Irishmen more — in the words of Ogden Nash: 'No MacTavish was ever lavish'.

Rather, in virtually guaranteeing employment to Irish labour, McAlpine's acted as a safety net for Irishmen in need of a start or experiencing hard times.

> *I never saw as many 'pinchers' in one pub as there was in the Jolly Smokers tonight. I heard it was a big new job that McAlpine was starting that brought them to Northampton. They looked pretty grimy, the lot of them — old 'donkeys' up to their ears, old moleskin breeches and rubber boots.*[7]

Local authorities maintained building departments for maintenance and for occasional small construction projects. Naturally this politically sensitive usage of direct labour tended to be mainly British although here again a 'steady' Irishman, once in, might, with application (and a low profile) rise through the ranks to a supervisory though still subordinate position.

As building technology advanced, more and more specialist services were subcontracted. These included not only traditional trades such as plastering, painting, plumbing, carpentry and joinery, but also electrical work, heating and ventilating, plant hire and roofing. Here again, the technically proficient English tended to monopolise the work and favour their fellow country-men whenever the assistance of labourers was called for. The traditional tradesman's prohibition on labourers 'handling tools' reinforced the exclusion of the un-skilled (see Chapter Seven).

At the level of 'general operative' or unskilled labourer, however, the Irish were predominant. Almost twenty years after Jackson's survey, one-fifth of all adult male operatives were general labourers, but by that time construction methods necessitated more skills than had been the case in 1951. At that time, unskilled on-site personnel would have been closer to a quarter. Since manpower in building and contracting totalled 1.8 million in 1948, Jackson's 1951 figure of 5.5 per cent adds up to a lot of Irishmen.

Had they been diffused throughout different aspects of building operations, their numbers would have been insignificant, but it was their concentration in groundworks which made them important. Here, teamwork, stamina, and dogged determination were vital, and in these the Irish excelled — so much so that they dominated these operations to the extent that, in time, it became almost impossible for the non-Irish labourer to compete. As F. Munnelly recalls:

Lads just wouldn't work alongside the English; they'd do anything to get rid of them ... walking around on site in mid-winter without a shirt on, carrying a hod, laughing and sneering at the English labourers dressed in shirts and jackets, driving them out.[8]

'Handling Tools'

Of itself, this 'bottom-drawer closed shop' was nothing new; it had been observed amongst the immigrant Irish of Mayhew's day, and before, although less so in construction than in stevedoring and other labour-intensive niches. Such monopolisation inevitably provoked the polarisation of roles and the concen-tration, wherever possible, in the hands of the native English, of the more highly skilled and financially rewarding building occupations.

One time in the gas-works, me and my brother were doing all the street-works ... the (Irish) boys would dig out the trenches — up to the seventies — and then there'd be an Englishman sitting in the van ... they'd put on their overalls and they'd come out and do a little joint (connection), go back again to their cup of tea, and that was their day's work done.

The English had little desire to do the 'dirty work' in any event. Since the introduction of compulsory education, in the late nineteenth century, they had been steadily moving away from unskilled manual occupations and, with the onset of full employment after the Second World War, this trend accelerated. In the construction industry, however, given the continu-ing necessity to concentrate operatives in the initial, labour-intensive, groundworks phase of every project, a clearly defined niche was always available to the unskilled Irish — and they seized it with alacrity.

Economic and educational handicaps notwithstand-ing, however, more and more Irish emigrants had, or soon acquired, the rudiments of a trade in the building industry. Concreting, kerb-laying, and basic joinery were easily improvised, and usually anyone with a trade would willingly pass on the basic techniques to a fellow-Irishman on site. According to Frank Munnelly: 'An Irish guy with a trade would "carry" you — let you learn enough to try on your own'.

The trademark of the 'Chippy' was the two-handled bag in which he carried his tools. This bag could not be closed because protruding from one end would be the spirit level, and from the other the panel saw, and the characteristic shape this gave the chippie's bag led to it being called 'the turkey'.

Consequently, it wasn't unusual for an unskilled Irish labourer, after a few weeks, helping a site carpenter, to remark:

Next job I go to, I'll have 'the turkey'!

It was equally common to see men, who had been happily doing 'first fixing' joinery, disappear off site as soon as the time for the more skilled 'second fixing' work — such as making and hanging doors, window sashes — came around.

'Time-Served Men'

There were, of course, the more traditional 'time-served men', who would not even take their tea-break on site in the same hut as a navvy, let alone permit him to 'handle tools', but these were usually British tradesmen, such as finishing carpenters or bricklayers.

The navvying gangs [were] *the men who dug the founds and the trenches and laid the concrete. With the various squads of tradesmen on the site we did not mix, and even their labourers kept apart from us. For all we had to do with them they might as well not have been there at all.*[9]

Another man who worked from the late 1940s on sites in and around London recalls:

Sewage works, Bala, 1957.

When we were on the tea break, the Cockney tradesmen would sit in one corner of the hut atin' sandwiches and talkin' football, while the Irish labourers would be in the other corner playin' games of '45', and there'd be no communication between the two.[10]

Learning 'on the job' was nevertheless a widespread postwar phenomenon in the industry and the foundations of several well-known Irish companies were laid in precisely this way by men who acquired the rudiments of trades such as bricklaying, timbering, or plastering in the late 1940s and early 1950s.

Between the 1930s and the 1960s, however, the majority of the Irish worked as direct labour for British companies. Kevin Stapleton from Ennis in County Clare, for example, was twenty-one when he was recruited by a Wimpey's agent for work on an airfield contract.

I took the boat to England, heading for Ilminster, near Taunton in Somerset. I had a wooden portmanchoo [sic] *with a clasp and key. The Lodging Allowance at the camp was £1 4s. and the rate was 1s. 6d an hour.*

Over the next forty-six years Kevin was to work for many major contractors including Wimpey, Mowlem, Bovis, Cubitt, D.I. Williams, Percy Bilton, Lehane, McKenzie & Shand amongst others. His was always direct rather than sub-contracted labour.

The importance and level of responsibility of the Irish in British construction, in those years, has been classified as follows, in a questionnaire completed by respondents retired from senior management positions with Tarmac Construction[11]:

Level of Promotion:
1. Navvy/Labourer/Trades Operative
2. Ganger
3. General Foreman
4. Works Manager/Site Agent

The hierarchy in the field went like this — you'd start as a labourer, and they were comparatively unskilled; after that things became quite skilled — for instance, you became perhaps a pipe layer, and that's a semi-skilled operation; then you became a timber man, and that was a very responsible job — lives depended on it.

Then, if you were a leader of men, you became a ganger. And above the gangers, we had 'Walking Gangers', and they would look after three or four gangers in the field. And above them you'd have the General Foreman, or Works Manager. And all of these came up through the ranks.

From 1960 onwards, your Trades Foremen, who built the bridges and so on, they were separate, but the Works Manager, and General Foreman, they came from the plant operators, because the important thing became how to handle plant, not men.... So my foremen quite often tended to be plant-oriented, having operated tractors, or scrapers, or something like that. (John Cox, former Chairman, Tarmac)

Importance of Irish Labour
Very Important — Especially in:
1. Ground Works — Direct or Sub-Contract
2. Form Work — Direct or Sub-Contract

In the initial stages of most contracts Irish labour figures highly in numbers on site.

Speaking from personal experience, most of my Works Managers and Gangers were Irish. I don't know of many Irish Site Managers. Mainly our Irish workforce was either on the labouring side — hourly and weekly paid — or, on a much smaller scale, they've gone into site administration — Site Clerk, Office Manager, Cost Clerk, etc.. (John Docherty, former Director, Tarmac. Supervised many major Tarmac industrial contracts — e.g., Pembroke Power Station.)

In my time, apart from the trades and machine men, the labour force from ganger down was predominantly Irish.... Some of them might be born and bred in England or Scotland, but they were unquestionably Irish. (John Cox)

On the motorways, when I worked for Dick Hampton's, the muck shifters, all the men driving the big 636's, the D4s, D6s, D8s, were all West of Ireland men. One time, when the Revenue men came on site and word went round, all the machines stopped, and men on false cards disappeared in all directions.

On the Thames Barrier, we had 2,500 men at peak, and I'd say 80 per cent were Irish — first or second generation; very few came directly from Ireland to that job. 95 per cent of the Woolwich and Bexley men were Irish; 60 per cent of those from Dartford were Irish. 70–80 per cent of the carpenters were Irish. (Dudley Barrat, Costain, Labour Officer, Thames Barrier, 1975–1982.)

Good & Bad Points of Irish Labour
Good
Hard Workers — Not worried about 'getting their hands dirty'. Reliable and 'Multi-Skilled' — especially at groundworks/drainage layers/ landscape work.

Dick Hampton, 'Muck Shifters', M4, 1963.

They'd come sideways up to the ganger — always thumbs turned out, for a good worker, and say, 'Any fear of the start?' That's the way they did it. A special breed.... (John Cox)

Bad

Few have achieved skills training; i.e. Apprentice-ship; Health & Safety

Occasionally you'd meet one who'd completed his schooling, and he could go far.... Tom Frayne came to me from a large family in Mayo, aged nineteen, and started as a Time Keeper. He then became a Site Office Manager, and then I taught him about quantity surveying. Then he started his own company, and he could buy and sell me now, ten times over. He has enough nous to own and run a very slick operation (Wreakin Construction). (John Cox)

Discipline

The men liked to be directed, and they liked strict discipline — no doubt about that. We (Tarmac Construction) built the main power station there (Pembroke), but another contractor — Taylor Woodrow — came in after us. Our discipline was very tight. To give you an example: at the ten-minute tea break, my foremen were in there at the end of ten minutes, chasing them out. Taylor Woodrow took on a lot of our labour, and one of my Irish foremen remarked to me one day that the men didn't like working for Taylor Woodrow because the discipline was too slack; they could sit in the hut for twenty minutes before anybody chased them out, and they didn't like it.... A lot of people, they like to be told what to do, and if they're told very firmly, they'll go and do it. But not to be left on their own. (John Docherty)

Strikes

I think the Irish were probably more strike-inclined than anybody else — certainly on the jobs I worked on — when I was running Pembroke Power Station I had two troubled times there and both of them were Irish-inspired, led by very vocal people who were Irish, but everybody got behind them completely. For

two or three weeks there was absolute loyalty to the strike leaders. As a matter of fact, I had to get rid of the lot of them — 2,000 men. (John Docherty)

We have little appreciation today of how bleak and spartan life for the general British public actually was in the immediate aftermath of the Second World War. The first postwar Labour government (1945–50) ran into economic difficulties in 1947. The niggardly American loan, negotiated by J.M. Keynes in 1945, was exhausted by July 1947 and the resulting crisis was compounded by the worst winter since 1880–81.

The coal industry proved unequal to the demands placed upon it, resulting in massive cuts in supply, and extensive temporary lay-offs occurred. At the same time stocks of materials were so low that many factories shut down for periods of time to allow them to build up again.[12]

The combination of terrible weather conditions and shortages of materials also badly affected the construction industry which was, under any circumstances, extremely weather-sensitive at that time. The housing programme was cut and the Scottish hydro-electrification programme was reined in although, by its very nature, the fuel crisis underlined the scheme's long-term strategic importance.

The cuts in the current power plant scheme mean about 25% less will be installed than hoped for. Total expansion from 1945 will be 60% rather than the hoped for 70%. The authorities have issued the following appeal to the public: Do not use electric fires during peak hours, if you have another form of heating. Peak hours are from 7 to 9.30 a.m. and from 4 to 6 p.m.

Mr. J. F. Field, Engineer and Manager, Edinburgh Corporation Electricity Department, says: 'Sir Stafford Cripps' programme of cutting out extensions (to power plants) was dangerous, and would seriously affect industry. The Cripps programme of cuts is going to mean that the present restrictions will continue for several years.[13]

The resulting lay-offs, which inevitably affected Irish workers, might explain the otherwise startling statement, in May of 1947, by the Irish Minister for Finance, Frank Aiken, that 'Wages in Eire are better than those in Britain'.[14]

At the request of the new Chancellor of the Exchequer, Sir Stafford Cripps, a policy of wage restraint was adopted by the trades unions. As a result, wages in 1948 were, in fact, lower in real terms than in 1947, and between then and 1950 they rose by only 5 per cent while retail prices rose by 8 per cent.

Cripps's declared priorities: 'First are exports ... second is capital investment in industry; and last are the needs, comforts and amenities of the family' meant that, when the new US Secretary of State, General George Marshall, assigned $1,263 million from the European Recovery Programme to Britain from September 1948, the construction and civil-engineering industries were able to benefit directly since industry required infrastructure, and workers required housing and services.

By January 1952 the new Tory Minister for Housing was able to empower local authorities to issue licences to private developers to build houses, in favour of the public sector, at a ratio of 1:1 instead of the previous 4:1. Two years later the private sector was responsible for nearly 30 per cent of new homes. 327,000 houses were built in 1953 and 354,000 in 1954.

Shortages of energy and materials had been a fact of life since the early war years, and the efforts made then to overcome them continued in the construction industry thereafter. American pre-fabrication methods and materials, encountered during the war, were adopted piecemeal.

Construction of a distribution system from the Falls of Morar Power Station for the Morar district, Inverness-shire, is in danger of stopping due to materials shortages.[15]

Constructional variations to save steel are mentioned [in the North of Scotland Hydro-Electricity Board's fourth annual report]*, including the use of pressure tunnels instead of steel pipelines, and reinforced concrete in place of steel girders. Economies of up to 20 per cent in the use of steel were thus attained.*[16]

The various 'pre-fab' systems, although scaled down from domestic to industrial and public service applications (such as site cabins or school extensions), evolved steadily and new composite materials were developed.

Concrete came in pre-cast reinforced frames, slabs, and ready-mix. Timber came precision-cut in the forms of roof-trusses, or in composite form as plywood and chipboard. Steel was adapted for framework, and plastics found a multiplicity of uses. Plasterboard and glass benefited from architectural innovation.

Services (light, heating, ventilation, communications), and their associated materials and techniques, became ever more sophisticated and complex so that new trades evolved and associated costs rose, but so also did overall efficiency.

These developments were matched by the increased use of plant on site. Again the war provided the impetus. Labour, which began by being scarce, became increasingly expensive, and contractors responded by gradually introducing machinery for such labour-intensive operations as earth-moving, materials handling, and concreting. Tower cranes (over 200 were in use by 1954), hoists, loaders and excavators appeared alongside concrete mixers, and these items were increasingly hired rather than purchased.

The need to hire meant the need to plan, and operations became better synchronised and less ad hoc. Management and their clients became less tolerant of wasted time and resources, and more appreciative of operatives with skills and intelligence. Cash incentives were offered for increased productivity: contractors, instead of saying to operatives, 'Work hard or starve', were now increasingly saying, 'Work hard and earn bonuses'. 'Rational Economic Man' was at last in the ascendant.

None of these developments took place overnight; change was gradual and incremental, but inexorable. As with the evolution of nineteenth-century railway building, over time it produced more responsive and responsible contractors and a more streamlined industry, within which operatives gradually declined in numbers but (for a time) enjoyed better pay and conditions. Thousands of Irishmen and their families prospered during this period.

By 1966, 36 per cent of Irish-born males resident in Britain were allegedly working in construction. Such figures do not, however, give a truly accurate picture of the Irish presence in the industry at this time. They omit the long-term resident Irish (officially classed as 'British'). They do not take account those of Irish-descent who were, and are, an important constituent of the Irish presence in the industry. They are usually based on the numbers applying in a given year or inter-censal period for National Insurance cards. And, finally, they omit those working on 'The Lump' (see below).

'On the Fiddle'

The difficulty with figures based on National Insurance cards issued to Irish construction workers was the widespread abuse of the system in the pre-computerised era of cumbersome centralised records and alphabetical card indexes. Men avoided tax not only by working under fictitious names, but also by buying or borrowing the cards of others who had returned to Ireland.

How Tony came to have national insurance cards to sell I did not ask.... Afterwards I was to find out the practice of working on somebody else's cards was fairly widespread amongst Irishmen and women in Scotland. One man I knew was working night shift on the cards of a man who had gone back to Ireland, while drawing benefit from his own in the labour exchange.[17]

To avail of tax allowances and refunds many Irish men claimed for non-existent dependants — wives, children, elderly parents — then 'signed off' after eleven months, and returned to Ireland with their tax rebates. Returning to Britain at a later date, they assumed a false name (for example, turning 'Gerald Fitzpatrick' into 'Patrick Fitzgerald'), took out new cards, and repeated the procedure.

Fellas was cheatin', and messin' around, and they didn't know how to do it properly; they'd go back to Ireland, and they'd come back then under their mate's name, or some relation that was in the village, and they had two ration books.... A man would be goin' under the name of 'Flynn' in one place, and 'Murphy' in another place, and — the thing was, someone that knew them as 'Flynn' would be callin' them that in the other place, and — Oh! They'd hit a shkelp on you for that.... So, in our time you'd be callin' them, 'Young Man', or 'Shkan ('Skin'), or 'Cock', or 'Horse'.... You could yell out, 'How's it goin', Horse ?', and a dozen men might answer![18]

So widespread was this practice that a man might actually forget which name he was currently supposed to be working under. A myth persists within the industry that men actually purchased the cards of returning navvies the moment they stepped off the Dún Laoghaire boat, but certainly anyone working on the cards of a complete stranger, wherever obtained, could well have difficulty remembering his name in a crisis.

On the hydro schemes we always insisted that the men who were working under assumed names let us know; this information would only be divulged if someone met with an accident and we needed to notify next-of-kin. Even so, a lot of men were buried anonymously.[19]

This evasiveness was well understood at staff level throughout the industry, and not allowed to become an issue.

Coming towards the end of the season, every man was given a £100 pay-off but we'd keep one week's wages. At the start of the next season, towards the end of March, we'd send each man a telegram to come back; if he turned up, he'd get the week's wages from last season, plus £150 start-up money.

A lot of them came back all right — but with new names and new insurance cards, even though that meant they couldn't claim the back money.[20]

The industry at the best of times was never conducive to regularity, probity, and conformity in the workforce. Since the Railway Age it had been characterised by vagrancy, and economic uncertainty. Even in the mid-twentieth century this had changed little, and the same fundamental evils — carelessness and ignorance, on the part of the men, and indifference to their long-term welfare, on the part of the employer, persisted.

Our pensions weren't portable — what's the point of joining the scheme if it isn't portable? For staff and operatives who appreciated being well treated, there was an incentive to stay for the non-transferable pension, but a lot of hourly- and weekly-paid men didn't bother to enter the pension scheme.

We had 2,000 operatives on Pembroke Power Station in the late sixties, many of them Irish, and I wouldn't say anywhere near 5 per cent were on a pension scheme. Virtually all the operatives on that job weren't; there were a few special 'Tarmac' men — mixer operators, pile drivers, and so on, that travelled 'round the country, but they were very few because this industry was all casual labour. The average job was about one to two years; Pembroke, which lasted seven or eight years, was an exception.[21]

It is perhaps overstating the case to blame the employers entirely with regard to pensions. The recently retired Pensions and Welfare Officer at Tarmac Construction, Edna Beasley, noticed an underlying tendency in the men themselves which exacerbated the situation:

A lot of our former employees from Ireland suffered from a lack of education; when confronted with a letter saying, 'You are eligible to join our pension scheme', their reaction was, often, 'Couldn't be bothered'. Now, whether they really couldn't be bothered or, because they felt ashamed of their illiteracy, they wouldn't come to someone and say, 'I don't understand — will you explain it to me?' I'm not sure, but several of them said as much to me later on.

Ten to twelve per cent of those on Tarmac's pension scheme are Irish — plant operators would be the majority: navvy drivers, pile drivers, fitters, timekeepers. Men who held responsible jobs....[22]

Navvy Values

Sociologist A.J.M. Sykes' two well-known articles about Irish navvies ought not to be accepted uncritically. Basing his remarks on a period of field work on a hydro scheme in the North of Scotland, in 1953, Sykes makes certain statements about the Irish navvies employed on the project with which none of my respondents with relevant experience could agree. These were all men who had themselves worked in various capacities, and at different levels of responsibility, on similar Scottish schemes (Sykes doesn't name the site on which he himself worked).[23]

Senior management figures, both English and Irish, responded with horror to Sykes' allegations concerning the attitude of management and staff towards the ordinary workers.

The management and staff interviewed ... made no attempt to hide their contempt ... they referred to the men as 'animals' and the kindest estimates of them placed them as people outside society [24]

John Docherty, for example, considered this 'far too extreme' but conceded that:

The real employers of the Irish were Wimpey and McAlpine, who weren't really interested in a navvy unless he came into the office before he started and asked for a sub (an advance on his wages).... That was his real standing; if he didn't ask for a sub then they thought you couldn't depend on him, because he might disappear the following day. But if he got a sub he was tied to the company; he wouldn't just walk away without paying it. It was almost like a pawnbrokers.... [25]

Sykes supports his allegations with quotations from navvies such as, 'It's every man for himself', 'You've got to be able to look after yourself', 'You get no quarter in this game'; and, from the management side, 'This is a hard life and we are tough'.

None of these statements, however, amounts to more than the normal macho boasting of rugged men in a tough, dangerous, and dirty all-male working environment. As Sykes himself says, 'Both sides took a pride in the toughness and brutality of the industry'.

Sykes is inclined perhaps to read too much into the traditional spirit of independence prevalent in the construction industry. As has been frequently re-iterated throughout this narrative, the intermittent and transient nature of civil-engineering contracts fostered casual labour, and militated against both collective bargaining and company loyalty, and Sykes himself acknowledges this when making comparisons with other industries. To characterise the resulting worker–management relationship as more than normally adversarial is, however, to overstate the case, black jokes like the following notwithstanding:

One time McAlpine was inspecting a bridge works when an Irish navvy, carrying a bag of cement, fell into the water. When the men went to help him McAlpine called out, 'Save the cement, lads — we can always get another Irishman'.

Civil engineering, as opposed to building, is inherently hazardous and, in the past, was much more so because the manual input (and human error factor) was greater. Both contractors and operatives had to take chances, if deadlines were to be met and bonuses earned. This was clearly understood by all concerned.

Some of Sykes' assertions are well-founded. Compensation claims resulting from accidents inevitably provoked resentment and hostility, but the men, by adopting macho attitudes and resisting unionisation as an infringement on their freedom, abetted employers inclined to disregard safety procedures.

Without unionisation there was little prospect of 'working to rule' as a lever on management, and this was exacerbated by the navvies' work ethic:

The navvies' high valuation of individual work ability precluded any collective action to limit production or impose uniformity of earnings.

Sykes may have encountered some of the old-time navvies who had become embittered by their experiences and who viewed themselves, as did Patrick MacGill, as an 'outlawed breed'. The typical Donegal navvy of the early postwar period, however, was content to treat the hydro schemes as a more profitable variant on the migratory farm labour cycle, and generally regarded both management and conditions as a considerable improvement on those encountered on the Scottish farms which had hitherto employed him.

Sykes also alleges that the Irish navvies, mainly small farmers or the sons of small farmers, would not have admitted to being navvies back in Ireland. There has indeed always been some concern amongst certain sections of Irish society to avoid being associated with labouring life in England, and a man, once associated with it, might afterwards be pejoratively labelled for life — 'The Digger Donovan', for example. The Donegal miners with whom Sykes associated, however, took pride in being 'one step up' from mere tattie hokers, and a man who returned from the hydro schemes was looked up to by his community.

It was Sykes' contention that a man who was seen to be saving, on the hydro schemes, wasn't considered to be 'a real navvy'.

It was clear that the men who were genuinely saving were but a tiny minority of those in the camp. Attitudes to these men varied: some were admired, others despised as being miserly, but in all cases they were regarded as being unusual, as only temporarily in the industry, and therefore not accepted as real navvies.[26]

In fact, an Irish navvy in such circumstances would, if he wished to save, have to take devious measures to hold onto his money. Prior to the mid-1960s contractors paid wages in cash, and the navvies, particularly in remote locations, often had to carry accumulated sums on their persons for long periods. For the navvies, confined to remote camps, and with little diversion when off work, gambling was an insidious temptation, and a clever man would avoid giving the impression that he had ready cash on him when the 'Crown and Anchor' sharks appeared.

We were paid on a Friday, and I saw many men losing their wages in half an hour. There would be professional card players coming into the camp, they'd work in pairs and get the lads who hadn't been there long and fleece them. The lads would earn big money and then squander it. I go back up to Glasgow now (1995) and see some of them in a bad way, particularly the fellas who never married.[27]

Another parasitic breed were the men who travelled from site to site with the sole intention of 'cadging' from their workmates and then disappearing before pay day. Evading these took forethought:

You could sub 10s- a day for the first week — for your grub.... After that it was Monday and Friday, if you wanted it, but we didn't need it — it was good money for the time, really good money. Still, my mate and myself would be in the queue on a Monday and Friday, even though we'd have a wad of notes on the hip. You'd always send a few quid home, that time, but if you didn't, some of the 'Wide Boys' would be tappin' you, if you weren't subbin' ... they'd be

Spaghetti Junction, 1972 — Fr Daniel Cummins on-site with Irish workers.

looking for money off you, whingin'. Some of these had no intention of workin'; they'd get a few quid off you, they'd jack then and gone ... and you'd be down the pound, or whatever.

So by you goin' in the queue, get a pound sub or whatever, no one ever bothered us. 'Twas easier than refusin', know what I mean?[28]

Another variant of this behaviour was commonplace in the urban centres frequented by Irish navvies:

Then we had ... the guy who didn't like work, the 'dosser' as he was commonly known, whose mother/father died suddenly twice or three times a year — a scam to raise money or, in some cases, to get money to finance holidays.[29]

Obviously, most married men were there for no other purpose than to save, but even single Irish men, working in construction, automatically saved by virtue of remitting money back to their families.

I was always savin' so much a week at that time. Every decent Irishman sent so much home at that time; whether you wanted to or not, it was expected of you. You didn't even think what they were doin' with it at home.... You felt good about it; it was a bit of a religion, sort of thing.

Then, after a while, you realised they didn't really require your money at all, and you stopped sendin' it, when you got to about twenty-seven or twenty-eight. All they were doin' with it was puttin' it in the bank themselves, or the post office. A married man would be different, obviously.... A strange life, but the women back in Ireland, and the men over there, just took it for granted — they didn't feel anything odd about it.[30]

Perhaps Sykes was on the Loch Sloy site and there met older men who may have been conditioned by the pre-war ethos of the original 'Tramp Navvies'.

Tunnellers were one of the many post-war shortages when the Hydro Board first began its work....

Advertisements in newspapers all over Britain brought only a trickle of recruits, most of them veterans of the Lochaber and Galloway schemes, the only two major hydro-electric projects undertaken in great Britain since the 'Dead-End' days at the beginning of the century [a reference to Patrick MacGill's autobiographical novel, *Children of the Dead End*, set in Kinlochleven during the construction of the dam there]. *No more recruits came because more did not exist ... rock tunnelling was a lost art so far as Britain was concerned.*

The contractors and the Board put their heads together and started training schemes, using the old hands from Lochaber and Galloway as instructors.... Loch Sloy is a good example. A heading was run into the rock face there and was used purely for instruction. Slowly teams of tunnellers were built up.[31]

Of the Lochaber or Galloway Schemes, it was said:

When you first went into these camps there was not even beds. You went into a hut, you had a bed of straw, and you lay on it and then you went out into another place to get your food, well, it wasn't fit for pigs. No, it was not. You got porridge in the morning and ye got tea and bread and there was no dishes washed, no nothing. But you were just used to the roughness. You just would soon fall into the same way as the whole lot of them. Now on a Saturday night some of them would sing and some of them were good singers.

And then they would fight and they might fight till morning and they would start gambling — that's how the money went — a lot went on the Crown and Anchor. When a man would lose he'd be angry, he'd smash the place up. And his money was gone.[32]

In the main, however, the older men working on the Scottish hydro schemes were married, with families in Ireland to whom they were very firmly committed, and the younger men, as we have seen, did 'what was expected'.

Isle of Grain, outside London. Note the fleet of buses in the foreground. A man who 'jacked' before his shift ended would face a long walk home.

No Irishman with whom I've spoken, who has experience of these projects, recognises Sykes' extraordinary contention that 'No man was ever acknowledged to be a "friend" of another man'. Sykes, however, is quite insistent on this point, and devotes considerable space to it. He concludes:

> It is no exaggeration to conclude that the men followed a systematic pattern of avoidance: if one worked with a man one did not sleep near him; if one went out with a man in the evening one avoided him for the next day or two; and one did not go out with men from the same hut. No man was ever heard to speak of having a friend or a 'mate', and no one was heard referring to any other man having one. Each man stood alone as an individual.[33]

It is difficult to understand how Sykes could have gained this impression when the norm amongst Irishmen throughout the industry is so totally at variance with it. References throughout my own interviews to 'mates' and collective socialising are too commonplace to bear repeating. Even the notoriously individualistic 'Long-Distance Men', who might shun the group activities of the younger men, and walk off a site without explanation, were redeemed in the eyes of the latter by loyalty to their own kind.

> For all that, they're very loyal to each other and what one of them has is shared with the other who hasn't got it.[34]

Clearly Sykes succeeded in finding a most unusual assemblage of Irish navvies amongst whom to conduct his study. They don't appear to have conformed either to the old 'Tramp Navvy' ethos or to that of the post-war generation. His findings therefore ought not to be used unquestioningly when making assumptions or generalisations about the Irish navvying experience.

Visionary Works

Major civil-engineering projects proliferated through-out Britain from the late 1940s onwards. It was a time of daring and visionary civil-engineering works, carried out in a spirit of enterprise and endeavour, with enthusiasm compensating for experience in an atmosphere reminiscent of the pioneering days of the canals and railways of the eighteenth and nineteenth centuries. Once again, British administrators and engineers were promoting great public works which created opportunities for those willing to get involved. All across Britain, many thousands of Irishmen wandered at will from site to site, pursuing 'the big money'.

I worked 'on the buildings' from 1966 to the late seventies. I varied working in normal jobs (McAlpines, Laing, etc.) to working for 'subbies' — On The Lump (cash in hand). The money was £30 to £40 a day, good money then, I had been working longer hours in a pub for £10 a week living-in.[35]

Wimpey ('We Import More Paddies Every Year'), along with Laing, Mowlem, and McAlpine, constituted the government's wartime civil engineering and construction planning and advisory body and these companies took full advantage of this position to manoeuvre themselves towards securing a substantial share of the government's strategic postwar public works programme. Each of these companies employed Irish workers in substantial numbers, using their extensive network of wartime Irish agents for recruitment.

The provision of energy was an essential element in the programme of postwar reconstruction. The Scottish hydroelectric schemes spanned a twenty-five-year period, and represented a significant investment, but they had little impact on the nation's overall energy requirements. A massive campaign began in the later 1940s to construct coal- and oil-fired generating stations throughout Britain. A decade later a further programme of nuclear power plant construction began.

Fawley Oil Terminal and Refinery, 1952.

Complementing the new oil-fired generating plants was a planned series of refineries designed to replace imported oil, in ready-to-use form, with home-refined product sufficient not only to supply the power stations but also to make the country almost completely independent of foreign refineries.

World consumption had increased, from 265 million tons in 1938 to 475 million tons in 1948, but Britain's output was still only 3,500,000 tons. The new refinery programme was intended to achieve an output of around 20,000,000 tons by 1953, for an investment of over £125,000,000.

Such refineries, of course, had to be located around Britain's coastline, to facilitate off-loading from tankers, and required enormous sites. These included Grangemouth, Stanlow, Milford Haven, Fawley, Isle of Grain, Thameside, Teeside, Cruden Bay and Flotta (the latter two dating from the later North Sea Oil phase).

The Irish were present in large numbers on all of these projects but two in particular are especially associated with Irish labour (possibly because of their proximity to the large Irish concentrations in London and the South-East): these were Fawley, and the Isle of Grain.

Fawley

A refinery had existed at Fawley, on the west bank of Southampton Water, since before the war. Yearly production, however, was only in the region of 900,000 tons. An annual target of 6,500,000 tons output by 1953 — amounting to around a quarter of Britain's projected needs — was set for the new refinery.

Fawley was conceived on such a scale that by 1951 it had become the largest refinery in Europe. It was located on a 450-acre site, on the west bank of Southampton Water, about ten miles from Southampton Docks. A marine terminal with a 3,200-foot jetty was built by Christiani and Nielsen to accommodate four tankers up to 700 feet in length and 39,000 tons. The excavations were carried out by Wimpey

Construction. Employment peaked in 1950 at around 4,500 men and the project was completed, six months ahead of schedule, in September 1951 at a cost of £37,000,000.

The refinery's energy needs alone were double the requirements of the nearby city of Southampton, and necessitated the construction, by the Esso Petroleum company, of a private power station for its own use, which became one of the largest privately owned generating plants in Europe.

As if this were not enough, what was then the world's largest oil-fired power station in Europe was begun nearby in 1963. At that time it was the largest contract ever awarded by the Central Electricity Generating Board (CEGB). The 2,000 mega-watt station, supplied by a direct pipeline from the refinery, cost £20,000,000 and was completed in 1968 at the same time as the 130 mega-watt Esso Company private power station. Mitchell's were the main contractors. All in all, works at Fawley stretched over a twenty-year period, and employed almost ten thousand men.[36]

Isle of Grain

The Isle of Grain, forty miles east–south–east of London, was another long-term civil-engineering project even more closely associated with the Irish. Work began here in 1950 and continued until 1962. Two years after commencement, 5,000 men were employed on construction work for Sir Robert McAlpine & Sons, George Wimpey & Co., Costain-John Brown Ltd., Matthew Hall & Co., and the Motherwell Bridge and Engineering Company. Wimpey's contracts alone accounted for no less than £70 million, over all three phases of construction, including construction of the largest catalytic reformer outside the USA.[37]

Because of its proximity to London this project experienced a very high labour turnover. Situated at the tip of the peninsula stretching between the Thames and Medway estuaries, the site was isolated and inhospitable. Camp life was unattractive and men

Isle of Grain, Kent, 1956. A bleaker site so close to London would be hard to find.

tended to remain only for short periods. They could get back to 'The Smoke' with relative ease, but so also could the contractors' agents.

Earnings were soon dissipated and anyone anxious to 'build up a stake' again could remove himself to the Big Money and small diversions of the Isle of Grain for another stint. According to Malcolm O'Brien,

To save money one had to go outside London and work on the remote projects such as dams, tunnels, major road works, hydro works or power stations.

In this way, the project gave employment to thousands of Irishmen and became something of a legend in Camden Town, Kilburn, Cricklewood and the various rival 'Capitals of Ireland' around London.

Towards the end of the 1950s, while these projects were underway and the Scottish authorities were still commissioning hydroelectric schemes, contracts were already going out for the first generation of nuclear power stations. At the same time, work was beginning on Britain's first motorway, the Preston Bypass. It was the high point of the postwar boom in British construction, as the following extracts from *Labour News* illustrate:

The total gross construction output for 1957 amounted to £2,150 million. One sixteenth of those in employment in Britain work in construction and one half of the nation's capital was committed to the construction sector.

The total employed, both male and female, in building and civil engineering is 1,414,000, while 1,061,000 work in actual building and construction firms. In April 1957 there were 66,290 general building firms, of which 50,240 employ from one to ten operatives. Only 180 employ over 500 men. 29,660 had working principals only. There were 28,830 specialist firm employing 283,000 operatives.

Total working days lost in all industries in 1957 equalled 8,412,000, with only 84,000 (or 1%) lost in the construction industry. (27 November 1957)

Some indication of the volume and variety of works which lie behind the statistics for that one year may be gathered from Appendix 1.

The boom continued in 1958, with *Labour News* highlighting further developments. By 1960, despite worsening labour relations, public works went on apace.

Era of Energy

The 1950s were the era of energy. The bulk of the Scottish hydroelectrification schemes were begun or completed in that decade. Unofficial figures for these projects are as follows:

- There is a total of 67 hydro-power stations
- Original capacity for conventional hydro stations was about 1,100MW, upgraded by refurbishment to around 1,100MW
- Annual output of conventional hydro stations varies between 2.4 GWh and 4GWh
- Pumped storage schemes are 300MW at Foyers and 400MW at Cruachan
- There are 94 dams
- 57 of the dams are large dams on the ICOLD (International Commission on Large Dams) world register of large dams (dams over 15m high)
- A total of 200 miles of piped and open aqueducts was constructed
- There are 47 miles of steel pressure pipeline
- The civil-engineering works have a current cost-capital replacement value of around £1,800 million (sterling)

Simultaneously the various refineries, power stations, and dams south of the border got under way although some of these, as has been shown, were spread over the entire decade. We can gain some insight into the scale and extent of civil engineering in this period by looking at the project lists of just two of the major players in the industry at that time, Wimpey Construction and the Mitchell Construction Company. Both were substantial employers of Irish labour. As with the projects mentioned above, the following are listed in Appendix 2 as much to revive old memories amongst those who worked on them as to inform the general reader of the awesome scope of British post-war construction.

The Mitchell Construction Company, which originated as an engineering consultancy in the 1920s, took over the respected tunnelling firm of Kinnear Moodie just after the war and began to compete for major civil-engineering work. In the pioneering climate of postwar reconstruction, the company learnt as it went along, and soon established a formidable reputation as one of Britain's foremost builders of power stations and dams.

It was overexposure on one of the latter, the Kariba Dam in Kenya, which brought about the company's downfall in 1972, after which it went into receivership and was taken over by Tarmac. Before that happened, however, it had accumulated one of the most impressive project lists in the history of British civil engineering (see Appendix 3).

Other Mitchell undertakings too numerous to list separately included large chimneys (300–650 ft.), marine works, piling & bridges, tunnelling, pipelines & aqueducts, and site camps. The company was a good employer and gave work to a great many Irishmen during their time as contractors.

It would, however, be misleading to suggest that Mitchell's and Wimpey's were the only big players in this area of construction. Taking one element alone, dams for example, The British National Committee on Large Dams lists forty-four projects and their builders for the period, 1963–1983 (see Appendix 4).

The total value of these contracts was in excess of £1,302,604,000! Bearing in mind that they represent, over a limited time-frame, only one aspect of the many public works being undertaken at that time, they give a strong indication, not only of the scale of British postwar construction, but of the size and capacity of the civil-engineering industry. Private ventures, including building proper, add another enormous dimension to the picture. Such a list puts the Irish input into perspective. It is worth pointing out, however, that £113,040,000, or one-tenth of the total value of these dam contracts alone, went to the Irish-owned firm of M.J. Gleeson plc.

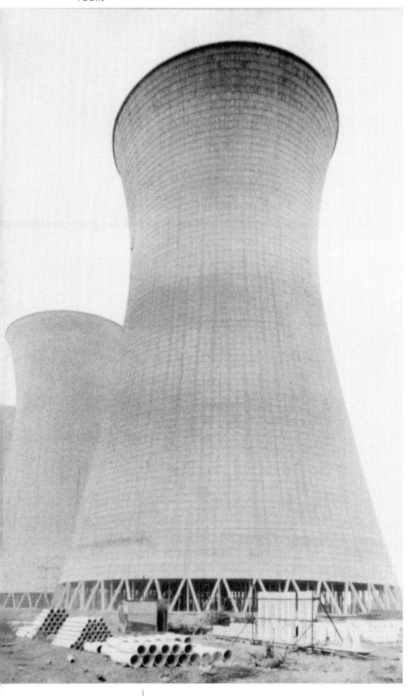

Above: Cooling towers — 'Only scaffolders with nerves of steel need apply'.

Motorways

The 1960s was the age of transport. This was the great period of motorway building in Britain, when British engineers and contractors for the first time confronted and overcame the difficulties inherent in this quantum leap in road-making, and work was attempted on a scale hitherto unknown outside Germany and the United States. Here again, the Irish were employed in large numbers.

It has been rightly pointed out that roads are unique amongst civil-engineering structures in that, firstly, a road never gets off the ground except on a bridge; and secondly, a road never gets out of the weather except in a tunnel.[38]

Therefore, building a road capable of withstanding the elements indefinitely, while accommodating ever-increasing loads and volumes, is an awesome challenge not usually appreciated by the general public.

Readers may have wondered why roads in Victorian and Edwardian tales are always 'dusty' or 'white' when roads are self-evidently black and smooth. They might consider the fact that not until 1930 was it possible for a British County Surveyor to announce that, 'All the existing main roads are now tarred for the first time in their history'. Even then, many secondary roads still had water-bound surfaces, as in Telford's day, while in urban areas wood blocks and setts were only beginning to give way to asphalt.

Coated macadam was coming into vogue but was still laid by hand — the average man laying 25 to 30 tons per day, the exceptional man achieving up to 45 tons. Given the unemployment crisis of the 1930s, it is understandable that men were favoured over machines, for road building, when the rate was only 1s. 2½ d. per hour. Consequently there was minimal emphasis on plant and a preponderance of picks and shovels.

Although some mechanisation occurred in the late 1930s — D8 s and 12-yard scrapers were in use on the Northwich Bypass in 1939, as were trenching machines, nevertheless,

... as late as 1939 it was possible to excavate narrow trenches as cheaply by hand as by machine.

Between 1939 and 1956 no major road works were undertaken in Britain. Petrol rationing wasn't ended until 1953 but the prioritisation of production for export, helped by priority allocations of steel, resulted in car manufacture jumping from 412,000 units in 1949 to 900,000 in 1955. By 1958 this figure had reached one million while a more favourable balance of payments, coupled with full employment, meant that much more output could be retained for the domestic market.

By 1959 British road mileage was only 16,769 miles more than it had been in 1911. The number of cars, however, had increased by 3,400 per cent over the same period. A clever illustration appeared in a British Road Federation booklet called 'No Road', in 1953, which showed a bicycle parked on the kerb of the A1 (Great North Road) in East Retford, reducing traffic on this major national trunk road to single lane working.

Pre-war plans for motorway construction had been shelved, but a ten-year programme, announced by Labour's Minister of Transport in 1946, included a provision for motorway construction. Even then it was necessary to pass the *Special Roads Act* of 1949 for this radical departure from the traditional 'all comers, all vehicles' philosophy of the Queen's Highway to achieve political respectability (especially during three successive Conservative administrations).

On 2 February 1955, plans were announced for government expenditure on road improvements of £147 million over a four-year period. These included motorways between London and Doncaster and between Birmingham and Preston. Preliminary design studies had been put in hand as early as 1951, with detailed design commencing in 1955, and construction (on the Preston Bypass) in 1956.

Given that '... a road depends upon the ground for support throughout its whole length, and for its entire life', little was known about the classification of soils and their behaviour under load. Soil mechanics was only in its infancy and site investigation, to determine

Above: Scaffolding inside a cooling tower.

the structure and geological history of soils, wasn't systematised until the Road Research Laboratory issued Road Note No. 29 in 1960.

Although only eight miles in length, the Preston Bypass, valued at £3,300,000, represented a historic undertaking in the history of British highway engineering. Necessitating two river and railway crossings, and the shifting of 3,000,000 cubic yards of muck, this project represented earthworks on a scale not seen in Britain since the great age of railway building.

Preston Bypass, 1959.

The Project Manager on this work was John Cox:

The Bills of Quantity made no provision for unsuitable muck, and when we had 14" of rain in the second month of the contract, it was bound to be difficult.... The plant for the earthmoving was that which had been used for open-cast mining and airfield construction and was not ideal....

There were Caterpillar D8s, Allis Chalmer HD 15s, International TD 20s, and Vickers Tractors with a variety of scrapers, together with Le Tourneau Model 'C' Rubber Tyred Scrapers, and a team of Euclid bottom dump wagons loaded by a Euclid Loader. Even an odd Sherman tank could be seen, as well as several large excavators from coal sites. Not a very easy contract.[39]

The London to Birmingham Motorway (M1), seventy-five miles in length, was

an outstanding example of civil engineering, completed at a rate of construction without parallel in Britain, and seldom, if ever, achieved abroad.

Begun on 24 March 1958, it was officially opened on 2 November 1959, nineteen months and nine days later; 183 bridges were built — an average of one every three days, and a mile of dual carriageway was completed every eight days. The cost worked out at between £250,000 and £300,000 per mile.

The Consulting Engineers were Sir Owen Williams and Partners of London and John Laing & Son Ltd was the main contractor. The work was offered to tender in four sections. Laing decided to tender for all four in expectation of receiving no more than two. However,

On 15 January 1958, the Author's Company were asked if they would be prepared to undertake the whole of the four sections. Although this proposal represented a commitment twice as large as that which they had originally contemplated and, in fact, was the largest single contract ever undertaken by one civil engineering contractor in Britain, they decided that they could accept it. On 20 January the Ministry of Transport awarded the contract for the four sections on a firm-price basis, for completion in 19 months and using flexible road construction.[40]

Given the unprecedented scale of the undertaking, and the relative inexperience of all concerned, this was a bold undertaking, brilliantly executed. That great authority on the history of mechanical and civil engineering, L.T.C. Rolt, described it as, 'an undertaking worthy to rank beside the great achievements of the pioneers'.

At peak, 4,700 men were employed, of whom so many were Irish that two special Catholic chaplains, Father Joseph Nolan (from Kerry) and Father Patrick McPartland (from Armagh), had to be appointed to look after their spiritual welfare. Father Nolan had responsibility for the men on Sections One & Two, and Father McPartland for Sections Three & Four.[41]

It was sometimes possible to say Mass in administrative huts, scattered along the route. But since the bulk of the workforce was housed in hostels and digs, scattered amongst the many towns and villages within busing distance of the works, and worked a seven-day week, disseminating information concerning the times of Masses and locations of churches was usually more practical.

This was achieved by contacting the workers on site, usually during tea breaks, and in the often harsh and bleak conditions Father Nolan found men grateful on the whole that someone other than company staff should show an interest in them and their welfare. He recalled the chaplains being frequently asked by Irish workers to write letters home for them. This says much for the level of education of these emigrant labourers. It was forty years after Ireland had attained independence, and some seventy years after Flora Thompson, then working as a country postmistress in Oxfordshire, recorded Irish harvesters coming to her in secret with requests to perform the same function for them.

Words came freely to the Irishman, and there were rich, warm phrases in his letters that sounded like poetry.[42]

Rolt makes the point that, while the average number of operatives employed per mile was seventy, the nearby London & Birmingham Railway required no less than 225 men per mile when it was built in the 1830s. The disparity is accounted for by the presence on the M1 of plant with a combined strength of 80,000 brake horse power.

By the early 1960s, motorways were costing £1 million per mile, and by 1970 this had escalated dramatically to £2 million per mile. It has been calculated that the 100,000 tons of building aggregates needed for each mile of motorway would have been sufficient to build 2,000 detached homes.

A508 Junction at Collingtree, on the M1, 1959.

The early rural motorways were themselves relatively simple affairs compared with those through urban conurbations such as the one-third of the 66-mile-long Midland Links Motorway linking the M1, M5 and M6, which was viaduct-carried through the heart of Birmingham. One three-and-a-half-mile section became Britain's longest continuous motorway viaduct.

The number of main contractors involved (ten) is indicative of the complexity of this undertaking. The famous 'Spaghetti Junction', at Gravelly Hill, Birmingham, was Britain's first multi-level inter-change. From a projected overall budget of £110 million, the route through the Birmingham conur-bation accounted for no less than £70 million.

One Tarmac estimator put the percentage cost of labour on a normal motorway project at 20 per cent.

by a consortium of Tarmac, Costain, and the Dutch company, HBM.

Thames Barrier

Each sector consists of a hollow steel gate, fabricated from 40mm curved steel plate, fixed to giant steel disks at each end. For most of the time the gates sit in concrete recesses, flush with the river bed. When high tides threaten, hydraulic machinery rotates the gates into a vertical position, with their curved surfaces facing the incoming tide.... It is one of the most distinctive maritime engineering structures of the 20th century.[43]

This project, the greatest 'dam' ever built in Britain, cost approximately £420 million over ten years, and Barratt estimates that Irish labourers took home approximately £170 million of it.

The labour force at peak was almost 80% Irish — first or second generation, although very few came directly to the project from Ireland. They were mostly star Men from Tarmac, Costain, Balfour Beatty, especially the 'travelling men' who operated plant (two of our crane drivers actually had wooden legs!) These got subsistence money wherever they went since they were, in effect, homeless.

Hiring was done largely on recommendation, and interviews were held in the 'Black Prince' pub in Bexley at 7 a.m. each day; if a man couldn't make the interview how was he going to make the job? We had the General Foreman, the Section Foremen, and a couple of local union reps. who could identify the 'toe rags' from the locality who might make trouble.

Early on we found out that some union reps were taking bribes of up to £500 to hire men from amongst the Dartford and Woolwich Irish populations, but we had to go carefully — a strike there could cost £1 million a day![44]

Above: Irish Chaplaincy scheme in action. Fr Nolan on M1 site with Laing machine and temporary parishioner.

This means that the labour content of the above project amounted to £25 million. The Irish are believed to have accounted for around 40 to 60 per cent of the workforce on most civil-engineering projects during the era of direct labour. Therefore it is possible that as much as £15 million went into the pockets of Irish workers on the Midland Links.

Dudley Barratt, a Londoner, worked on the M4 for muckshifters Dick Hampton & Co. where he claims the drivers of the 636s, D4s, D6s, and D8s 'were all West of Ireland men'. This is the firm which features in Philip Donnellan's film, *The Irishmen*. In the early 1970s he moved to Costain's where he was appointed Labour Officer on the Thames Barrier project which was built

Preston Bypass, 1958.

Spenser Steelworks, Llanwerh, South Wales, 1962.

Model of the Thames Barrier.

Militants

Most of this money was earned by people in the metal trades — such as welders, steel fixers and steel erectors, — and it is Barratt's belief that much of the labour unrest of the period originated with them.

> *Any site, of any size — power stations especially, were 100% unionised. The very militant metal trades were infiltrated by Trots. The rates for the same trade differed between civil and mechanical engineering and each had its own Working Rule Agreement. Civil engineering is defined as all works up to ground level, and is typified by motorways, roads, harbours, etc. Typical mechanical engineering projects would be power stations, refineries, oil pipelines, etc. A lot of the steel erectors on Fawley Power Station were Northern Irish.*[45]

The unionisation of the trades elements of the construction industry was widespread and effective in the 1960s. John Docherty recollected having to deal constantly with union officials on the major projects which he managed at that time.

> *I used to spend at least one day a week in Transport House, dealing with the unions, but that was all settled when two things happened: Maggie got tough with them, and Nissan came into this country. They showed us how to handle labour; they said, 'Look, we're dealing with one union, no more! If you don't agree, then we don't come here'. On an average construction job we had to deal with at least three or four unions.*[46]

How well or badly labour relations proceeded on a given site, however, had much to do with the attitude of the employer. Mitchell's, a company with an excellent reputation as an employer, fared very well in those years of labour militancy. One Mitchell contract heavily reliant on the metal trades was Fawley Power Station.

> *Excavation for the foundations descended to 75 feet and the basement structure was so large it would have been possible to float two liners the size of the Queen Mary side by side within its walls. Because the station was located on the low-lying foreshore, the construction called for extensive coffer dams and similar works: one sheet steel pile envelope alone enclosed an area of nearly 10 acres.... In spite of the difficulties on the site and the often appalling working conditions, we were able to reap the benefit of our good labour relations. In the three years we were working at Fawley we did not lose a single day through strike action. The response of the men to their own achievement was magnificent and we were, in fact, asked by the CEGB if we would take over the erection of the structural steel work because, apart from ourselves, labour relations on the site were very strained. We had to decline because this would have involved us with another union and good labour relations are not a question of instant gimmicks: they have to be built up in a spirit of mutual confidence over a long period.*[47]

Barratt's 'Trot' accusation may have had some basis in fact; certainly the British Communist Party seems to have been remarkably active in the construction industry if Brian Behan is to be believed.

> *I was elected to the National Executive Committee of the Communist Party ... what we wanted was control over the site so that we could use the union machine to put over our particular brand of socialism.... Actually, if the employers had started behaving decently ... we'd have been most disappointed and would have set about inventing some grievances.... For my efforts on the Festival [of Britain] site I had received the knighthood of election to the Communist Party Executive.... It was either the sack or give over control of the site to us, with the firm simply doing whatever we told them. In any case, a lot of our effort was to pose as 'militants' even if we gained nothing else. This pose would give us the support of the workers in their unions.*[48]

Perhaps the most famous strike in the industry in those years was the South Bank strike during the building of the Shell Centre by Sir Robert McAlpine & Sons. The strike, which lasted six weeks, gained support from construction workers at site from Abbey Wood Housing, the Belvedere Power Station, and the *Daily Mirror* site amongst others. McAlpine sacked all 2,000 workers from the site. This was, arguably, Brian Behan's finest hour.

> *I only had eyes for organisation. Four thousand men, five years a-building. Link them to the Isle of Grain, the Atomic Power Station at Bradwell, and you had an army of twelve thousand. Imagine 12,000, enough to run a newspaper, buy a loud-speaker van or to cost over £100,000 a week if they all went slow together.*[49]

The extent of Behan's influence is reflected in the fact that the *Glasgow Herald*, so far removed from the scene of the action, saw fit to print the following on 31 October 1958:

Steel erectors, 1960s.

Brian Behan, brother of Brendan, was yesterday expelled from the Amalgamated Union of Building Trade Workers for his unofficial activities connected with the stoppage at the Shell building site at South Bank, London.

'Brutish and Boring'

By 1971, when the M25 orbital motorway around London was under construction, there was still plenty of civil engineering work available for the Irish but the specialised manual skills, along with the challenge and mystique, had gone out of it. Someone like Bob Geldof could apparently stroll over from Dublin, and step into a T23 muck-shifter on that project, without even knowing how to drive.[50]

Amongst the men in the motorway camps, Geldof encountered 'an unmistakable warmth and clannish-ness', to which the unconventional middle-class city boy responded enthusiastically. He saw them as 'cowboys ... a wild collection of men ... who had come to terms with a kind of living'. Many, though not all, were Irish. He had no inclination to emulate their lifestyle.

> *... despite its humour and its rewards and the fact that I was making a lot of money, ultimately I found it brutish and boring. I didn't want to live outside the constraints of society, I wanted to live within society, ignoring the constraints that bothered me, or perhaps changing them.*[51]

By the early 1960s motorways were costing £1 million per mile and by 1970 this had escalated dramatically to £2 million per mile. It has been calculated that the 100,000 tons of building aggregates needed for each mile of motorway would have been sufficient to build 2,000 detached three-bedroom homes.

Victoria Line

The other great transport-related projects of the post-war period were the electrification of the main line rail system, and London Underground's Victoria Line. Electrification proceeded throughout the 1960s and 1970s and both conversion and refurbishment generated employment for thousands of Irish labourers and sub-contractors. Both Domhnall MacAuligh's book, *An Irish Navvy*, and John O'Donoghue's biographical work, *In a Strange Land*, contain vivid descriptions of the ubiquitous railway plate-layers, who were almost a throwback to the Railway Navvies of the Victorian era.

The Victoria Line, 11.5 miles long from Walthamstow to Victoria, was 'the first new tube across central London for over half a century' and came twenty-one years after the last section of tube railway to be built by London Transport.

Eighteen months before work began, two experimental lengths of twin tunnel, one running from Finsbury Park to Manor House and the other from Netherton Road (Tottenham) to Manor House, were built at a cost of £1 million. The Finsbury Park–Manor House section was lined with concrete block segments of a new pattern, and the other section used a flexible-jointed cast-iron lining without bolts. No grouting was required with either system. A rotary type of shield, known as a 'drum digger', previously only used to excavate a sub-aqueous tunnel, was introduced and speeds of three and a half feet per working hour, a world record in clay soil, were achieved. This was double the speed achieved using previous techniques.

Work on the Victoria Line proper began on 20 September 1962, six months prior to the centenary date of the world's first underground railway, the Metropolitan from Paddington to Farringdon in London, and the new line was formally opened by Queen Elizabeth II on 7 March 1969.

This project gave employment to thousands of Irishmen, most especially tunnellers, and attracted much press coverage at the time. What everyone wanted to write about were the soft-ground miners, 'Kings of the underworld', and the majority of these seemed to be Irish. 'I'm telling you', said pit-ganger Tubby Buesden, half Cockney, half Australian, 'If it wasn't for the Irish there wouldn't be a single bloody tunnel built in England'.

London Transport was paying John Mowlem £2 million to build the three-and-a-half-miles of tunnel between Victoria and Oxford Circus in 1966. According to site agent John King, many of the miners were

earning five times as much as some of his site engineers.

The men worked in gangs — seven for a 30-foot diameter tunnel, five for a smaller one — and appointed a 'ganger' to negotiate contracts on a section-by-section basis with the General Site Foreman, Sid Eastoe. Each section was known in the trade as a 'Workshop' and was let to individual gangs for an agreed price.

The basic rate in early 1966 was 6s. 8½d. per hour. The question to be decided was how many hours Eastoe, known as 'The General', was willing to pay for a given section. That in turn was determined by the tunnel diameter, which dictated the number of rings required to line it, and the rate of progress measured in rings per shift. For example, a five-man gang, working a twelve-foot diameter section, could be expected to complete three rings per shift on average.

The gang might then be offered eleven hours per ring per man. This would give each man 33 hours at the basic hourly rate, or a day's pay of £11 1s. 4½d. or a week's wage of £55 6s 1½d. A 30-foot tunnel might be offered at a rate of 60 hours per ring per man. A normal shift was eleven hours, plus two half-hours for breaks, but the gangs worked flat out and often achieved more than the agreed target. The men would, in fact, expect to average £100 per week, or more, and often did.

For the men's part, the determining factors were the conditions — the width of the section, how far the 'workshop' was from the shaft, how many skips for loading the 'muck', how many 'pony men' to shift it, what the track was like below. The ganger would use this information to decide what rate his gang would accept.

They took the sixty-degree heat sixty feet down as a given, and expected to flout the safety regulations by ignoring the hard-hat rule, while wearing only knotted handkerchiefs, vests, old trousers and heavy boots. What they were going through was sand or gravel or, usually, London Blue Clay — in reality, dark milky brown and the consistency of hardening putty.

The pneumatic drill shovels weighed nearly 50lb and were operated from a platform of planks when digging out the upper part of the section. The clay lumps were thrown by hand onto other planks and shovelled into skips. The noise was so loud that instructions were given by hand signal. Once the correct width and height had been excavated, the rings were put in place and bolted together. These segments, weighting from 6cwt. to a ton, were placed by a hydraulic 'ram', although it was traditional to put the topmost, final ring in position with head and shoulders.

The macho ethos of the Irish soft-ground tunnellers, mainly from Mayo and Donegal, brought them big financial rewards, but their disregard for health and safety often proved disastrous in conditions where compressed-air workings exposed them to the risks of 'the bends' and bone necrosis disease.

Chaplains

Many of the projects mentioned above carry names to conjure with. They have gone down, in the annals of construction history, as landmarks in the lives of thousands of Irishmen and, indeed, of their families. The late Father Joe Taaffe recalled his experiences as chaplain to the Irish working on Pembroke Power Station in Wales:

Shift break, tunnel crew, Victoria Line, 1964.

Above: Wylfa Power Station, North Wales, 1964. Navvy guard of honour for Bishop John Pettit. On his left is Fr Kieran O'Shea, Chaplain at Wylfa from 1964 to 1969. Note that only the clergy are wearing black shoes.

I was brought to Wales ... as a chaplain in one of the workers' camps housing the workers who were building the power stations at the time.... I had a room in one of the huts, same as the men themselves.... You would have had up to 1,000 living on the camp. The majority of them were Irish....

It was a very lonely life, particularly for the married men. It was very hard for them. Coming up to holiday time, to Christmas time, the atmosphere was electric.... Some of them used to get home a long weekend every six weeks, some got that every eight weeks, it varied according to the firm. But it was a different story the night they came back. On the coach coming back from Holyhead there would not be a word, not a word, heads down.

These would have been hard, tough men.... Sometimes in the summer their families would come over for two weeks' holiday to the locality (staying in caravan parks)....

The men who came into the camps first were men who had worked on other sites and they were solid men... In this camp they could get home every eight weeks or so. But in the years before this, when they worked up on the hydros in Scotland, they couldn't get home. They led a strange and lonely life, unnatural — and their wives had to be father and mother to the children, which was tough on the women as well. When the father came home, he had presents for the children, but once he went back the task fell completely back on the women.[52]

Fr Owen Sweeney, chaplain on the McAlpine-run Llanwern Steelworks project at Newport in South Wales from 1959 to 1962, spoke of the Irish on site as follows:

> I came to appreciate the inestimable value of their contribution to human well-being. I came to regard them as the true nobility of society, humble, hard-working men who rarely complained about their lot.[53]

'Unnatural'

The ramifications of these 'unnatural' domestic arrangements were far-reaching, and often harmful to all concerned. John Healy noted some of the consequences:

> [W]ho, even to this day, dares put words on the social evil of the young wife left a prey in a lonely hill home for ten months of the emigrant year?[54]

The children of these intermittent marriages, not unlike those whose fathers were in the armed forces abroad during the two world wars, had their own special experiences to relate:

> From childhood until well into my teenage years my father worked in England to support us. We could not survive on the sixteen acres.... The small pale blue envelope ... arrived every two weeks. The few pages of a letter and the postal order. It was our financial lifeline.
>
> My father normally came home twice a year, in summer and at Christmas.... There was a fixed routine to the annual journeys back home by my father.... My mother made sure the four of us — three sons and a daughter — had our faces scrubbed to angelic brightness with a towel lathered with Lifebuoy soap before we piled into the van for the trip to town.
>
> My father's first stop was Moran's pub in Rush Street, Castlebar. It was something of a ritual....

> Many of the gathering there at Christmas were themselves just home from England. Men in wide pin-striped suits, hair Brylcreemed down.... The talk was of Wimpey's, McAlpine's, Murphy's, Taylor Woodrow, the big firm my father worked for. Of hydro-dams, power stations, undergrounds, motorways, the chances of a start on big contracts soon to begin....
>
> I always found the first few days awkward. The routine we had followed week in and week out was disrupted. There was now a 'MAN' of the house. A man taking over the bits of jobs I did every day around the house and farm. A man to divert mother's attention away from us.
>
> And often it seemed that, just as my childish huffs had been overcome and we had melted into a complete family again, it was time for him to go.
>
> We came to know the tell-tale signs: a full array of shirts flapping and straining on the clothes line. Mother and father talking in low, serious tones.... Clutching at words of reassurance.... 'The months will fly by'. The pile of washed shirts ironed and stacked neatly. The suitcase taken down from the top of the wardrobe.... And then he was gone....[55]

It is interesting that Tom Rowley identifies his father's work in England over many years with one specific firm, Taylor Woodrow, suggesting the continuity and relative security of the 'company man'. Yet the family was not 'brought over', and the holding sold, as was the case with very many families in similar situations in the 1950s and 1960s.

Even seasonal migration took its toll on families:

> Seasonal migration robbed me of a father.... My parents were living for nine months as if they were separated. My mother reared us on her own — she had all the work to do. There was children, there was women, there was no men — they were all away.

The same childhood estrangement experienced by Tom Rowley blighted these lives also:

When he was away we'd look forward to all the lovely presents, but initially he was like a stranger. You had the big clean-up before he came, but we had to get to know him all over again.[56]

It sometimes happened that a man, deciding to return or just in need of access to his savings, found that the money had been squandered. Some wives were spendthrifts, or bad managers, while others used these resources to finance their escape from an unbearable situation and set up house elsewhere with another man.

We can tell you about people where the man scraped and scrounged and worked all the hours God gave, and sent the money home, and then, at the end of his working life, or maybe before that when he went home, there was nothin' — it was gone!

There was a man livin' in Tamworth, near Lichfield, Billy — I can't tell you his surname, but he was married, and he had a family, his wife had left the convent, and that fella was a demon for work — he worked all the hours God gave, and sent everything home, and he was on 'The Lodge' as well — getting subsistence.... And eventually the job finished, and he went home, and she had gone — and everything with her.

We have heard of several instances where men had gone home, and there was nothing in the bank, the wife had just frittered it — after years.... It must be devastating for a man to have that happen.

The life they were leading led to a lot of marriages breaking up, because the wife was at home, with the children, and in a lot of cases took up with another man....

It's a very lonely life for a woman — if she's not on the spot, with the husband. You become very, very independent and it's very hard to adjust, when the man does come home, because you've been used to doing your own thing....

We found this difficult ourselves, and I can honestly say — hand on heart, that it's only in this last twelve months that we have really settled.[57]

An estimated 43,000 adults and 44,000 children returned to Ireland in the 1970s as a result of the short-lived turnaround in the economy. Young couples seized the opportunity to return and raise their children in what they perceived to be a better environment. For many, however, this was a time of disappointment and bitterness as work petered out, or small businesses failed, and many returned to Britain to start again.

'Company Men'

However, a number of older men, possibly with families in Ireland who had not migrated, did resettle successfully. These were in the main steady men who had worked hard and saved their money. Many others, however, chose to settle in Britain and either married or, if they had families, brought them over from Ireland. Apart from the few successful entrepreneurs almost all would have been 'company men'.

It is for this reason that Sykes' controversial contention, that a man who gave anything approaching long service to an individual firm was regarded by his fellow navvies almost with contempt, is hotly disputed by veterans of the industry with whom I have discussed the issue. There may have been some element of truth in it while 'on the job', but there is little doubt that, beyond those confines and in reflective moments, such men were often envied by their fellows.

The large numbers of Irish navvies who did stay with one firm or settle down in a specific locality often enjoyed a modest prosperity and live fulfilled lives.

The majority decided to put down roots, and provide for their families. Without exception, those who have chosen to settle in England, and not go back to Ireland, have subsequently purchased their council houses. You go into their houses and they've altered and renovated them — absolutely smashing.... And there are photographs on the sideboard of their sons and daughters, who've gone to university in England, and really made good, and they're absolutely thrilled to tell you how well their kids have done.[58]

This, of course, is the opinion of only one person, expressed in limited terms, but founded on a lifetime's experience attending to the welfare needs of Irish workers in one of Britain's largest construction companies — an experience that would have been replicated across a range of British firms throughout the industry.

These are the 'silent majority' amongst the postwar Irish construction workers — neither wealthy 'subbies' nor sad derelicts, but solid, responsible citizens with comfortable homes and successful children. It is impossible to quantify them, but they have left their mark on Irish communities throughout Britain in the form of well-supported schools, social clubs, associations, welfare centres and charitable institutions.

They retain their loyalty to Ireland but are generally well assimilated and respected within the wider society. There may in some instances be question-marks over their relationships with wives and children, but these are secondary to their success as emigrants. They are neither alienated from their own kind, like so many successful contractors, nor marginalised by the host society, like the numerous homeless, alcoholic, or otherwise disadvantaged casualties of the construction industry in Britain.

They can justly claim to have found 'gold in the streets' — not a fortune, but a modest prosperity sufficient to hold their own on either side of the Irish Sea. Their reward was modest indeed in proportion to their efforts. When we consider the scale and extent of their achievements, we could do worse than quote Wren's epitaph:

Si monumentum requieres, circumspice
[If you seek a monument, look around]

9 Private Fortunes

Oh Mary, this London's a wonderful sight
With the people all workin' by day and by night
They don't grow potatoes, nor barley, nor wheat,
But there's gangs of them diggin' for gold in the street.
(Percy French)

Between 1951 and 1961 over 400,000 Irish emi-grated from the Republic to Britain, in almost equal gender proportions. The numbers leaving in the 1950s were of an order of magnitude not seen since the peak years of post-famine emigration.

In 1955, 48,000 emigrated; by 1957 the annual figure had risen to 58,000; and in 1961, when the population reached an all-time low of 2.8 million, as many were leaving as were being born.

The entire country, both rural and urban, was affected but the collective trauma being experienced by large numbers of the rural Irish was comparable only to that of their Famine-era forebears. This fresh exodus was also comparable to that of the mid-nineteenth century in that, coming at a time when British labour was 'trading up' from manual and servile to skilled and sedentary work, uneducated Irish emigrants were leaving home equipped only 'to labour and to serve'.

Poet and academic Brendan Kennelly recalled young men coming to him in County Kerry in those years requesting that he write them a ballad as a memento of their 'home place'.

The ballads I wrote were simple and straight-forward — and all for men. No woman ever asked me to write one. It was a time of bleeding; the villages and countryside were bled, week after week.[1]

Journalist Sean Duignan, speaking at the Parnell Summer School in 1996, described an assignment in the late 1950s to cover the train–boat–train journey being taken by hundreds of young emigrants bound for London or the English Midlands — an area described complacently in the Irish school history books of the time as 'A country of slag heaps and dirty-looking canals.'

To carry out his assignment, Sean took the train from Sligo to Dublin on a Monday morning in April

1957. As he travelled through the little towns and junctions of the west he saw the carriages fill steadily with morose youths and red-eyed girls carrying cheap suitcases. As home receded, with each passing mile they gradually lapsed into silent reveries, punctuated by bouts of weeping.

He spoke of ageing fathers painfully parting with their sons on station platforms, their eyes haunted by the bitter knowledge of failure; and of mothers pleading with daughters to 'write regularly and keep the faith'. John Healy's grandmother, whose daughters all emigrated to the United States, in contrast exhorted each of them to, 'Keep your mouth and your legs closed, and send home the slates'. This was code for the remittance money which, amongst other things, would finance home improvements like the replacement of roof thatching with the more durable slates.

Later the same evening on the Holyhead boat, Sean Duignan witnessed other, older men, the landless siblings perhaps of those same fathers, and veterans of many partings, trying to comfort these young girls while holding down their own quiet desperation.

John Healy recalled similar scenes from his own boyhood in a small Mayo town:

> *The train would pull into Charlestown to a crowded platform ... the mothers who had come down to see a son and daughter off ... bit their lips when they saw the still-crying strangers from down the line.*[2]

Above: Catching the *Cambria* at Dún Laoghaire.

Above: A last sight of land.

The following unsolicited letter, written by Jack Foley in June 1999, gives this more than adequate corroboration:

> *I come from Charlestown, County Mayo, and my part of the country was full of emigrants to England from the forties to the sixties. Of course, during the war years and before there was some emigration, but it was mainly to 'The Farmers'. After the war workers went into the Building Industry because work was easier — you had a bed to sleep in instead of a bale of straw, and there was the company of the pub....*
>
> *I grew up with stories of Long Distance Kiddies who would ask for 'A Pint or a Light' in a pub of a Saturday night, but who could still put in a good day's work on Monday....*
>
> *Of my own family of nine all emigrated except two. One of my most poignant memories is of my parents saying goodbye to my oldest brother, Tom, as he left to catch the bus at the end of our boreen. As the bus took off and my brother waved up at the house, my mother ran down the road calling for him to come back.*
>
> *I was about six at the time and I went to my mother and asked her why did she let him go if she wanted him to stay? By the time the last of us had left, I'm sure the pain had dulled.*

Beyond some rudimentary personal networking if they were lucky, most of these young people, often little more than children, received no meaningful training or preparation for this traumatic move.

'Connaughtmen and Horned Cattle to the Far Platform, Please'

All they knew was that they were following a well-trodden path, and that the signposts were many; the caustic cry of the railway porter, 'Connaughtmen and horned cattle to the far platform'; 'Paddy's Milestone', the huge column of rock in the Clyde Estuary; and the midnight train from Stranraer to Glasgow, locally named 'The Paddy'.

One of the most emotive was 'The Irish Mail' from Holyhead to London, with its mantra of stations — Holyhead, Chester, Crewe, Stoke, Rugby, London Euston. Camden Town, just up the road, known as 'The Capital of Ireland' because it was, allegedly, 'the farthest an Irishman can walk with two full suitcases'.

For thousands of Irish men and women these names had a resonance which, in this age of shuttle flights and transnational contracts, may be difficult to comprehend. Met with in that order, they represented degrees of despair, but when reversed — Euston, Rugby, Stoke, Crewe, Chester, Holyhead, the sequence became the rhythm of the rails, and gladdened Irish hearts as it drew them closer to the boat for home.

No one who experienced it will easily forget the pungent smell of frightened cattle, fouled with dung and urine, being herded onto the boat at Dublin's North Wall, bound for Liverpool, while their human equivalents tried to suppress the unreasoning urge to fight their way back onto Irish soil before the gangway was finally withdrawn.

St Brendan's Hostel, Barnes, London, 1962.

For decades these boats were miserable tubs with a bearable first-class section, which few could afford, and a chaos of second-class 'accommodation' which, for many, translated into finding just enough space to lie down — in cabin gangways, on luggage racks, or on hardwood seating out on deck.

> The Liverpool boats were the cattle boats. The cattle were let out first; the cattle were treated better than the people. I used to find that very depressing. The cattle were down below in the hold, you could smell them. The passengers were just sort of up above, on open decks, it was very primitive.... Other people just wouldn't understand this experience of going across the water on that boat.... 'People slept wherever people could sleep, on the toilet floor, on the stairs, on the tables.[3]

The crossings were often rough, the passageways sometimes awash with puke and porter, but if the boat was bound for home, the little bar would ring with songs, fiddles, accordions and laughter, while sometimes rangy men, with west-of-Ireland faces, cut a few spirited steps in wide-legged trousers out on the swaying floor.

Going 'over', almost the only comfort they had was the certain knowledge that they would find work. In those long decades of economic hardship, unemployment, 'closed shop' trades union practices and fee-paying schools, young Irish labourers arriving in Britain all started off more or less on the same level playing field. All they had was energy, enthusiasm, the strength and stamina for unremitting outdoor labour — and an enormous demand for what they had to offer.

'Paddy's Bible'

As defined by Sir Malcolm McAlpine, the golden age of the Irish navvy in British construction was the 1940s through the 1960s. Labour News, by then known affectionately as 'Paddy's Bible', carried a list of subheadings indicative of the range and extent of the work available to them:

> Building News
> Public Works (Water Supply, Sewerage & Sewerage
>   Disposal, Roads & Bridges)
> Around London
> North-eastern Developments
> Scottish News
> Educational Buildings & Extensions
> Government Contracts
> Contracts To Tender
> Local Authorities Housing Plans
> Contracts Placed
> Classified

The advertisements were correspondingly varied (see Appendix 5 for a random selection from 1956).

The first of these advertisements indicates a most useful service which enterprising navvies, anxious to rise above mere labouring, might avail of to put in bids for work, without actually having mastered the intricacies of estimation and bidding.

The last advertisement shows the remarkable progress already made over the previous decade by two such men, Joseph and John Murphy of Caherciveen, County Kerry. Theirs was to be perhaps the best known example of the spectacular rise to wealth and influence of the postwar Irish navvy. It is a great pity that neither of them has ever evinced any willingness to see their story told.

At the height of his powers in the early 1960s, Joseph Murphy is reputed to have told a precocious young management consultant:

> If I didn't earn £2,500 every hour, of every day, of every week of every year, I'd be bankrupt![4]

Labour News also carried advertisements for hostel accommodation, which many single men preferred to either 'rooms' or digs, especially in the 1940s and 1950s (see Apeendix 5):

These commercial hostels were a welcome innovation because, by the 1950s, the old Victorian Model Lodging Houses ('The Models') had been demolished. This was a great loss to the remaining Long-Distance Men or Tramp Navvies who were still active in the industry. Most of these men were now in their late fifties or older and, if they were still moving about, had no family or permanent address.

Pincher Kiddies

Bill Brennan (who found a home in Arlington House and a place in the *British Medical Journal* as the only individual on record with ten clubbed fingers, smashed on site) came under the influence of the old 'Pincher Kiddies' as a youth. He learned the techniques of tramping from them, in England, in the 1940s:

> The Pinchers never advised any of us younger men, 'Learn a trade, don't settle for this'.... They'd never take another man's tools.... Each had his own, washed and spotless, tied up with a leather strap — their own 'graft', fork, foot-iron.... These were often pawned in Ryan's of Warren Street on a Saturday. The foot-iron was a great thing; you strapped this strip of steel under your boot between sole and heel to protect the leather from the digging. Out in a place like High Wycombe, flinty ground, boots without the foot-iron wouldn't last a week.
>
> They had a kit bag, with a billycan, and a ball of twine and a six-inch nail for hanging up your billycan when you were sleepin' out. The best place to 'skipper up' [sleep out] was always under a palm tree — the water was all carried out to the ends of the leaves and wouldn't drip down on your clothes. The old Pinchers always told me, 'When you're in a town, always walk to the kerb, not near the doors, so if someone comes out at you, you can dodge'....
>
> They knew where everyone was — if there was a job, they'd tell you, better than today. But they had the wanderlust — no matter how good the money, or

the job, how well they were treated, for no reason they might say, 'I'm jackin' — I'm off'. He might be diggin', you might be chasin', and he'd just look up.... 'Ah, it's time I was movin' on', and he'd just walk away.... You mightn't meet him again for two or three years.

> They were a great race of people — a mighty people. Regimental men — not educated, but they knew their work ... better than any machine today. Neat, and tidy, and yet they'd maybe be sleepin' under hedges. You'd know them by the neck-scarf, and the moleskins, and the 'Yorks', and the hobnail boots.[5]

Jim Gallagher also commented on the legendary footloose character of the Long-Distance Men, with whom he worked in the 1950s, saying that such a man might be beside him in the trench, when,

> The head would come up, and look around, and he'd reach over for his jacket, and be ready for the off, like the mountain yew [the nomadic hill-country sheep of the west of Ireland].[6]

These men were unsuited to the new-style hostel accommodation, which was run along military lines, and often staffed by ex-servicemen. Only the Rowton Houses, such as Arlington, still retained to some degree the sort of semi-charitable system that had characterised the pre-war lodgings of the tramping fraternity.

> *A lot of men went into digs that shouldn't have been there at all — they'd wet the beds, an' all that, they couldn't help it. The 'Pincher Kiddies' — the 'Milestone Inspectors', their kidneys were weak from years of sleepin' out under hedges.*

Damping Down the Bed

The younger generation weren't always suited to good-quality accommodation either, but for different reasons. The pernicious habit of 'damping down' the bed was widespread amongst heavy drinkers. This weakness for drink, frequently coupled with unfamiliarity with the niceties of indoor sanitation, may have been at the root of some of the notorious 'No Blacks, No Irish' accommodation signs the 1950s and 1960s.

Such problems also plagued those responsible for providing sleeping quarters in the camps connected to the major civil-engineering works — hydro schemes, refineries, motorways and power stations. Conditions in these camps, as shown above, were often bad in the early stages but, as Malcolm O'Brien's career path illustrates, they improved steadily as time went on.

Malcolm is the perfect example of an Irishman rising 'through the tools' to a senior position within the industry after the Second World War. Born in Limerick in 1932, he was educated to Intermediate Certificate level by the Irish Christian Brothers, then attended Limerick Technical College where he obtained Building and Civil Engineering Certificate grades 1, 2 and 3. What that amounted to in the real world emerges below:

1. *1947 — Commenced apprenticeship as Carpenter/ Joiner Limerick. Contractor — O'Sullivan Builders.*
2. *Building houses. Foreman Carpenter. Sub-contractor Steve Fitzgerald.*
3. *Shannon Housing Society. House building. Site Manager.*

MOVED TO LONDON 1950

1. *North Thames Gas Works. Foreman Carpenter — Shared site caravan with General Foreman.*
2. *London Ferro-Concrete — Foreman, Pre-cast Concrete Erection. Lived in Digs.*
3. *Annan Power Station, Chapel Cross, Scotland — Chargehand Carpenter building concrete Cooling Towers. Large Work Camp. Conditions good. Food plentiful but very plain: Mince & Mash; Soup in plenty. Long hours. Very wet weather. Large work force travelling by bus from all over south Scotland and northern England.*
4. *Blue Streak Rocket Range, Gilsland nr. Carlyle (Wimpey) — Foreman, Rocket Range.*
5. *London — Southern Gas Board, Foreman Scaffolder; Walker & Slater, Multi-storey Office Blocks (Foreman); Wimpey, fourteen-storey Office Block, Edgware Rd. (Site Foreman). During this period I lived in a flat at Finsbury Park, London.*

London postwar — No problem with getting work — shortage of labour. Carpenters & Masons esp. required everywhere. Normally one lived in a 'room' — Bed & small wardrobe. One had one's meals in a café. Most Irish spent their leisure time in the pubs.

Daily Progress — Rise early — work twelve hours. A few pints after work — and food if you had any money left. No one saved any money (maybe, very few). The landlady might give you a 'sub'.

6. *Aberystwyth, Wales — Dam, Capelbangor. Chargehand Carpenter. Lived in pub at Capelbangor.*
7. *Oban — Loch Awe Hydro Electric Scheme — Chargehand Carpenter. Very rough job. Bad Camp. Nissen huts & Gas Heaters. Grass carpet in summer, mud in winter. Mostly Irish & west of Scotland men — very hard workers. Poor local labour.*
8. *Tawse Dam (Edmund Nuttall): — Chargehand Carpenter — tunnel work underground — not very safe. No site canteens here — you had your break where you stood.*

9. *Trawsfynydd Nuclear Power Station, mid-Wales — Chargehand Carpenter. Now we have better working conditions. We are now looking after the men's welfare. The works camp is first class. General all-round better working conditions. Work force from all over Great Britain & Ireland.*

10. *Aultboy, Rosshire, northwest Scotland (NATO Base): I built a very big camp here, prior to the work commencing; things were getting better.*

Malcolm O'Brien joined Tarmac Construction in 1963. His career continues:

1. *Pembroke Dock. Regent Oil Refinery. Lived in digs.*
2. *M5 Motorway Birmingham. Lived in flat in Birmingham.*
3. *Monmouth bypass. Working on the river Wye. Lived in cottage in Trelleck.*
4. *Hamilton bypass, Scotland. Lived in Manor House — Botwell Park House.*
5. *Derby Link Road. A61 & 6, Allestree. Lived in Tarmac caravan site.*
6. *Gloucester bypass. Lived in Tarmac caravan site.*
7. *A74 (Carlyle). Major road works through bogland.*
8. *A23 London/Brighton. Major Fly-Over.*
9. *Yemen. Roads Project (1971) — Tarmac/Trapp/Heilkamp. Lived in Tarmac Camp in Yarin with family. Worked most of the time in 'Fly Camps'. 3,000 men on this project. Many killed in accidents. Project prepared for 'Ex-Pat' deaths; had my coffin stored at British Embassy!*
10. *Oman, Persian Gulf (19 Power Stations Project).*
11. *Masirah Island, Indian Ocean — A hurricane destroyed the oil installation. I set sail from Muscat, Oman, on a landing craft, the 'Tarmar', with 60 Asian workers. We towed our camp behind us (approx. 10. No. Living Units). We successfully carried out repairs to the installation and returned to Muscat 9 months later.*

12. *United Arab Emirates — Abu Dhabi, Dubai, Sharjah, Al-Ain.*
13. *Oman — Salalah on Sth. Yemen border. Complete & hand over Airport Project.*
13. *United Arab Emirates — Sales of plant & equipment in Gulf Area.*
14. *Saudi Arabia — completion of Residential Complex, Jubail.*
15. *Algeria — Completion of 21 No. Sites Med. Coast to Southern Sahara.*
16. *Channel Tunnel Trackwork (1991).*
17. *M6 widening Project.*
18. *Rochdale Town Centre Bridge (world's widest).*
19. *Tarmac Railway Division — Refurbishment of twenty-five rail sites in Cornwall.*
20. *1997 — Retired from Tarmac.*

Malcolm was awarded the MBE in 1994, in recognition of his services to the British construction industry.[7]

Malcolm O'Brien's story would have many parallels throughout the industry. He got off on the right foot with a trade, prior to leaving Ireland, and made his way in the industry by gaining wide experience all over Britain. This made him a valuable asset to a major construction company with international contracts and many different divisions. In the nature and extent of his achievement he represents the quintessential Irish 'company man'. In the course of his early career, however, particularly during 'the London years', he flirted with the more uncertain world of the 'lumper', which attracted and held so many of his generation.

Once a man had 'found his feet', and knew his way around construction work, he had ready access to employment and simply had to decide whether he wished to work 'on the cards' or 'on the lump'.

'On the Cards'

Working 'on the cards' carried many advantages; a man would enjoy reasonably good working conditions such as canteens, wet weather gear, and transport subsidies.

He would receive holiday and national insurance stamps and, in most cases, the benefits of trades union agreements. The downside was registration with the Revenue Commissioners, weekly rather than daily wages, occupational demarcation, and pay restrictions determined by the industry's negotiated rates. Bonus and overtime earnings would follow a curve, from start to finish of a job, and the 'big money' would be on offer for only a relatively short time on any given project. A man who elected to stay with the firm couldn't simply 'jack' to follow the big money elsewhere.

Above: 'Looks good!' Pay day on site.

'On the Lump'

Working 'on the lump' gave a man cash-in-hand on a daily basis and, often, a negotiated bonus determined by output. He avoided the payment of income tax, and was able to decide if and when he would work, without reference to a boss. If he was a good worker and put in the hours he might, given a good employer and abstemious habits, amass large sums of money quite quickly. According to Tom Durkin, 'People on "The Lump" — working outside the Agreement — got paid better money at the end of the week for the measured-up work'. Smart men bought houses for cash in the larger cities, when property was cheap, and rented these out to other Irishmen.

The downside was vulnerability to exploitation — 'No money if you stopped for the rain', poor working conditions, typified by the absence of wet weather gear or covered transport, abuse by agents and gangermen, and the complete absence of any holiday, sickness, pension or unemployment benefits. The absence of these cost many a man dear in later life. The greatest demand for casual labour was in the major urban centres where pub culture predominated and many men developed a dependency on drink, which undermined both their welfare and their health.

A lot of men moved freely between these two situations according to the availability of work, rates of pay, and personal inclination, at any given time:

> *I worked 'On the Buildings' from 1966 to the late seventies. I varied working in normal jobs (McAlpine's, Laing, etc.) to working for Subbies 'On the Lump' (cash in hand). The money was £30 to £40 a day, good money then; I had been working longer hours in a pub for £10 a week living-in.*
>
> *It was 'hard going' with the subbies; most wanted 'everything done today' — presumably they were trying to stay one step ahead of the revenue people!* [8]

Malcolm O'Brien refers to the fact that, in this environment, 'The Irish spent most of their leisure time in the pub', and acknowledges that 'no-one saved any money' and they ate only 'if they had any money left'. Those who wanted to save money went outside London to remote camps where there were fewer opportunities to spend it.

Some of the reasons why the pub was the favoured recreation centre have already been alluded to and included peer pressure, loneliness, and inhospitable accommodation:

> *The Irish, when it came to drink, were no better or worse than many other races. It was the old 'Give a dog a bad name' bit.... They were not really wanted by the landladies. They were forced to live in rooms where they looked after themselves, caravans when*

possible on sites; they were forced to the pub by loneliness, lack of identity, culture shock and, very often, the language was a problem.[9]

A fundamental reason for the popularity of the pub was, of course, a simple love of drink. But there were others:

'The Crown' in Cricklewood was our Mecca. If you wanted a job, or wanted to know where work was coming up, or if you were known as 'A worker', you could always get drink 'on the slate' or a loan of a few quid, 'til you got back on your feet. Or, if you were stuck for a place to stay, you had a word with the guv'nor (from Galway) and there was always 'A room upstairs for a couple of nights'.

There was an unwritten rule — you could rob a bank or whatever ... but you did not 'welsh' on a loan, and you fixed up your drinks bill when you got 'the start' on some job.

'The Crown' was like 'Rick's Café' in Casablanca — everyone went there, sooner or later. People who moved around got their letters from home addressed to 'The Crown'; it was basically a rough 'n' ready sort of place.[10]

For the Irish navvy the central place of the pub in the life of the labourer could be a mixed blessing. There were less benign views expressed to me about it than those set out above:

Many Irish manual workers were exploited by the major companies and, to a lesser extent, by their very own in the pubs, the digs, etc.

'The slate' was quite common in a lot of the pubs; couple that with a feed of bacon and cabbage and, before long, the bill had grown to quite a bit, especially when multiplied by six or seven days.

Another racket was charging the desperate worker ten shillings to cash a cheque, so that, by the end of the week, many unfortunates had very little to draw after wiping the slate clean on a Thursday or Friday. They had no choice but to start another, and so on....[11]

From the mid-1970s onwards, when payment by cheque became standard industry practice, many publicans changed cheques for the men. A favourite 'office' in London, for example, was McGovern's on the Kilburn High Road (Peter McGovern, coincidentally, had been guv'nor of The Crown from the late 1950s until the early 1970s). While this establishment may have been exemplary, there were many complaints, often from the wives of Irish labourers, about the practice of giving a man so much off his cheque, early in the evening. 'I can only let you have so much now, Sean; there's a dozen men up there ahead of you' (which was probably true), then he would be left to drink the bulk of it while he waited for the rest, until maybe ten or eleven o'clock that evening.

Other pubs noted for cashing building cheques were 'The Grove Tavern' and 'Biddy Mulligan's' in Hammersmith. In the former men put their cheque, through a pigeonhole-sized hatch, and awaited the outcome, which could take all evening.

Bill Brennan, understandably, took perhaps the most jaundiced view of pubs and publicans:

Payouts in the pub — Subbies'd say, 'I haven't enough to pay you it all now; I'll give you the rest here tomorrow'. So you'd drink what he gave you, and still have to come back to the pub again the next night to get the rest.... Instead of payin' you abroad where you were on the job.

I was workin' for 'X' (a publican-cum-contractor) below in King's Cross, on the railway, when the gangerman, who was sound, said to me, 'How much is X payin' you?', and I said, £17 a day, which was good money I thought. And he said, 'I'm bookin' in £28 a day for you to the Railway'. X never came near that job; he paid me out in his own pub in Camden Town. So you were conned every way; the landlady, the subbie, the fella in the boozer....

Nowhere to dry your clothes.... If you came in a bit excited, with a few bevvies on you, and the landlady

The Crown, Cricklewood — a Mecca of the Irish navvy.

didn't like it, she'd throw you out then and there without any rent back, knowin' she had plenty more tenants, just to hang onto your few pounds....

Jumpin' out of a van in the evenin', soakin' wet, into the pub — no such thing as goin' home to change, and the rain soakin' into you.... That's why all the old men (most of them are dead now), you see them goin' around with sticks and crutches. When you were young it didn't seem to affect you, but now it's got into their bones, dried into them....

You'd often see the steam — they had the open fires those times, see the steam comin' out of their clothes, or even drippin' out of the old donkey jackets down onto the floor.

And, with a few bevvies on you you'd get the wrong change — give in a ten pound note, get back change for five, complain and get thrown out....[12]

English *v.* Irish

There were many adverse comparisons made between the Irish and English operatives in this regard. Generally, although the Irishman was regarded as the harder worker, the Englishman was considered to be a steadier individual in terms of dependability and lifestyle. One Irish subbie, now retired, gave me his views on the subject:

The Irish were able to work; it was a case of 'brute force and ignorance'; they had stamina, they were young, they were used to workin' out of doors at manual work.... The English were a bit softer — eatin' out of chip shops and so on, but a good English worker — and there were plenty of good ones — could be better than an Irishman.

They had schoolin', for a start — they could read; so if someone dropped a load of a thousand bricks they could read the note and know what was delivered. They were conscientious — not always drunk in the mornin's; the Irish were often that drunk, you'd have to carry them into the wagons.

The English were steadier — they had no axe to grind; they were at home already.[13]

Asked why, therefore, the Irish were in such demand in preference to Englishmen, this man put it in a nutshell with a few succinct sentences:

Most of them left Ireland with no education, no money, just to get away from fleas, and hunger, and clay floors. The hungry people emigrated; they would do twice the work, for half the money, and they would do it faster!

Frank Munnelly, now a college lecturer living in Dublin, was the third generation of his family to leave Mayo to earn a living as a labourer in England. While Billy O'Grady subbied through the 1960s and 1970s, Frank worked 'on the buildings' in the 1980s. Nevertheless, in this regard, the fundamentals had not changed. As Frank put it:

The English weren't 'cute hoors'; they wouldn't recognise an opportunity, a 'double bubble' — a job that might be stretched into Saturday double time, in the making.... they just wanted a 9 to 5 job; they would say, 'I need a job', whereas the Irishman would say, 'I don't want a job — I want to make twice the amount of money I'm making now, but in half the time'.

There'll always be a job there for somebody who will do a job which nobody else wants to do, if you can do it quickly![14]

This begs the question, of course, of what the Irishman did with all this money. A 'company man' could reasonably hope to invest in a home and his children's education, and perhaps a pension, and

tunnellers had a reputation for saving (witness the lovely modern homes dotted around west Donegal). The footloose navvy on the London or Manchester or Glasgow scene, on the other hand, working 'on the lump' for subbies, was a different story. Bill Brennan was in no doubt about which route he should have chosen:

You were only workin' for the drink — clothes and digs; the rest went on 'Bevvy'. Worse than slavery.... If I had my life to live over, I'd have taken a trade or I'd have gone with some big firm, and when my day was finished I'd get my little pension....

With McAlpine, they had a system which was very good, I think ... you could save what you wanted — £5 or £10 or whatever, out of your wages; 'twas kept back, and they put it in the bank or post office for you. A lot of people done it and built up a nice little bit against old age.[15]

Eileen Doyle recalls the relative consideration shown by Sir Robert McAlpine & Sons towards their permanent workforce in this regard as early as the 1930s:

I do know the firm was always ready to help their staff. As a child when my parents were in Crete and my grandmother and her daughter were living in our house, I can remember that cheques would come from company HQ for a part of my father's salary to cover household expenses such as rates, etc., and my school fees.[16]

Bill Brennan was clear as to which nationality took the wiser course:

The Englishman had a different system. He said to himself, 'Right — so much for the Old Woman, so much for the fares, so much for the fags, so much for the papers...' and that was all put away. If he had the price of a couple of pints left, he'd have a couple of light ales; Paddy would laugh at that and say, 'Its only a cod, them oul' light ales'. Paddy was drinkin' big pints of strong beer or stout, wolfin' them down him, but the Englishman was sober in the mornin', while Paddy was as sick as a pig.

Paddy was a 'Hero', but the Englishman had his system — Paddy had no system, except put the hand in the back pocket on Monday mornin', and only when it was empty did he have a system, 'That won't happen next week' ... But next week it was the same....[17]

Subbies

As Liam Walshe put it,

The routine was, we got paid on the Thursday, and got 'The Sub' the following Monday, and our time was spent in the pubs and the bookies, and our rooms were only for sleeping in. Our mission in life was to shovel....[18]

Yet there were other Irish navvies who neither went to seed, nor became contented company men, but showed initiative and pulled themselves up out of the trench and, in some cases, into a Mercedes.

Achieving this, however, was no easy matter and called for qualities of energy, ambition, even ruthlessness. Such qualities were practically all that distinguished these men from the thousands of their contemporaries who left similar backgrounds in Ireland with no money, few skills, and little education, seeking a 'start' in the construction industry. How did they do it?

'You need a bit of "go" in you — a bit of arrogance, even stupidity. It's no good being made of milk and honey!' was Billy O'Grady's typically forthright answer.

Tom Durkin from Mayo was a veteran of the hungry 1930s, and a lifelong socialist. Nevertheless he took a typically pragmatic view of the forces driving such men:

An Irish contractor, to be competitive, he's not a philanthropist, he can't be.... and some of them are the worst because they've come up through the exploitation themselves, and feel it's fair game — 'we're on top now and we'll do the same'.[19]

Billy O'Grady was quite adamant as to the psychology at work in these situations:

If an Irishman gets on top of you at all, he'll use his hobnail boot to keep you down; they go alone....

He went on to describe leaving Ireland as a boy emigrant in 1954, aged thirteen, with his entire family:

We had no house here — all's we had was hunger and fleas. We come from oul' farmers' 'Love Children', not registered, nor named, nor nothin' ... 'Round here (South Wexford) they took all these children — priest's children and the like, up to Barnacoille. They were brought up there where no one knew who they were.... It wasn't unusual in them days for someone to give away a daughter's love child to a friend or neighbour. The first child always went to the grandmother to rear — the parents weren't married then, because they had nothin'.... When the second one came they got married then. The first child was never any good — they got too much!

In Manchester we lived over a butcher's shop; my Saturday job when I was at school was delivering the horsemeat from the butcher to the 'Bombay' restaurant....

A natural businessman, Billy worked his way up from labourer to subbie, with various entrepreneurial detours along the way:

Most of the contracts I had in England were for eighty to a hundred houses — there was very little money in it. They were only givin' you enough to pay your wages.... They'd count how many men you had on site — say you had 50 men in one week, at £3 each per day; they'd say, 'OK — 50 x £3 is £150; plus £20 for his van, we'll give that, plus £20 for himself'. You wouldn't make much....

You'd maybe give the Quantity Surveyor a tenner a week for himself, and he'd put you down for another £30's worth of work. Take him out for a meal, get him drunk, any oul' backhander.

If a Clerk of Works was causin' too much trouble, he might be set up; they'd cut a plank part through, and put it across a water-filled trench on a wet site, so it'd give way under him. Send him off home to have a good wash!

Counties by Merit

He was an astute judge of men who formed firm opinions as to the relative merits of the different counties' manpower:

If you were diggin' out a road, you'd mark off every thirty-five yards with a piece of chalk, and tell a new man: 'If you can't finish that before this evenin', don't come in tomorrow.'

You'd ask a guy where he came from, to see if he can work.... Donegal — a bit fiery, but a good worker; Roscommon — intelligent, decent, and a reasonable worker; Leitrim — probably OK; Cork — let him stand at the gate, lettin' the wagons in and out! Limerick — a bit of a buzz, orators....

The higher and hillier the ground the better the workman — like the mountain hare....

On this last point Billy's judgement echoes that of Charles Jones, the continental agent for the great Victorian railway contractor Thomas Brassey:

It is found that all the people born in the mountains, and on poor lands, have more virtue than those who are born in the plains, and in luxurious places.

Importance of the Navvy

Also echoing this informed opinion, from the golden age of the railway navvy, is Billy's insightful assessment of the importance of the humble navvy in the wider scheme of things on site:

A navvy on a construction site in England is probably the most intelligent man on the site. A roofer puts roofs on; A brickie — it's one on top of two....

A navvy — he's got to know where to unload things, so's they're not in the way; He's got to control the site; he's got to take levels; he's got to put ducts in; he's got to concrete; he's got to put services in; he's got to bench the manholes; he's got to put the pipes in....

He doesn't just make up a shovel of 'muck' — although he can do that too.... A proper navvy has to do a million and one jobs. You have to be quite intelligent to know the different jobs — start a dumper; make sure there's oil and diesel in it; mix 'compo' for brickies; get a load out on the scaffold; make sure there's not too much 'stuff' on it; keep the Trades goin'; organise unloadin' gangs; don't unload stuff where it'll have to be put back on the wagon, and shifted again, in the mornin'.

A good groundworker's job [the term 'navvy' was dropped from official usage in 1960] *is more complicated than that of any tradesman....*

Pride

Asked to explain their motivation, Billy said, simply, 'They liked to get things right — it should look 'Right'; it was a matter of pride.' This pride, as reflected in the old navvies' care and treatment of tools, has been remarked on in earlier chapters. The issue of pride goes very deep. There is a great emphasis on it amongst men who have put long years of service in the construction industry behind them. It underlies their approach, not only to their work, but also to their social relations. It has its roots in the enforced egalitarianism of poverty, and the collective responsibility to which this gives rise.

Billy O'Grady, who probably knows more about humble beginnings than most men I've interviewed, refers back to the 1930s to explain it:

In the thirties the only thing that was keepin' people goin', who had nothin', was to try and keep themselves clean, and keep themselves out of the limelight.... Pride was the only thing they had to keep the head goin'; Bless themselves, and be proud.

The phrase, 'keeping themselves out of the lime-light', is also very significant. In the small, tightly knit rural communities from which most of these men emerged, such enforced proximity carried both positive and negative implications. The positive implication was that they developed a very strong sense of 'belonging'; the negative implication was that they carried a concomitant obligation to conform.

Most of the time all this rested lightly upon them. Once in Britain, however, the situation became fraught with tension. The family was replaced by the fraternity of the workplace. In that community your name was your mission statement — get a bad name, and you were nothing.

A 'bad name' could come about for many reasons; theft from your comrades, viciousness, unreliability in teamwork, failure to look after your dependants, or a

desire to be 'different'. The best protection against this fate therefore, it was believed, was never to stand out from the crowd.

Perhaps the most conspicuous form of being 'different' was to manifest ambition. Frank Munnelly was also a student at the time when he was working on site in England. However, he was very careful not to allow his workmates to learn this:

If they knew you were a student, that you had ambition, they would consider that you were using them, their whole world, as a mere stepping-stone to something better. Far from endorsing your value system, however, they would consider you as less than they were and turn away from you.

Gangermen

Another route to finding a surrogate 'family', however, was to become a 'company man' — not in the sense used here formerly, but as the agent of an Irish employer.

The pecking order.

Any subbie who possessed leadership qualities recognised that he needed one or more devoted lieutenants — and that the best motivator is ambition. However, he would already be aware that his own attempts to better himself had put him outside the community of his fellows, and would therefore realise the difficulty which must be presented by bringing others along with him, while keeping them in a subordinate position.

The next step was to make this new status official by publicly raising his wages and giving him the status of 'ganger'. From that point on the man, unless he went out on his own, had a foot in both camps. His life was spent on site with his men, but his status placed him in authority over them. Nevertheless, in common with the other employees, he remained a subordinate.

Such men often gave total loyalty to one employer, serving him for a lifetime, without accruing any

Cross-country cable laying near Carlisle, 1952.

A good judge of character would choose men who desired to have more than their mates — whether money or status — but lacked either the intelligence or initiative to go after it alone. A subbie, for example, might single out one individual, and secretly offer him a personal bonus for increased output. That man would then find ways to push his fellow workers and, if he had a dominant personality, would in time become their unofficial leader.

significant wealth for themselves, because the organisation was now their 'family'. They were, however, in a sort of No Man's Land, and depended on the loyalty of their employer for that feeling of 'belonging' so crucial to the psychological well-being of the rural Irish.

Nevertheless, these agents and gangers could only serve well by driving their erstwhile workmates, and so ran the constant risk of making themselves deeply unpopular. Some were fundamentally decent men, and successfully walked this tightrope all their lives. Both Sean O'Ciarain and Bill Brennan have already referred to men of this type. But most earned a well-deserved reputation for brutality, ignorance, and callousness, which was made all the more outrageous for being directed against their own countrymen.

When I was a Junior Engineer with McAlpine's, there was a perception that, when an Irish labourer was promoted to ganger, he was the sorest ganger of the whole lot, on his own people, people he'd worked with before he was promoted. I always thought that came from an attempt to curry favour with the employer.[20]

Sean O'Ciarain's observations, made at close quarters while working as a navvy, bear out John Docherty's managerial perspective on this issue:

The Irish navvy ganger would not be long thinking about telling a man to go down the road, and without much regard for the rights or the wrongs of the matter ... he was like the rooster on the top of the dunghill. And he showed no mercy to the fowl scraping about below him....

The main attribute of a typical ganger man was often not so much his knowledge as his ignorance. A man with a dominant personality, coupled with servility towards his bosses, was ready-made for the job, toadying up to those who were over him and bullying those who were under him, and that is how the majority of them were.... The straight decent man was to be found amongst them, but he was in the minority, and taking them in general, a Scottish ganger was a better man to work under than an Irish one.[21]

The behaviour of the Irish seems to have compared badly with that of their British counterparts. Bill Brennan felt strongly about this:

If you were workin' for an English foreman, and you were on an extra rate for somethin', the Englishman would see you got it; but Paddy would book it in all

right, then put it in his own pocket, immaterial of counties, like....

That's what caused all the trouble in the pubs and dancehalls.... Everyone was just duckin' and divin'. One Friday night in 'Auntie's Bar' in All Saints, Manchester, Paddy Noonan and a couple of other lads who had been workin' on a priced job for Murphy out in Bury came in to get paid off by Hartnett, Murphy's agent.

Hartnett told them, 'That's not what we agreed at all, lads — You're not owed that much'. Noonan knew Hartnett always carried a big ball of notes in the back pocket, so he tore the pants off of Hartnett, took out what he was owed, and told the lads to do the same, and give him back the rest. The guv'nor had to loan Hartnett a pair of pants to go home in'.

The majority of the Irish navvies and 'RB1s' with whom I discussed this issue held views similar to Bill's. They reserved their strongest criticism for those gangers employed by Irish sub-contractors (and for the 'subbies' themselves), most of whose work was with the main public service providers — Post Office, Gas Board, Electricity Board, rather than with the major civil-engineering contractors.

Paddy Flavahan, himself a former subbie, says of British versus Irish foremen:

If you done your work for a British foreman he treated you all right. Some Irish foremen were clannish and wanted to know what county you came from, and how much you could drink.

Irish sub-contractors exploited their own people; they picked them up and dropped them off at the pubs, and if you weren't a drinker you were the 'odd one out'. One sub-contractor from Birmingham went back to Ireland owing a lot of money to little people, including a friend of mine who supplied building materials — a very honest man; this sub-contractor went back owing him thirty thousand pounds — a lot of money for a 'One Man Band'.

Me and my partner went bust in 1969, through no fault of our own, but we paid all the one-man bands — little people that we knew depended on it to feed the family. Tarmac & Roadstone had to wait for their money.

We finished on a Friday. I started up again on Monday with a gang of five men. Me and my partner are still the best of friends. We kept small after going bust. We ended up all right; we still go out and supervise jobs for friends.[22]

Probably the best-known and most notorious of Irish gangers from the postwar period was 'Elephant' John O'Donoghue, from Caherciveen, County Kerry. Born in 1934, he emigrated to Britain aged sixteen. He began his working life as a labourer with fellow-Caherciveen man John Murphy. Six feet two inches tall, and weighing seventeen stone, he soon became a ganger and eventually an agent for Murphy. He died in 1999 after 45 years' service to the Murphy Company, with whose management he was reputedly very close.

It is interesting to note the conflicting opinions expressed about this man following his death. The firm contented itself with a short statement to the effect that he would be 'sadly missed by his family, friends and colleagues'.

The *Irish Post*, in a piece by reporter Ronan McGreevy, quoted a long-time friend and colleague, 'Concrete Mick' O'Sullivan at some length:

If you worked hard and did a good day's work, you got well treated. He got things done and people respected him for it. He was known across the length and breadth of Britain. I have found that the people who didn't like him were those who didn't know him. If you did know him, you would have found him to be one of the nicest people you could meet.

He was quite simply a legend and a great character. He had a wonderful sense of humour, loved playing practical jokes, and he was very generous if one of his men came into bother or needed money for an emergency.[23]

This piece prompted a letter from the widow of a former employee of Murphy's, a woman named Mariad Ó Suilleabhain, in which she recounted many kindnesses shown by 'Elephant John' towards her and her family following her husband's incapacitation and subsequent death. She concludes: 'He was someone his family and friends should be very proud of'.[24]

A quite different response to the same article emanated from a veteran of the industry called Dan Casey from Harrow in Middlesex. It echoes similar sentiments expressed to me by other former Murphy employees. While it doesn't list any specific actions of 'Elephant John', it does reflect the ethos of this sector of the industry and its consequences for those involved, and is therefore worth reproducing in full:

*I could not believe my eyes when I read the article on Elephant John (*Irish Post*, 31 July).*

He became notorious, not for his generosity of spirit to his fellow man but for the manner in which he abused and humiliated his fellow countrymen on behalf of his boss.

The Elephant, and his counterparts who worked for the other Irish contractors McNicholas, picked up fellow Irishmen in the mid-fifties and sixties in Camden Town, Elephant and Castle, and Cricklewood at 6 a.m. and took them to various parts of the country.

If they could not keep up with the pacemakers and the leading hands, they were sacked on the spot, did not receive any payment and had to make their own way home, quite often many miles away and with no money.

These Irish contractors were used to rebuild Britain after the war. They are now competing to be among the richest families in these isles. Where is the generation of Irishmen that worked for them?

Many got maimed and killed at their work places. Those that survived can be seen in Camden Town, Cricklewood and Kilburn suffering from rheumatism, bronchitis, arthritis and other diseases that have arisen from not being provided with protective equipment.

A large proportion are on state benefit because they did not pay any National Insurance contributions and, of course, paying tax was out of the question. These contractors have been found guilty in the courts for their tax evasions.

Elephant John, his counterparts and the people they worked for, who are the main culprits, abused and humiliated as many if not more of their fellow countrymen than the Christian Brothers.[25]

Billy Brennan took a dim view of Elephant John, as a result of seeing him in action on several occasions:

He should have been killed long ago with the things he done.... I seen him above in Sheffield with the Connies — young lads, catchin' them by the hair of the head, pullin' them out of the trench, a kick up the hole and send them down the road with a pound thrown after them; and they were doin' as much as anyone.

Now he's doin' well. Good luck to him! Good luck to any man that got on, but they exploited all of us people'.

Above: Payment sheet to Paddy Flavahan for sub-contract, 1958.

'Murphy's Volunteers'

The following account of life as a casual labourer with an Irish sub-contractor thirty-odd years ago typifies the many experiences related to me verbally or in writing in the course of five years' research amongst the Irish in the British construction industry:

In the sixties, when working for Murphy's, no protective wear was provided by the employer. On one occasion, whilst digging out for cable, the trench was full of water and we had no wellington boots. There was a building site nearby, and our ganger-man went onto this site, and found a heap of old discarded wellies in a drying-room.

They were all sizes, filthy, and very smelly. He gathered them together, brought them to us, threw them onto the floor and told us to help ourselves — so much for hygiene! We didn't have much option but to wear them or to paddle around with water over our short leather boots.

There were no toilet facilities provided and we had to make our own arrangements [Alastair McAlpine in his autobiography, Once a Jolly Bagman, refers to the ubiquitous galvanised bucket with which each floor of the firm's multi-level sites was equipped for the men to urinate in!] One bucket of cold water was for washing everyone's hands and, talking of hands, there were no protective gloves available. Hands became extremely cold in the winter and callused.

The men were taken to work in an open wagon, regardless of weather conditions, and the hours were from 7.30 a.m. until 6 p.m. Wages were from £2 to £3.10s. a day in the early sixties. We had to work in all weathers and you could be sacked if you refused. Some of the workers in the late fifties, early sixties, slept rough in old huts or wherever they could find a bit of shelter.

On one occasion two older men asked Elephant John for 'the start' and were told to jump onto the moving wagon. They made several attempts to get on the back of the vehicle but were unable to do so. The agent threw them 2/6d. and sarcastically told them to 'Go and get a bus; it will be lower down and easier for you' — meaning, 'Go home!'

Some of the firm's agents had their own pubs in Liverpool, and allowed and encouraged the workers to sub money every day from their wages, just so they would go into the pub and spend money there. If you did not sub — the chances were you'd be sacked!

Murphy's men always spent a good deal of money at the local butcher's shop where they would buy steak, chops, sausages, etc. The 'Can Lad', the person who 'Shackled up' [cooked] would be sent to the shops each morning with the shopping list from the men and, on his return, would cook in an extremely large frying pan (as big as a roundabout) over a fire in a drum in the road. If we happened to be working near a field of potatoes we'd probably have boiled spuds in their jackets.

Most of the men lived in digs where the firm's wagon would pick them up in the mornings. One particular landlord never used to waken his men up until the very last minute — this would save him from cooking them breakfast.[26]

The Murphy brothers, from Caherciveen in County Kerry, reputedly came to London as labourers in the 1940s. Within a short time they had established separate companies (the 'Green' and the 'Grey' Murphy) which undertook large cable-laying contracts for the Post Office and the CEGB.

Bill Brennan, who epitomises the Irish casualties of this saga, speaks with respect of these well-known Irish sub-contractors and gives them a better press than might be expected:

One time two hundred of us was down in Croydon, pullin' cable, and there was this agent for Murphy, Gill was his name, and he was shoutin', 'Hi-Hup, One-Two, Hi-Hup, One-Two', and John came along and said, 'Don't be shoutin' Hi-Hup, One-Two, give the men a break'. He was a decent skin.... Murphy got it by hard work, and choosin' the right men; Mossy Riordan was with him through thick and thin. He was an agent, but a gentleman. I seen Mossy when he was wearin' the foot iron.... John himself was a gentleman; he'd treat you well.... It goes back again to the gangermen. They hadn't a clue.... It was, 'Skull–drag this', and 'Skull–drag that'. They couldn't see the easy way ... they knew nothin'; they'd never check for cables, pipes, anythin' — just, 'Dig here' or 'Dig there'.

'Pincher' Mac

He took a similarly benign view of the founder of the McNicholas dynasty:

Old Pincher Mac was all right — it was the people that was over you — the gangers; Pincher's son, Tommy, was all right too. You'd meet him on a contract somewhere up the country, and he'd come up to you and say, 'What price is the hoors up here?' ... things like that.

Michael 'Pincher' McNicholas from County Mayo got his 'start' in bomb-damage repair work, in the mid-1940s, and within a decade had progressed to cable-laying as a sub-contractor for the Central Electricity Generating Board. 'Pincher' was in partnership with his brother, Pat, for their first decade in England and,

when the partnership was dissolved, Pat retained their existing GPO contracts while Michael took over the Electricity Board work. This was an astute and intelligent division of labour and ensured the growth of two successful sub-contracting firms instead of one. These firms celebrated their fiftieth anniversary in 1999.

Michael Clancy, from County Clare, emigrated to London in 1948 and, after a period as a labourer, began subbing for the Water Board. He founded M.J. Clancy & Sons Ltd in 1958. The Clancy Group was formed in 1998, encompassing five separate companies, and now has an annual turnover close to £100 million. The company has acquired a reputation as a leader in the field of trenchless technology in the UK. It still remains an independent, privately owned, family business.

'Pateen' Lowry, from Connemara, began work as a railway navvy in 1947 and founded a company in 1950 that progressed to win cable-laying contracts from Pirelli and BICC around Britain. It has grown exponentially into a mainstream civil-engineering firm over the intervening decades.

The Kennedy brothers, John and Joe, from County Sligo also began as labourers, in Manchester, in the late 1940s and progressed to sub-contracting for the Gas Board. They also divided their forces and formed separate companies (the 'Blue' and the 'Green' Kennedy) to cater to different areas in the public sector. John Kennedy was able to follow Joe into retirement in 1998, following a management buyout valued at £22 million.

These companies have all grown enormously in the years since they were established, embracing many different aspects of civil engineering, and now enjoy annual turnovers in the hundreds of millions. Some have become household names. Their founders would all claim to have succeeded by their own efforts, and, to a great extent, that is true, but essentially the 'engine' of these efforts in almost every case was Irish labour.

Undoubtedly there were many decent Irish contractors, who treated their men well and tried to look out for them. Billy O'Grady, for example, would always start a new man off with easy jobs indoors, out of sight of the agent or engineer, so that he could watch the experienced men at work through the windows and get some idea what to do. Similarly he would put a hungover man on a soft job until he'd recovered and could pull his weight. It was, of course, in Billy's interest to be seen to have competent workers, but he might just as easily have sent them 'down the road'.

Nor is there any reason to doubt Bernard McNicholas's claim to have given many employees advice and assistance in obtaining mortgages or saving for retirement. If they chose to ignore this advice, sleeping rough or in hostels and drinking their pay away, the contractor could hardly be held responsible.

As in many walks of life, however, those in authority also have to make choices — to show consideration and care, or indulge in exploitation and abuse.

Working conditions (on a hydro scheme) were very rough indeed and not at all comparable with those to be found in manufacturing industry or even on building sites.... Both sides took a pride in the toughness and brutality of the industry; as one manager summed it up: 'This is a hard life, and we are tough'.[27]

The 'subbies' had a vast army of Irish labourers at their service in the boom years of the 1950s, 1960s and 1970s. It is difficult to envisage the extent of the Irish labour pool at that time. In Scotland, the Midlands, and the South-East of England there was a multitude of rural Irish males whose world was bounded by the site, the pub, the bed-sit and the digs frequented by their fellow countrymen.

The 1951 census quotes a figure of 46,080 Irish 'Workers in Building & Contracting'. Occupational Order XIV of the Standard Industrial Classification System listed Sub-Groups 582, 584, 591 & 599 — embracing Builders' Labourers, Bricklayers' Labourers, Labourers on Railways, Roads, etc., Tunnel Miners and Navvies.

In 1960 these occupations were reclassified and modernised to take account of technological and organisational changes in the industry. Occupational Order XV now included, in addition to the traditional builders' labourers and tradesmen, Sub-Group 098:

> *Construction Workers (persons performing the duties of a number of building trades; covering & repairing roof structures, laying sewage, water & gas mains, underground conduits & cables; paving & repairing roads by hand; cleaning the exterior of buildings; applying heat or acoustic insulating materials; working under water; working as steeplejacks; demolition workers; sewermen; contractors' timbermen; handymen & maintenance men not otherwise classified.*

Occupational Order XVII – 'Drivers of Stationary Engines, Cranes, etc.' — included Sub-Group 104: 'Operators of earth-moving and other construction machinery not otherwise classified'.

Order XVIII – 'Labourers not otherwise classified' —included Sub-Group 106: 'Railway Lengthmen (Persons Laying & Maintaining Railway Permanent Ways). In 1960 the time-honoured term 'navvy' was finally dropped from official classifications.

In the 1961 census report, these three Orders taken together account for an official Irish labour force of 63,050. By 1971 the comparable figure was 70,790.

The Irish were then thought to represent 12.5 per cent of the national total but this, given the nature of the industry, cannot have been much more than an educated guess. For example, there was a marked discrepancy between the Census Report figures, and those of the Ministry of Labour, for that year. Construction workers classed as 'Employees', plus 'Out of Employment', plus 'Signing On' were returned by the Census Report as totalling 3,657,000. The Ministry of Labour estimated the same categories at 4,188,000. These figures also omit those of Irish descent — an increasingly important component of the construction industry workforce, especially amongst tradesmen and plant operators.

Whatever the actual figures, there was certainly an inexhaustible supply of labourers available to the Irish subbies, and they took full advantage of it. The opportunities were great and the profits enormous.

The Gas Industry

In the gas industry, for example, openings were created which the Irish were uniquely placed to exploit. This industry, which had been in serious decline with the ever-increasing use of electricity for domestic use, enjoyed a renaissance in the 1960s with the inception of the fashion for so-called 'G' Plan furniture, and the incorporation of the gas fire as a focal point of living-room furniture. Sales improved and renewal work had to be done throughout the system, from the late 1950s onwards.

This necessitated lots of cut-and-cover work, excavations, and tunnelling to fit valves sectoring off urban districts and 'governors' on people's meters. The Gas Board didn't have enough direct labour to meet the demand or, more correctly, couldn't afford to hire it on union terms. The restrictive work practices within the industry boiled down to what the Board saw as 'a lot of money for not enough work', which didn't hold out much hope for a revitalised industry. The answer was contracting out so much work for a given price. The labour rate then became the concern of the contractor, not the Board.

The British workforce, however, did not show much interest in sub-contracting. Perhaps worn down by the war years, those who weren't already in secure employment within the nationalised industries or for main contractors seemed content to work for themselves as small builders/repair men, and weren't attracted to the hard graft of public works.

The Irish, on the other hand, had the individualism, the energy, and the hunger for work, which were so conspicuously absent from their English counterparts. Men who had been in Britain since the war, either self-employed or even with the Gas Board, tapped into the home network and brought over labour for the new contracts which were coming on stream.

The Irish had a much more 'flexible' system: money into the back pocket for work well done. 'You get paid for the shit you shifted' was the slogan of the day. The bigger the trench, the more they earned — if they could do it fast enough. Because the men weren't 'on the books' they could be laid off if the work wasn't there, something unthinkable in the ranks of direct labour. The men, for their part, could always go 'down the road' and get another start. The unions were very strong at that time, and the Board was obliged to negotiate a ratio of contract/direct (in-house) labour of the order of 60:40 in favour of the unions.

When natural gas was discovered within viable reach of mainland Britain there was huge demand for contractors to install it. There were three pressure regimes. The gas landed ashore and distributed to the cities was at pressures of 1,000 pounds per square inch, and required the laying of thirty-six-inch steel pipes, the big 'Spine Mains'. Next it was reduced to a series of 350 to 450 p.s.i. pipes for distribution on the outskirts of cities. Finally it was distributed to individual households via the old-fashioned low-pressure 'domestic' system. Of the Irish contractors, only Murphy was by this time big enough to take on the national mains work, but there were many smaller contractors available and willing to tender for the rest.

Don Wilson, former Contracts Manager for British Gas Northwest, informed me that 'Contractors such as John Kennedy, P.N. Daly, D.J. Ryan, and Vince Connaughton, as well as John Murphy on the national scale, were the backbone of the labour force in the Gas Industry in the north-west'. To these might be added the names of Fintan Kirwan, Tim Kilroe, John Donnellan, Jim Ennis and P.J. Bourke, amongst others.

A series of large explosions led to the holding of the King Inquiry and the introduction of a national policy of wholesale pipe renewal. This of course precipitated a boom. Schedules of work were drawn up; a profile of what was wanted was presented; and a price was determined for the various operations. Contractors would then submit a quote per gang of

three men plus. A large contractor such as Kennedy might have as many as eighty gangs, covering specific service areas such as Manchester or North Cheshire.

Once a contractor was engaged, he just had to send his agents to the various depots where work was apportioned by the Gas Board Engineer. In effect, the contractor was simply providing the raw labour; the company provided the expertise. The Irish input was all brawn; no brain was necessary. Nonetheless, they all did extremely well out of it.

The renovation budget for Northwest Gas in 1978, for example, was £20 million a year, over seven years. This was divided, 60:40, between contractors and company staff. The contractors, however, did the bulk of the renovation. The money was divided into one-third for pipes etc.; one-third for reinstatement; and one-third for labour. This translated into approximately £7 million per year for the contractors. In the late 1970s this was a big pie when divided between the local Irish contractors.

That budget in turn was multiplied by a factor of eight to cover the entire country's gas network. Of the other utilities, Water also generated employment for contractors, though on a lesser scale, but both Electricity and Telecommunications spent much bigger money. Murphy, McNicholas, and Lowery, amongst

many others, had been picking up contracts from utilities such as the Post Office and the Electricity Boards since the early 1950s. The telecommunications industry is still generating work for Irish contractors of every size....

'Less Brawn, More Brain'

By the late 1970s, however, the slogan, 'Less Brawn, More Brain' began to be heard. It had been costing, say, £10 for the pipe, £10 to dig the hole, and £10 to put it back. Now the JCB, with its specialised 'back actor' shovel, was able to make the digging and reinstatement so much less labour-intensive that the profit for the contractor was going out of it and he faced the prospect of going the way of the dodo.

The more intelligent Irish contractors saw the writing on the wall. Already some of them had shown initiative by avoiding harmful competition — John Kennedy concentrating on Gas and Water work while Joe stayed with Telecom and Electricity; Murphy and McNicholas did likewise. Murphy alone is credited with having involuntarily given 'the start' to innumerable Irish sub-contractors who began as Murphy agents in various parts of Britain. These sub-contractors went out on their own when they realised the amount of work that was on offer, and the folly of merely doing it for someone else's benefit.

Now, in the North-West, the Irish contractors began to co-operate with the Gas Board. The region quickly became, in industry terms, a 'Centre of Excellence'. Dan Ryan developed 'PIM' burst-pipe technology, which was exported to the United States and earned them substantial royalties. Kennedy's started supporting a polymer chemist, Phil Marshall, at the University of Manchester Institute of Technology. Marshall subsequently joined Kennedy's. From this partnership revolutionary technologies emerged which became the norm, first in the gas industry, and later in other utilities. Henceforth Irish contractors of substance consistently employed knowledgeable people and competed at the cutting edge of construction and civil engineering.

Don Wilson is a no-nonsense Yorkshire countryman with no Irish connections. He belongs to a generation that got on, through the Depression era, without the benefit of third-level education, fought a war, and rebuilt their country after it (John Cox is another of that ilk). He holds no brief for the 'victim' school of diaspora Irish history in Britain, but he admires and respects the Irish, and it is his belief that Irish contractors in Britain today are at the forefront of their profession.

He considers that they got there by dint of pure native intelligence, an inborn ability to move with the times, to listen, to see where the opportunities were, to know how to exploit a situation, and to know, basically, 'whether to do the bloody job, or not!' He maintains that because they come from an agricultural background they 'have an innate sense of what is "right", an ability to "make things do", to "fettle things"', which the increasingly urbanised English have gradually lost.

An anecdote told by the late Joseph Murphy provides a perfect example of this instinct. Anxious to secure a contract to build a causeway to an island off the coast of Northumberland, Murphy eschewed the deployment of divers, geologists, aerial photographers, and other specialists, as favoured by such competitors as Taylor Woodrow and McAlpine, and simply took direct action:

> I drove up on my own one day and walked the land and watched how the tides were running. I put in a tender that sunk them all. And I'll make good money out of it as well.[28]

This may be characteristic of the pioneering generation that founded these companies, but few of them today are headed by men from such traditional backgrounds. Top management is now largely in the hands of college graduates, often second generation, and few consider a career in the industry possible without a professional qualification.[29]

To assess the status of the Irish in British construction today, we need only look at the turnovers of some of the leading Irish-owned companies in the UK:

Durkan Group	£75.0 million
Clancy Group	£99.8 million
McNicholas plc	£100.1 million
Kennedy Construction	£103.2 million
Fitzpatrick plc	£138.8 million
J. Murphy & Sons	£157.7 million
McNicholas Construction	£169.9 million
O'Rourke Group	£188.0 million
M.J. Gleeson	£298.1 million [30]

The personal fortune of John Murphy is estimated at around £40 to £60 million, and the company is credited with having spawned innumerable businesses established by erstwhile employees who saw opportunities to go out on their own whilst in John Murphy's employ.

To put these figures in perspective, it is useful to quote the 1999–2000 turnovers of six well-known non-Irish companies:

Taylor Woodrow	£1,504.0 million
George Wimpey	£1,525.9 million
John Mowlem	£1,608.5 million
John Laing	£1,791.7 million
Balfour Beatty	£2,904.0 million
Amec	£3,100.8 million

Many of these companies are, of course, large consortia, and figures may include a share of joint ventures. This would apply to a much lesser extent to most of the Irish-owned companies listed above.

These figures place Irish-owned construction companies in the second rank of the industry, and, in light of these figures, who can dispute that the Irish in British construction today have, incontrovertibly, 'arrived'.

When one considers the scale of operations required to make any impression on the British construction industry nationwide, and the advantages enjoyed by established indigenous firms, the achievements of those Irishmen who came to Britain with nothing and created these major companies have to be unreservedly applauded.

Perhaps a subtler yardstick might be that provided, with great sincerity, by Don Wilson in an aside:

> Only two contractors have ever been proposed for the highest honour which the Institution of Gas Engineers can confer, the title of 'Companion'. Those two are Irish — John Murphy and John Kennedy. In the case of John Kennedy in particular, it is a testament both to his standing in society, and to the affection in which he is held throughout the industry.

This is not to say that there wasn't a seamy underside to the success of some Irish contractors. The depth and ferocity of anti-subbie feeling amongst Irish labourers towards certain of their Irish employers, which doesn't seem to have diminished despite the passage of time, suggests that there has to be some fire behind the smoke.

Similarly, the construction industry has always been prone to scams and financial subterfuges. Nineteenth-century commentators referred to this as 'scamping'. One major player was suspected of paying railway navvies the lodging allowance agreed on a large contract, in lieu of wages, and thereby capitalising a critical phase of expansion. Since then, the Irish in British construction have been credited with inventing more than a few scams of their own.

> Isn't the crowd we're working for here getting two pounds nine shillings a week for every man jack on the job and instead of paying it out to the men, as is intended, aren't they putting it in their pockets and giving us maybe ten shillings' worth of sandwiches in the week? [31]

Anecdotal evidence throughout the industry suggests that large numbers of Irish labourers, with their built-in anti-social bias when in Britain, practised tax evasion at the most basic level by claiming non-existent dependants in Ireland, and by regularly fleeing the country before they became liable for tax, later returning under false documentation to repeat the process.

Off-Shore Accounts

Sources claim that, at a later stage, as contractors, many tax-evaders used false Irish addresses to claim non-resident status. This may have accounted for the widespread familiarity throughout rural Ireland thirty and more years ago with the concept of the 'off-shore account'. Small-town financial advisors, seeing large sums of money lodged in otherwise modest banking establishments, may have cottoned on to the technique as being ideally suited to their local up-and-coming entrepreneurs, anxious to avoid high rates of Irish income tax. If so, then some of the current financial scandals rocking Irish society may have originated with the scams of the Irish abroad.

Such a possibility, coupled with the culture of corruption that grew up around the Haughey-led Fianna Fáil Party, and the suggestion that Charles Haughey himself may have been bank-rolled initially by returned Irish contractors — as alleged by Patrick Gallagher – would certainly put Irish 'subbies' in a new light, vis-à-vis their contribution to the building of Britain!

Everyone at or close to management level in Irish construction circles in Britain has a fund of stories around financial scams executed by subbies and their 'accountants'.

Given the possibility that there may be some truth in these various allegations, it is not surprising that so few Irish contractors welcome someone casting a backward look at their careers. In construction, as in any walk of life, legitimacy and respectability are dearly won. The purpose of this book, however, is to show what was built with the stones, rather than what is to be found underneath them. That work can be better left to others.

An important part of this task, however, is to show what price was paid for all this glory, and by whom.

10 Forgotten Men

But now I am bent and my fire has turned cold,
In another four years I'll be fifty years old
Now I'm worn out and finished,
But what do they care,
For they've had all they want
From the Rambler from Clare.

The great nomadic armies of Irish navvies, who manned the building sites of Britain from the 1950s through the 1970s, were centred mainly in the larger cities such as Glasgow, Liverpool, Manchester, Coventry, Birmingham and, especially, London.

In the latter there were huge concentrations — in Hammersmith, Camberwell, and Fulham, south of the Thames, and in Islington, Holloway, Paddington, Acton and Camden Town, north of it. The 1966 Census showed almost 300,000 Irish-born residents in the city, with perhaps twice as many of Irish descent, officially unrecognised as Irish but nonetheless, in the construction industry particularly, very much part of the Irish community.

Dudley Barratt believed that as much as 80 per cent of the peak-time workforce on the Thames Barrier was Irish-born, or of Irish descent. He calculated that, of the £250 million earned by the Irish on the Thames Barrier over its ten-year construction period, no less than £170 million made its way back to Ireland.

> *Most of the lads on the site, if they're not straight from Ireland, then they're second-generation Irish. We've a load of second-generation lads from the Midlands. There are very few genuine Englishmen about the place, but then that's the problem with England. At the end of the day, when it's all trawled out, there are very few real Englishmen in the country.*[1]

It was the Irish-born, however, who set the tone for these communities. No one who lived in Britain during those years could fail to recognise a west-of-Ireland labouring man — the unfashionable clothes, the ruddy complexion, the big build and the bad teeth. Such men were described by one observer, who recalled seeing them walking to and from Mass on a Sunday morning in Oxford Road, Manchester, as, 'Like migrating swallows, in their dark suits and white shirts, brown shoes and bright red ties'.

Another observer remarked that a certain traffic island in Camden Town, close to a popular Irish pub, was known as 'Penguin Island' because of the many Irish, similarly dressed, who assembled there on a Sunday morning waiting for twelve o'clock opening.

For all the alleged wildness and enthusiasm for drink and confrontation of the Irish, the images which survive on film and in print from that time depict naïve, warm, and enthusiastic individuals eager to please, keen to work, and anxious to present a good appearance — this despite concerns expressed amongst Tory ministers of the day about unrestricted Irish access to employment in Britain.

In 1961, Cabinet members were canvassed to make Irish emigrant workers subject to the same work-voucher system as those from the New Commonwealth, or else to make it a criminal offence for them to take up employment without express permission from the Ministry of Labour. Sir Norman Cook, the then Cabinet Secretary, circulated an internal memorandum noting that, 'Some people feel that too many Irishmen come over here, that they are a drunken and undesirable lot, and that we should do better to keep them out.' In the event, the Irish were exempted from the 1962 *Commonwealth Immigrants Act*, which imposed the work-voucher system, on the pragmatic grounds that, 'It does not make any sense, in practical terms, to try to control movement from this to other parts of the British Isles.' Another attempt, in 1964, to raise the issue was having more success in Cabinet but in that year the Tory government fell and the matter was shelved.[2]

Most of the Irish immigrants lived in digs or hostels and few showed any inclination to become welfare recipients. Contrary to the myth that the Catholic Irish are work-shy, they considered an admission that one was 'on the dole' as a humiliation to be avoided at any cost.

Heathen England

The Irish Establishment, ironically, was expressing an equal level of anxiety concerning Irish emigrants to Britain at this time, prompted by fears that they would lose their morality and be corrupted by 'heathen England'. In a letter to the then Taoiseach, Sean Lemass, the Catholic Hierarchy sought a ban on emigration to Britain by persons under eighteen years of age. The government was requested to consider the fact that one in five emigrants to Britain was under eighteen and, if possible, to introduce an identity card that would result in those under age being stopped at their point of exit.

The letter referred to England as a pagan and amoral environment. Why the Hierarchy, with its all-pervasive control of social and educational facilities in Ireland, weren't taking steps to prepare young people in a practical and constructive manner for inevitable emigration, was not clear. To be fair, however, it must be acknowledged that the Irish Emigrant Chaplaincy Scheme was one substantial gesture of concern for the Irish in Britain, which emanated from the Irish Hierarchy.

In the event, Lemass argued that, while the government shared the concerns of the Hierarchy for the welfare of vulnerable Irish emigrants, nonetheless:

> *Legislation to prohibit the emigration of young persons under penalty of committing an offence would, even if it were constitutional, operate to discourage the return to Ireland of the offenders. It would also seem to involve interference with normal and justifiable travel where no danger to the young persons in question was involved.*[3]

Opposite page: Men's Mission, Quex Road, Kilburn, in the 1950s. During the church's postwar heyday, Mass had to be broadcast over a PA system to include those outside unable to find room within.

In fact, the extent to which Irish men and women in Britain, from all walks of life, attended to their religious duties in this period was quite remarkable. Sykes' article on the social relations of the Irish navvies on a Scottish hydro scheme in 1952 is quite specific about their religious habits:

> *The Irish navvies were very devout; many prayed openly night and morning, and displayed religious pictures in their lockers; all of them attended mass on Sundays.*[4]

The urge to conform to the traditional Irish patterns of religious observance was often reinforced by Irish landladies. Sean O'Ciarain described lodging-houses operated by two such landladies, in Glasgow, in the early 1950s:

> *Everybody in the digs was obliged to go to Mass on Sundays, like it or not. To satisfy the landlady you had to be a chapel goer.... I might as well have a lump of a bullock, lying in there in the room, as a man who won't go to Mass....*[5]

Domhnall MacAuligh's book is peppered with references to churchgoing:

> *I borrowed a bike this morning and went to first Mass so that I was able to be back on duty at half past seven ... Mike Ned and I went to confession tonight and it was badly needed ... Holy Communion this morning, thank God. Sunday is the day we like best here in Northampton. All the Irish gather here in the club after Mass.... I went out to the job in the morning for I had been told that Mass could be had out at the aerodrome.... To Mass in Highbury this morning.... We got a bite to eat near the station and we went off to Mass in Camden Town afterwards.... Off to Mass in Daventry at eleven. Father Collins gave a good sermon.... Mike Ned, Tom, Corcoran and I went along to the ten o'clock Mass....*[6]

Irish priests, working in Britain under the auspices of the Irish Emigrant Chaplaincy Scheme (1957–1982), sent regular reports back to the Scheme's patron, Archbishop McQuaid. Their assessment of the religious observance of Irish emigrants was that 60 per cent were excellent, 30 per cent ranged from good to careless, and 10 per cent were completely lapsed.[7]

The Irish were fond of dancing and socialising amongst their own, but neither the Irish commercial ballrooms nor the Catholic parish clubs, which hosted these events, served alcohol. It might be that men would have a few drinks to get up 'Dutch courage' before attending; once inside, however, soft drinks became the order of the day.

This was a restriction which was recognised as being in everyone's best interests, and which seemed to sit lightly on those concerned, even those many men who seemed unable to socialise without getting 'tanked up' before entering the dance hall.

I needed the alcohol to be able to ask a woman to dance.... I had to have a massive amount of alcohol drunk over there in 'The Good Mixer' pub before crossing the road to 'The Buffalo'....

'The Buffalo' was pretty much set up the way it was in Ireland — all the men along one side of the room, all the women along the other, and the men had to go across to them. It was so difficult, man, so fuckin' difficult.... The Irish culture was still there; it was so rigid.

I was goin' across and no one would dance with me, because I was mad drunk, and I was saying, 'What the fuck is wrong with me? I'm young, and I've got a three-piece suit on, and I've got a few bob in my pocket — what the fuck's going on?' And of course the answer was, I was totally drunk.

A woman at that time would inquire who you were, what you'd done, who you knew from her part of the country, who was in charge of such-and-such a job — if you couldn't give clear answers to those questions you were totally screwed. I'd come away totally frustrated; I wasn't socially able to make any of these moves towards a normal life, which any normal human being should have, without alcohol....[8]

Many Irish people in that era were, in fact, 'teetotallers' — members of the Pioneer Total Abstinence Association. At dances, young women would be invited by admirers to 'take a mineral'. 'Taking the mineral' was tantamount to inviting intimacy and much could hang on the response to such an invitation.

For many of the young immigrant Irish of the 1950s and 1960s, the dance halls were their main source of recreation, and a woman's income was often divided into rent money, food money, and dance money. There was a strictly enforced dress code in operation. The men dressed in navy blue suits, with a white shirt and a blue or red tie (in 'The Gresham', as elsewhere, a tie could be rented for a shilling at the door prior to admission). The women wore ballroom dresses or, in

Pioneer's Total Abstinence Association outing, 1961, organised by Church of the Sacred Heart, Quex Road.

Above: The Gresham Ballroom, Holloway Road, London.

Above: The modern dancing ballroom of the Galtymore — jiving had become acceptable.

The Galtymore, Cricklewood, in the 1960s.

the 1960s, skirts with three-tier stiffened petticoats underneath to make them stand out from their bodies.

There was a multitude of these Irish dance halls in Britain. In Manchester, perhaps the best known were 'The Ardrí' and 'The Ardilaun', with parish clubs such as 'St Kentigern's' providing a clerically super-vised alternative. In Birmingham 'The Shamrock' competed with 'St Chad's' and 'St Catherine's'. Liverpool, Leeds, Coventry and Luton all had their equivalents. The greatest concentration, inevitably, was in London. The most popular of these were 'The Blarney' on Tottenham Court Road, 'The Hibernian' on Fulham Broadway, 'The Four Provinces' at Manor House, 'The Gresham' on Holloway Road, 'The Round Tower' in Camden Town, 'The National' on Kilburn High Road, 'The Forum' in Kentish Town and, perhaps the best-known of all, 'The Galtymore' in Cricklewood. 'The Shamrock' on Tottenham Court Road was one of several more refined venues which held 'Tea Dances' on Sunday afternoons ('They're all Connemara people that come here and it would go hard with you to find a word of English there').[9]

Above: The New Ardrí Ballroom, Manchester.

Liam Walshe has vivid memories of these establishments:

The Irish dance halls? Well, some of them were good craic, others were best avoided! I used to go to the 'The Gresham' on Monday nights. I wasn't into dancing really (two left feet!) but that was where the women were! Being unconventional by nature, I might go up to a girl and say, 'I'd ask you to dance, but I can't dance, so can I just sit down and talk to you?' If I got a frosty glare, I moved on; if I got a smile, I sat down. Overall, an effective chat-up line!

If you wanted to be sure of getting 'a claim' for the night, you went to 'The Buffalo' in Camden Town. It was said that if a man (any man) couldn't get a woman in 'The Buffalo' the best he could do was — lie down and die!

John Moran actually met his future wife in 'The Galtymore' where she was working part-time as a cloakroom attendant. He later became a cashier in this establishment. 'The Galtymore' had two separate halls — a Céilidh Hall and a Modern Dancing Hall.

You wouldn't find the same crowd in both, although you only had the one Admission; the Céilidh Hall was frequented by the ones from Galway, Mayo, and Kerry.... It could get rough at times; there was rivalry between some of the small sub-contractors and they might cause trouble. Things changed in the late '60s — the work moved out, and these lads followed it.[10]

Dysfunctional

Often somewhat better educated and consequently perhaps relatively more refined, some Irish women were more open to liaisons with non-Irish partners, particularly if these held out the possibility of 'betterment'. One correspondent wrote to me:

We had some Irish girls working at the hostel. They were not very friendly with the Irish men — especially if they had desk jobs.

However, the majority, whatever their social pretensions in the small communities whence they originated in Ireland, usually reacted to Britain's alien social environment with new-found feelings of solidarity towards men from their own part of Ireland:

There was a great levelling-off at Holyhead.

As Domhnall MacAuligh observed:

Provincialism is long gone — Achill marries Kildare, Galway marries Waterford. What does it matter? The kids born here have Northampton accents.[11]

Women's opinions of the Irish in the British construction industry have proved most elusive. A public appeal produced only four replies — two of them from the same person. Overall their verdict on the behaviour of Irish navvies in Britain is not very flattering:

I have a limited recollection of my father's life as a navvy. I remember he would get a 'draw' on his wages early in the week — having spent a great portion of his pay check the previous weekend in the pubs.... I'm afraid my father wasn't very articulate on his return home at the end of the day. After his meal he fell asleep. However, had I been able to follow him after work to 'Ward's Irish House,' 'The Queen's Elm', or 'The Lord Pakenham' I'm convinced I would have found out a lot more about his day on the job ... by today's standards mine and many other Irish families in England would be classified as 'dysfunctional' — so be it.[12]

I am a Pensioner from the West of Ireland, and the poor women in my young days had very hard lives. Lots of them were treated like slaves by their husbands.... Their lives were all hard work and

hardly any money. They could not leave and come with their sons. Lots of them had big families in those days. I do know that the navvies slept in barns, not in a house, so where could a woman with a big family go to? She could not stay with her sons, and she would not be taken into lodgings. They had no money — there was no social security then and the Irish government did nothing for poor people years ago.

Some of the poor women were forced into marriage because the match was made. They had no say in it, and after a while their spirit was broken anyway.

Some of the women went to America to earn their fortune, and worked as maids, and saved and saved so they could get a husband. If they did not get the fortune, they could not get a man.

And a lot of Irish men, even today, I find, think that women are inferior to them. They are there to cook and clean for the men....[13]

I was a child migrant out of Ireland in the early fifties. The Irish men, young and old, were drunken thugs who disgraced themselves in every city they worked in. They had no respect for their women at home or on the streets. They used to brag to their mates about shoving women up the stick.... The homes for unmarried mothers was full of Irish women in this country during the fifties. Paddy would not marry — he carried the status of a hard case. He made dirt of his own women in a foreign country....

Construction was run by Irish men. They worked their own men into the ground, and paid them poorly, and today those men that are lucky enough to be still alive are without money and in poor health because of those Irish contractors....

A migrant is only a second-class citizen in any country and if you don't stand by your own, and have respect, you just become DIRT.

The Irish girls coming from Ireland — most didn't drink, smoke or dope. They worked to get a bit to eat and clothes on their back.

They used to suffer a lot of verbal abuse, the poor things; they could not better themselves, as they had no education. Marriage was the beginning and end to the so-called life they had to endure.[14]

Certainly there were very rough men amongst the Irish in the industry in the two decades following the Second World War. As one man described it, 'England in those years was a brutal place — there was an awful lot of drinkin' done.'

A toughness bordering on callousness pervaded the poorer sections of society, in both Britain and Ireland, up to recent times, which is little understood today. Many people lived lives of considerable hardship and deprivation, with few expectations, leavened only by a high degree of solidarity and a determination to enjoy to the utmost whatever consolations life had to offer. One such, ironically, was the almost total unavailability of credit and the consequent freedom from that chronic anxiety which debt brings in its wake.

One need only consider the innumerable instances of children of large families being divided out amongst relations, or committed to 'care', to appreciate the difficult decisions which parents took, with pain and fortitude, in order to survive. Amongst the poor, family and community were central to any successful strategy for survival; the psychological stress consequent on being isolated from these support systems, characteristic of many Irish men on the margins of the construction industry, remains to be properly researched.

Not everyone, however, went down this road. Even in those harsh years a hard-working 'company man', perhaps operating plant, or one who concentrated on house building could live and work in decent conditions and earn a modest living.

Polish and Irish Tunnellers, break through, Lough Sloy, Scotland 1949 — 'The Pole keeps the money and throws away the pay packet; Paddy throws away the money and keeps ...'

Subaqueous tunnel, River Avon, Bristol.

The Tunnel Tigers

The really big money was earned in two particular sections of the industry — tunnel work, and cable laying. Here time was of the essence, conditions were tough and often dangerous, and production bonuses and lots of overtime could bring earnings to way above the average. In 1964 wages on the Clyde Tunnel averaged £70 per week, compared to the tradesman's wage at the time of £11, but the risks were commensurate with the rewards.

Sean O'Ciarain encountered the pioneers of the postwar tunnelling fraternity in Glasgow in the 1950s. They were then working on the Scottish hydro schemes but later 'followed the shilling' to England and the power stations and transport tunnels:

The 'Tunnel Tigers', as they were called, came down at the weekends, all rough and scruffy, and badly in need of a bath, but with plenty of money in their pockets....

The Irishmen were noted for flashing the pay-slips. A pay envelope showing a high figure of money for a week's work was a thing to keep for showing in pubs in order to impress people.[15]

Tunnellers depended on teamwork for effectiveness, and the resulting discipline often extended to personal abstemiousness and a savings habit that maximised the benefits of their high earnings. Known in the industry as 'Tunnel Tigers', they were mainly from Donegal, with a strong Mayo representation amongst the 'soft tunnelling' fraternity (men who worked in clay, sand, or gravel as opposed to those who worked in rock).

Tunnellers traditionally earned the highest wages in the industry but, because they operated in teams and in a controlled environment, there were no opportunities for entrepreneurs to amass personal fortunes. Nevertheless most tunnellers made very good money and used it to provide for themselves and their families before they got too old for such demanding work.

With the money that I've been making, I've been able to buy a house in London and a house back in Donegal. I rent that one out to a young family there....

A couple of the lads who came out with me have done very well. One of them has now got his own timber business in Tyrone.... I'm here to make money and I never forget that. I've got a good-sized house in Bristol, and two houses back in Donegal with fifty acres of land. I rent the houses out.[16]

In the pursuit of big money, however, there was a tendency to take chances and cut corners with safety procedures. This could prove disastrous where men were working in compressed-air environments as in tunnels under water, such as the Clyde, Tyne, Blackwall and Dartford Tunnels where compression was necessary to keep ground water out of the workings.

The dangers of 'Caisson Disease' — 'the bends', had been recognised since the nineteenth century. These were widely publicised in *Dangerous Trade*s (edited by Thomas Oliver), published in 1907, and used as primary evidence in drawing up the provisions of the *United Kingdom Workmen's Compensation Acts*.

Provision was made by contractors to enable men working in compressed air to re-adjust to normal pressures using decompression chambers. These chambers allow air pressures to be equalised gradually between compression levels below ground and those outside so that nitrogen, which dissolves in the blood while men are working underground, could be exhaled slowly from the lungs rather than popping out violently in the form of bubbles. If the process is cut short, the popping bubbles cause pain in joints, muscles and other parts of the body (Type 1 bends) and, in some cases, more serious symptoms such as loss of vision, unconsciousness, dizziness, paralysis and death (Type II bends). The pain has been described as, 'like 20,000 men trying to hammer their way out of your body'.

Occasionally employers increased pressures in emergencies beyond the recognised safety limits. One miner was working on a tunnel under a river when the contractor had to deal with a sudden breach in the roof of the tunnel:

The pressure was turned up and up and up to keep back the deluge, way beyond the safety limits. Blood was coming out of some blokes' ears, noses, and even their arses.

COMPRESSED AIR WORKER

IF BEARER IS TAKEN ILL SEND AT ONCE TO- MEDICAL LOCK, THE TYNE TUNNEL BRINKBURN STREET, EAST HOWDON, WALLSEND ON TYNE, AND PHONE EDMUND NUTTALL WALLSEND 624567

Above: Inscription on Tyne Tunnel miner's 'Dog Tag' — worn on or off duty.

Sometimes the miners themselves took short cuts with the decompression procedures. One man remembers that during the Tyne and Wear Metro construction navvies were known to pay the airlock controller £10 to run the cycle through quickly so they could get to the pub before closing. The outcome was sometimes serious, but was understood and accepted by both management and men as the likely consequence of taking a calculated risk.

When miners, for whatever reason, suffered attacks of the bends they were told to take painkillers or exercise. 'I used to cycle round the estate in the middle of the night.... You would get home, go to bed, and then the pains would start. You would have to decide how bad they were.' On the Tyne Tunnel miners were given a metal dog tag by the contractor inscribed with the message, 'If taken ill, return at once to the medical lock, Tyne Tunnel.' This was to enable them to be reprocessed through the decompression chamber, which usually alleviated the symptoms.

Nevertheless many totally compliant individuals suffered subsequent health problems after unknowingly contracting a condition known as bone necrosis, or 'bone rot'. Bone necrosis was caused when the nitrogen bubbles blocked off blood supplies to the bones in joints, especially shoulder and hip joints, Deprived of blood, the bones effectively died, and began to crumble.

This condition, usually contracted by frequent sufferers from the bends, in most cases went undetected for many years. Inevitably after such a lapse of time it was very difficult to establish any connection between the chronic condition and the original project, although expert opinion held that even one attack of the bends was sufficient to contract bone necrosis.

Even when a case was brought by former Clyde tunnellers in 1965, only five years after completion of that project, they were denied compensation on the grounds that their employers had observed and enforced the safety regulations as they then stood. Some men accepted small three-figure out-of-court settlements in the belief that they would not get justice. The leading contractors who specialised in tunnelling in those years included Charles Brand, Edmund Nuttall, Balfour Beatty, John Mowlem and Leonard Fairclough.

However, in 1994 Ray Cox, a Lancashire miner who had worked on the Dartford road tunnel for two years in the mid-1970s, received an out-of-court settlement of £200,000 from Balfour Beatty for having contracted bone necrosis whilst in their employment. Balfour Beatty did not accept liability but x-rays, interpreted by experts, showed that damage to Cox's hip was contracted during the Dartford project while a similar condition in his shoulder joints was a result of work done later in Hong Kong for another contractor. This was because a specific amount of time had to elapse before the condition reached a particular stage. These calculations undermined the arguments of Balfour Beatty that Mr Cox's ailment was contracted in someone else's employ.

A major breakthrough in the fight for compensation occurred when Bill Lawrence, then occupational health and safety adviser and campaigner for miners' compensation at Wallsend People's Centre, Newcastle, tracked down the records of the Decompression and Sickness Register to Newcastle's Royal Victoria Infirmary. They had been stored in a disused basement of the hospital laundry. This register contained not only the names of all those employed on the Clyde Tunnel but also x-rays of 1,700 tunnellers collected by orthopaedic surgeon Dr Dennis Walder as part of a twenty-year Medical Research Council study into the effects of the bends. In the early 1980s the government withdrew funding for the project and the records went into storage and were forgotten.

In 1995 Irish ex-tunnellers formed the Clyde Tunnellers' Association to fight for compensation on behalf of bone necrosis sufferers who had worked on both the Clyde and Tyne tunnels. A Donegal man, Michael Gara, was elected chairman.

With the precedent of the Cox case established, substantial out-of-court settlements of similar cases have since become the norm in the industry, but money cannot compensate for the ruined bodies and blighted lives of the victims. There are tragic stories behind the façades of many of the well-built homes of Donegal.

Tunnellers were prey to many serious medical conditions, apart from bone necrosis, and an accumulation of these could and often did lead to premature death. This was the case with Derry-born Con Docherty, a leading miner and tunnel boss and, for many years, one of best-known Irish tunnellers in British civil engineering

In December 1969, near Lakenheath in Essex, a gang of twenty-eight tunnellers, led by Con, broke the world record for soft-earth tunnelling, on the Ely-Ouse water pipeline, by two hundred feet. The consulting engineers, Binnie & Partners, sent a congratulatory telegram addressed to 'Docherty, Murphy, and Ryan', the leading miners. The names speak for themselves. Eighteen months later, in May of 1970, in recognition of their achievement; Con and his immediate superiors were presented to the Queen.

Five years and six months later, on 25 November 1976, Con was dead. Cause of death was as given follows:

Pulmonary embolism
Pulmonary fibrosis and emphysema
Pulmonary sarcoidosis[17]

Above: Nuttal's were the tunnelling contractors on the Ely–Ouse project.

Above: Con Docherty meeting Queen Elizabeth II.

Con had worked on the Mersey and Tyne tunnels, and in rock, clay, sand, and shale, above ground and under water, all his life. Born in 1936, he was eleven days short of his fortieth birthday when he died.

Laying Cable

Cable-laying, which could also pay well in certain circumstances, was more individualistic work, and encouraged a quite different mentality.

The cable work was the best of the lot — especially if you liked a bit of travellin'; if you were with a good subbie on the cables, the money was as good as anywhere.

Unlike the tunnellers, however, cable men were not team workers, and neither did they have the same urge to save, because so much of their free time was spent in pubs or 'on tramp'.

You'd jump out of a job as quick as anything — if you didn't like the look of the foreman, or he didn't like the look of you; or you didn't like the site, or the beds were bad, or there was nothin' happening on the job.

The hordes of 'lumpers', working casually by the day or on piecework, were like mercenaries, and their world was equally tough and uncompromising. Most of their work was with utilities such as the GPO and the Electricity Board. Their very names were redolent of the 'Mad Max' ethos of the trade: 'Hairy Frank', 'Diesel Tom', 'Mad Muldoon' (who had two missing fingers and would order a round of drinks by holding up his maimed hand and shouting, 'two pints and two halves!'), 'The Tin Can', 'Mad Mountjoy', 'Punch Donnellan' and 'The Ball of Muck'.

Living Conditions

Billy O'Grady recalled a job in Reading where he collected a crew every morning who were sleeping rough in an old orchard. He claims it was commonplace to meet Irishmen who were virtually squatters:

Lads were living in attic spaces in the roofs of terraces; cooking with a camping stove and gas bottle — a hole in the slates to let out the smells. Piss in a bucket. Sleeping on old mattresses on the floor. They lived cheap, and made good money, but they drank and gambled it away.

Malcolm O'Brien, who was to end his career with an MBE, began in London in the 1950s taking what he could get because, as he put it,

In those days one 'followed the shilling'. You'd arrive in London, check the paper, phone up a number.... 'Any chance of a start?' 'What can you do, Paddy?' 'I'm a joiner'; 'Right — start in the mornin' Paddy'. No interview....

Once on site he would meet some other Irish lads, get chatting in the tea break, and perhaps be told: 'We have a room — there's four of us in it, but there's an extra bed (or mattress on the floor). You can move in with us.' This would cut the cost of the room all round but very often, in Malcolm's words,

It was rough; they were like animals, I'm sorry to say — most of them didn't have any hygiene. In Ireland, even in the city where I came from, 90 per cent of the houses didn't have an internal toilet. They damped the beds or, at best, pissed in the sinks. When I came over to London my mother was ashamed to say I was in London because, in Limerick, a fella in trouble would be given the choice by the courts of either gaol or England....

Sharing a room also often involved sharing a bed. This practice could take two forms: men on alternate shifts might take turns sleeping in the one bed on their own or, particularly in the early postwar period, they might sleep two to a bed. Malcolm recalled this experience with a shudder of horror:

It's an awful feeling when you move in the night and touch another man who probably, like yourself, is sleeping in the buff.

Bed sharing was also often 'officially' sanctioned by greedy landladies who had no qualms about putting complete strangers into the same bed, sight unseen:

Con relaxing at his home.

I got the room all right, but I had to share it with five others, three beds in the room and two in each bed. In the next room it was the same arrangement, and you never knew what kind of a man was going to be put in beside you. The landlady's word was law. If a man was good enough to stay the night in her house he was good enough for you to share a bed with. And anyone who did not like that knew where the door was. It was either accept it or go. Nobody was forced to stay against their will.[18]

Domhnall MacAuligh was also a 'two-in-a-bed man' from time to time:

I made my way down the Harrow Road until at last I found a place to stay.... Up I went to the bedroom that the landlady offered me. But I found a man in the bed already and damned if I knew what on earth to do. Anyway, he told me to get in beside him, which I did, as I didn't think I could get anywhere else at that time of night.

A bloody big fellow he was too and I nearly fell out of the bed as soon as I got into it. Talkative too ... after I got his life story — a Murphy from Cork he was — he started giving out the Rosary and I answered him. I must say ... this is the first time I have come across two strangers in the same bed saying the Rosary together.[19]

A young emigrant's fate could be decided simply by the contacts he made in the first forty-eight hours after his arrival. He could be led astray, or get put on the right road. Having met so many men who became victims of the Irish navvy sub-culture it came as almost a shock to meet someone as uniformly fortunate as was John Moran of Westport.

John, the eldest of the family, left Westport at the age of twenty in March of 1957. He was able to travel in the company of a local man who was returning to London and this made the journey a less lonely experience. John's brother, who had 'gone over' the previous year and taken a live-in job in a hotel, had found him a room in Paddington.

I was lucky — the landlady, Madge Durkin, was from Sligo and she was very good to me. It was like a home from home. She'd look after you if you were sick, or anythin', and she kept in touch with us all. A lot of people went into rooms; it could be awful lonely inside in a room. You knew, if you went out, no one'd say 'hello' to you ... you'd just have to make you own way — go to the pub, or not ... nobody knew where you were.

John was quite content to have his own room, with a gas cooker, bed, wardrobe and wash-hand basin. A metered gas fire provided heating. He remained at this address in Paddington for ten years before getting married.

Once settled, John contacted another Westport man who was working on a very large housing project run by Unit Construction, at Abbey Wood on the borders of Kent. This man got John the start, on the following Monday morning, and he spent the next eight years with this firm on the same project.

Abbey Wood was a well organised, unionised site, and conditions were excellent. The labourers were supplied with work boots, and clothing which could be left overnight in the firm's drying-room. There was an excellent canteen, and both food and travel allowances were paid. John observed that the bricklayers were mostly English and time-served men, while the labourers were Irish (little had changed since Denvir's day). Overall, however, John observed that there were not many Irish working with house-building firms in London in those years.

It was steady work with few worries. One such was getting to work on time:

In the early years, lads would run you to work in a van. Sometimes, when the van wouldn't start, you'd be waitin' at the corner, and gettin' into a panic. Then a bus would go by, and some lad you knew would lean out the back and shout, 'Van's broke down — make your own way to work!' That could take up to an hour and a half, by bus across London.

'Pulling cable', 1952.

Another problem, which all Irish emigrants had in common, was coping with exile.

Everyone went home for Christmas — not so many in the summer at that time. Goin' back after the holiday, your heart would be in your boots; everyone was very quiet on the boat. The winters could be quite severe — January, February, March were often so rough the buildin'd stop. It was hard, facin' back into it after Christmas.

John knew how fortunate he was:

I was lucky that I was kept on, that I never had an accident, that I didn't have to go out pullin' cable. I got smaller money than on the big jobs, but there the work was very rough; heavy goin', no wet gear, work in all conditions. I wouldn't have been able for it.

Murphy's contracts were heavy work — mostly cable work, hard ... out in all conditions. Casual work; on the lorry at half six in the mornin', open wagons.... Men would work a few days, then disappear. It was a question of what you went in for....

Although a Mayo man, John was obviously not made in the mould of the true navvies, the Long-Distance Men, such as those from Donegal, Achill, or Connemara. He told me Cricklewood was the home of the Achill people:

Phelim McGinty was a building contractor, who had his office on Cricklewood Broadway, and he was from Achill. All I knew of the Connemara men was seein' them at the dances: fine, powerful men. They chased the big money, and were well fit for it — it was sort of natural to them. They were great for whoever they worked for. You'd hear them of a Sunday evenin', on the No. 16 bus from Kilburn to Cricklewood, talkin' Irish and sometimes singin'.

Domhnall MacAuligh also praised the Connemara men's appetite for hard work. He described them as 'the heavy diggers, or muck-shifters':

We were getting off the bus when this old, battered lorry belonging to McNicholas passed by, loaded with 'Connies'. Some of our lads decided to taunt them, but they got their answer: 'Ah, go away, ye shower of paupers,' they said to us. These lads wouldn't do any other type of work, except muck shifting or navvying. [Where he was being paid £4 a day as a 'company man' on a Northampton site in 1966, the Connemara men were making up to £6 or £7 with 'subbies']. *Some of them are worked to the bone like dogs. When they reach the age of forty, they've had it. The work they do is very heavy.... Only those from Connemara, Mayo, and Kerry will do it.*[20]

Unaccustomed demands were made on these young Irishmen, living away from home. As John Moran recalled:

You had to go out, learn to shop, do your own cookin'. For lads not used to it this was an awful shock. You'd buy a big piece of meat — steak, bacon, mutton, priced according to size, and take it home and boil it up or fry it. 'Twas time consumin', too. Often in the evenin', you wouldn't have the patience for it — you'd go out to the cafe. Irishmen had big appetites, and it could work out expensive. A favourite place to eat was Kane's, in Kilburn.

Digs were the usual alternative for those in work. Noel O'Donnell recalled a typical Camden Town lodging-house.

We were stayin' in digs in Camden Town, in a place run by a lovely lady, Mrs Prunette, with a lot of Sligo men. There was Paul Mannion, and Bobby Carey, both from Collooney, and they worked on the pile-drivin'. They'd be markin' out the work on a pile of mashed potatoes at the dinner table — you'd have to watch out, comin' in the door, in case there'd be a big hole dug just inside it!

Many lodging houses weren't equipped with baths and, every Saturday, Irish labourers would go down to Percy Road Public Baths where, according to John:

There'd be a queue outside — up to thirty or forty lads. You paid goin' in, got a towel and soap, ran your cold water, and told the fella outside how much hot water to let in. Once he'd stopped, that was your lot; if it got cold, you got no more. Shirts went to the laundry.

Left: Matron to student nurses before a dance:
'Have nothing to do with those Irish navvies, girls. It's just the grace of God that keeps their trousers up!'

Sunday Mass was an important occasion. A favourite venue was Quex Road, Kilburn, described by John Moran as 'A real Irish church, with great priests. You'd always meet someone you knew. A big plus was the numbers of Irish girls would go there.... 'Twas somethin' you had with you, that you didn't want to lose.' Domhnall MacAuligh also attended Mass in Quex Road, and remarked on the number of Connemara men and women he met and recognised there. During Lent many Irish went to Quex Road for evening Mass. For men on bonus in the building trade, who started early each day and worked the weekends, these evening Masses were ideal.

John managed to live a remarkably normal life, not dissimilar in many respects to that which he might have lived at home. He joined the Parnell Gaelic Football Club and played most weekends, in season: 'That was good steady company — always someone to talk to, and mix with....'

He was a teetotaller and had a part-time job with 'The Galtymore' ballroom in Cricklewood. The extra work was both a means of earning additional cash and a way to meet people. Instead of squandering his earnings, he was able to save and, in this, he was assisted by his mother in Westport.

My mother was always determined that I would come back; when this house, only two miles from home, came up for sale she and my father did all they could to help me buy it. My mother had all the money I'd sent back saved in the Post Office.

I was married by this time, with two little girls in school, and I decided to move back but, for myself personally, I had it hard to leave London. I was happy with my life....

A place of your own is worth a lot, after sharin' a house in London. You can walk out your own front door, and it's your own — that's worth a lot. Privacy, and so on.... I have my health — not many do. A lot of men I worked with, and knew in London, are dead now.

John's only regret was that he didn't invest in a property in London, when prices were low, as a nest egg for his retirement. He was deterred by fears that the Revenue Commissioners would somehow penalise him for it: ''Twas an opportunity lost; there was a great fear of the taxman amongst the Irish in England.' Unquestionably, had he taken that chance, John would not have been the kind of exploitative Irish landlord referred to by Malcolm O'Brien:

The smarter ones saved, bought houses, and rented them to the unfortunate single men, and they were heartless....

Lumpers

The world of the 'lumper' in London consisted of colonies of Irish men and women in places such as Kilburn, Cricklewood, Camden Town, Fulham and Hammersmith. Their landmarks were the 'Irish' pubs, the 'workmen's cafes', and the hiring stands of Camden Town, Cricklewood, Hammersmith and the Elephant & Castle.

Here every morning men waited, from six o'clock, to be selected by Irish gangers and agents, who would pick their quota of 'skins' and load them into open wagons which might then drive them anywhere within a two-hour radius of the capital.

Before I ever left home I knew all you had to do was go to Camden Town and you'd get work; just pick a colour — whatever colour you liked ... RSK was brown, Murphy was green or grey, Lowry was blue, Pincher Mac was green....

You wouldn't inquire where, what time, how long, what price [in the early 1960s it was £3.50, £4.00, £5.00 a shift] — just jump on a wagon and away you went....

It was a fabulous old time really. If you stood in the middle of Camden Town there was a road goin' up — Kentish Town Road, and on each side of the

Above: Camden Town — 'Capital of Ireland'.

road there'd be nothin' for two, three hundred yards but vans and lorries — Thames Traders with the little canopy — and they'd be all Lowry's; then, if you turned around, and looked down Camden High Street towards Mornington Crescent it was all RSK wagons; if you turned north again, towards Chalk Farm, it was all John Murphy's wagons.... Then, on the side roads off Camden High Street, there'd be a rake of other contractors, mostly on Post Office work — small cable work....

But you wouldn't get a lot of the buildin' workers there ... all these lads were what they called 'The Heavy Diggers'. The other lads, that'd be workin' for Taylor Woodrow, for John Laing, for Mowlem, they'd be all gone off on the Underground for different parts of London.... They wouldn't entertain what my father called, 'them savages'.

He worked for a company called Wates, and he used to leave Camden Town around twenty to eight in the mornin', travel maybe half an hour on the Underground to work. He got the three breaks every day, and he'd still be home for the tea at six o'clock. And he got changin' facilities on the job, and holiday pay — stamps for that, and he got a contributory pension....

We'd be comin' back to Camden Town at eight o'clock at night; we got no stamp — nothin'. I don't know the reason, because you could have demanded your stamp, but you wouldn't go against the crowd anyway.... Lads now, that went to England in, say, '55 or thereabouts, they're sixty now, if they're still alive, and they don't have a contributory pension — they have to beg one off the State....

But it was fabulous that time, as a young man, to see all those men in the Greek cafes 'round Camden Town, packed in — 'Double Egg, Bacon and Sausage', 'Egg and Bobble', 'Fish and Bobble' ['Bobble' was mashed potatoes and cabbage mixed together]. You'd get a lovely piece of smoked haddock there in the mornin' and, especially if you'd had a few pints the night before, it was lovely — there was great cuttin' in it!

But it was a funny thing; if you went into one of them cafes in the mornin' — and they'd be packed, from one end to the other, you wouldn't hear a gig, not a word, out of any of them; well, you wouldn't want to be talkin' to anyone at half five in the mornin', would you?

And there'd be thousands of men there every mornin' — if you weren't there between half six and quarter to seven, there wouldn't be a wagon left in it....

Down to Reading, or Chatham, or up to Chelmsford, Ipswich, even Peterborough, in those small little Transit vans, and all packed with men smokin' away....

Once in a lifetime that thing happened — when thousands of Irishmen congregated in those places, in Camden Town, Birmingham, Manchester, all aged between fifteen and forty, from 1954/55 up to about 1970.

There was no other work compared; there was buildin's, and power stations, and so on, but there was no other situation — no crowd of Irishmen that came together on one particular job — no Englishmen, strictly Irishmen — men from the west of Ireland — Mayo, Kerry, Connemara, Belmullet, Arranmore Island, Gweedore, Falcarragh; hundreds of Irishmen every mornin', jumpin' on wagons.... It's part of history now — it'll never come again....[21]

Joe McGarry, who came from Armagh, took a more jaundiced view of the Irish recruiting system.

If you came from a certain county, you'd be employed by a contractor from that county — it didn't matter if the other guy was a better worker.... You could go out from Camden Town every day for a week with a different contractor ... Camden Town, Cricklewood, Elephant & Castle; you got known as a hard worker, if you wanted to be goin' out the next day.... I liked goin' to different places, it gave me an idea of what England was like.

Above: Waiting for breakfast in Camden Town — 'Double egg, bacon and sausage'.

'Any fear of the start?'

Below: 'You could pick your colour.' Jumping on wagons, Camden Town, 1964.

It was a weird thing — no one in Camden Town ever asked for a job — it wasn't done. A subbie might come along needin' ten men — ten 'Skins', but you couldn't ask — you stood, and you were picked, or not, and when all the vans were gone, there were an awful lot of rejected souls still standin' there....

At that time, a ganger might come around the pubs in the evenin', and deal you out a pound for the breakfast in the mornin', so that meant you could blow your money in the pub the night before, because once you got that pound you knew you'd be goin' on that wagon in the mornin', and you'd earn another four pound for the shift....

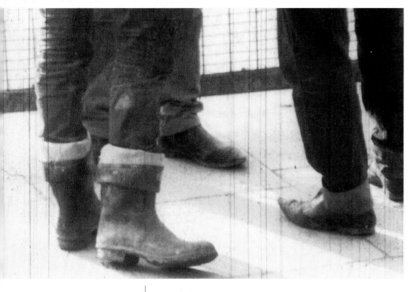

Above: Gangers picked 'skins' by looking at their boots ...

I did an awful lot of what I knew were stupid things, but I didn't say anything, I just did what I was told, because the ganger had the money in his pocket, right there, to pay me that evenin', and if I didn't do whatever he said, I wouldn't be goin' out the next day....[22]

The sub-contracting system wasn't *designed* to oppress labourers, but labour supply was its core business and, even inadvertently, it did so nonetheless.

One of the commonest forms that this exploitation took was the running of 'Dead Men'. This operated as follows:

A main contractor needed a job done which required sixty men on site for seven days. He was offering to pay those men two pounds per hour for a minimum of eight hours each day. He did not, however, wish to be responsible for their National Insurance stamp, holiday pay, tax deductions, etc. so he employed a labour-only sub-contractor to provide them.

The sub-contractor hired the men for a pound per hour, thus guaranteeing himself eight pounds per man per day profit, which, over the seven days, netted him £3,360 without having to lift a finger. On top of that he got his employer's cut.

The main contractor, however, needed an Agent to supervise the contract; the sub-contractor in turn needed a Ganger actually to engage the men, deliver them on site, and oversee the work.

The Ganger, however, only engaged fifty men for the contract, but wrote down sixty names on his timesheet, thus leaving ten men's wages unclaimed — unless by himself. However, the timesheet had to be countersigned by the Agent, so the Ganger agreed to share the wages of the ten 'Dead Men' equally with the Agent. This amounts to £1,120 at the contractor's original agreed hourly rate of £2 per man per hour. Thus they each gained £560 a week, over and above their actual wages, without doing any extra work for it.

Nevertheless, the work was such that sixty men's labour needed to be expended to meet the deadline, so the Ganger now had to get the work of sixty men out of the fifty he actually had on site. This was where the brutality comes in.

If the men (or enough of them — the 'critical mass', one might say) needed the job badly enough, they delivered their labour, and the scam worked. The contractor got the agreed service on schedule, the sub-contractor got the agreed price, and everyone got rich — except the navvy! Those fifty men got a total of £2,800 between them for their week's work. The main contractor, however, paid out £6,720 in wages for their labour plus that of the ten 'dead men'. Incontrovertibly therefore, in the words of Joe McGarry:

An awful lot of Irishmen made an awful lot of money off the backs of an awful lot of other Irishmen.

Whether or not cable laying was exploitative is very much a matter of perception. For example, there was a tradition in London in the 1950s and 1960s of 'the Sunday shift'. Often, where weekday traffic or essential commercial activities impeded normal work, contractors would earmark such jobs for Sundays. This was welcomed by many of the Irish labourers, who were usually broke by Saturday night, and were eager to earn a day's wages to finance the remainder of the weekend's drinking.

Malcolm O'Brien recalls how the Sunday shift system worked:

I used to work occasionally on a Sunday morning for Murphy, pulling cable. On a Saturday night, a ganger would come into the 'Half Moon' pub on Holloway Road, and ask did you want a shift in the morning. If you did, you had to guarantee him a drink the next night. Well, of course everyone did, because it was Sunday only, and it gave you money for your beer, and maybe a good meal of bacon and cabbage.

The shift might last from seven o'clock until half past twelve, for about five pounds a shift. No documentation — just a bundle of fivers in the pub, and pay the men out. Afterwards, when you were driven back to London in the wagons, the foreman came in with you and he had possibly ten shillings off each man, and he drank all day free, and if you didn't go along with that, no more Sunday shifts.

While the men might have suffered from the nefarious practices of the gangers, the 'Sunday shift' was inherently beneficial, and it is probably for this reason that John Kennedy of Manchester spoke happily of hiring 'A *meitheal* of men to pull cable on a Sunday morning'.[23]

Clearly John, in his later years, liked to view this practice as philanthropic. Perhaps he employed a more humane type of agent or ganger than some other Irish sub-contractors: ''The Bull' Cauley was an agent for Manchester Kennedy, and he was a fair guy, not like some of the blackguards Murphy had'.[24]

Successful Irish contracting firms today tend to see the employment policies of their founders as perhaps more benign than they actually were at the time. For example, a spokesman for McNicholas Engineering, one of the firms derived from old 'Pincher' Mac's original company, commenting in *The Irish Post* on the controversial correspondence generated by the death of Murphy's notorious agent, 'Elephant John', wrote as follows:

With high unemployment in the '50s and '60s, times were hard for many labourers, but the reward for those in employment was an income well above the national average wage.

It is not clear whether the phrases 'high unemployment' and 'an income well above the national average wage', as used here, were intended to refer to the employment situation then current in Ireland, or in Britain. If the references are to Ireland, then the statement certainly holds true, but the men were working in Britain, not in Ireland, and at times of virtually full employment there.

Christopher Powell, in his economic history of the British building industry, quotes some interesting statistics in relation to this issue:

As actual earnings exceeded basic pay, so actual hours worked usually exceeded hours agreed nationally between employers and operatives. In 1948 the average weekly earnings (as distinct from wage rates) for a 46.6-hour week were £6.44, almost exactly double that of 1938, when average hours worked were fractionally less. By 1958 averages had reached about £12.07 for 48.2 hours ... but far more significant were changes in the cost of living. From an index of 100 in 1937, this moved to 170 in 1948,

Above: A shuttering carpenter was an important man — lives depended on him.

Opposite page: Lowry & Co. laying cable, Ipswich, 1962.

and 265 in 1958. Overtime payments enabled operatives, whose basic rates were several pence an hour less than the average for manufacturing and other industries, to bring up their earnings to the national average.... In 1973, retail prices increased 9.2% and average weekly earnings of adult manual workers in construction were £41.41, which was 11p less than those in manufacturing industry.[25]

In other words, if a labourer was prepared to work longer hours, he could hope to equal or exceed the average industrial wage. But if he worked for an Irish sub-contractor as a day-labourer, whatever the going rate, he probably wasn't getting the benefit of national insurance stamps, wet weather gear, subsidised canteens, or any of the other perks of unionised employment with a monetary value.

Manpower in building and contracting, in Britain in 1968, was around 1.8 million but the numbers employed 'on the lump' by Irish sub-contractors fulfilling public utilities contracts is not known. Referring to the mainstream building and civil-engineering sections of the industry, Christopher Powell states that 'High general labour turnover and some site management of doubtful quality, were thought to have helped the growth of "the lump" to something approaching 200,000 men by the later 1960s.'

Skins

Malcolm O'Brien, with the advantage of a broader industrial perspective than John Kennedy, and the clear conscience of the lifelong employee, recognised that the system was fundamentally exploitative of the common labourer, whether he was called a 'Skin', a 'Navvy', an 'Operative', or an 'RB1'.

On every site, Wimpey had a 'sub-clerk' who went around the site every day, sayin': 'Do you want a sub?'.... The clever ones said 'No', but the firm didn't like it ... if you subbed a man half his day's pay, he couldn't leave the job because he was broke every pay-day. And on a Saturday the first thing he'd have to do was look for a sub on next week's wages. So he couldn't survive, or move away, because he had no money....

Wimpey employed a 'Walking Pelter', or Senior Ganger, whose duty was to give the work to the other Gangers.

The Walking Pelter was usually a Mayo man, or a Donegal or Connemara man. They were all six foot-plus, totally uncouth, and pitiless. They walked that site from morning 'til night and, if they saw any-one in a trench idle, they fired them on the spot. I've never met with them anywhere else except Wimpey's.

Asked what the British companies valued most about the Irish, Malcolm replied:

We were always there as a labour force; we enjoy working and we're physically fit. We come from an open-air environment — no industrial pollution, whatsoever, and well-fed on spuds and milk. And we were easier to handle than any other emigrants in England.

Left: The Archway Tavern, London.

Opposite page: The Half Moon pub, Holloway Road, North London. Pubs had served as labour exchanges for the British construction industry since the nineteenth century.

I was surprised at this, given the Irish reputation for belligerence, and asked Malcolm to elaborate:

We're a very servile-type people. Apart from being pleasant, we accept orders. It's different now — we're educated and we want to be the boss. But, from the turn of the century right through the 1960s, we were servants — and loyal servants. I could name you a lot of men, who worked for Tarmac, who would die for Tarmac! Thirty, forty-year men, Irishmen.... There's not many left now, because they're all retiring.

They followed the caravan sites, with their women and children.... They were totally dependent on the construction industry, because it was easy to get into, and you needed no training. A lot of it was brute force and ignorance....

But there aren't so many Irish in it today — less and less. The 'Travelling Man' has almost disappeared. Englishmen run it. The Englishman is one of the best bosses one could possibly have, because he can look at a situation and assess it in a calmer light than we can. We're aggressive people really, which is why they employed us. We won't let a job get the better of us, but we sometimes can't see the forest for the trees. I think we haven't reached that state of stability yet. We're not in the top echelons yet — we're almost there, but not quite....

For many Irish construction workers, however, the industry represented a free and independent lifestyle, which more than compensated for its brutality and callousness. Often, in fact, money mattered less than is popularly supposed:

Money never crossed my mind — I didn't care about money; you'd have your ten yards marked out for you, at ten shillings a yard, and you'd have your fiver made in the day. All I wanted money for was the weekend. Many a Long Distance Man walked out of a good job and into a bad one, just for the sake of being able to jack.[26]

The peculiar mystique of the 'Travelling Man' is the most important factor linking Britain's navvies over the past two centuries — from the Canal Age to the Motorway Era. Such Irish as were attracted to that way of life in the first hundred and fifty years, are virtually undocumented. But the earliest evidence of a significant Irish minority amongst the Tramp Navvy fraternity is found in the writings of Patrick MacGill, especially in *Children of the Dead End* and *Moleskin Joe*. References to them can also be found in Sean O'Ciarain's, *A Farewell to Mayo*, and *Dialann Deoraí* (An Irish Navvy) by Domhnall MacAuligh.

They shared many characteristics with the travelling artisans, the journeymen of the nineteenth century, and with the hobos and tramps of the first half of the twentieth. Latterly, however, the term 'Travelling Man', as used by men like Dudley Barratt and Malcolm O'Brien, generally refers to plant operators who live in on-site company caravans, but it could equally apply to many of the Irish navvies who travelled all around Britain laying cable.

Men who got a reputation as a hard worker, whatever their vices, were often asked by agents to go to distant parts of the country, and saw little difference between pulling cable in London or Manchester and doing likewise in remote parts of Wales or rural

Lincolnshire. Connemara man Noel Ó Domhnaill acquired a taste for 'long-distance' travelling in this way.

An agent might come up to you on a Monday morning in Camden Town, and say, 'Would you be interested in a week in Shropshire?' or wherever, and you'd just head back to your room, get your gear, and be in a van headed out the country before dinner time.

There were miles of 23,000-volt cables put underground. No high-tension cable was brought into or across towns or cities except underground. At Portmadoc, in Wales, we put miles of it underground, from Wylfa Power Station in Anglesea.

If you went down the country you'd be confined to a little room in a house somewhere. There might be a sink in the corner, or maybe only a basin. There might be a bathroom downstairs but there'd be a rake of men usin' it.... A lot of the towns had public baths, and you'd use them....

And you might be sharin' that room with two or three other lads, and maybe two of them you wouldn't like, or they mightn't like you, and the only place to go was out for a few pints, so you'd get into that rut then....

We had a great old time.... In London you'd go out with an Irish girl, but down the country it was all English girls we went out with. One time we went to Hull, with Murphy out of Leeds, and all the pubs was packed with women for the first week. Then, the second week, there were no women at all in the same pubs. So I asked the governor, 'Where are all the women?' and he told me, 'The trawlers are back. Wait a week, and they'll be in again.'

It seems when the poor buggers of fishermen were away up off Iceland, or wherever, their wives were out spendin' their money, and showin' us Irish lads a good time. I felt sorry for them — but you don't look a gift horse in the mouth!

Connemara men were often attacked by their fellow-Irishmen on account of the habit native speakers had of conversing together in Irish, even when others present didn't have Irish. Noel's explanation for this seeming rudeness is enlightening:

It was the done thing amongst native speakers. English to me was the language of the 'Big Shots' — there was a lot of misunderstanding about this, but it was regarded as bad manners not to speak to another Irish-speaker in his own language, if you had it yourself.

It was of course safer to attack a fellow-Irishman than risk arrest for violent behaviour towards an English person and, seeking an outlet for their frustrations, many men vented their anger on each other.

In contrast with the many Irish who expressed contempt for the more docile English, and often indulged in unprovoked aggression towards them, Noel Ó Domhnaill showed considerable insight into the reasons behind the seeming placidity of the average English-man in those years.

An Englishman was as tough as any man. What we didn't realise was that a lot of the older English were just out of the army. They'd been in Dunkirk,

North Africa, Germany, and Burma. They were so happy to be home with their families, their wives, that if a row started they'd just go next door to another pub....

These guys had seen real violence — they'd seen their buddies killed next to them, and there we were arse-holin' around the country, thinkin' we were big shots.

Where them fellas were comin' from, they didn't have to have the big money, or the big car — they were quite content to be alive and able to survive, like the old people in Ireland years ago. There was a lot of content in Ireland long ago — there was a lot of emigration, but there was a lot of contentment too....

The ordinary Englishman was no different to ourselves; any that had done their 'O' Levels, and gone to grammar school, you didn't ever meet them. At the end of the day, like any man, you go to bed, and you get up in the mornin', and you go to work — and it's as simple as that!

The touchiness of the rural Irish in Britain in the 1950s and 1960s stemmed from a strong sense of inferiority, exacerbated by the petty snobbery endemic in Irish society at that time, combined with the legacy of colonialism.

And then coming to England with the lads and sticking together, being afraid to talk to the English girls, and all the time this brooding thing of history ... well, it didn't help, you know, in so-called integrating.[27]

An awful lot of Irishmen — some of the finest of men, 18, 25, 27 years of age, really handsome men, afraid to talk to a woman or an English person, riddled with fear.... I've seen them go into a cafe and, if there was a young woman of their own age behind the counter, they could not talk to her. They had to knock each other out to prove they weren't afraid. And it was Ireland that did that to them.[28]

A different form of inferiority complex dogged the youth of Tyrone man Joe McGarry who, like Noel, also ended up 'taking the boat', working on sites in England, and becoming an alcoholic.

Growing up in the North, as a Catholic, I was destined to be a labourer. I didn't intend to — I wanted to learn a skill, but you soon learned your place.... 'Who is this Fenian, wantin' to be a tradesman — who is he?' You're a Catholic, a teenager, with acne, who can't talk to girls except your own sisters; you come up through poverty; you have no true sense of self.

The people who did have a sense of self, who were true individuals, became the millionaires, while I was standin' down a hole, to get money, to buy drink, so that I could fit in, belong, be 'normal', be 'one of us'. If you didn't maintain this 'together-ness', you weren't part of 'our little group'; you were one of 'them', whoever they were. If you didn't drink your money at night, you were seen as 'mean' — there was somethin' wrong with you.

And eventually you ended up homeless — sleepin' rough, turnin' up each mornin' in Camden Town, lookin' for 'the start' so's you'd get a pound to buy a breakfast. But you'd be in the 'Offie' as soon as it opened, if you were anywhere near one that day, and you'd have the liquid lunch. The Englishman or Scotsman who was skipperin' out would be on the dole, but that wasn't in our culture; Paddy would work for his drinkin' money, even when he didn't have a bed....

There is a depth of pain that finds its level, amongst a group of men, in a pub, in a park, homeless and drunk, who recognise each other's pain.... Now I know I'm an island of self, between two places, and I have to identify my own self — what I am, what I can do.[29]

Noel Ó Domhnaill took another route. In his case it was not an inferiority complex, but pride, which drove him to the life of the tramp navvy. He didn't leave

Connemara from economic necessity. Like so many others of both sexes, from the 1960s onwards, he was motivated by the example of his peers, and the need to escape the stultifying boredom of a moribund society.

I was sixteen — the second youngest. I was goin' to the Tech. — I didn't have to leave. But I saw the lads comin' home with the serge suits — black, and blue, and green, and everythin', and the Brylcreem, and you wanted a part of that, and it was exciting.

Rock 'n' Roll was comin' out, Bill Haley, and Radio Luxembourg every Sunday night — the Top Twenty. Usually it was Elvis Presley, and it was dynamite — just the sound of it would get you goin'; and all we had was Paddy O'Brien the accordion player, or Joe Burke, or the Walton's programme – 'If you feel like singing, do sing an Irish song'.... Only in them days it wasn't even in Irish on RTE, it was English — Joe Lynch, or Bridie Gallagher, or Brendan O'Dowda, or someone....

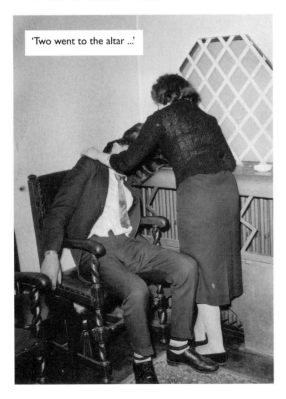

'Two went to the altar ...'

Once established in England, and into the work–drink–sleep cycle of the 'lumper', the issue became whether he could continue drinking to excess, while maintaining the standards of output he'd set himself when he first 'came over'. Inevitably, he couldn't....

When you went to England first, you'd start at seven in the mornin', and work till night. Pride kept you goin' — you wouldn't want to be caught dossin'. Then, as the drink took hold, you couldn't keep up the pace, and your pride wouldn't let you accept that, so the only answer was — 'jack up and move on'. So, at first you'd be runnin' away from the situation, and then you'd end up runnin' away from yourself.

All a Lie

In the construction industry, even the soberest of Irish men seemed to be always in some sense running away from themselves. 'Katherine', a former nurse with three children, married for thirty years to an Irish construction worker, looks after the health and welfare of disadvantaged Irish people in a large English city. Much of her work involves helping Irishmen who formerly worked in construction but have ended up ill, or alone, or homeless. More outspoken than many health professionals, her understanding of these men's predicament is acute:

When I looked at my husband, and looked at all the rest, and at my children's friends, I thought it was me, then I thought it was England, and eventually it dawned on me that it was Ireland, had done all this to them.... I realised that the harm was done before they ever left. England added to it, but it wasn't the cause of it....

The Irish woman controls; the man thinks it's him, but it isn't. But it's done in an underhand, sneaky way.... But it doesn't help anything, because their children can see it, growing up; years and years of thoughtlessness, and cruelty, and selfishness, and they're confused....

One son given the land, maybe because he came back first, or never left, but the other sent money home every week, and ended up with nothing. And the parents have done this without bringing them together and saying, perhaps, 'Well, you didn't want the land, and you're settled with a family in England, so we'll give the land to your brother, because he has nothing', or whatever. Not just do it behind his back....

A lot of the Irish girls who came over in the fifties went into service, most into nursing, and met what they thought was the right fella, got pregnant and got dumped, and had to go into homes, and have the children adopted, and they couldn't write home about this....

England used to be full of Adoption Homes, up and down the country, run by nuns or the Local Authority. And these women are now the secret drinkers....

And the fellas were living a lie too; they weren't supposed to be men, out drinking and dancing and chatting up girls, or whatever.... They just don't know how to face anything, because they were never told about anything, and they were never allowed to ask for anything; because if you asked, you were a failure. You should have been able to do it yourself. Or you're letting the neighbours know you needed to ask. It's sad, and stupid, and pathetic....

The men won't face reality; if they can't get the material things, have it there on show, they live in dreams — all in the mind.... And the more stable ones eventually crack up; it's not that they crack up, they come to their senses, wake up to reality. They've been living under this stress for so long, and it suddenly dawns on them that they were tricked — 'My parents had me believe in — whatever; the priest had me believe in — whatever; my boss had me believe in — whatever....' — and it was all a lie....

And while they were told that England was a place where you could be yourself, they found out that, if you're Irish and need the support of your own kind to survive, as the 'Westies' who work in construction always do, then you can't be yourself — they won't let you. You want to make a stand, and speak out against it, and they won't let you speak out; so you become an outsider....

Whatever way they were brought up, there's a lot of bitterness, and spite, and jealousy in them.... So much so that it can eat away at them, and it can destroy them, and any relationships they might have.... They end up old, and bitter, and alone; they've worked so hard for something better, but they never get that thing that's better, because of their own selves....[30]

This applies to some degree, not only to the ordinary 'navvy', but even to many of the successful self-made contractors of those times. Jackson observed this in an acquaintance who had risen to ownership of a major construction company and suggested that it also applied to others in a similar position.

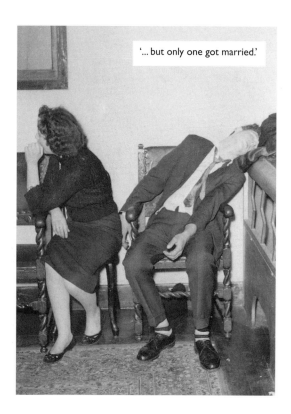

'... but only one got married.'

The narrow concentration upon the mechanics of building, the long hours, the incessant travel, and the near-total immersion of energy in the business has left many of these men materially wealthy but culturally impoverished. [They] cling on, in spite of all medical or family advice to the contrary, for their companies are their lives' work, and often the only 'real' thing in their lives, the prop-up of vanity and of their very personalities. For them, work takes the lion's share of their energies, leaving them as powerful builders of motorways and housing estates and, by the same token, painfully inadequate in many other areas of social and cultural activity.[31]

Jackson is to be commended for giving a voice to such men, at a time when the average Irish historian preferred to relegate the Irish labourer in Britain, successful or otherwise, to the safe and sterilised realm of statistics; but he overlooks the emotional repression governing such men's lives. This often underlay all else, and informed their attitudes towards their children.

And these men, if they're married, are puttin' their sons through what they went through, so where have the lessons been learned, and why do they refuse to learn? Is it badness — 'I suffered, so you should suffer too'?

It's beyond badness — it's something deep that's there, and it destroys them; and it turns their children against them. They don't hate their fathers — they pity them, but they can't go on living with them....

When they're together they all say the same things; they can tell you what their fathers are going to say, after they've had a few pints — 'You're not a man — unless you're out there on 'The Buildings', like I am....'

I can remember my son, at sixteen, changing overnight.... 'Don't expect me to wear the sky-blue suit, and stand at the bar talking about machines, because I won't do it! If that's what you're expecting, don't — because I won't do it. And I won't put on a false show'. And, in their hearts, the fathers know they're right, and wish they'd had the courage to make a stand, but they never did....

'On affairs of state ...'

My husband's a plant operator, and he came home one day with mud up to his knees from a new site and said, 'That's what the men have to work in'; But then he's complaining that his boy isn't the son he should have been, because he isn't out working alongside of him....

He talks about the contractor's two sons being out — one's a grand lad, but the other one's 'shoutin' and roarin' about the place all day long'. And I said, 'I'm not surprised; I'm sure he hates it — that's why he's shoutin' and roarin' at everyone'. And, in years to come, neither of them will thank their father.... 'Ah,' he says, 'but their mother feeds them well; you should see the big lunches....'

I said, 'I bet she does — feed them well! Because as long as they're well fed they can earn more money — for her!' They're being well fed now, while they're young, but in ten years' time, when their health's gone, who'll feed them then?'

And what'll they do? They'll have no interest in any thing, because they weren't encouraged to have an interest.... If they have long-term illness, they can't even sit down and read a book to pass the time, because they've never done it. Half an hour, with a book, they cannot do!

So illness to them is a kind of living death; they'll tell you themselves, they're better if they die, because they have no interests. Because they were never encouraged to do anything, other than earn money — and that cannot be normal. These mothers have a lot to answer for.... There comes a point where we have to stand up and say, 'It isn't necessary to do that anymore — there has to be a better way'....

A Heavy Burden

At the heart of the problem, for many of these men, was poor self-esteem. Unlike the old-style navvies, they took no pride in the traditions of their calling. In fact, they were at pains to avoid being labelled as 'navvies'. At the same time as they enjoyed their 'wild man' status, within the industry, they strenuously rejected society's negative image of their occupation. In this respect, at least, Sykes' observations whilst working amongst Irish navvies in Scotland in the early 1950s are spot on.[32]

Not infrequently, the navvy has been judged as harshly, and with as little discernment, in the twentieth century as he was by the commentators in the nineteenth century, who condemned him for his failure to observe middle-class mores.[33]

Consequently they felt inhibited socially while at the same time glorying in their Legionnaire-like image as hard-drinking, fighting, gambling and risk-taking tearaways. Few of them accepted that they might remain in the industry indefinitely, and aspired to saving sufficient money to leave, while at the same time cultivating a spendthrift image which usually resulted in continuing bondage to the day-wage system so characteristic of the industry.

Many, prior to the phasing-out of direct labour in the 1970s, were spared the worst consequences of this irresponsibility by virtue of being 'company men' whose National Insurance Stamp was paid for by the firm. Provided that they remained in Britain long enough, they could eventually retire on a State Pension, and receive the benefits of the National Health System.

If however, like so many, they placed a premium on anonymity, independence, and freedom of movement, and worked primarily 'on the lump', their only hope of security in later life was either to become subbies or to buy property when they were 'flush', as an investment against old age.

The postwar Irish navvy, however, was often at pains to deny his occupational status to those 'at home' in Ireland, insisting that he was only in the industry temporarily, before moving on to better things. Consequently he avoided making a commitment to life in Britain, but instead vaguely expected to achieve material success as a preliminary to repatriation.

Failure in this, many believed, made it impossible ever to return to their home place. These are the men who, after thirty or forty years' absence from Ireland, inhabit the 'no man's land' of institutions such as Camden Town's Arlington House.

This is in marked contrast to the pre-war men, part of the migrant harvester tradition, who were expected only to make modest gains and were understood by all to be navvying abroad in order to do so. Many, of course, found the life of the wandering labourer more congenial than peasant life in Ireland. Such men decided that the opprobrium of society was more than compensated for, amongst the working class at least, by the pride and freedom of the 'Long-Distance Men' whose antecedents had built the canals, roads, dams and railways of Britain and, always, retained their independence.

The postwar Irish navvy, in stark contrast with both of these traditional role models, was constrained by the negative stereotype of the Irish labourer — the 'all-brawn–no-brain navvy'. He was also put under pressure by the exaggerated expectations of material success which the new-found dominance of the Irish within the British construction industry had engendered amongst those at home in Ireland. A great deal was being asked of him, and it is to his credit that, in so many instances, he succeeded in establishing a middle ground.

Wagons Looking Down on Wheelbarrows

Both the industry and the Irish became progressively more 'civilised' as time went on. From the 1950s onwards the more successful Irish joined with their priests in establishing social centres where their countrymen could meet and relax and enjoy their own cultural activities. Sometimes these new centres were hotbeds of petty snobbery, characterised by one observer as 'wagons looking down on wheelbarrows'.

But usually these displays of wealth took more wholesome forms, such as funding their own GAA teams. Mainly, however, the Irish centres were just warm islands of Irish conviviality and custom in an alien, indifferent, or even hostile society. The Federation of Irish Societies, based in London, provided a national umbrella organisation to promote their interests.

Of course what was initially a natural and comforting inclination to close ranks and turn inwards, as a defence against loneliness and xenophobia, could become unhelpful in terms of the wider assimilation and development of the individual. This collective introversion occasionally resulted in cultural isolation from both the host society and a changing Ireland.

In some of the Irish clubs and centres around Britain, by the late 1970s, stagnation had set in and many became little more than drinking clubs for the older Irish-born members. Some centres, however, were broader in their vision, providing a dynamic environment for the evolution of Irish culture in ways more compatible with the norms of the new society. Many also performed an important welfare function. One such was the London Irish Centre in Camden Town. In 1955 a committee led by Fr Tom McNamara, purchased premises at 51 and 52 Camden Square and set up the Centre. The Centre's aims were as follows:

1. To form a social service bureau to give advice on various problems and to keep a register of decent lodgings for men and women.

2. To provide a hall for social and recreational functions.

3. To provide temporary hostel accommodation.

To their credit, more than one Irish contractor contributed men, money, and materials to the refurbishment and expansion of the Centre. The John F. Kennedy Memorial Hall, for example, was built in 1964 by M.J. Gleeson plc, then led by the founder's son, Jack Gleeson.

Forty years later, the London Irish Centre has three large halls with catering facilities, a fully staffed Advice and Information Centre, and the largest Irish Housing Association in Britain. The bulk of their current case workload has to do with accommodation, with 39 per cent focused on welfare benefits, 10 per cent on employment and 9 per cent on health. Most, but not all, clients are Irish-born.

In the North-West, similar functions are performed by the Irish World Heritage Centre in Manchester and its related welfare organisation, Irish Community Care. Today these organisations receive substantial funding from the Irish government-sponsored DION Emigrant Welfare Committee.

Until relatively recent times, however, repeated requests from concerned Irish emigrant organisations — such as the Irish Bishops, beginning as long ago as 1948 with an appeal by the Irish Priests' Committee for State aid for emigrants — fell on deaf ears. This despite the incessant election-time references by Irish politicians down the years to 'The Curse of Emigration'.

It seemed, for a brief period in the 1970s, that this curse was finally being lifted from the Irish. During the decade 1971–1981, 43,000 adults and 44,000 children returned to Ireland to enjoy that country's new-found prosperity. The 'boom', however, was short-lived and a net out-flow of 9,000 in 1984 had increased to 46,000 — a figure only comparable with those of the late 1950s — by 1989.

Despite the popular perception of hordes of 'illegals' entering the United States in those years, and the daily queues throughout the decade outside the American and Australian embassies in Dublin, it is clear from National Insurance registration data — 31,816 in 1989 — that the majority went to Britain. Many others, who already held British PRSI numbers, were returning immigrants who had failed to re-establish themselves in Ireland. In addition to these, it is very likely that a substantial minority of Revenue 'illegals' still existed in the construction industry who don't appear in official statistics.

Fortunately for those seeking work in the building industry, Britain was about to enter a period of spectacular growth in private-sector construction. The work generated by the discovery of North Sea oil and gas was, of course, on-going, as was a somewhat curtailed motorways programme, but most of the new building was private-sector driven, and aimed at providing commercial accommodation. As such, it was largely concentrated in the South-East, particularly in and around London.

An estimated 14.3 per cent of working Irish males in 1985 were in construction (down from the 17.85 per cent given by Jackson in 1963, but in a less buoyant building industry). This was a much higher proportion than the national average — a mere 6.6 per cent.[34]

Above: Fr McNamara opens the London Irish Centre, Camden Town, 1955.

Above: Jack Gleeson, Chairman of M.J. Gleeson plc, signing contracts for the construction of the John F. Kennedy Memorial Hall, London Irish Centre, in 1964.

The downside to this picture was the reaction of the British government to the proliferation of tax evaders. Consequent on the phasing out of direct labour by the main contractors, self-employment in the industry increased by 56 per cent between 1970 and 1985, as did the predominance of unregistered subbies hiring undocumented, predominantly Irish, labour. In 1985 half of all manual-building workers were self-employed. This statistic could be misleading, however: in 1980 Wimpey, with an annual turnover of almost £2 billion world wide, still retained 15,000 employees.[35]

The response of the Inland Revenue was to introduce '714' Certificates, enabling their holders to get paid without deductions, and 'SC 60s' which resulted in workers having tax at a flat rate of 25 per cent deducted at source. Holders of these certificates paid tax on a self-employed basis. Because they could deduct their expenses they paid less tax than under the PAYE system. It was thought that this incentive would induce them to register.

Employers, of course, benefited by avoiding the payment of National Insurance contributions and holiday money. This gave them a competitive edge over contractors employing direct labour. Also, since they could hire skills to match contracts, their contracting range increased correspondingly. Their workforces could be kept small, pricing by subbies was keen, and the risks of fluctuating demand could be passed over to the sub-contractors.

An abundance of sub-contractors on large, fast-track sites, on the other hand, made greater managerial demands on the main contractors. Also, the insistence by private-sector clients on fast completions could result in rising labour costs (private-sector work accounted for no less than 68 per cent of all contracts in 1985).

Subbies had to contend with underpricing, delayed payments, and ensuing difficulties meeting VAT demands, resulting in many business failures (usually followed by their rapid re-emergence under a new trading name) but they stood to make large profits in busy periods. The building industry had always offered Irish emigrants an almost unique opportunity for upward mobility but, by the 1980s, small men attempting to go out on their own for the first time rarely survived.

Veteran 'lumpers' from the 1960s, however, often became eight-figure turnover companies in the 1980s. The 'big names' from the postwar boom were soon joined by a new generation of Irish-owned companies such as McGinley, Gulmanda, O'Keeffe, O'Rourke, Byrne Brothers, Fitzpatrick, Gallagher, Hennelly, Durkan Brothers, Norwest Holst, Kilroe, and Wrekin Construction, amongst others. Many English also re-entered the industry in those years, attracted by the new 'loads-a-money' economic climate, but few stayed the course. Indian contractors also began to make an appearance in the industry at this time, one such using the advertising slogan, 'You've used the Cowboys — now try the Indians!'

In boom times, such as the late 1980s, wage rates rose but the drawback for the new 'self-employed' workers was the lack of protection from health and safety regulations and industrial tribunals, as well as loss of unemployment, injury, and disability benefit, and pensions.

It was inevitable that, in such a climate, many employers would largely ignore both training and safety. In the heady days of full employment these drawbacks were often regarded as a small price to pay, particularly where Irish men clung to the fantasy that they would be 'going home next year', rather than facing permanent residence, retirement, and old age in Britain.

When the 'bust' came again, as it did in the early 1990s, it was the casual labour sector that was hardest hit. Direct employment had shrunk from 59 per cent in 1975 to 39 per cent in 1993. Of 195,000 firms then in the building industry, 98.3 per cent employed fewer than twenty-five people, and almost 70 per cent of workers in construction were skilled. The 31 per cent who were unskilled labourers were the ones who suffered most from the casualisation of the industry.

By this time, labour in the construction industry was pretty much polarised between the élite elements, working in excellent conditions on projects associated with North Sea Oil and the Channel Tunnel, and the exploited and abused casual day-labourers in the cities.

I arrived in Flotta on a cold January morning, to take on the job of site office manager for one of the many construction companies working there, mainly building an oil terminal to service the Piper and the Claymore oil fields. Apart from leave periods this was to be my home for the next three years.

Above: Fr Eamon Casey at the London Irish Centre, 1969. Fr Casey pioneered important housing initiatives for the London–Irish community and is remembered with great affection by the Irish in Britain.

Flotta is one of many islands that make up the Orkneys. It is four miles by two and is inhabited by twenty-two families. Before the oil they existed on sheep farming, cutting peat for heat and cooking, and government relief.

Between Flotta and Stronness lies famous Scapa flow, where the Germans scuppered their fleet at the end of the First World War. On a calm, clear day (a rarity) one can see the hulks sticking up out of the water.

We had 500-plus men on our books, mostly Scots, but about 150 Irish and the remainder from the north east of England. The working day was seven a.m. to seven p.m. seven days per week, and in the early days we worked six weeks without a break.

The food and accommodation was excellent — first class. It was provided by Grand Met Catering. Four meals per day — breakfast, lunch, dinner, supper; a huge choice of everything, top quality and unlimited helpings. We had two large dining halls — one for the staff members and one for the rest.

We had two bars — one for the staff and one for the rest, all drinks at cost price; the best of beers, wines, whiskey, gin, etc. Once a week we had a cabaret — a sort of singsong. We hired some reasonable artistes, and usually a good time was had by all.

I have many happy memories, and one or two scary ones, of my time on Flotta. I overheard a little 'jock' one day complaining about the food — too many T-bone steaks, he said; too rich for his fish-and-chip stomach. Another time two Glaswegians came up to work for us, dressed in baseball boots and T-shirts — on the edge of the Arctic Circle!

Then we had Big John, from Donegal, who had lived in Glasgow for years. He just wouldn't fly. We tried everything — getting him drunk, pep talks etc., all to no avail. Every time he went out on leave it took three days; one and a half going and the same coming back, by car and boat. He could have made the same return journey by air in three hours max. I'm told he is still waiting to make his first plane trip!

And yet, in my three years up there, we didn't have one serious accident, either coming or going or during our working time on the island. Having said all that — the son of a well-known shop steward and senior plant operator tried his utmost to rectify that, by driving a 22RB off the end of the jetty and into Scapa Flow. No one hurt — a miracle!

Before I conclude, I must pay tribute to one Joe Mangan, from Belmullet in County Mayo who, at the tender age of sixteen, more than held his own with the best. Joe was a General Operative (First Class), who had spent six months at Kishorn building the Rigs before coming to Flotta. He was, indeed, a throwback to the true grafters from the turn of the century.[36]

Joe Mangan, whether he knew it or not, was a lucky man. Given that he hadn't obtained either vocational or academic qualifications, being only sixteen when he came to Flotta, he had obviously started his career in the right place and at the right time.

Thousands of his contemporaries, equally young, equally unskilled, and equally anxious to work in construction, were, however, very clearly in the wrong place and time. These were the youths who went to London, and other big British cities, in the late 1980s and early 1990s and took the traditional route of the casual labourer working 'on the lump'.

By the mid-1990s the increasing casualisation of the industry had undermined both training and health and safety. Subbies, to compete, were cutting corners and taking risks. At the same time increasingly widespread technological applications and innovations throughout the industry were making the unskilled labourers almost redundant. Certainly where mere muscle was required, it mattered little to either contractor or client which men were selected, and what low levels of pay and conditions they were obliged to accept.

According to an article in the *Independent on Sunday*, on 2 February 1996, the tradition continues:

Fifty scrappily dressed men — most of them Irish, some East European — solicit passing vehicles in a suburban street. A blue Transit van rolls to a halt beside the kerb. The driver, a thickset, cropped-haired 'gangerman', is here to pick 'Skins', men who will work on his building-sites for fifteen pounds for a twelve-hour day. Those touting for work are recruited 'on the lump', no questions asked, no ID required, cash in hand....[37]

One young man referred to a 'tradition' amongst Irish male emigrants to Britain of seeking employment in construction. It is doubtful whether he understood just how long-lived this tradition is. It has produced, not just the casualties seen in places like Conway House, but countless thousands of modestly successful men, and a respectable sprinkling of millionaires.

We have seen how well represented the Irish were on the building of the Manchester Ship Canal — 'The greatest engineering feat of the Victorian Age'. Exactly a century later, it was estimated that Irish-born men and men of Irish decent accounted for no less than one-third of the 15,000-strong work force on the construction of the Channel Tunnel. Leading figures from the industry recently voted this the single most important project in the entire history of British civil engineering – 'The biggest project since the Pyramids'. (*Construction News*, Centenary Edition, 1996.)[38]

Young construction workers, Daventry, 1958.

In that same time-span the Irish have risen in the British construction industry, from mere labourers, to 'the second rank' as owners of major companies. A glance at *The Sunday Times* Rich List, 2001, reveals a clutch of well-known names from the ranks of Irish-owned construction companies in Britain:

Fitzpatrick, Pat	£35 million
Kennedy, Joe & John	£70 million
Murphy, John & Family	£87 million
Murphy, Joe (Jr) & Family	£40 million
O'Rourke, Ray	£60 million

Attrition

Yet, in 1997, Father Paul Byrne, OMI, Chairman of the Episcopal Commission for Emigrants, wrote a sobering article for the Simon Newsletter, describing the sad shadow-side to the success story of the Irish in 1990s Britain.

Of the 29,000 who left Ireland during 1996/97, no less than 18,000 were aged between 15 and 24. While allowing for the fact that Ireland has the youngest cohort of graduates in the EU, it is probable that, given the low threshold of 15 years, there are many who are naive, unqualified, vulnerable and young.

The problem is that basic information about our emigrants is very sparse. How many of the 18,000 were only sixteen, or even fifteen? How many had no qualifications at all? How much money, if any, did they have with them? We know something about where they went — just 13,000 of the 29,000 went to Britain — the vast majority, it seems, to London.

Clearly young Irish men seek work in many occupations other than construction, but the casual and nomadic nature of that industry makes it both accessible and attractive, and that, in itself, may ultimately prove detrimental to their long-term welfare. Paul Byrne gave tragic examples of the sad fate that can still befall the homeless Irish even in the 1990s:

Recently the City Morgue in Birmingham had no less than five unidentified corpses believed to be Irishmen, including a 23-year-old who died homeless. In the same city, 'Paidi' died homeless in a remote corner of a car park and was only found as a skeleton.... Fr Frank Ryan of the Irish Welfare Centre in Birmingham found his full name and date of birth from Salvation Army hostel records. He had come from a Gaeltacht area and is buried there now. Ironically, Paidi died with over two thousand pounds in obsolete sterling notes in his pocket....

A recent influential study by Professor Mary Hickman and Dr Bronwen Walter, on behalf of the Commission for Racial Equality, details the following stark facts about the Irish in Britain:

* *Irish-born people are more strongly clustered in social class V, the lowest grouping, than any other major ethnic group in Britain;*
* *Measures of social mobility suggest that the Irish-born category do not share upward mobility to the same extent as the population as a whole;*
* *Percentages of Irish-born people with no qualification are well above the average;*
* *Irish people are under-represented as home-owners — 21 per cent are in council housing with the national average standing at 16 per cent;*
* *Rates of overcrowding are twice that of the population as a whole and Irish people live in the worst housing.*

In the study referred to by Father Byrne, it is also alleged that Irish men, alone amongst migrants, have a higher mortality rate in Britain than in their home country. The study states that the largest number of Irish-born workers in Britain are in the forty-five to fifty-nine age group, and are employed in traditional sectors — domestic work for women, and building work for men.

Above: Arlington House, Camden Town. The final destination for too many Irish construction workers.

Pressure on Irish welfare agencies in Britain is increasing, as the problems of the older generation — mainly emigrants from the 1940s through the 1960s — begin to emerge around retirement age. According to the 1991 Census the number of Irish-born males over the age of sixty-five in the Greater London area was 18,393. The number of Irish-born females over sixty was 37,370. Across England and Wales the equivalent figures were 71,354 males over sixty-five and 134,634 females over the age of sixty.

It would not be stretching credibility to suggest that the huge disparity, and the correspondingly high mortality rate, amongst older Irish-born males is a direct consequence of the conditions and lifestyle associated with the construction industry, which employed the majority of Irish-born male immigrants in Britain since the war.

Both the British and Irish governments need to put in place comprehensive policies to deal with issues of ongoing emigration, and also to give concrete recognition to the contribution of older Irish emigrants to their societies, and the special problems which they are encountering in later life. Those wishing to end their days in Ireland, particularly, ought to be enabled to do so. Both Ireland and Britain owed them that much.

At its most extreme, the problems of the disadvantaged older Irish in Britain are symbolised by the 130 progressively ageing and vulnerable Irish men currently resident in Arlington House in Camden Town, where Irish labourers have been given shelter since 1905. Their plight was highlighted in a 1997 report by the current custodians of the hostel, Bridge Housing Association, the concluding paragraph of which reads:

The Irishmen of Arlington House are now facing difficult times in a changed world. The Camden Town of their youth has disappeared, as the working-class Irish community, with its pubs, has moved on and been replaced with what has become one of North London's trendiest and busiest areas.

The world of casual building work and full employment has gone for good. However, the patterns of unsettled lifestyles, transient work, and hard manual labour, have left behind them ill health, homelessness, and — for some, alcohol dependency. Without pensions or savings, men who worked to lay the infrastructure of modern London face an uncertain future in a world which is openly hostile to them and their home.[38]

At least in Arlington House they live, and sometimes die, in a caring environment amongst sympathetic friends and staff who understand them and the world that they inhabit. These men are some of the contemporary casualties of the Irish experience in 'building Britain' over two-and-a-half centuries. They suffer the chronic ill-health of a lifetime spent working outside, in all weathers, in an industry notorious for its toughness and brutality. Many also still suffer the pain of exile.

Even men who carved out comfortable and successful lives in Britain through the construction industry sometimes found that they could not escape this sense of alienation. In 1966 Domhnall MacAuligh, with a book to his credit, journals publishing his articles, and a wife and two children around him, still felt deep unhappiness after fifteen years living in Northampton:

There was a freeness about expatriation once. You told yourself it wouldn't be forever — that it was a holiday.... It would be over sooner or later; but that's no longer true; all that's ahead of you is the time you have left on earth. Spend it here, in loneliness and desolation. I came here in 1951, and I've never felt at home here in all that time....[39]

'Nobby' Clarke, the Long-Distance Man from County Galway who was the first Irish navvy I interviewed, told me his life story early one Sunday lunchtime, in 1993, in the South London Irish Centre in Wimbledon. He had started his career as a harvester before the war, made his way into construction, and all his life thereafter worked the cycle of the old-time

Tramp Navvy, going from farm to site and back again, according to his moods and the rhythm of the seasons.

He was a big man, bent now but with a huge frame, and his hands were like shovels. His presence somehow still emanated strength and when he spoke, the younger men around him listened, hard.

> *'Twas a great life, but 'twas tough. You were only three, or four, or five weeks at the one job; you weren't content to stay anyplace for long – 'twas a change, you know, for your body. The farmin' was the best — you paid no tax; but on the buildin's you were with your own. 'Twas a rough oul' life, but I'm none the worse for it. I'm seventy-nine gone — I can stoop down an' put me shoes on, an' shave meself, an' close the buttons on me shirt, but barely. I can take me pint, and whatever else you'd put in front of me, and I'm content....'*

'I'm content' — I doubt if many of those Irishmen who started off where Nobby started, and ended up as millionaires, could hope to say more when they reach his age. In any event, both he and they, and all the other Irishmen who bore the name of navvy, are proud men and part of a proud tradition. That much they all have in common.

Epitaph

Despite the hype, it would be going too far to say without qualification that the Irish alone 'built Britain'. Undoubtedly, over the two centuries between the building of the Newry Canal and the end of the Second World War, the British did the lion's share — the entrepreneurs, the civil engineers (the world's first and finest), the visionary merchants, the great contractors, and especially the railway navvies.

But all around them, all the time, the Irish in their thousands were 'digging it out, and throwing it well back', in every place where muck had to be shifted, and foundations dug by hand. And in the twentieth century, from the 1940s to the 1990s, the ground works aspects of Britain's construction and civil-engineering industries were completely dominated by the Irish — the peasant Irish, the 'culchies', the 'thick Paddies', so long belittled and despised, on both sides of the Irish Sea.

While it could be argued that the Irish did not, by themselves, build Britain, it must be asked whether, without them, it could ever have been done. In the nineteenth century, as the Industrial Revolution press-ganged the rural poor into the mills and factories and urban ghettos, the Irish were Britain's indispensable mobile reserve of supplementary labour. In the twentieth, as British living standards rose, they were the muck-shifters and the grafters who would get down, and get stuck in, when no one else would touch such work. Sir William McAlpine has given me his personal assessment of the importance of the Irish to the British construction industry. Few would question the authority of his opinion:

> *Since the late eighteenth century, the Irish have played a major part in the expansion of British industry and of the country's canal, road and rail network. The success of the British construction industry owes a great deal to Irish skills in excavation and construction, and their contribution to the development of the industry has been immeasurable.*[40]

Perhaps the Irish navvies' greatest accolade was paid them, appropriately, by an old English navvy. Charlie Williams of Fallowfield, who worked as a 'Nipper' on the building of the Manchester Ship Canal over one hundred years ago, said of his Irish co-workers:

> *My navvy-ganger always preferred Irishmen — they were more robust, and strong as bloody lions; The Salt of the Earth — THEY were MEN!*[41]

I could not have put it better myself.

The final irony — official Irish recruiting poster from 1997.

Notes

Introduction

1 Bagwell, P.S., *The Transport Revolution*, p. 1
2 Cullen, C.M., *An Economic History of Ireland*, p. 96
3 Bagwell, op. cit. pp. 7–10
4 Burton, A., *The Canal Builders*, p. 155
5. This pattern was to be repeated, two centuries later, by many of the successful Irishmen who came to prominence in British construction after the Second World War — except that the Irish became contractors rather than engineers.
6. 'NAVVY —
   1. A drain-maker's spade with a stout, narrow, gouge-like blade, a "graft"
   2. Verb: To work as a "navvy"
   3. With "on": To struggle on through difficulties."
   (*The English Dialect Dictionary*, Vol. IV (Oxford University Press, 1961)).

1: The Culture of Migration

1 Redford, A., *Labour Migration in England 1800–1850*, Manchester University Press, 1926
2 MacLaughlin, J., *Ireland: The Emigrant Nursery and the World Economy*, Cork University Press, 1994
3 Fitzpatrick, D., *Irish Emigration*
4 Hosbach, W.A., *A History of the English Agricultural Labourer*, 1894, p. 259
5 Cullen, L.M., *An Economic History of Ireland since 1660*, 1972, pp. 117–121
6. Ó Gráda, C., 'Seasonal Migration & Post-Famine Adjustment in the West of Ireland', in *Studia Hibernica*, No. 13 (1974)
7. Irish Folklore Commission
8. House of Commons, *Poor Inquiry*, Appendix D, 1836, vol. 1, pp. xxxi
9. Cullen, op. cit., pp.111–2
10. Moran, G., 'A Passage to Britain: Seasonal Migration and Social Change in the West of Ireland,1870–1890', *Saothair* 13, (1982), p. 26
11. Cullen, op. cit., pp.119–120
12. Ó Gráda, C., op. cit., p. 73
13 Condor, S., *The Men Who Made Railways*, 1868, p. 169
14 Smiles, S., *Lives of the Engineers*, 1858, p. 89
15 Irish Folklore Commission
16. Mullins, T., in John Burnett (Ed.), *Useful Toil*, 1974, p. 64
17 Ó Duibheanaigh, S., Irish Folklore Commission, MS. 477: 394–6, in O'Dowd, A., 'Seasonal Migration to the Lagan and Scotland' in *Donegal History Society*, Geography Publications (Eds. W. Nolan, L. Ronayne, M. Dunleavy), 1995, p.p. 645–6 (M.S. O'Dowd's trans.)
18 Neary, J, *Memories of a Long Distance Kiddy* (1994), p.32

19 O'Hara, J., Conversation with the author, Manchester, 1995
20. Clarke, N., Conversation with the author, London, 1993
21. *Labour News*, August 30, 1871
22. Moran, G., 'A Passage to Britain: Seasonal Migration and Social Change in the West of Ireland, 1870–1890', *Saothair* 13 (1982) p.26
23. Neary, J., Conversation with the author, London, 1995
24. Fitzpatrick, D., *Irish Emigration 1801–1921*, 1994, p.21
25. Healy, J., *No One Shouted Stop* (1988), p. 45
26. MacGill, P., *Children of the Dead End* (1995 edition), pp. 117, 174
27. Neary, J., op. cit.
28. Moran, G., op. cit., p.30
29. Delaney, E. *Demography, State and Society* (2000), pp. 244–8; see also Brody, H., *Inishkillane: Change & Decline in the West of Ireland* (1973)
30. Delaney, op. cit., p. 176; for the obverse of this attitude, and its consequences, see MacLaughlin, J., *Ireland: The Emigrant Nursery and the World Economy* (1994), p. 27
31. *Doohoma*, RTÉ, 1972

2: Canals, Bridges, Embankments and Cuts

1. See Davis, G., 'The Irish in Britain, 1815–1939', in *The Irish Diaspora* (Ed. Andy Bielenberg), 2000; see also Herson, J., 'Irish families in Victorian Stafford', in R. Swift & S. Gilley (Eds.), *The Irish in Victorian Britain: The Local Dimension*, 1999, 'Catholics from other provinces were a mixture of the skilled and less skilled', p.163
2. Chinn, C., 'The Irish in early Victorian Birmingham', in R. Swift & S. Gilley (Eds.), *The Irish in Victorian Britain: The Local Dimension*, 1999, p. 64
3. Ibid., p. 56
4. Neal, F., 'Irish settlement in the north-west and north-east of England', ibid., pp. 90–100
5. Handley, J.E., *The Navvy in Scotland*, Cork, 1970, pp. 48, 54, 55
6. Neal, F., op. cit., pp. 83, 99–100
7. O'Dowd, op. cit., pp. 30–31
8. Handley, J.E., *The Irish in Modern Scotland*, Cork, 1947, pp.175–177; see also Turton, J., 'Mayhew's Irish: The Irish poor in mid-nineteenth century London', in *The Irish in Victorian Britain*, op. cit., p. 131
9. Ó Gráda, C., 'The Irish in Nineteenth Century Britain: Problems of Integration', in R. Swift & S. Gilley (Eds.), *The Irish in the Victorian City* (1980), pp .13–14
10. Kennedy, Robert (1973), quoted in Glynn, Sean, 'Irish Immigration to Britain, 1911–1951 : Patterns and Policy', *Irish Economic and Social History*, vol. 8, 1981, p. 51
11. Handley, J.E., *The Navvy in Scotland*, 1798–1845, Cork 1943, pp. 54–55
12. Handley, J.E., ibid. p. 127

13. Evidence of Superintendent Dowling, Liverpool Commissioner of Police, to the House of Commons Select Committee on Railway Labourers, 1846 (530), xiii, 425, pp. 3056–3057
14. Public Record Office, Copy 1/398
15. Jackson, J.A, *The Irish in Britain*, 1963, p. 13
16. Handley, J.E., *The Navvy in Scotland*, p. 48
17. Cf. The numerous statements on this subject in the many Parliamentary Reports dealing with Emigration, the plight of the Irish Poor, Railway Labourers, etc.
18. Handley, J.E. *The Navvy in Scotland*, pp. 80–81
19. Helps, A., *Life and Labours of Mr Brassey*, 1872 (1969 ed.), p. 76
20. This is a fundamental difference between European and American railway building. In Europe land was expensive and labour cheap, so routes had to be as direct as possible, even if this necessitated huge amounts of labour-intensive works such as tunnelling. In America, in contrast, land was cheap and labour costly, so that lines could meander around obstacles, proceeding comparatively slowly, provided labour costs didn't rise significantly above projections.
21. Bagwell, op. cit., p. 38
22. Handley, J.E., *The Irish in Modern Scotland*, p. 143
23. See Handley, J.E., *The Irish in Scotland, & The Irish in Modern Scotland*; also Mayhew, H., *London Labour and the Labour Poor* (4 vols., London, 1861–2; reprinted New York, 1968)
24. Smiles, S., *Lives of the Engineers*, 1858
25. Ashton, T.S., *Economic & Social Investigations in Manchester, 1833–1933*, 1934, p. 117
26. *Eccles & Patricroft Journal*, June 8, 1888 (re building of Manchester Ship Canal)
27. Conder, F.R., *The Men Who Made Railways*, 1868
28. Helps, Arthur, *Life and Labours of Mr Brassey*, 1872, pp. 77–78
29. Coleman, T., *The Railway Navvies*, 1965, p. 63
30. Tremenheere, M., Commissioners' Report, Board of Agriculture, 1867, in Hosbach, W.A., *A History of the English Agricultural Labourer*, 1894, p. 259
31. Coleman, op. cit. p. 27
32. Francis, J.R. *A History of the English Railway*, 1851, vol. 2, p. 67, Smiles, op. cit.
33. Bagwell, P.S., op. cit., p. 100

3: Paddy and the Big Ditch

1. Carlyle, T., in Coleman, op. cit., pp. 24–25
2. Various Parliamentary Reports (Ref. Handley) Report on the State of the Irish Poor in Great Britain, 1835, pp. xxxvi–vii, 68
3. Sullivan, D., *Navvyman*, 1983, pp. 3–22
4. Brooke, D., 'Railway Navvies on the Pennines,' 1841–71, in *Journal of Transport History* (N.S.), Vol. 3 (1975–6), pp. 45–6
5. *Manchester Guardian*, 3 March 1888
6. Delaney, R., *Ireland's Inland Waterways*, 1984, pp. 172–3
7. Brooke, D., 'The "Lawless" Navvy: A study of the crime associated with railway building', in *The Journal of Transport History*
8. Barrett, Rev. D.W., *Life And Work Among the Navvies*, 1880, p. 82
9. Lecount, P., 'History of the Railway Connecting London and Birmingham' quoted in Coleman, op. cit., p. 22
10. *Eccles & Patricroft Journal*, 8 June 1888
11. 'They Brought the Sea to Manchester', *North-West Sound Archive*
12. Williams, F.S., *Our Iron Roads: their History, Construction, and Social Influences*, 1852, p. 419
13. MacGill, P., *Songs of The Dead End*, 1912

14. *Manchester Guardian*, 29 February 1846
15. Conder, F., *The Men Who Made Railways*, 1868, pp. 89–91
16. Redford, A., op. cit., p. 151
17. Brooke, D., *The Railway Navvy: 'That Despicable Race of Men'*, 1984, pp. 110–119
18. For a discussion of the current scholarly thinking on the subject of Irish labour and wage levels see Turton, J., 'The Irish poor in mid-nineteenth century London', in *The Irish in Victorian Britain: The Local Dimension*, op. cit., pp. 131–9
19. Cahalan, C., Letter to the author, 19 April 1999
20. Brooke, D., Letter to the author, 26 October 1997
21. Brooke, D., ibid., Table V; 'Railway Navvies On The Pennines, 1841–71', in *Journal of Transport History* (N.S.) Vol. 3 (1975–6), pp. 41–53; 'The Railway Navvy of the 1881 Census', in *Quarterly Journal of Social Affairs*, 1986, 2(4) pp. 363–377
22. Patmore, J.A., 'A Navvy Gang of 1851', *Journal of Transport History*, Vol. V, p. 10 (1962)
23. Brooke, D., *The Railway Navvy*, p. 28
24. Ibid., p. 167
25. Brooke, D., Letter to the author, 26 October 1997
26. Public Record Office, RG 10/4252, f. 31 verso
27. Sullivan, Dick, *Navvyman*, p. 120
28. Brooke, D., Letter to the author, 26 October 97
29. Westhoven, W., The Forth Bridge, (1890), quoted in Mackay, Sheila, *The Forth Bridge: A Picture History*, HMSO (1993 edition), p. 27
30. Trebel, J.H., 'Irish Navvies in the North of England, 1830–1850', in *Transport History*, VI (1973), p. 228–9
31. Handley, J.E. *The Navvy in Scotland*, p. 16
32. Fitzpatrick, D., 'Irish Emigration, 1801–1921', *Economic & Social History Society of Ireland*, 1984, p. 31
33. Doyle, E., Letter to the author, 16 April 1998
34. McAlpine, Malcolm H.D., Letter to the author, 28 May 1998
35. During the Second World War Joe Doyle, who had left the firm, was requested by McAlpine to take all photos and plans relating to Heraklion still in his possession to the Admiralty in London in connection with proposals to use Crete as a staging post in the invasion of Europe. According to Eileen:

    The information given to the Admiralty re the sea-defences, tides, depth of water & seasonal storms, etc., would only have confirmed that a sea-borne landing was not feasible.

    Since the Germans had previously secured Crete by means of airborne landings presumably the British would not have been able to take them by surprise by doing likewise.
36. Lecount, P., in Coleman, T., op. cit., p. 35
37. Conder, F., *The Men who Made Railways*, 1868, pp. 89–91
38. Proceedings of the Institution of Civil Engineers, (1914–15), Part 1, vol. 199, p. 42
39. MacGill, P., *Children of the Dead End*, 1985 ed., p. 187
40. Select Committee on Railway Labourers, 1846, Q. 427
41. *Glasgow Herald*, 16 December 1822, quoted in Handley, J.E., *The Navvy in Scotland*, 1970, p. 127; *Kilmarnock Journal*, quoted in *Glasgow Herald*, 25 July 1842, in Handley, p. 137
42. *The Commonweal* 28 January 1888
43. *Daily Graphic*, London Supplement, 'Views of the Manchester Ship Canal: Sketches round about Eastham', p. 5
44. *Eccles & Patricroft Journal*, 24 February & 2 March 1888
45. Cowley, U., 'Paddy & The Big Ditch', 1994 (Unpublished Commissioned Report)

46. *Manchester Guardian*, 3 March 1888
47. *Manchester City News*, 16 April 1888
48. Gray, T., *A Hundred Years of the Manchester Ship Canal*, 1994, p. 28
49. Brooke, D., op. cit., p. 139
50. Coleman, T., op. cit., p. 1

4: The Long-Distance Kiddies

1. Rolt, L.T.C, *The Making of a Railway*, 1971, p. 87; *Victorian Engineering*, p. 100
2. Helps, Sir Arthur, *Life and Labours of Mr Brassey*, 1872, pp. 218–219
3. Ibid, pp. 219–220
4. Handley, op. cit., p. 69
5. MacGill, P., *Children of the Dead End*, 2nd ed., Calibah, 1995, p. 213
6. Dickens, C., *Dombey and Son*, 1836
7. Select Committee on the State of the Irish Poor in Great Britain (1835)
8. Handley, op. cit., p. 24.
9. Lee, J., 'Ireland in the 20th Century', *Sunday Tribune*, 24 September 2000
10. Foster, R., *Modern Ireland: 1600–1972* (1989 ed.), pp. 371–2
11. Harris, R.A., *The Nearest Place That Wasn't Ireland*, 1984, pp. 123, 159
12. Hobsbawm, E., 'The Tramping Artisan', *Economic History Review*, vol. 3, no. 32, second series, 1951, pp. 34–35
13. MacGill, P., *Moleskin Joe*, 1921, pp. 15–16
14. MacGill, P., *Songs of the Dead End*, 1890 (1984 ed.) p. 59
15. MacGill, P., *Moleskin Joe*, pp. 43–44
16. MacGill, P., *Children of the Dead End*, 1995 Ed., pp. 152–153
17. Ibid, pp. 153–154
18. Ibid, p. 194
19. Fitzpatrick, D., *Irish Emigration*, 1801–1921, 1994, p. 21
20. MacAuligh, D., op. cit., p. 55

5: Twilight of the Navvy

1. Moran, G., "A Passage to Britain': Seasonal Migration and Social Change in the West of Ireland, 1870–1890", *Saothair* 13 (1982), p. 28
2. Fitzpatrick, D., 'The Disappearance of the Irish Agricultural Labourer, 1841–1912'
3. Moran, op. cit., p. 26
4. Ibid., p. 30
5. Thompson, F., *Lark Rise to Candleford*, 1973 ed., pp. 207–208
6. Fitzpatrick, D., *Irish Emigration*, 1801–1921, pp. 7–8
7. Ibid, p. 40
8. Foster, R., *Modern Ireland, 1600–1972*, p. 539
9. Morgan, D.H., 'The Irish Harvesters', in *Harvesters and Harvesting*, 1840–1900, 1982, Hosbach, W.A. (ed.), p. 83
10. Ó Tuathaigh, G, 'The Irish in 19th Century Britain: Problems of Integration', in R. Swift & S. Gilley (Eds.), *The Irish in the Victorian City*, p. 17
11. Public Record Office, RG 10/4252 f. 3
12. 1 verso. Sullivan, D., op. cit., pp. 5, 50, 120
13. Coleman, T., op. cit., p. 31
14. Brooke, D., op. cit., p. 37
15. Handley, J.E., *The Navvy in Scotland*, pp. 151–158
16. Flynt, J., *Tramping with Tramps*, 1969 ed., p. 250
17. MacGill, P., *Moleskin Joe*, 1918
18. Neary, J., *Memories of a Long Distance Kiddy*, p. 42
19. Orwell, G., *Down and Out in Paris and London*, 1940, p. 126, 179–181

20. Ibid., p. 116
21. Kavanagh, P., *The Green Fool*, 1984 ed., p. 254
22. Hilton, J., in Jack Common (Ed.), *Seven Shifts*, 1938, pp. 36–37
23. McAlpine, M.H., Unpublished letter to the author, 1998
24. Childers, J. Saxon, *Robert McAlpine*, 1925, pp. 82–83
25. Joby, R.S., 'Three Phases of Railway Contracting', Institution of Civil Engineers, 7th Annual Seminar, July 1988, Outline, Section 10
26. Brooke D., 'The Railway Navvy — A Reassessment', *Construction History*, Vol. 5, 1989, p. 35
27. World Register of Dams, 1977, p. 11
28. See: Robinson, B., *Walls Across the Valley — The Building of Howen & Derwent Dams*, 1993; also Sutton, G.E., *The Story of Birchinlee: A Memento of Twelve Years in the Workmen's Village*, Derwent Valley Waterworks, Derbyshire, 1914
29. *Building Magazine*, 150th Anniversary Issue, February 1993
30. *Wonders of World Engineering*, 1938, Vol. 1, pp. 175–185; Vol. 2, pp. 1115–1124

6: The Haemorrhage

1. Glynn, S., 'Irish Immigration to Britain, 1911–1951: Patterns & Policy', *Irish Economic and Social History*, Vol. VIII (1981), p. 67
2. Neary, J., Conversation with the author, November 1994
3. Brooke, D., 'The Railway Navvy — A Reassessment', *Construction History*, Vol. 5, 1989, p. 35
4. Healy, J., *Death of an Irish Town*, 1967, p. 22
5. O'Hara, J., Conversation with the author, 1994
6. *World War Two, Official History*, Ch. XX, p. 339
7. Jenkins, A., *On Site: 1921–1971*, pp.33–34
8. Duffy, J., Kildorrery, Co. Cork (personal reminiscences)
9. Quinn, P., Unpublished letter to the author, 27 February 1999
10. Flavahan, P., Letter to the *Irish Post*, 1999
11. Curran, M., in Pam Schweitzer (Ed.), *Across the Irish Sea*, 1991, p. 58; 'Mary Anne' in Anne Lynch (Ed.) *The Irish in Exile: Stories of Emigration*, p. 15
12. Duffy, C., Conversation with the author, November 1993
13. *World War Two, Official History*, Ch. XVII, pp. 365–366
14. Cox, R., Presidential Address, ICE, 1982
15. *World War Two, Official History*, p. 174
16. Reported in *Irish Democrat*, June, 1946
17. Conversion Calculations supplied by Office of National Statistics, G.B.
18. Healy, J., op. cit., pp. 23–24
19. Ibid., p. 26
20. *Irish Democrat*, January 1946, April 1946
21. Quinn, P., op. cit.
22. Jackson, J.A., *The Irish in Britain*, 1963, p. 106
23. Gallagher, Jim, Conversations with the author, 1998
24. Banks, G.,' North of Scotland Hydro Electric Board', in *Glasgow Herald Trade Review*, January, 1948
25. Gallagher, J., op. cit.

7: McAlpine's Men

1. Griffin, J., in P. Schweitzer (Ed.), *Across The Irish Sea*, 1991, p. 80
2. Meenan, J., *The Irish Economy since 1922*, 1970, p. 344; O'Brien, J. (Ed.), *The Vanishing Irish*, 1955.
3. Gilland, E., Unpublished letter to the author, 1999
4. Burke, P., in *Across The Irish Sea*, op. cit., p. 35
5. 'Mary Anne', *The Irish in Exile*, op. cit., p. 15
6. Burke, P., ibid, p. 25
7. MacAuligh, D., *Dialann Deorai* (The Diary of an Exile; English transl. entitled *An Irish Navvy*), 1966 ed., p. 182

8. Fitzgerald, A., 'Reservation No. 2', *Report of the Commission on Emigration*, 1954, p.222
9. Meenan, J., op. cit., p. 347
10. Investment in Education Report, 1964, Table 3.2
11. Lyons, F.S.L, *Ireland Since the Famine*, 1976 ed., p. 653 (quoting from 9 above)
12. Healy, J., op. cit., p. 26
13. Harris, R.A., op. cit., p. 17
14. Jackson, J.A., op. cit., pp. 71–74
15. Glynn, S., 'Irish Immigration to Britain, 1911–1951: Patterns and Policy', in *Irish Economic and Social History*, Vol. VIII, (1981), p. 57
16. MacAuligh, D., op. cit., pp. 36–7
17. Report of the Commission on Emigration and Other Population Problems, 1948–54, Dublin, 1956, pp. 136–137
18. Healy, J., op. cit., p. 25
19. Carroll, D., Conversations with the author, 1994
20. O'Ciarain, S., *Farewell to Mayo*, 1991, p. 119
21. *The Irish Democrat* (journal of the Connolly Association), 1945–47
22. O'Hara, J., Conversation with the author, 1994
23. O'Hara, J., Conversation with the author, 1994
24. McNicholas, B., 'The Irish in Britain', BBC Radio One, 1995
25. Durkin,T., ibid.
26. Bill Brennan, Arlington House, Camden Town, Conversation with the author, 1996

8: Public Works

1. Powell, C, op. cit., p. 177
2. *The Irishmen: An Impression of Exile*, (Philip Donnellan, Director), BBC, 1965
3. Barratt, D., Former Labour Officer, Costain. Conversation with the author, 1997
4. O'Brien, M., Conversation with the author, 1997
5. O'Neill, R, Letter to the author, 1999
6. Cox, J., Conversation with the author, 1997
7. MacAuligh, D., op. cit., p. 82
8. Munnelly, Frank, conversation with the author, 1999
9. O'Ciarain, op. cit., p. 141
10. Anonymous Questionnaire respondent, 1998
11. Respondents: Doug Goodsir, John Cox, John Docherty.
12. Sked, A. & Cook, C., *Post-War Britain*, 1994 ed., pp. 28–35
13. *Glasgow Herald*, 8 December 1947; 10 December 1947
14. Aiken, F, Dáil Éireann, quoted in *The Irish Times*, 14 May 1947
15. *Glasgow Herald*, 5 March 1947
16. Ibid., 22 June 1947
17. O'Ciarain, op. cit., p. 99
18. O'Hara, J, op. cit.
19. Hennety, P, conversation with the author, 1998
20. Barratt, D., op. cit.
21. Docherty, J, conversation with the author, 1997
22. Beasley, E, conversation with the author, 1997
23. Sykes, A.J.M., 'Navvies: Their Work Attitudes'; *Sociology*, 3, 1969, pp. 21–35; 'Navvies: Their Social Relations', *Sociology*, 3, 1969, pp. 157–172
24. Sykes, op. cit., p. 23
25. Docherty, J., op. cit.
26. Sykes, op. cit., p. ?
27. Sweeney, P., in 'Working Lives: The Irish in Britain', Holohan, Anne, *Irish Post*, 1995, p. 147
28. Gallagher, J, conversation with the author, 1998
29. Cahalan, C., unpublished letter to the author, 1999
30. Gallagher, J, op. cit.
31. *Colville's Magazine*, Winter, 1961, pp. 18–19
32. Kay, B, *From the Gorbals to Gweedore*, p. 4
33. Sykes, 'Navvies: Their Social Relations', *Sociology*, 3, 1969, pp. 157–160
34. MacAuligh, D., op. cit., p. 35
35. Walshe, L., unpublished letter to the author, 1999
36. *Engineering*, 28 September 1951
37. Ibid.
38. Summerfield, K., 'Design and Construction', in *Journal of the Institution of Highway Engineers*, June 1980
39. Cox, J, op. cit.
40. Cox, J., op. cit.
41. O'Shea, Fr K., *The Irish Emigrant Chaplaincy Scheme in Britain, 1957–82* (1985), pp. 32–33
42. Thompson, F., *Lark Rise to Candleford* (1973 ed.), pp. 470–472
43. Institution of Civil Engineers Exhibition, 2000
44. Laing, WK., 'Luton–Dunchurch: Construction', Paper No. 6439, Institution of Civil Engineers, 3 May, 1960
45. Barratt, D., op. cit.
46. Docherty, J., op. cit.
47. Morrell, d., *Indictment: Power and Politics in the Construction Industry*, 1987, p. 63
48. Behan, B., *With Breast Expanded*, 1964, pp. 131–136
49. Ibid., p. 152
50. Geldof, B., *Is That It?*, 1986, p.65
51. Ibid., p.66
52. Taffe, Fr. J., in 'Working Lives: The Irish in Britain', op. cit., pp. 151–152
53. Sweeney, Fr Owen, *Irish Post*, 10 March 2001
54. Healy, J., op. cit., pp. 64, 73
55. Rowley, T., 'The Journey Home', *Sunday Miscellany*, RTÉ Radio One, 1999
56. *Doohoma*, RTÉ, 1972
57. Plant, Ronnie & Frieda, conversation with the author, 1999
58. Beasley, E., op. cit.

9: Private Fortunes

1. Kennelly, B., Unpublished letter to the author, 1999
2. Healy, J., op. cit., p. 45
3. Jean' & 'Eleanor', 'The Irish in Exile', *Hammersmith & Fulham Community History Series* No. 1, pp. 18 & 2
4. Boyd, W., 'An Irishman's Diary', *The Irish Times*, 14 August 2000
5. Brennan, B., Conversation with the author, 1997
6. Gallagher, J., Conversation with the author, 1997
7. O'Brien, M., Conversation with the author, 1997
8. Walshe, L., op. cit.
9. Cahalan, C., op. cit.
10. Walshe, L., op. cit.
11. Cahalan, C., op. cit.
12. Brennan, B., op. cit.
13. O'Grady, B., Conversation with the author, 1999–09
14. Munnelly, F., op. cit.
15. Brennan, B., op. cit.
16. Doyle, E., op. cit.
17. Brennan, B., op. cit.
18. Walshe, L., Unpublished letter to the author, 1999
19. Durkin, T., *The Irish in Britain*, BBC Radio Five, 1996
20. Docherty, J., op. cit.
21. O'Ciarain, S. op. cit. pp. 155–6

22. Flavahan, P., Unpublished letter to the author, 1999
23. McGreevy, R., *Irish Post*, 31 July 1999
24. O'Sullibhan, M., *Irish Post*, 22 August 1999
25. Casey, D., *Irish Post*, 14 August 1999
26. Corish, P., Unpublished letter to the author, 1999
27. Sykes, A.J.M., *Navvies: Their Work Attitudes*, op. cit., p. 23
28. Fielding, J., *The Success of the Irish in the Construction Industry*, 1996
29. *Construction News, Top 100 and Financial Review, 2000*, September 2000, pp. VIII–X
30. Fielding, J., *The Success of the Irish in the Construction Industry*, 1996
31. MacAuligh, D., op. cit., p. 167

10: Forgotten Men

1. Barratt, D., op. cit.
2. British Cabinet Papers released under Thirty Year Rule, *Independent on Sunday*, 1 January 1995
3. Irish Cabinet Papers released under Thirty Year Rule, *Irish Post*, 1995
4. Sykes, A.J.M., 'Navvies: Their Social Relations', *Sociology*, 3, 1969, p. 161
5. O'Ciarain, S., op. cit., p. 148
6. MacAuligh, D., op. cit.
7. O'Shea, Fr K., op. cit., p. 38
8. McGarry, J., Conversation with the author, 1997
9. Walshe, L., Unpublished letter to the author, 1998
10. Moran, J., Conversation with the author, 1996
11. MacAuligh, D., *'Céad Slán le Mary Horan': Donal MacAuligh in Northampton,* RTÉ, 1966
12. Hanlon, K., Unpublished letter to the author, 1998
13. Unpublished letter to the author (Name withheld), 1998
14. 'Páidrigín', unpublished letters to the author, 1998
15. O'Ciarain, S., op. cit., pp. 130–131
16. McGettigan, P., 'The Road from Donegal', *Independent,* 10 October 1992
17. Death Certificate, North Tyneside East, 19 November 1976
18. O'Ciarain, S., op. cit., p. 94
19. MacAuligh, D., op. cit., p. 73
20. MacAuligh, D., *'Céad Slán...'*
21. O'Donnell, N., Conversation with the author, 1999
22. McGarry, J., Conversation with the author, 1997
23. *Meithea*l is a Irish word for mutual aid — a voluntary community labour force, such as was commonly used in the Irish countryside in the absence of machinery to harvest crops or, where money was scarce, to build a house for a newly-married couple.
24. O'Donnell, N., op. cit.
25. Powell, C., op. cit., pp. 183–184, 178
26. O'Donnell, N., op. cit.
27. Jackson, J.A., *The Irish in Britain*, pp 72–3
28. Ibid., p. 73
29. McGarry, J., op. cit.
30. 'Katherine', Conversation with the author, 1974
31. Jackson, J.A., op. cit., p. 124
32. See Sykes, A.J.M., 'Navvies: Their Social Relations', *Sociology*, 3, 1969, pp. 157–172
33. Brooke, D., 'The Railway Navvy of the 1881 Census', *Quarterly Journal of Social Affairs*, 1986, 2(4), p. 363
34. Labour Force Survey, 1985
35. Powell, C., op. cit., pp. 220–2
36. Cahalan, C., Unpublished letter to the author, 1999
37. Green, J., *Independent on Sunday*, 2 February 1996
38. 'One Better Day', Bridge Housing Association, 1997
39. MacAuligh, D., op. cit.
40. McAlpine, Sir W., letter to the author, May 2000
41. 'They Brought the Sea to Manchester', North West Sound Archive

Appendices

Appendix 1

Mitchell Construction have been awarded three contracts totalling £4.5 million. The first, valued at £2.5 million, with the North of Scotland Hydro Electricity Board, is for over thirteen miles of tunnelling on the Teillin section of the Breadalbane Scheme, in Perthshire, plus eight miles of pipeline aqueducts, access roads, intake weirs, and shafts. The work is expected to employ up to 600 men over a three year period.

The second contract, with the South of Scotland Electricity Board, is for £1.25 million and entails construction of a generating station at Kincardine, Fifeshire, over three and a half years.

The third, worth £750,000, calls for construction of three cooling towers, the largest in the world, at the new power station at High Marnham, Nottinghamshire. (1 March 1957)

Hydro electric power schemes worth £14.25 million have been announced by the North of Scotland Hydro Electricity Board. Two power stations are to be built at Kilmorack Gorge and two at Strathfarrar over the next five years, giving peak employment of 1,000 men. (8 March 1957)

A rubber factory is to be built by John Laing & Son Ltd. At Fawley near Southampton. (12 April 1957)

The Central Electricity Authority has authorised the construction of a £15 million hydro electric scheme at Blaenu Ffestiniog, Merionethshire, by Sir Robert MacAlpine & Sons. A quarter-mile long dam will be constructed for the scheme and the pumping station will have the world's largest pump installed. (3 May 1957)

The Central Electricity Authority has announced the siting of the world's largest coal-fired power station at Thorpe Marsh, about four miles north-east of Doncaster, in Yorkshire. Construction is planned for the early 1960s and will cost an estimated £40 million. (17 May 1957)

British Petroleum announces an expansion scheme at its Grangemouth refinery costing £4 million; also construction of a super-tanker jetty at Loch Long, Finnert, costing £1.5 million, to be completed by the end of next year. (24 May 1957)

The North of Scotland Hydro Electricity Board announce their Awe Project (Constructional Scheme No. 28). This includes the first large-scale pumped-storage hydro electric development in Scotland. It will utilise 324 square miles of the River Awe catchment area.

This development will occur in three sections — Inverawe, Cruachan, and Nant.

The Cruachan pumped storage works will have a total installed capacity of 450,000 kilowatts, and will cost an estimated £24.5 million.

Inverawe will have a low barrage, from which water will be conducted through a tunnel to a power station at the mouth of the river.

The Cruachan power station will be used at night and on weekends, when the system load is low, to absorb surplus energy from atomic or high-efficiency steam systems, by pumping water from Loch awe up to a high reservoir, formed in the corrie on Ben Cruachan at a height of 1,300 feet. The reservoir will be connected by shafts to an underground power station and water will be conveyed to and from Loch Awe by a horizontal tunnel.

A dam at the outlet of Loch Nant will supply water from the reservoir by tunnel and pipeline to a power station near Inverinan on the shore line at Loch Awe. (26 July 1957)

Work begins shortly at Milford Haven oil terminal on a tanker jetty at Popton Point. (16 August 1957)

The Central Electricity Authority announce the selection of Trawsfynedd, Merionethshire, as the site of their fourth nuclear power station, costing between £30 and £40 million. (30 August 1957)

The Ministry of Transport has invited tenders for construction of the Luton to Dunchurch (M1) Motorway, a distance of 53 miles. (27 September 1957)

A contract for construction of a £3 million chemical plant at Fawley, covering a 52-acre site, has been awarded to George Wimpey & Co. (4 October 1957)

Work has begun on the £6 million BP oil refinery at Grangemouth. (20 December 1957)

A £14,250,000 Dam scheme at Loch Monar, Loch Beannacharan, and the rivers Farrar and Beauly, providing five dams and four generating stations, fed by a catchment area of 350 square miles, proposed by the North of Scotland Hydro Electricity Board, has been approved by the Secretary of State. (13 June 1950)

The contract with Higgs & Hill for South Uist Rocket Range, in the Outer Hebrides, has been modified from the 1957 £20 million contract to one of only £5 million. Excess plant will be shipped home. Between 250 and 400 operatives are nevertheless still required. (27 August 1950)

Esso signs contract for construction of a 3,500 foot jetty, for the £18 million Milford Haven Oil Refinery, with Foster Wheeler Ltd. (10 September 1950)

Esso is seeking planning permission for a 75-mile pipeline from their refinery at Fawley to a new distribution depot near London Airport with a 20 million-gallon capacity at a cost of £2.5 million. This will be the first large-scale refined-oil pipeline in Britain, with an initial capacity of 1.5 million gallons daily. (8 January 1960)

The London-to Yorkshire motorway, which is currently costing £395,000 per mile, is expected to cost an average £418,000 per mile over its entire length of 160 miles, for a total cost of £60 million. (13 February 1960)

Agreement has been reached to build a 70 mile pipeline to supply ethylene via a pipeline from the Esso refinery at Fawley to the ICI plant at Severnside in Gloucestershire at a cost of £800,000. (26 February 1960)

A £60 million nuclear power contract has been awarded to the Nuclear Power Group by the Central Electricity Authority. Work is begin next month at Dungeness, on a 112 acre site. This is a shingle promontory, six miles by five miles, projecting into the sea. The labour force is estimated to peak at 1,800. (22 July 1960)

The Birmingham link to the M1 Motorway, which will run on stilts above the city for a distance of two and a half miles, has been approved at a cost of £3.8 million. (5 August 1960)

Appendix 2

Wimpey Projects
Dams & Hydro Electric Works
1. The Awe Project, Argyllshire, Value £1,750,000
2. Pitlochry, Perthshire, Value £1,656,000

Industrial Buildings & Depots
1. Milford Haven (Esso Refinery) 1950+ Value £430,000

Civil Engineering
1. London Airport, 1944+, Value £13 million
2. London Airport Extension, 1961+, Value £5,500,000
3. Spadeadam Rocket Establishment, 1957–1960

Collieries & Mining

1. Parkside Colliery, Lancs., Value £800,000

Railways

1. Kent Coastline, Value £2.5 million

Roads

1. Gateshead–Felling Bypass, 1960, Value £635,000
2. Torryburn Bypass, Fife, 1962
3. M2 Motorway, Kent, 1961+ Value £6 million
4. A1 Improvements, Yorks., 1961, Value £750,000
5. Coventry Inner Ring Road, 1960, Value £73,000
6. Greater Missenden Bypass, 1961, Value £147,000

Thermal Power Stations

1. Ferrybridge 'B' Yorks., 1954–1956, Value £1.25 million

Pipelines, Tanker Jetties, Storage

1. BP Terminal, Finnart, Loch Long, 1959, Value £750,000
2. Milford Haven to Llandarcy Pipeline, 1958–1959
3. BP Refinery, Isle of Grain, 1951–1960, Value £70 million

Chemical & Petro-Chemical Works

1. Brotherton Chemical Works, 1954–1956, Value £400,000
2. Union Carbide, Hythe, Hants., 1960,
3. Grangemouth Petrochemical Plants, 1947–1861,

Road Surfacing

1. M6 Motorway

Appendix 3

Dams

1. Monar Dam, Inverness-shire (Strathfarrar Scheme)
2. Loighel Dam, Awe Barrage, Argyllshire (Inverawe Scheme)
3. Loyne Dam, Inverness-shire (Glen Moriston Project)
4. Cluanie Dam, Inverness-shire (Fionain Intake, Nant Scheme)
5. River Earn Intake (Beadaalbane Scheme)
6. Nant Dam, Argyllshire

Power Stations

1. Brimsdown 'B' Power Station (Pre-war, North Metropolitan Power Station Company)
2. Thornhill Power Station (Yorks. Electricity Board)
3. Portishead 'A' Power Station (Bristol Corporation Electricity Department)
4. Ironbridge Power Station (W. Midland Joint Electricity Authority)
5. Goldington-Bedford Power Station (Central Electricity Generating Board; 100-acre site; 5,800 piles cast on site)
6. Kincardine Power Station (South of Scotland Electricity Board)
7. Thorpe Marsh Power Station (Central Electricity Generating Board — CEGB)
8. Drakelow Power Station (CEGB)
9. Blyth 'B' Power Station (CEGB)
10. Methil Power Station (South of Scotland Electricity Board)
11. Carolina Port Power Station (North of Scotland Hydro-Electricity Board — NSHEB)
12. Peterborough Power Station/s (1923, 1925, 1945)
13. NANT Underground Power Station (NSHEB)
14. Culligran Power Station, Inverness-shire (NSHEB)
15. Strathfarrar Power Station (NSHEB)
16. Deanie Power Station, Inverness-shire (Glenstrathfarrar Scheme; 6-mile supply tunnel, NSHEB)
17. St Fillan's Underground Power Station, Loch Earn, Perthshire (Breadalbane Scheme, NSHEB; 19 miles of tunnel — world tunnelling record, 557 ft in one week)
18. Ceannacroc Underground Power Station, Inverness-shire (NSHEB)
19. Fawley Power Station (Largest contract ever let by the CEGB)
20. Chapelcross Nuclear Power Station (First in Scotland; UK Atomic Energy Authority)

Cooling Towers

1. Walsall (CEGB)
2. Capenhurst (UK Atomic Energy Authority)
3. Wigan (British Electricity Authority)
4. Chapelcross (UK Atomic Energy Authority)
5. High Marnham (CEGB, 5 x 340 feet high)
6. Castle Donington (CEGB)
7. Padiham 'B' (CEGB, two towers cooling 7 million gallons per hour)
8. Skelton Grange (CEGB)

9.   Willington 'B' (CEGB, 3 x 300 feet high; 10 million+ gallons per hour)

Appendix 4

Large Dams, UK

1.   Airyholm, Newcastle-on-Tyne, 1978–1979, Gleeson Civil Engineering Ltd., Value £1 million

2.   Alton, Ipswich, Suffolk, 1972–1976, Gleeson Civil Engineering Ltd., Value £6.3 million

3.   Arlington, Eastbourne, Sussex, 1968–1972, Higgs & Hill Civil Engineering Ltd., Value £1.5 million

4.   Backwater, Perth, Scotland, 1964–1969, Balfour Beatty Construction (Scotland) Value: £3.3 million

5.   Bakethin, Newcastle, 1978–1979, George Wimpey & Co. Ltd., Value £3 million

6.   Balderhead, Darlington, Northumbria, 1961–1964, Richard Costain (Civil Engineering) Ltd., Value £3 million

7.   Bewl Bridge, Tunbridge Wells, Kent, 1973–1975, Gleeson, Value £2 million

8.   Boothwood, Huddersfield, 1967–1970, Sir Lindsay Parkinson & Co. Ltd., Value £2.3 million

9.   Bough Beech, Sevenoaks, Surrey, 1967–1969, Gleeson, Value £1.9 million

10.   Bradan, Ayr, Scotland,1970–1973; Gleeson, Value £1.5million

11.   Brenig, Denbigh, Clwyd, Wales, 1973–1976, Sir Lindsay Parkinson, Value £12.1 million

12.   Brianne, Swansea, 1968–1972, George Wimpey, Value £6.1 million

13.   Castle Hill, Perth, Scotland, 1975–1978, Value £3.3 million

14.   Celyn, Bala, Gwynedd, Wales, 1960–1965, Tarmac Civil Engineering Ltd, Value £3.2 million

15.   Clunas, Nairn, Scotland, 1969–1971; Tarmac; Value £410,000

16.   Clwyedog, Llanidloes, Powys, Wales, 1963–1967; Reed & Mallik Ltd., Value £5 million

17.   Colliford, Bodmin, Devon, 1981–1984; Gleeson, Value £6 million

18.   Cow Green, Penrith, Durham, 1967–1970; Mitchell Construction Ltd., Value £2.4 million

19.   Craignafeich, Kilfinan, Scotland, 1970–1972, RH Cuthbertson & Ptners, Value: £120,000

20.   Crowdy, Bodmin, Devon, 1971–1972, Tarmac, Value £400,000

21.   Cruachan, Loch Awe, Scotland, 1962–1965, James Williamson & Ptners, Value £1.5 million

22.   Derwent, Durham, 1960–1966, John Mowlem & Co., Value £5.3 million

23.   Diddington, Cambridge, 1962–1965; W&C French Ltd, Value £2 million

24.   Dovestone, Manchester, 1960–1966, AE Farr Ltd, Value£1.7 million

25.   Draycote, Coventry, 1967–1968, Lehane, Mackenzie & Shand Ltd, Value: £1.8 million

26.   Empingham, Peterborough, 1971–1975, Gleeson, Value £30 million

27.   Errwood, Manchester, 1964–1968, Lehane, Mackenzie & Shand, Value £1.49 million

28.   Glen Finglas, Glasgow, 1963–1965; Mowlem, Value £644,000

29.   Grimwith, Harrogate, Yorks., 1976–1982+, McAlpine, Value: £20 million

30.   Kielder, Newcastle, 1976–1982, Balfour Beatty/ Fairclough Joint Venture, Value £66.5 million

31.   Llys-Y-Fran, Milford Haven, Wales, 1968–1972; Sir Lindsay Parkinson & Co. Ltd, Value £3.6 million

32.   Marchlyn, Bangor, Wales, 1976–1980; Gleeson, Value £16.5 million

33.   Queen Mother & Wraybury, 1969–1974, Laing, Value £5.6 million

34.   Scammonden Water, Yorkshire, 1966–1969, Alfred McAlpine, Value £5.4 million

35.   Sibleybach, Cornwall, 1967–1969, Gleeson, Value £0.6 million

36.   St Ithians, Cornwall, 1962–1965; Gleeson, Value £0.54 million

37.   Thames Barrier, Woolwich, London, 1974–1983, Costain/Tarmac/HBM (J.V.), Value £42 million

38.   Thruscross, Leeds, Yorks., 1961–1966; Holland & Hannen/Cubitts Ltd Joint Venture, Value: £1.6 million

39.   Turret, Perthshire, 1961–1964, Lehane, Mackenzie & Shand Ltd, Value £10 million

40. West Water, Edinburgh, 1962–1967, Reed & Mallik, Value £1.35 million
41. Wet Sleddale, Cumbria, 1963–1966, Gleeson, Value £2.2 million
42. Whiteadder, Edinburgh, 1965–1969, Carmichael Ltd, Value £1.6 million
43. Wombleball, Devon, 1975–1979; Bovis Civil Engineering Ltd, Value £12.6 million
44. Winscar, Huddersfield, Yorks., 1972–1975; Gleeson, Value £35 million

Appendix 5

Sub-Contracts Wanted: Experienced Tunnel Miners and Navvies available for Headings and Deep Excavations within 100 miles of London. Reasonable Rates. Box 687, Labour News Offices, 69, Fleet Street, London EC4. (6 January 1956

West Hartlepool. Good experienced navvies required immediately for Post Office ductwork contract. Apply to Agent on site at junction of Albert Street and Stockton Street, West Hartlepool. North Midland Construction, Nottingham. (20 January 1956)

Experienced deep trench timbermen urgently required, with plenty of overtime and every alternative weekend working. Top rate of wages paid and subsistence according to the Working Rule Agreement. Apply by letter. GW Bell, Agent, Lehane, Mackenzie & Shand, Oyston Reservoir, Oyston Lane, Higham, Derbyshire.

Experienced timbermen and navvies for deep sewer work. apply — Hussey, Egan & Pitmore Ltd., nr. Euston Road Station, Morecambe. (27 January 1956)

The Northwest Construction Company Ltd., Litherland, Liverpool 21
require the following key personnel for Post Office work between Taunton and Barnstaple. Only men experienced in Post Office ductlaying work should apply:

    Gangers
    Concrete Manhole and Box Builders
    Ductlayers
    Rammer Operators
    Labourers
op rates, lodging allowance and opportunity to earn bonus. Applications should be made to the Agents for the various sections on the sites between Taunton and Barnstaple. (14 March 1956)

Business Opportunities:
Directorship offered in Limited Company engaged on GPO and other engineering work. To young man, energetic, capable and good organiser, willing to travel and take charge of outside work and control labour (profession not essential); capital outlay about £1,000. Good opportunity for expansion. Replies treated confidentially. Box 759, Labour News Offices. (12 April 1956)

Sub-Contracts Wanted—Contracts Wanted
Labour Only: Groundwork Excavations, Concreting, Pipe-laying, Site Clearance, Earth-moving and Transport. Experienced Men, good references, keen prices. —
Treacy, 81, Horn Hill Road, Maple Cross, Herts. (27 April 1956)

Warm Rooms, Club Bar, Television, Billiards, etc. And 15 Meals a Week for £3.0.0
Industrial Catering Ltd., London:
Colney Hostel,
St. Albans
Bowmans Green 3104
Bicester Road Hostel
Aylesbury 806 (20 January 1956)

15 Substantial Meals
Good Rooms
Television
Billiards, Etc.
£3. 0. 0 Weekly.
(£2. 17. 0. For Women)
Industrial Catering Ltd.
Westwood Hostel
Peterborough 3962

Woodlands Hostel, Baldock
181, Stratton St. Margaret
Swindon (21 September 1956)

ACCOMMODATION (LIVERPOOL):
Sharing Double Rooms.
Room Charge with 5 Meals 33/9d.
Room charge With 15 Meals 61/3d.
All rooms centrally heated. Licensed Bar, Lounges,
*   Shower, Etc.*
The Residential Club,
Kirby Industrial Estate,
Nr. Liverpool

HOSTELS WITH A FRIENDLY ATMOSPHERE
Industrial Catering Hostels are pleasant places to stay.
They are well run, comfortably furnished, and provide a
number of recreations and amusements: billiards, TV,
snack bars and reading rooms. The food is good and the
helpings substantial, and a man, even on the heaviest
work, need never go hungry. And all at rates you can
afford.
Weekly Rate £3. 2s. 6d.
B. & B.   £1. 0s. 6d.
Weekly Rates include breakfast and evening meal
*   everyday, and lunch on Sunday.*
Industrial Catering Ltd.,
199, Knightsbridge,
London SW7 (12 April 1959)

Bibliography

Ashton, T.S., *Economic and Social Investigations in Manchester, 1833–1933*, 1934

Bagwell, P.S., *The Transport Revolution from 1770*, London: Batsford, 1974

Barrett, Rev. D.W., *Life and Work among the Navvies*, 1880

Behan, B. *With Breast Expanded*, London, MacGibbon & Kee, 1964

Brody, H., *Inishkillane*, London: Allen Lane, 1973

Brooke, D., *The Railway Navvy: 'That Despicable Race of Men'*, London: David & Charles, 1983

Burton, A., *The Canal Builders*, London, 1972

Childers, J. Saxon, *Robert MacAlpine*, 1925

Coleman, T., *The Railway Navvies*, London: Hutchinson, 1965

Conder, S., *The Men Who Made Railways*, 1868

Cullen, C.M., *An Economic History of Ireland since 1660*, London: Batsford, 1972

Delaney, E., *Demography, State and Society*, Liverpool University Press, 2000

Delaney, R., *Ireland's Inland Waterways*, 1984

English Dialect Dictionary, The, Vol. IV, Oxford University Press, 1961

Flynt, J., *Tramping with Tramps*, Maryland: McGrath, 1969 edition

Francis, J.R., *A History of the English Railway*, 1851

Geldof, B., *Is That It?*, London, Sidgwick & Jackson, 1986

Handley, J.E., *The Irish in Modern Scotland*, Cork University Press, 1947

Handley, J.E., *The Navvy in Scotland*, Cork University Press, 1970

Healy, J., *Death of an Irish Town*, Cork: Mercier Press, 1968

Healy, J., *No One Shouted Stop*, Achill: Healy, 1988

Helps, A., *Life and Labours of Mr Brassey*, 1872

Hilton, J., in *Seven Shifts*, Jack Common (ed.), London, 1938

Holohan, A., *Working Lives: The Irish in Britain*, London: Irish Post, 1995

Hosbach, W.A., *A History of the English Agricultural Labourer*, 1894

Jackson, J.A., *The Irish in Britain*, London, 1963

Kavanagh, P., *The Green Fool*, 1984 edition

Kay, B., *From the Gorbals to Gweedore*, Edinburgh, 1964

Lecount, P., *The History of the Railway Connecting London and Birmingham*, 1839

Lynch, A. (Ed.), *The Irish in Exile: Stories of Emigration*, Hammersmith and Fulham Community History Series, No. 1

Lyons, F.S.L., *Ireland Since the Famine*, London: Fontana, 1976 edition

MacAuligh, D., *Dialann Deoraí (An Irish Navvy)*, London: Routledge & Kegan Paul, 1966

MacGill, P., *Children of the Dead End*, London: Caliban, 1995 edition

MacGill, P., *The Navvy Poet, The Collected Poetry of Patrick MacGill*, London: Caliban, 1984

MacGill, P., *Moleskin Joe*, London: Herbert Jenkins, 1921

MacLaughlin, J., *Ireland: The Emigrant Nursery and the World Economy*, Cork University Press, 1994

Meenan, J., *The Irish Economy since 1922*, Liverpool University Press, 1970

Morrell, D., *Indictment: Power and Politics in the Construction Industry*, London, 1987

Mullins, T., in *Useful Toil*, John Burnett (Ed.), London: Allen Lane, 1974

Neary, J., *Memories of a Long Distance Kiddy*, London, 1994

O'Brien, J., *The Vanishing Irish*, London: W.H. Allen, 1955

O'Ciarain, S., *Farewell to Mayo*, Dublin: Brookside, 1991

O'Donoghue, J., *In a Strange Land*, London: Batsford, 1958

Orwell, G., *Down and Out in Paris and London*, London: Penguin, 1940

O'Shea, Fr Kieran, *The Irish Emigrant Chaplaincy Scheme in Britain, 1957–1982*, Naas, 1985

Redford, A., *Labour Migration in England, 1800–1850*, Manchester University Press, 1926

Schweitzer, P. (Ed.), *Across the Irish Sea*, London: Age Exchange, 1991

Sked, A. and Cook, C., *Post-War Britain*, London: Penguin, 1994 edition

Smiles, S., *Lives of the Engineers*, 1858

Sullivan, D., *Navvyman*, London, 1983

Thompson, F., *Lark Rise to Candleford*, London: Penguin, 1973 edition

Winchester, C. (Ed.), *Wonders of World Engineering*, 1938, Vols I & II, London: Amalgamated Press

Articles

Brooke, D., 'The Railway Navvy — A Reassessment' in *Construction History*, vol. 5, 1989

Brooke, D., 'The Railway Navvy of the 1881 Census' in *Quarterly Journal of Social Affairs*, 1986

Brooke, D., 'Railway Navvies on the Pennines' in *The Journal of Transport History* (NS), Vol. 3 (1975–6)

Chinn, C., 'The Irish in Early Victorian Birmingham' in R. Swift and S. Gilley (Eds.), *The Irish in Victorian Britain: The Local Dimension*, Dublin: Four Courts Press, 1999

Davis, G., 'The Irish in Britain, 1815–1939' in *The Irish Diaspora*, Andy Bielenberg (Ed.), Cork University Press, 2000

Fitzpatrick, D. 'Irish Emigration, 1800–1921', Dublin: Economic and Social History Society of Ireland, 1984

Glynn, S., 'Irish Immigration to Britain, 1911–1951: Patterns and Policy' in *Irish Economic & Social History*, Vol. VIII (1981)

Herson, J., 'Irish Families in Victorian Stafford' in R. Swift and S. Gilley (Eds.), *The Irish in Victorian Britain: The Local Dimension*, Dublin: Four Courts Press, 1999

Joby, R.S. 'Three Phases of Railway Contracting', Institution of Civil Engineers, 7th Annual Seminar, July 1988, Outline, Section 10

Moran, G., 'A Passage to Britain: Seasonal Migration and Social Change in the West of Ireland' in *Saothair* 13 (1982)

Morgan, D.H., 'The Irish Harvesters' in *Harvesters and Harvesting*, 1840–1900, 1982 edition

Neal, F. 'Irish Settlement in the North-west and North-east of England in the mid-nineteenth century' in R. Swift and S. Gilley (Eds.), *The Irish in Victorian Britain: The Local Dimension*, Dublin: Four Courts Press, 1999

Ó Duibheanaigh, S., Irish Folklore Commission, MS 477, 394–6 in A. O'Dowd, 'Seasonal Migration to the Lagan and Scotland' in W. Nolan and M. Dunleavy (Eds.), *Donegal History Society*, Geography Publications

Ó Gráda, C., 'Seasonal Migration and Post-Famine Adjustment in the West of Ireland, 1870–1890' in S*tudia Hibernica*, No. 13 (1974)

Ó Gráda, C., 'The Irish in Nineteenth Century Britain: Problems of Integration' in R. Swift and S. Gilley (Eds.), *The Irish in the Victorian City*, London, 1985

Ó Tuathaigh, G., 'The Irish in 19th Century Britain: Problems of Integration' in R. Swift and S. Gilley (Eds.), *The Irish in the Victorian City*, London, 1985

Sykes, A.J.M., 'Navvies: Their Work Attitudes' in *Sociology 3*, 1969

Sykes, A.J.M., 'Navvies: Their Social Relations' in *Sociology 3*, 1969

Turton, J., 'Mayhew's Irish: The Irish Poor in Mid-Nineteenth Century London' in R. Swift and S. Gilley (Eds.), *The Irish in Victorian Britain: The Local Dimension*, Dublin: Four Courts Press, 1999

Official Publications

UK

Official History of World War Two

Report on the State of the Irish Poor in Great Britain, 1835

Report from the Select Committee on Railway Labourers, 1846

REPUBLIC OF IRELAND

Investment in Education Report, 1964

Labour Force Survey, 1985

Report of the Commission on Emigration and Other Population Problems, 1954

Newspapers & Magazines

Building Magazine

Colville's Magazine

Construction News

Eccles and Patricroft Journal

Engineering

Glasgow Herald

Independent (UK)

Irish Democrat

Irish Times, The

Irish Post

Independent on Sunday

Journal of the Institution of Highway Engineers

Labour News

Manchester Guardian

Sunday Times, The

Television & Radio Programmes

Doohoma, RTÉ, 1972

The Irish in Britain, BBC Radio Five, 1995

The Irishmen: An Impression of Exile, BBC, 1965

Sunday Miscellany, RTÉ Radio One, 1998

Céad Slán le Mary Horan: Dónal Macauligh i Northampton, RTÉ, 1966

Unpublished Theses

Fielding, J., *The Success of the Irish in the Construction Industry*, Unpublished dissertation, University of North London, 1996

Haren, E., *Builders, Chancers, and the Dole*, Unpublished dissertation, University of North London, 1993

Lowther, E., I*rish Leisure Activities of the Nineteen Fifties and Nineteen Sixties, with Reference to the Dancehalls*, Unpublished Dissertation, University of North London, 1996

Index

(Page numbers of illustrations are in
italics)

Abbey Wood, 224
Aiken, Frank, 159
air-raid shelters, *117*
Archway Tavern, London, *234*
Arlington House, 97–8, 188, 242, *248*, 249
Ardree Ballroom, Manchester, *216*

Bagwell, 67
Baker, Benjamin, 65
Balfour Beatty, 11, 125, 221, 261
Ballard, Stephen, 44
bankers, 17
Barratt, Dudley, 175–7, 211, 235
barrow runs, 39, *40*, *68*
Beasley, Edna, 161
beer tickets, 52
Behan, Brian, 177
Ben Nevis Hydroelectric Scheme, 104,
    123–4
bends, the, 220–1
Berry, Henry, 15, 17
*Betty and Billy — a Child's Tale of the
    Ship Canal*, 85
Bevan, Aneurin, 148
Birchinlee, 100
Blyth, Benjamin, 60
bomb damage, 119, *119*
bone necrosis, 221–2
bonuses, 160
Bourke, P.J., 206
Brand, Charles, 221
Brassey, Thomas, 13, 44, 59, 196
Brennan, Bill, 188, 192, 194, 199, 201–2
bricklayer' labourers, 98
bridge construction, 57, *57*
Bridge Housing Association, 249
Bridgewater Canal, 15–6, *15*
Bridgewater, Duke of, 15
Brindley, James, 17
Bristol Aeroplane Company, 118
British Communist Party, 177
British Medical Journal, 188
Brooke, David, 49–50, 55–7
Buchanan, Robert, 66
Building, 135

building construction, 94, 98, 117, 120–2,
    139
    job levels in, 156–7, 245
    workforce, Irish proportion of,
        151–2, 155, 157, 160
building workers, *246*
    and hostels, *119*
Burke, Pat, 134
Burton, Anthony, 16
Byrne, Fr Paul, 247–8
Byrne Bros, 245

cable laying, *198*, 202, 204, 222–3, 225,
    225, 231, *233*, *236*
Caledonian Canal, 35–6
Camden Town, 186, 227–30, *228–9*, 249
canal construction, 11, 13, 37–42, *43–5*
canals, commercial, 14–5
cards, working on the, 190–1
Carlyle, Thomas, 47
Carmichael, A,M., 125, 263
Casey, Dan, 200
Casey, Fr (later Bishop), Eamon, *245*
casual labourers, transient, 34, 45, 47–8,
    58, 82–5
Catholic Hierarchy, the Irish, 212
Cauley, The Bull, 231
Ceannocroc Underground Power
    Station, *127*
cement mixing, *107*
channel construction, 17
Channel Tunnel, 245–6
chaplains, 172–3, *174*, 179–81, *180*, 212–3
chemical plants, 260
Chew Valley Reservoir, 39, *39*
Children of the Dead End, 85, 94, 235
Chinn, Carl, 33
civil engineering industry, 94, 113, 115
Clancy, Michael, 204
Clancy & Sons Ltd, M.J., 204
Clarke, Nobby, 27–8, 145, 249–50
class discrimination, 134–6
Clyde Tunnel, 219, 221
Clyde Tunnellers' Association, 221
Coleman, Terr,. 92
Commission for Racial Equality, 248
Commonwealth Immigrants Act, 1962,
    212

company men, 181–3, 190, 19
compressed air, 220–1, *220*, 241
conacre, 21, 23
Conder, F.R., 44
Cong Canal, 49
Connaughton, Vince, 206
Connor, Winifred, 63
Construction News, 102
Conway House, 246
Cook, Sir Norman, 212
cooling towers, *170–1*
Cooper Committee, 124
Cordingly, W.S., 63
Corsham, 118
Costain-John Brown Ltd, 167, 174, 262
Cox, John, 153, 172, 207
Cox, Ray, 221
Cox, Ronald, 118
Crown, The, Cricklewood, 192, *193*
Cuthbertson & Partners, R.H., 126, 262
Cullen, L.M., 20
cutting construction, 15, 17, 37

Dale Dyke Dam, 73
Daly, P.N., 206
dancing, 213–6, *215–6*, *226*, 227
Dangerous Trades, 220
Dargan, William, 36
dead men scam, 230
decompression, 220–1
delousing, 117–8
demolition work, *139*, 145, *147*
Denvir, John, 80, 98
Derry Boat, *25*
Derwent Valley waterworks, 100, *101*
Dialann Deoraí, 235
DION Emigrant Welfare Committee, 243
Ditch, the Big, 67–70, see also
    Manchester Ship Canal
Docherty, Con, 222, *222–3*
Docherty, John, 161, 176, 199
dock work, 82
docks construction, 11, 35–6, 100, 108,
    108
dole beef, 112
Doncaster Bypass, *145*
Donnellan, John, 206
Donnellan, Philip, 152, 175

Down and Out in Paris and London, 96
Doyle, Eileen, 194
Doyle, Joe, 59, 139
Doyle, P.J., 58
drilling, 41, *41*
Dublin–Liverpool boat, 186–7
Duffy, Charlie, 116
Duffy, Joe, 116
Duignan, Sean, 184–5
dumpers, 72
Duncan Logan, 125
Dún Laoghaire–Holyhead mail boat, 185, *185*
Durkan Bros, 245
Durkin, Tom, 150, 191, 195

Eastoe, Sid, 179
Eccles and Patricroft Journal, 63–4
Economic War, 112
Education Act, 1967, 134
Elan Valley Reservoir, 73
Ellesmere Canal, 36
embankment construction, 17, 37, *41*
emergency coupons, 146–7
emigrant journey to London, 184–6, *184*
emigrant remittances, 29, 31, 34, 86–7, 89, 120
emigration trends, 81, 103, 122, 135–9, 184, 205, 211, 243, 247
Emigration from the United Kingdom, Select Committee on, 53
energy, era of, 169–70
Engels, Friedrich, 83
England's Motorways, 37
Ennis, Jim, 206
Episcopal Commission for emigrants, 247
excavators, *72*, *145*

Fairclough, Leonard, 221, 262
Famine, the Great, 20, 24, 80
Farewell to Mayo, A, 235
farm labourers, *26*
Farnham, Joseph, 66
Farr, A.E., 103, 262
Fawley Oil Terminal and Refinery, *166*, 167, 176
Federation of Civil Engineering Contractors, 115
Federation of Irish Societies, 242
field-hospitals, 66, 68
Fitzpatrick, David, 58, 91
Fitzpatrick, Pat, 245, 247
Flavahan, Paddy, 199
Flynt, Josiah, 95
Folan, Paddy, 31
Foley, Jack, 185
food tickets, 52
foremen, British v Irish, 199
Forth Bridge, 57, *57*
Foster, Roy, 9

Fuller, Bill, 145
Fylde Water Authority, 100

gaffers, 25
Gallagher, James, 137
Gallagher, Jim, 188
Gallagher, Matt, 137
Gallagher, Patrick, 210
Gallagher Group Ltd., 137, 245
Galloway Power Scheme, *106*, 108, *110*, 123
Galtymore Ballroom, Cricklewood, *215*, 227
gangers, 49, 179, 197–201, 230–1, 234
Gara, Michael, 221
Garnett, Mrs Elizabeth, 69
gas work, 76–7, 82, 205–7, *206*
Geldof, Bob, 177
Gilmore, Thomas, 64
Glasgow Herald, 60, 177
Glasgow subway, *94*
Gleeson, Jack, 242, *244*
Gleeson plc, M.J., 99–100, 122, 126, 139, 169, 242, *244*, 262–3
graft, 18
Graham, James, 58
Grand Trunk Canal, 15
Great Central Railway, 71
Greathead, James Henry, 78
Greenford Park Estate, 102
Gresham Ballroom, Holloway, *215*
Grey, Earl, 43
Griffin, Julia, 132
groundworkers *see* navvies
Grove Tavern, Hammersmith, 192
Gulmanda, 245

Haley, George, 69
Half Moon pub, Holloway, *235*
halfway house, *101*
Hall & Co, Matthew, 167
Hampstead Garden Suburb, 102
Hampton, Dick, 152, 157, *157*, 174
Handley, J.E., 35–6, 42, 58, 73–4, 79, 94–5
harbour construction, 11, 35–6
Harris, Ruth Anne, 82, 136
Harrison, Capt. Henry, 120
harvesters, 45, 47, 58, 83–4, 91–3, 109, 113, 138
harvesting, *32*, 34, 139
Haughton, E.E., 85
HBM, 174, 262
headings (tunnels), 28
Healy, John, 29, 111–2, 120, 137–8, 141, 181, 185
Hennelly, 245
Hickman, Prof Mary, 248
hill farm, *134*
Hobsbawm, Eric, 82–3
Holyhead Road, 36
homestead, abandoned, *30*

hostels, 97–8, *119*, 145–6, *146*, *186*, 187–8, 242, *248*, 249
house building, 102, 111, 137, 148–9, 158, 224
Housing Acts, 1946 and 1949, 148
housing estates, *148–9*
hydroelectric schemes, 122–5, *124*, 158, 166, 169, 179, *180*, 259
  Scottish, 58, 60, 74, *77*, *93*, 104–8, *105–6*, *110*, 123–5, *125*, *127*

In a Strange Land, 178
Industrial Christian Fellowship, 70
inheritance, 28, 31, 91
Independent on Sunday, 246
Inland Navigation System, the, 13, 16–7
Institute of Highway Engineers, 118
IRA bombing campaign, 111, 116, 133
Ireland's Own, 135
Irish Community Care, 243
Irish Democrat, 102, 121, 146
Irish Emigrant Chaplaincy Scheme, 212–3
Irish in Britain, social situation of the, 248–9
Irish in Britain, 53
Irish labour,
  British compared with, 193–5
  demand for, 53–4, 82
  discipline and, 158
  good and bad points of, 157–8
  living conditions of, 52, *53*, 60–6, 118, 128–9, *130*, 145–6, *146*, 150, *153*, 164, 223–7
  nomadic, 152–4
  prejudice against, 132–4
  pub recruitment of, 150
  railway construction by, 55–60, 82
  settling down in Britain, 182–3
  strike-breaking by, 54–5
  strikes and, 158
  wartime recruitment of, 113–30, 133, 139
  willingness to work of, 212
Irish Mail train, 186
Irish Navvy, An, (Dialann Deorai),178
Irish Post, The, 30–1, 200, 231
Irish Times, The, 135
Irish World Heritage Centre, 243
Irishmen, The, 152, 174
Irish-owned construction companies, turnovers of, 209
Irwell, River, 17
Isle of Grain Oil Refinery, *165*, 167–8, *168*

Jackson, J.A., 49, 53, 137, 151, 155, 239–40, 243
Jericho navvy village, 92
Johnson, Thomas, 124
Jones, Charles, 196
Jones, Robert, 66

Kariba Dam, 169
'Katherine', 238
Kavanagh, Patrick, 98
Kennedy, John (Manchester) and Joe, 204, 206, 209, 231, 234, 247
Kennedy Memorial Hall, J.F., 242, *244*
Kennelly, Brendan, 184
Kensington Palace Hotel, 119
Keynes. J.M., 158
Kilgarriff, John, 63
Killylane Dam, 39
Kilmarnock Journal, 61
Kilroe, Tim, 206, 245
Kilsby Tunnel, *40*
King Inquiry, 206
King George V Dock, London, *74–5*
King, John, 178
Kinlochleven Dam, 58, 60, 74, *77*, *93*, 104, 124
Kirk, Tom, 62
Kirwan, Fintan, 206

Labour News, 28, 89, *90*, 100–2, 168–9, 187–8
Laggan Dam, *105*, 105–6
Laing & Son Ltd, John, 11, 122, 139, 147–8, 166, 172, 259
land drainage, 115
land holding and survival, 20–3, 34
Lark Rise to Candleford, 91
Lawrence, Bill, 221
lazy beds, *21*
Lecount, Lt Peter, 50, 59–60
Lemass, Sean, 212
Lind & Co Ltd, Peter,103
List, Alfred, 60
Liverpool Port, 67
Llangollen Canal, 36
Llanwen Steelworks, 181
Loch Katrine Scheme, 74
Loch Treig reservoir, 104–7
Lochaber Power Scheme, 104, 123
lock construction, 17
lodging-houses, common, 97
London–Birmingham Railway, 50, 59, *81*, 173
London Irish Centre, 242–3, *243–5*
long-distance men (kiddies), 27, 46, *86*, 110, 130, 150, 165, 188–9
Lowery Construction, 206
Lowry, Pateen, 204
lump, on the, 191–3
lumpers (skins), 150, 190, 222–3, 227–34, *229–30*, 241, 245
and drink, 191–2

McAlpine, Alastair, 201
McAlpine, Alfred, 118, 262
McAlpine, Sir Malcolm, 59, 99, 119, 187
McAlpine, Sir Robert, 99, 154
McAlpine, Sir William, 250

McAlpine & Sons, Sir Robert, 11, 55, 59, 66, 74, 102, 139, 147, 154, 166–7, 177, 181, 194, 207, 259
McAlpine's Fusiliers, *8*, 11, 59, 99, 132–50
MacAuligh, Domhnall, 87, 135, 178, 213, 217, 224, 226–7, 235, 249
McDermott, Denis, 63
McGarry, Joe, 229, 231, 237
MacGill, Patrick, 29, 51, 58, 60, 74, 83–5, 87, 92, 94, 96, 104, 162, 235
McGinley Construction, 245
McGovern's, Kilburn, 192
McGreevy, Ronan, 200
McNamara, Fr Tom, 242, *243*
McNicholas, Bernard, 149–50, 204
McNicholas, Michael Pincher, 202–3, 231
McNicholas, Pat, 202–3
McNicholas Construction, 145, 149, *203*, 206–7, *208*
McNicholas Engineering, 231
McPartland, Fr Patrick, 172–3
McQuaid, Archbishop J.C., 213
M1 motorway, *12*, 172–3, *173–4*
M25 motorway, 177
Mahoney, John Rodgers, 66
Manchester and Liverpool Railway, 42, 62, 67
Manchester and Sheffield Railway, 51, 75
Manchester Ship Canal (the Big Ditch), *14*, *16*, *35*, *41*, 42, *43–5*, 50, 62–3, *64*, 65–70, *67–8*, *70*, 71
casualties in construction of, 68–9
district, census enumerator's return for, *61*
Mangan, Joe, 246
marriage in rural Ireland, 91
Marshall, Phil, 207
Marx, Karl, 83
Mayhew, Henry, 79, 155
Meenan, Prof. James, 135
Mersey, River, 15, 17
Mersey Tunnel, *104*
Methil Dock, *102*
Midland Links Motorway, 173–4
migration, 19–32
seasonal, 19, 24–8, 32, 88–9
Militia Camp Programme, 115
Ministry of Labour, 116–7, 120–1, 145, 212
Ministry of Supply, 117–9
Ministry of Works, 115, 117
Mitchell Construction, 103, 125, *130*, 167, 169, 176, 259, 262
Model Lodging Houses, 94–6
Moleskin Joe, 84, 235
Moran, John, 216, 224–7
Motherwell Bridge and Engineering Co, 167
motorways, 37, 71, *163*, 168, 170–4, *172–5*, 260
Moule, Rev. Lewis, 69

Mowlem & Co., John, 11, 139, 166, 178, 221, 262
muck-shifting, 44, 226
mulberry harbours, 118
Mulligan's, Biddy, Hammersmith, 192
Munnelly, Frank, 155, 194, 197
Murphy, Joseph and John, 187, 200, 202, 207, 209, 247
Murphy Company, 200–2, 206–7, 231, *240*

Nash, Ogden, 154
National Insurance cards, 160–1
National Registration Identity Card, *122*
National University of Ireland Club, *138*
navvies, *13–4*, *16–7*, *137*, *188*
behaviour of, 47, 50–1, 165, 189
domestic arrangements of, unnatural, 180–2
drinking among, 51–3, 83, 191–3, 217–8
emotional inadequacies of, 240–1
hard work of the, 44–5
importance of, 196
living conditions of, 52, *53*, 60–6, 189, 192–3
macho attitudes of, 162, 217
marriage and drink among, *238–9*
motivation of, 196–7
origins of the, 17–8
resistance to unionisation by, 162
self-esteem of, 238–9, 241–2
social inadequacies of, 238–9
strength and physique of the, 44, 49–51, 250
traits of, by county, 196
tramp, 82–5, 93–5
values of, 162–5
wages of, 53–4
Navvies' and General Labourers' Union, 68–9
navvy, definition of, 13–4
Navvy's and General Labourer's Guide, 69
Navvy Mission Society, 69–70
Navvyman, 49, 56
Neary, John, 25, 28, 29, 31, 96, 110–1
neutrality, 133
New Towns Act, 1946, 149
Newry Canal, 15–7
Nolan, Fr Joseph, 172–3, *174*
North Sea oil and gas, 126, 243, 245–6
Northwest Holst, 245
Northwich Bypass, 170
nuclear power stations, 125, 166, 168, *170–1*, 260
Nuttall Construction, Edmund, 118, 125, 221, *222*

O'Brien, Malcolm, 154, 168, 189–91, 223, 227, 231, 234–5
O'Ciarain, Sean, 144, 199, 213, 219, 235

O'Donnell, Eddie, 30
O'Donnell, Noel, 226, 236–7
O'Donoghue, John, 178
O'Donoghue, Elephant John, 200–1, 231
off-shore accounts, 210
O'Grady, Billy, 194–5, 204, 223
O'Hara, John, 26–7, 112, 137, 146
oil refineries and terminals, *165–6,*
    166–8, *168,* 259–60
Oliver, Thomas, 220
Once a Jolly Bagman, 201
O'Neill, Owen, 66
O'Neill, Peter, 153
Onslow Square Hostel, 146
O'Rourke, Ray, 245, 247
Orwell, George, 96–7
O'Shea, Fr Kieran, 180
Ó Suilleabhain, Mariad, 200
O'Sullivan, Daniel, 66
O'Sullivan, Concrete Mick, 200
Our Navvies, 69

Pall Mall Budget, 62
Passenger Traffic Order, 1842,
    rescinding of, 121
Patmore, J.A., 55
pay day, *191*
pecking order on the site, *197*
Pembroke Power Station, 179
pensions, 161
Percy Road Public Baths, 226
Peto, Samuel Morton, 13, 45, 59
Pettit, Bishop John, *180*
pincher kiddies, 188–9
Pioneer Total Abstinence Association,
    214, *214*
pneumatic axe, *128*
potatoes, 20–1, 23–5
Powell, Christopher, 231
power schemes, 166–7, 179, *180,* 259
prefabs, 148, 159
Preston Bypass, 168, 171–2, *172, 175*
Prevention of Violence Act, 1939, 111
Price, F., 66
public houses, 192, *193, 234, 235*
public works, 24, 34–6, 48, 71–8, 94, 100–3,
    113, 141, 151–83
puddling, 38–9, *38–9,* 74

Quarterly Letter to Navvies, 69–70
Quex Road Church, Kilburn, *213–4,* 227
Quinn, Peadar, 121

railway construction, 11, 13, 40, 42–6, *82,*
    89
    casualty rate in, 41, 51
Railway Labourers, Select Committee
    on, 60
*Railway Navvy, The,: 'That Despicable
    Race of Men',* 55
ration books, 146

RB1 (shovel), 144–5, *144*
reconstruction, 147–8
recruitment to return to Ireland, *251*
Redford, Arthur, 19, 53–4
Reed & Mallik, 125, 262–3
Registration for Employment Order, 114
Reilly, Harold, 62, 64
religious practice, 212–4, *213–4,* 227
remittance men, 86–7
Rennie, John, 17
Report on Emigration, 1954, 140
reservoir construction, *38–9, 39,* 73, 100
Ribblehead Viaduct, 92
Ricour, Paul, 13
road construction, 11, *17,* 36–7, *37,* 71, *82,*
    140, 142–3, 145, 153, 154, *163,* 168,
    170–2, *172–5,* 260
Roberts, Samuel, 49
ROF 16, 118
Rolt, L.T.C., 67, 71, 172–3
Rowley, Tom, 181
Rowton, Lord, 97
Rowton Houses, 94, 97–8, 188
Royal Victoria and Albert and King
    George V Docks, *74*
Ryan, D.J., 206
Ryan, Thomas, 56

St Brendan's Hostel, Barnes, *186*
St Fillan's Underground Power Station,
    125
Salvation Army hostels, 97
Sankey Brook Navigation, 15, 17
scaffolding, 171
scams, 160–1, 209–10
Scottish hydroelectric schemes, 58, 60,
    74, *77, 93,* 104–8, *105–6, 110,* 123–5,
    125, 127
Settle–Carlisle railway line, 92
Severn Tunnel, 65–6, 69
sewerage construction, *133, 156*
Shell Centre, 177
Shrewsbury Canal, 36
shuttering carpenter, *232*
sickles, *22,* 24, 27
Silent Valley Reservoir, 39
skins, 234–8 *see also* lumpers
Smiles, S., 23, 42
Smith, Margaret, 63
Snow, Dr John, 100
social centres, 242–3, *243–5*
Spaghetti Junction, 163, 173
spailpins, 23, 27, 112, 123 *see also*
    harvesters
Special Roads Act, 1949, 171
Spenser Steelworks, 175
Spike, the, 94, 96–7
spoil filling, 35, 39–40, 45
Stapleton, Kevin, 156
steam cranes, 73
steam navvy, 35, 44, 68, 71

steel erectors, 177
Steers, Thomas, 15, 17
Stephenson, George, 17
Stephenson, Robert, 50, 59
stevedores, 35
Strathfarrar Hydroelectric Scheme, 125,
    125
subcontractors (subbies), 150, 154–5,
    195–9, 202, 204, 207–34, 245–6
    payment sheet, *201*
sugar beet campaigns, 121–2
sugar beet workers, 92, 109–11, 113
Sullivan, Dick, 49–50, 56–7, 84
Sunday shift, 231
Sunday Times, The, 247
Sweeney, Fr Owen, 181
Sykes, A.J.M., 161–5, 182, 213, 241

Taaffe, Fr Joe, 179
Talla Reservoir, 74
Tarmac Construction, 11, 126, 154, 156,
    161, 169, 173, 262
tattie hokers, 23, 27, *27,* 29, 31, 34, 103,
    113, 123, 162
tax dodges, 160–1, 209–10, 244
Taylor, Frank, 115
Taylor Woodrow, 11, 115, 139, 147, 181,
    207
Team Valley Trading Estate, 103
technical development, 141–3, *142–3,* 159,
    170–2, 207
Telford, Thomas, 36, 170
Thames Barrier, 174, *176,* 211
Thirlmere Reservoir, 73
Thompson, Flora, 91, 173
tommy shops, 52–3, 80
tradesmen, 155–8
    militancy of, 176–7
tramp navvies, 82–5, 139, 164, 188–9,
    235–6
    self-banishment of, 87
    dress of, 84
    signs of, 84, *85*
tramping artisans, 82–3
Transport History, 57
transport revolution, the, 14–6
travel identity cards, *113*
Trebel, J.H., 57
trenches, 144–5, 206
trenchless technology, 204
Trevelyan, G.M., 45
Tucker, James, 66
tunnel construction, *40, 76,* 104–8, 123,
    126–30, 126–30, 178, 205, 219–222,
    218–221
Tyne and Wear Metro, 221
Tyne Tunnel, *220,* 221
Tyssen, 125

underground railways, 78, *79, 94,* 111,
    111, 117, 152, 178–9, *178–9,* 221

unemployment benefit, 145

Vanishing Irish, The, 132
Vermuyden, 18
Victoria Line, 178–9, *178–9*
Vyrnwy Reservoir, 73

wages, 231–4
Walker, Thomas A., *53*, 64–6, *65*, 69
Walker's fragments, 66–7
Walsh, Liam, 216
Walshe, Liam, 195

Walter, Dr Bronwen, 248
Waterford–Rosslare Railway, 59, 99
Wates, 147–8
Weaver, River, 17
Welwyn Garden City, 102
Wembley Stadium, *98*, 99
West Highland Railway, 99
Westhoven, Wilhelm, 57
Williams, Charlie, 250
Williams, E. Leader, 67
Williams & Partners, Sir Owen, 172
Williamson & Partners, J., 126

Wilson, Don, 206–7, 209
Wimpey Construction, George, 11, 102–3, *103*, 139, 148, 153–4, 156, 166–7, 169, 244, 260–2
Woodhead Reservoir, 39, 75
Woodhead Tunnels, 40, 51–2, 75
work permits, 113–5
workmen's compensation, 145, 220–2
World War II, 112–5
Wrekin Construction, 245
Wren, Sir Christopher, 183
Wylfa Power Station, *180*

Photographic Acknowledgements

pp. 6, 12, 174, HMSO

pp. 13, 22, 25, 26, 27, 82, 218, National Museums of Scotland

pp. 14, 16, 35, 40 (bottom), 41 (bottom), 43, 44, 45, 48, 53, 65, 67, 68, Manchester Ship Canal Company

pp. 13, 52, 70, 97, 193, 228, 234, 235, 240, 248, the author

pp. 15, 17, 140, Local Studies Unit, Central Library, Manchester

pp. 21, 30, Patricia Howard Cowley

p. 28, John Neary

pp. 32, 138, 186, 213, 214, 215, 226, 238, 239, 243, 244, 245, Paddy Fahey, Cricklewood Archive

pp. 38 (top & bottom), 101, North West Water Authority, Derbyshire

pp. 37, 39, 72, 79, 128, 129, 130, 142, 148, 149, 170, 171, 172, 173, 175 (top), 219, Institution of Civil Engineers

p. 40 (top), National Railway Museum, York

p. 41 (top), Sonia Wickham

pp. 57, 74, 75, 99, 105, 106, 110, 124, 143, Wonders of World Engineering (Amalgamated Press, 1936)

p. 61, PRO, London

p. 64, Riley Archive

pp. 76, 94, 98, 102, 104, 108, 111, 117, 133, 139, 145, 147, 165, 166, 168, 175 (bottom), 177, Sir Robert McAlpine Ltd.

pp. 77, 93, Jim Bailey

p. 81, Science Museum, London

p. 85, Ruanne Cowley

pp. 86, 152, 153, 157, 178, 179, 185 (top & bottom), 188, 189, 229, 230, 236, 247, British Film Institute, London/BBC

pp. 90, 144 (top), Construction News

p. 107, Bethell & Sons, Manchester

pp. 113, 122, 137, 156, 201, P. Flavahan

pp. 119, 146, *Irish Democrat*

pp. 125, 127, 131, Tarmac Construction

p. 126, Bernard Rogers

p. 134, Mike Harding

pp. 144 (bottom), 197, 198, 203, 208, 225, 232, 233, front cover, McNicholas Construction

p. 163, *Irish Post* Archive

p. 176, Dudley Barratt Archive

p. 180, Fr Kieran O'Shea

p. 206, Terry Smith

p. 216, Irish World Heritage Centre, Manchester

p. 220, Bill Lawrence Archive

pp. 222 (top & bottom), 221, Mrs C. Docherty

p. 251, Construction Industry Federation

The publishers have made every reasonable effort to contact the copyright holders of photographs reproduced in this book. If any involuntary infringement of copyright has occurred, sincere apologies are offered and the owners of such copyright are requested to contact the publishers. For permission to reproduce the copyright material we gratefully acknowledge the above.